Language of Conflict

Also available from Bloomsbury

Constructions of Migrant Integration in British Public Discourse, by Sam Bennett
European Identities in Discourse, by Franco Zappettini
Intercultural Crisis Communication, edited by Christophe Declercq and
Federico M. Federici
The Language of Brexit, by Steve Buckledee

Language of Conflict

Discourses of the Ukrainian Crisis

Edited by
Natalia Knoblock

BLOOMSBURY ACADEMIC
LONDON • NEW YORK • OXFORD • NEW DELHI • SYDNEY

BLOOMSBURY ACADEMIC
Bloomsbury Publishing Plc
50 Bedford Square, London, WC1B 3DP, UK
1385 Broadway, New York, NY 10018, USA
29 Earlsfort Terrace, Dublin 2, Ireland

BLOOMSBURY, BLOOMSBURY ACADEMIC and the Diana logo are trademarks
of Bloomsbury Publishing Plc

First published in Great Britain 2020
This paperback edition published in 2022

Copyright © Natalia Knoblock and Contributors, 2020

Natalia Knoblock has asserted her right under the Copyright, Designs and Patents Act, 1988,
to be identified as Editor of this work.

Cover design by Rebecca Heselton
Cover image: © bullet74/ shutterstock

All rights reserved. No part of this publication may be reproduced or transmitted in any form or
by any means, electronic or mechanical, including photocopying, recording, or any information
storage or retrieval system, without prior permission in writing from the publishers.

Bloomsbury Publishing Plc does not have any control over, or responsibility for, any third-party
websites referred to or in this book. All internet addresses given in this book were correct at the
time of going to press. The author and publisher regret any inconvenience caused if addresses have
changed or sites have ceased to exist, but can accept no responsibility for any such changes.

Library of Congress Cataloging-in-Publication Data
Names: Knoblock, Natalia, editor.
Title: Language of conflict: discourses of the Ukrainian crisis / edited by Natalia Knoblock.
Description: New York: Bloomsbury Academic, 2020. | Includes bibliographical references and index. |
Summary: "Exploring the ways in which language and conflict are intertwined and interrelated, this
book examines the changes that have taken place in the public discourse of the Ukraine and Russia
since 2014 and the beginning of the 'Ukrainian Crisis.' Through analysis of the narratives constructed
by different social groups in Ukraine, Language of Conflict shows how discourse can illuminate the
competing worldviews and the conflicting positions of the various stakeholders in this conflict.
Through critical discourse analysis and multimodality, this book explores the prevalent narratives
and the linguistic features of the salient discourses surrounding this conflict. Using Russian- and
Ukrainian-language texts from traditional and social media, contributors from Ukraine, Russia and
beyond investigate discourses surrounding the most important topics of the crisis: its causes and
goals, the sides, and the values and ideologies of the opposing parties. Highlighting the ways
in which the stress produced by social discord, economic hardship and violence, is reflected
in verbal aggression, slurs, insults and profane language of extraordinary linguistic creativity,
Language of Conflict provides insight into the ways people think about, respond to and
experience the reality of conflict in their everyday communication"– Provided by publisher.
Identifiers: LCCN 2020004399 (print) | LCCN 2020004400 (ebook) | ISBN 9781350098565 (hardback) |
ISBN 9781350098626 (epub) | ISBN 9781350098619 (ebook)
Subjects: LCSH: Ukraine Conflict, 2014- | Ukraine–Foreign relations–Russia (Federation) |
Russia (Federation)–Foreign relations–Ukraine. | Crimea (Ukraine)–History–2014- |
Rhetoric–Political aspects–Ukraine. | Discourse analysis–Political aspects–Ukraine. | Rhetoric–Political
aspects–Russia (Federation) | Discourse analysis–Political aspects–Russia (Federation)
Classification: LCC DK508.852 .L36 2020 (print) | LCC DK508.852 (ebook) |
DDC 947.7086–dc23

LC record available at https://lccn.loc.gov/2020004399
LC ebook record available at https://lccn.loc.gov/2020004400

ISBN: HB: 978-1-3500-9856-5
PB: 978-1-3501-9288-1
ePDF: 978-1-3500-9861-9
eBook: 978-1-3500-9862-6

Typeset by Deanta Global Publishing Services, Chennai, India

To find out more about our authors and books visit www.bloomsbury.com
and sign up for our newsletters.

Contents

List of illustration vi
Notes on contributors viii

Introduction *Natalia Knoblock* 1

1 Discourses of conflict: Cross-linguistic corpus-assisted comparative discourse study of Russian and Ukrainian parliamentary debates of 2014 *Tatyana Karpenko-Seccombe* 11

2 Metaphor, identity and conflict in political discourse: A case study of President Poroshenko and President Putin's speeches *Liudmila Arcimavičienė* 45

3 The image of the Ukrainian crisis in the Polish-language media in Ukraine *Ewa Szkudlarek-Śmiechowicz and Izabela Błaszczyk* 65

4 Blended names in the discussions of the Ukrainian crisis *Natalia Beliaeva and Natalia Knoblock* 83

5 The antagonistic discourses of the Euromaidan: *Kolorady*, *Sovki* and *Vatniki* versus *Jumpers*, *Maidowns* and *Panheads* *Olga Baysha* 101

6 The Ukrainian nation – stepmother, younger sister or stillborn baby?: Evidence from Russian TV debates and related political sources (2013–15) *Daniel Weiss* 117

7 Who are 'they' for Ukrainians in Ukraine and in the diaspora? Othering in political discourse *Natalia Beliaeva and Corinne A. Seals* 137

8 Discursive practices in online media: Language ideologies in Ukraine in a time of crisis *Alla Nedashkivska* 157

9 Unrecognized holidays: Old and new 'state' traditions in the self-proclaimed republics in the east of Ukraine *Yulia Abibok* 177

10 Andriy Biletsky's Ukrainian order: Discourse, actions and prospects of democracy in Ukraine *Halyna Mokrushyna* 195

11 The art of the insult: (Re)creating Zaporizhian Cossacks' letter-writing on YouTube as collective creative insurgency *Alla Tovares* 213

12 Fighting fear with humour: The linguistic-pragmatic aspects *Yaroslava Sazonova* 233

13 Assimilative representations of Ukrainian refugees in the Russian and Ukrainian press: A 'burden' or a 'gain'? *Ludmilla A'Beckett* 253

Index 271

Illustration

Figures

2.1	Graphic representation of violence in political discourse	47
2.2	Metaphorical violence by kind in President Poroshenko's sample	52
2.3	Metaphorical violence by kind in President Putin's sample	55
2.4	Both leaders' conflict metaphorical styles	60
4.1	Emotional value of verbs used in the sentences with target words as subjects, by corpus and the structure of target words	92
4.2	Emotional value of modifiers of target words, by corpus and the structure of target words	94
4.3	A decision tree analysis of the contexts of the keywords in RPP and UPP	95
4.4	A decision tree analysis of the content of the contexts of the keywords in RPP and UPP, with the main predictor (blend) removed from the model	96
8.1	Language as a national symbol	164
8.2	One nation – One language	165
8.3	Distancing Ukrainian from Russian	167
8.4	Language choice: Do you speak Ukrainian?	168
8.5	Switch to Ukrainian: Language as a defense weapon	169
11.1	Ilya Repin. 'Zaporožcy/Zaporozhians' also known as 'Reply of the Zaporizhian Cossacks to Sultan Mehmed IV of the Ottoman Empire' (1880–1891) The State Russian Museum, St. Petersburg, Russia	216
11.2	YouTube video 'Letter to the Tzar[sic] / List do Carâ / Pis'mo k Carû', Babylon'13	221
11.3	Embedded (and blended) frames	227
11.4	Overlapping frames	227

Tables

1.1	Summary of Corpus Sizes	13
1.2	First 100 Keywords of Rada Corpus	34
1.3	First 100 Keywords of Duma Corpus	36
1.4	Thematic Groups of Keywords in Rada and Duma Corpora	38
1.5	Equivalent Keywords Shared between Two Corpora	15
1.6	Keywords of War, Aggression and Conflict in Both Corpora	39
1.7	Frequencies of Lemma *Separat*/ Separat** in the Rada Corpus and *Separat*/Separat** in the Duma Corpus	16
1.8	Frequencies of the Word *Krim*/ Crimea* in the Rada Corpus and *Krym*/Crimea* in the Duma Corpus	20

Illustration

1.9	Top 50 Collocates of Krim*/Crimea in Rada Corpus	40
1.10	Top 50 Collocates of Krym*/Crimea in Duma Corpus	41
1.11	Frequencies of Lemma *Aneks*/Annex** in the Rada Corpus and *Anneks*/Annex** in the Duma Corpus	21
1.12	Themes of Collocates of Krim*/ Crimea in Rada Corpus and Krym*/Crimea in the Duma Corpus	42
1.13	First 25 Collocates of Rosìâ/Russia in Rada Corpus	42
1.14	Themes Emerging from the Collocates of *Rossiâ/Russia* in the Ukrainian Duma Corpus	23
1.15	Comparison of Processes Associated with *Rosìâ/Russia* in Rada Corpus and *Ukraina/Ukraine* in Duma Corpus	26
1.16	Themes Emerging from the Right-hand Nominal Collocates of Rosìjs'k*/Russian in Rada Corpus and Ukrainsk*/Ukrainian in the Duma Corpus	43
2.1	Data Summary	49
2.2	Metaphor Frequencies in President Poroshenko's Speeches	50
2.3	Metaphor Frequencies in President Putin's Speeches	51
3.1	The Word Frequency: *Majdan, Demonstracja, Protest, Rewolucja, Rewolucja Godności, Euromajdan, Godność, Solidarność, Wolność* in the RC and the CC (per Million Words)	70
3.2	The Word Frequency List Developed on the Basis of the Reference Corpus (Places 1 to 10)	71
3.3	The Frequency of the Prepositional Phrases: *na Majdanie, na Majdan, na majdanach* (Per Million Words)	72
3.4	Verbs Underlining the Locative Aspect of the Term *Majdan* (Per Million Words)	73
3.5	The Frequency of Collocations Important for the Event-based Profile of the Term *Majdan* (Per Million Words)	74
3.6	The frequency of collocations important for the temporal profile of the term *Majdan* (per million words)	76
3.7	The most frequent collocations of the lexeme *solidarność* (per million words)	78
4.1	Frequencies of Use of the Target Words in RPP and UPP	89
4.2	The Percentage of Negative Verbs and Modifiers Used with Target Words in RPP and UPP	90
4.3	The Distribution of Verbs Used in Sentences with the Target Words as Subjects in RPP and UPP	92
4.4	The Distribution of Modifiers of Target Words in RPP and UPP	93
7.1	In-groups and Out-groups in the Discourse of Ukrainians from Different Regions of Ukraine (N Refers to the Number of In-group or Out-group Marking Pronouns in the Excerpts Analysed for the Present Study)	151
7.2	In-groups and out-groups in the discourse of Ukrainians in the diaspora (N refers to the number of in-group or out-group marking pronouns in the excerpts analysed for the present study)	152
11.1	Examples of strategies used to cause insult	224

Contributors

Ludmilla A'Beckett, PhD, is a research fellow at the Unit of Language Facilitation and Empowerment, University of the Free State, Bloemfontein, Republic of South Africa. Her main research interests are public discourse, intercultural communication and language policy in post-Soviet countries.

Yulia Abibok is a journalist and researcher from Donetsk, Ukraine. She is writing a dissertation at the National University Kyiv-Mohyla Academy on the transformation of the Donbas regional identity in 1989–2013 and is working on a book about the Second World War events in Powiat Trembowelski/Terebovlia rayon in eastern Poland/western Ukraine. She is a 2019–20 Institute for Human Sciences junior research fellow and lives in Kyiv, Ukraine.

Liudmila Arcimavičienė is an associate professor of English Linguistics at Vilnius University of Lithuania, teaching discourse analysis and political discourse at the Faculty of Philology, Institute of Foreign Languages. Her research interests lie in critical metaphor analysis, critical discourse analysis, ideological framing in the media, conflict scenarios and populist metaphor use in political discourse.

Olga Baysha is an associate professor at the National Research University 'Higher School of Economics', in Moscow, Russia. Olga Baysha earned her MS in Journalism from Colorado State University and her PhD in Communication from the University of Colorado at Boulder. Previously, she worked as a news reporter and editor in Kharkiv, Ukraine, and then as an editor-in-chief of a documentary production company in Kyiv, Ukraine. Her research centres mainly on political and cultural aspects of globalization, with an emphasis on new media and global social movements for justice and democratization. Dr Baysha is especially interested in analysing inherent anti-democratic tendencies of the discourses of Westernization employed by post-Soviet social movements.

Natalia Beliaeva specializes in word formation (in particular, lexical innovation such as blending and complex shortening) and morphological productivity, her most recent works being on blending as a morphological process (an invited contribution to The Oxford Encyclopedia of Morphology, Oxford University Press) and on factors that influence morphological productivity (a co-authored article in Zeitschrift für Wortbildung / *Journal of Word Formation* 3(1)). Natalia is also interested in second language acquisition, conducting research on the acquisition of multiword units, developing and delivering ESOL classes for learners with refugee background.

Izabela Błaszczyk obtained her doctor's degree in Slavic Linguistics from the University of Regensburg, Germany. Her research interests focus on heritage linguistics, modality and sociolinguistics. She is the author of two scientific monographs on heritage Polish and several articles on Polish language, culture and history.

Dr Tatyana Karpenko-Seccombe is a senior lecturer at the University of Huddersfield. She teaches English for academic purposes to international doctorate students. She completed both her MA in Language Studies and her doctorate in Linguistics at Lancaster University. Tatyana joined the University of Huddersfield in 2009. Prior to that, she taught translation studies at the City University of London. Tatyana has had interests in several linguistic disciplines, including corpus analysis, text and discourse analysis, cognitive linguistics and translation studies, as well as data-driven learning and teaching academic writing through corpora.

Natalia Knoblock is an associate professor of English at the Saginaw Valley State University in Michigan, USA. Her research interests lie mostly in political and cognitive linguistics, sociolinguistics and discourse analysis. Some of her queries focused on the US presidential debates, xenophobia and aggression in online communication, and the cognitive process of frameshifting in insults and propaganda.

Halyna Mokrushyna, Ph.D., is an independent researcher and writer. Her research interests include the challenges of the post-Soviet transition in Ukraine; social and economic inequality in the post-Soviet context; historical and cultural divisions within Ukraine; social memory and politics of memory; and relations between Russia and Canada and the broader context of the post-cold war world and relations between the East and the West. Her articles on these subjects were published on Counterpunch, Truthdig and Truthout websites. She currently teaches Ukrainian and Russian as foreign language to Canadian diplomats and develops teaching curriculum and testing materials.

Alla Nedashkivska is a professor of Slavic applied linguistics in the Department of Modern Languages and Cultural Studies, and a director of the Ukrainian Language Education Centre at the Canadian Institute of Ukrainian Studies at the University of Alberta. She publishes in the areas of Slavic linguistics, discourse analysis, gender linguistics, and political and media language, as well as language pedagogy and second language acquisition in Ukrainian. She authors Ukrainian language textbooks: *Ukrainian Through Its Living Culture*, University of Alberta Press 2010; *A Window into the World of Business: Ukrainian for Professional Communication*, University of Alberta Press/Pica Pica Press 2016; *PodorozhiUA*: Beginners' Ukrainian via the Blended-learning Model, forthcoming.

Yaroslava Sazonova, Ph.D., is Associate Professor of H. S. Skovoroda Kharkiv National Pedagogical University. She has about forty articles published in Ukraine, Poland, Lithuania, Check Republic and Russia. The latest printed work (2018) is a monograph *The Phenomenon of Fear in Horror Texts of Ukrainian and English-speaking Literature: Lingual Pragmatic Aspects*.

Corinne A. Seals is a senior lecturer of Applied Linguistics at Victoria University of Wellington in New Zealand. Drawing upon her Ukrainian heritage and research into Ukrainian language and identity, her most recent book is *Choosing a Mother Tongue: The Politics of Language and Identity in Ukraine* (Multilingual Matters, 2019). Her other recent books include *Embracing Multilingualism Across Educational Contexts* (Victoria University Press, 2019) and *Heritage Language Policies around the World* (Routledge, 2017). She is also Director of the Wellington Translanguaging Project and Translanguaging Aotearoa, and Board Member of the Ukrainian Educational and Support Trust in New Zealand.

Ewa Szkudlarek-Śmiechowicz is a linguist; she is a professor at the University of Lodz and Head of the Department of Contemporary Polish Language, University of Lodz. Her interests are linguistics of text and discourse, pragmatics, political linguistics, media studies and linguistic axiology. She is the author of two scientific monographs (*Wskaźniki nawiązania we współczesnych tekstach polskich* Łódź 2003; *Tekst w radiowej i telewizyjnej debacie politycznej. Struktura – spójność – funkcjonalność*, Łódź 2010) and over fifty scientific articles and chapters in monographs. She is also a co-editor of four scientific monographs (*Słowo we współczesnych dyskursach*, Łódź 2014; *Negacja w języku i komunikacji*, Łódź 2018) and an editor of the scientific journal *Acta Universitatis Lodziensis Folia Linguistica*.

Alla Tovares is Associate Professor in the Department of English at Howard University in Washington, D.C. Her main research interests include Bakhtin's theorizing on dialogue and carnival, language ideologies and digital communication. She is the co-author of *How to Write about the Media Today*; her articles have appeared in the *Journal of Language and Social Psychology*, *Text & Talk*, *Narrative Inquiry*, *World Englishes*, *Discourse & Society* and *Discourse, Context & Media*.

Daniel Weiss is a professor emeritus of Slavic Linguistics at Zurich University, Switzerland. He held chairs of Slavic linguistics as a full professor at the Universities of Hamburg, Munich and Zurich. Among his current research interests are the syntax of colloquial Russian and Polish and political discourse in contemporary Russia and Poland within a pragmatic and discourse-analytical approach. The last two of the five scientific research projects he directed were devoted to this domain. He has authored more than 150 scientific papers including one monograph and several (co-)edited volumes.

Introduction

Natalia Knoblock

Language of Conflict: Discourses of the Ukrainian Crisis is a collection of thematically unified chapters that examine the reflection of social, political and military conflict in public discourse. The volume elucidates discursive practices prompted by the situation of crisis, and it investigates the trends in language aggression, evaluation, persuasion and other elements of conflict communication from a discourse-analytical perspective. It describes the patterns and unique features of communication devoted to the situation in the Eastern European country of Ukraine, thus, bringing scholarly attention to a conflict that has largely escaped the linguistic community's scrutiny.

The conflict has provoked a flurry of propaganda, as well as emotional and sensational material, from both professional media and amateur content creators. Multiple works have examined the latest Ukrainian revolution's ideological and political implications from the point of view of political science (e.g. Lendman 2014; Sakwa 2015; Wilson 2014; Yekelchyk 2015). The Ukrainian crisis has also inspired stimulating research in the field of communication studies (e.g. Baysha 2017, 2018; Bohdanova 2014; Boyd-Barrett 2017; Pantti 2016). Nevertheless, linguistic and discourse-analytic studies related to the conflict are rare, and the language of the Ukrainian conflict remains understudied. That is unfortunate because the situation is unique in many ways, including a special set of ethnic, national and linguistic dynamics; in-group and out-group relations; and cultural phenomena influencing the discourse.

This volume focuses on the mediated aspects of conflict, recognizing the critical role language plays in instigating and communicating conflict. It has long been recognized that language is not only an instrument for describing events but also a part of events itself, shaping their meaning and helping to shape the social and political roles of communicators. This understanding of the role of language is common in sociolinguistics. An influential quote by Fishman (1972: 4) highlights that language is not merely the carrier of content, but can serve as content itself:

> Language is not merely a means of interpersonal communication and influence. It is not merely a carrier of content, whether latent or manifest. Language itself is content, a referent for loyalties and animosities, an indicator of social statuses and personal relationships, a marker of situations and topics as well as of the societal goals and the large-scale value-laden arenas of interaction that typify every speech community. (Fishman 1972: 4)

Language as content is specifically powerful in the time of conflict. Researchers have highlighted the discursive nature of warning signs of dangerous changes in social climate. For example, Classification ('us versus them'), Symbolization (labels or symbols of second-class citizenship) and Dehumanization (referring to humans as animals or inanimate objects) are listed by Stanton (2006) as the first three stages that preclude the slide towards genocide.

The power of language is also emphasized in the rich tradition of critical discourse analysis, which views discourse as a form of social action (Fairclough and Wodak 1997) and as a reflection of the way social power abuse, dominance and inequality are enacted, reproduced and resisted in the social and political context (van Dijk 2001: 352). Language is seen as both a reflection of and a tool for asserting power (Fairclough 2001). Text and talk are understood as possessing the ability to control people's minds, and, therefore, discourse is approached as one of the means to indirectly influence people's actions (van Dijk 2006).

With power comes danger – language has great potential to antagonize, hurt and polarize both individuals and groups. The longer a conflict lasts, the more discourses that demonize opponents get imprinted in collective memories and influence group ideologies. As can be learned from protracted conflicts, the lasting division and lack of interaction between antagonistic factions may lead to the creation of dehumanized and monstrous images of the 'other', which greatly complicate reconciliation (Doudaki and Carpentier 2018; Newman 1997). Language can be moulded, formed and manipulated in order to serve vicious, oppressive and ultimately catastrophic functions as easily as it can be used to spread goodwill. Therefore, a continuous and adaptive study of language is necessary to understand the ways it can contribute to alienation, dehumanization and violence.

Importantly, the relationship between language and conflict is at least two-way. First, language can function as a mirror reflecting the conflict. As speakers strive to make sense of threatening, complex and often chaotic situations, their cognitive processes are reflected in discourse through articulation of antagonism and of ethnic, social and political identities, and through categorization and framing of the conflict and its driving forces, aspects and participants. It can also serve as an instigator and facilitator of conflict, being a powerful instrument for antagonizing disagreeing factions. Both these functions are attended to in this book, where the relationship of conflict and language is approached from two main vantage points: how conflict is presented in the discourse under study through various linguistic means, and how it shapes communication while serving as a driving force of antagonistic language use.

The complex situation in Ukraine has produced discourses that provide analysts with valuable information for the study of language of conflict. In the winter of 2013/2014, *The Revolution of Dignity*, also known as *Euromaidan* or simply *Maidan*, replaced the Ukrainian government and initiated sweeping political and social reforms. The ensuing events split the society into disagreeing factions, plunged the economy into a deep recession and produced persisting military action, putting immense strain on the society. Predictably, the stress caused by the social discord, economic hardship and violence is reflected in hostile communication abounding in verbal aggression. The harsh conditions have also prompted discourses of coping, wherein speakers utilize various strategies to explain and rationalize their confusing and chaotic reality.

The title of the volume uses the word 'discourse' in the plural because one salient feature of communication related to the Ukrainian crisis is the multiple, often contradictory, visions of the situation. There appears to be little consensus about the state of affairs. The participants of the conflict, and their alleged goals, strategies, methods of action and other circumstances are presented differently depending on stance of the communicator, and they are hotly contested by the members of the discourse community. There is also a noticeable difference between official and unofficial communication, where official sources tend to be more unified and unofficial ones to be significantly more diverse. The discursive image of the crisis is dynamic and flexible, and it is contingent on the interpretation by interlocutors, who make judgements about the people, things and events they deal with, constructing their own 'truths' from their particular viewpoints.

The volume illuminates these competing worldviews and the conflicting positions of the stakeholders in the political and social developments of the country through the study of their discourse. It recognizes the importance of the issues of power and identity in the construction of the discursive image of the current situation, and it scrutinizes the many factors relevant to it, such as politics, culture, language and history. The chapters identify how these underlying forces shape the current discourse in Ukraine and study the role these factors play in transmitting communicators' particular worldviews. They highlight the role of culture in crisis communication and they connect the current events to historical phenomena relevant to the communicators. The studies in the volume acknowledge clashing perspectives on the realities of the social, political and military conflict that has been unfolding in Ukraine since 2014, and they address the role of discourse in reflecting existing views. The chapters also analyse how various social groups in Ukraine respond to the crisis, and how this response is reflected in their narratives.

Additionally, the volume acknowledges communicators' active role in constructing the (often incompatible) discursive images of the conflict. It examines the categorization and framing of the various aspects of the Ukrainian crisis as the communicators shape their own versions of the situation. It also focuses on the conscious, strategic use of linguistic resources in negative and aggressive discourse, and several chapters explore lexical and morphological phenomena, highlighting the features of communication unique to the Ukrainian discourse of conflict.

Readers of this volume will become immersed in the current state of Ukrainian affairs through the study of prominent narratives in the Ukrainian public sphere, and they will get a sense of the current problems and of the means and strategies employed to address them. Informed by the volume's chapters, readers will consider the divergent views expressed at different levels of society through various media sources. The chapters address the most salient topics of the conflict – its causes and goals, the sides, and the values and ideologies of the opposing parties – and focus on categorization, stance, positioning and framing, (de)legitimation, manipulation, and strategies for coping with antagonism and war. They analyse how various social groups in Ukraine respond to the crisis through the reflection of their response in their narratives. Concentrating on the linguistic features of the salient discourses of the Ukrainian conflict, this volume illuminates conflicting positions and worldviews of the stakeholders in the country's developments through the study of their discourse; highlights the role of culture in crisis communication and connects current events to the important historical phenomena salient for the communicators; examines the categorization and framing of the various aspects of the Ukrainian crisis as the communicators present multiple, often conflicting, discursive versions of reality; and includes contributions from authors in Ukraine as well as from outside of the country who provide diverse points of view on Ukrainian crisis communication. The discussion addresses and advances the understanding of the relationship between language, discourse and society by highlighting the complex interrelation of linguistic and extralinguistic phenomena in a time of crisis. Moreover, it draws attention to the discourse participants' active and deliberate communicative activity.

The multidisciplinary research presented in the volume utilizes a broad range of approaches and methods. The majority of studies fall within the critical discourse analysis and critical metaphor analysis, and some contributions also employ corpus-linguistic or multimodal approaches. This book offers a range of case studies that examine the multiple facets of the situation of post-Maidan Ukraine. Focusing mainly on informal communication and the material gathered from online sources, the collection provides insight into the ways people directly affected by the crisis think about, respond to and experience the conflict in everyday settings.

Through methodologically diverse case studies of a wide range of topics, the volume assembles a multifaceted perspective, one that provides broad insights into the complex interplay of culture, conflict, politics and language. While it would be overreaching to say that the full variety of discursive patterns of today's Ukraine are reflected in the book, the chapters do give readers a glimpse of the richness and range of discourses coexisting and competing in modern Ukraine. To deploy an art metaphor, the picture these chapters paint is not so much a painting as it is a mosaic. Each piece is independent and different from the rest, and each one contributes valuably to the overall image. Each reflects distinct communicative features, and only when taken together can the chapters begin to approach the task of representing the manifold, fragmentary and often contradictory reality of the Ukrainian discourse and the conflict upon which it centres.

It is difficult to categorize the studies simply, because the concepts they explore are multifaceted and involve complex and overlapping aspects. However, the chapters can be roughly grouped as doing the following: framing the conflict (Karpenko, Arcimavičienė, Szkudlarek-Śmiechowicz and Błaszczyk), analysing elements of verbal aggression (Beliaeva and Knoblock, Baysha, Weiss); identity work (Seals and Beliaeva, Nedashkivska, Abibok, Mokrushina); coping strategies (Tovares, Sazonova), and calls for compassion to refugees and internally displaced persons as the victims of the conflict (A'Beckett).

Tatyana Karpenko-Seccombe contributes a comprehensive corpus-linguistic study of the Ukrainian and Russian parliamentary debates of 2014. The analysis highlights representative keywords and their collocates to identify the main themes of the debates, such as war, aggression, violence and a negative presentation of the 'other side'. The chapter reveals the prevalent ideologies and attitudes of politicians of the two parliaments at the time of crisis by looking into the framing of the dominant themes. The results help to understand the respective visions of the conflict by tracing similarities and highlighting differences, confirming and quantifying them, in the official discourse of the two countries. **Liudmila Arcimavičienė** continues the comparative approach by scrutinizing the metaphor use in the speeches by Presidents Poroshenko (of Ukraine) and Putin (of Russia) devoted to the political conflict between Ukraine and the Russian Federation in their addresses to domestic and international audiences. She applies the critical metaphor analysis to the reflection of ideology and identity and emphasizes the differences between the two speakers in the use of violence-related metaphors. The study addresses the complexity of discursive political violence that integrates identity, ideology and metaphorical violence categories. The chapter by **Ewa Szkudlarek-Śmiechowicz and Izabela Błaszczyk** examines the discursive representation of Maidan, one of the most important concepts related to the revolution of 2013/14 that acquired a symbolic status. They bring into discussion the point of view that is often overlooked. In addition to Ukrainians and Russians, Ukraine is home to several other ethnicities, such as Jewish, Rusyn, Tatar, Bulgarian, Hungarian, Polish and more, each with their own rich culture and history. The chapter presents a snapshot of the views of the Polish minority on the current situation in Ukraine by exploring the use of the word 'Maidan' in Polish-language Ukrainian media. It represents the voices of people who are affected by the crisis by the virtue of being Ukrainian residents and who have a unique outlook because of their special position and the particular cultural lens through which they see the events.

The chapter by **Natalia Beliaeva** and **Natalia Knoblock** addresses innovative word formation in hostile communication as it concentrates on morphological blends and their contexts in the discussions of the Ukrainian crisis. The chapter compares blended insulting nicknames for Presidents Poroshenko and Putin to the uses of actual names, and it draws conclusions about the special aspects of use of blended names in Russian and Ukrainian news posts, blog posts and forums. The study explores the relationship between the semantics of blended and non-blended names, and their role in political discourse. The chapter by **Olga Baysha** considers the role of dehumanizing metaphors in promoting and intensifying radicalization. She describes several slurs that emerged in the course of the conflict to designate and insult opponents, and claims that features of social network communication facilitate radicalizing antagonisms. She argues that such communication allows the barrier between self and other to become solid and impermeable, which makes the prospects for peaceful dialogue between the disagreeing factions unlikely. **Daniel Weiss** shares a discussion of metaphorical mappings of family metaphors applied to the relationship of Ukraine and Russia. The chapter highlights the conventional family metaphors referring to Ukraine, stemming mostly from Russian TV talk shows, and relates them to Ukrainian metaphors revealing a similar cognitive frame. It traces the conceptualization of Ukraine as somewhat inferior and dependent rather than as a full-fledged independent nation. While revealing an inconsistent pattern of mappings, it discusses the persuasive force of metaphors and argues that the metaphorical representation of Ukraine as a younger, weaker or dependent family member is detrimental to productive dialogue between the nations.

The issues of identity find their reflection in the chapter by **Natalia Beliaeva and Corinne A. Seals** who focus on the use of pronouns like 'we' and 'they' to trace the borders their informants draw between in-groups they identify with and out-groups they distance from. The researchers highlight their interviewees' negotiation of in-groups and out-groups according to several factors, and discuss the issue of national, ethnic, linguistic and other identities of Ukrainians and ex-Ukrainian emigrants. The chapter exemplifies the complexity of the concept of a Ukrainian identity by showing that a national border is not a sufficient or even an adequate characteristic for classifying a person's identity. The role of language in the Ukrainian identity is examined in **Alla Nedashkivska**'s chapter that concentrates on various discursive practices that relate to the position of the Ukrainian language and to its coexistence and competition with Russian in public and private sphere. The study analyses different discursive strategies of social and traditional media that are ideologically invested and are reflective of a multiplicity of language ideologies in Ukrainian society. It focuses on the role, status and functions of the Ukrainian language in Ukraine as the country is struggling to forge a unified national identity while simultaneously giving some recognition to national diversity. **Yulia Abibok** brings into spotlight an out-of-the-mainstream discourse as she examines the texts of congratulatory addresses produced by leaders of break-away territories in Ukraine's eastern region. Her chapter traces the efforts to create a new identity in those areas through prominent topi and through strategies of self- and other-presentation as it deconstructs the discursive strategies in commemorative speeches used to transform and partly dismantle old local identities and to construct new ones. The far-right, ultraconservative vision for Ukraine is reflected in the discourse-analytic study by **Halyna Mokrushina** who analyses Andriy Biletsky's blogs. The discourse of a Ukrainian activist turned insurgent, turned military commander, turned politician represents the nationalist views on the current situation and paints a picture of an ideal Ukraine according to that sector of the society. Mokrushina argues that verbal aggression is dangerous due to its tendency to normalize such discourse and desensitize the society to it, which prepares people to accept physical aggression as a fact of life rather than a violation of the norm.

The case study by **Alla Tovares** focuses on a video in which Ukrainian soldiers recreate a scene from an iconic nineteenth-century painting. She treats the resemiotization processes involved in staging of the video as creative insurgency when Ukrainian soldiers collaboratively perform an insult towards the Russian president and Russian policies towards Ukraine. The study demonstrates how social actors draw on multimodal intertextual resources of a culture to utilize them to relieve stress. By drawing on a famed and culturally important scene from the past, the soldiers emphasize the link between themselves and the heroic past of their country, which helps them to cope with the harsh reality of war. Another study that presents a coping strategy analyses the use of humour to mock and insult the opponent. The material was collected by **Yaroslava Sazonova** from a popular blog that represents a middle ground in at least two ways: it is written in Surzhik, a highly stigmatized mix of Russian and Ukrainian languages, and it strongly attacks the Russian side while still occasionally criticizing the Ukrainian citizens and authorities, thus standing neither with the 'victory' nor the 'betrayal' polarized discourses prevalent in the Ukrainian public sphere. The author identifies several strategies of humorous verbal attacks: to emphasize the abnormality of the threatening object, delegitimize it and distance from it; and to minimize the threatening effect and provide psychological comfort and support for one's allies, and to unite them against the antagonist. **Ludmilla A'Beckett** discusses the representation of refugees and internally displaced persons (IDPs) in Russian and Ukrainian formal and informal media. The results of the study demonstrate that prevalent discursive patterns observed in the media of Western Europe are not representative of the Russian and Ukrainian patterns of discussing refugees and IDPs. Her study shows that the topos of large numbers, described by the Western researchers as dehumanizing, does not necessarily have the same negative connotation in Russian and Ukrainian sources. Thus, it further highlights the role of extralinguistic factors in evaluation, which is not inherent in a language system but emerges from the reality speakers describe.

The material for the studies comes from a wide variety of sources. It represents official communication, such as speeches of the respective countries' presidents or parliamentary debates, collected from official webpages of state representatives and institutions, and from addresses by the leaders of breakaway 'republics'. The authors also draw sources from traditional media such as newspapers or magazines, online news sources and television, as well as from informal online sources, such as blogs or social networks. Some data were collected in direct interviews with Ukrainian citizens or emigrants. An important requirement for the essays' inclusion in this volume was that they must concentrate on the discourses originating from Ukraine or Russia, and that outsiders' evaluations and interpretations are left for further investigation.

The authors make sure to note which languages they worked with in their projects. The majority of the chapters use Russian and Ukrainian as the material of analysis, with the exception of the Polish media study, the chapter which works with English-language interviews of Ukrainians, and the study that included President Poroshenko's speeches delivered in English. It is necessary to mention that the Russian and Ukrainian languages in the sources are sometimes mixed. The linguistic situation in Ukraine is such that the Ukrainian language is the sole official language of the country and dominates the public sphere, but Russian continues to be used in informal communication. Since many of the studies are conducted on the material collected from informal sources, many of them work with Russian and Ukrainian material mixed in different proportions.

It is self-evident that conflicts are always socially and culturally embedded, and that studying one is impossible without familiarity with its broad context. However, this volume attempts to refrain from making judgements about the situation, with the goal of remaining ideologically neutral and focusing exclusively on the linguistic side of the happenings. Luckily for readers who are unfamiliar with the specifics of the conflict and want to educate themselves about the political, social and military events in Ukraine, there is a rich and abundant scholarly literature on those topics. In the field of political science, multiple studies offer analyses of the latest Ukrainian revolution's causes, chronology and results, two of the most-cited monographs on the topic being Sakwa (2015) and Wilson (2014). The readers who are interested in the historical background of interrelation and interaction between Ukraine and Russia can refer to Kubicek (2008), Magocsi (2010), or Subtelny (2009), among numerous other studies of Ukrainian history. Finally, questions of Ukrainian linguistic policies and linguistic ideology continue to appear in the works by Bilaniuk (2005, 2016), Kulyk (2011), and others.

One of the consequences of the effort to avoid ideological engagement as much as possible is that different authors use different terms to categorize what is happening in modern Ukraine. The terms 'crisis', 'conflict' and 'war' have been politicized and are sometimes perceived as markers of a scholar's ideological leaning. The contributors to this volume were free to choose the term they felt was most fitting. A similar attitude was adopted in regard to the words 'rebels', 'separatists', 'self-defence', 'ATO', 'Maidan', 'anti-Maidan' and such. The chapter authors applied the terms they felt reflected the situation most effectively. I hope the readers will judge their contributions by the quality of their research rather than by their perceived affiliations and political and ideological preferences.

Staying away from the politics of the conflict, however, does not equate to irrelevance. While 'the results of violent conflict tend to outlast the physical confrontation, continuing to feed antagonistic perceptions' and undermining true reconciliation (Doudaki and Carpentier 2018: 2), scholarly attention to the conflict's aspects might help Ukraine to overcome its challenges. Studying discourse of crisis might aid its resolution because communication can serve not only as a tool for initiating and managing conflicts but also as a means to resolve them (Chilton 1997). An old quote applies here: 'Not everything that can be faced can be changed. But nothing can be changed until it is faced' (Baldwin, 1962). Therefore, there is hope that shedding light on the linguistic aspects of the Ukrainian crisis might play a positive role in resolving it. By highlighting potentially problematic discursive practices of actors in Ukraine and elsewhere, this research could nudge people towards reducing verbal aggression, promote the more responsible use of language, encourage attention to different points of view and build the will to compromise.

A note on transliteration

This volume is a collection of writings from scholars from different fields and different backgrounds, one of the consequences of which was a variety of transliteration systems and conventions they preferred. To unify the text, avoid switching from one trilateration convention to another in every chapter and broaden the potential readership, the chapters used translations into English where feasible. Short quotes incorporated into the text of the chapters were transliterated using the international standard system, but when a point could be better made by reference to the original, Cyrillic was used and translations were provided after the block quotations. To keep personal and geographical names recognizable, this volume preserves them in their common anglicized version, such as Ukraine, Poroshenko, Putin, Kyiv, Moscow, Donbass, Crimea and so on.

References

Baldwin, J. (1962), 'As Much Truth as One Can Bear; To Speak Out About the World as It Is, Says James Baldwin, Is the Writer's Job', *New York Times*. Available from: https://www.nytimes.com/1962/01/14/archives/as-much-truth-as-one-can-bear-to-speak-out-about-the-world-as-it-is.html

Baysha, O. (2017), 'In the Name of National Security: Articulating Ethno-Political Struggles as Terrorism', *Journal of Multicultural Discourses*, 12 (4): 332–48.

Baysha, O. (2018), *Miscommunicating Social Change: Lessons from Russia and Ukraine*. Lanham: Lexington Books.

Bilaniuk, L. (2005), *Contested Tongues: Language Politics and Cultural Correction in Ukraine*. Ithaka and London: Cornell University Press.

Bilaniuk, L. (2016), 'Ideologies of Language in Wartime', in Olga Bertelsen (ed.), *Revolution and War in Contemporary Ukraine: The Challenge of Change*, 139–60. Stuttgart: Ibidem Verlag.

Bohdanova, T. (2014), 'Unexpected Revolution: The Role of Social Media in Ukraine's Euromaidan Uprising', *European View*, 13 (1): 133–42.

Boyd-Barrett, O. (2017), *Western Mainstream Media and the Ukraine Crisis: A Study in Conflict Propaganda*. London: Routledge.

Chilton, P. A. (1997), 'The Role of Language in Human Conflict: Prolegomena to the Investigation of Language as a Factor in Conflict Causation and Resolution', *Current Issues in Language & Society*, 4 (3), 174–89.

Doudaki, V. and Carpentier, N. (2018), *Cyprus and Its Conflicts: Representations, Materialities and Cultures*. New York: Berghahn Books.

Fairclough, N. (2001), *Language and Power*, 2nd edn. Harlow, UK and New York: Longman.

Fairclough, N. and Wodak, R. (1997), 'Critical Discourse Analysis', in T. A. van Dijk (ed.), *Discourse as Social Interaction*, 258–84. London, UK: Sage.

Fishman, J. (1972), *The Sociology of Language*. Rowley, MA: Newbury.

Kubicek, P. (2008), *The History of Ukraine*. Westport, CT: Greenwood Press.

Kulyk, V. (2011), 'Language Identity, Linguistic Diversity and Political Cleavages: Evidence from Ukraine', *Nations and Nationalism*, 17 (3): 627–48.

Lendman, S. (ed.) (2014), *Flashpoint in Ukraine: How the US Drive for Hegemony Risks World War III*. Atlanta: Clarity Press.

Magocsi, P. R. (2010), *A History of Ukraine: The Land and Its Peoples*. Toronto: University of Toronto Press.

Newman, D. (1997), 'Creating the Fences of Territorial Separation: The Discourses of Israeli-Palestinian Conflict Resolution', *Geopolitics and International Boundaries*, 2 (2), 1–35.

Pantti, M. (2016), *Media and the Ukraine Crisis: Hybrid Media Practices and Narratives of Conflict*. New York: Peter Lang.

Sakwa, R. (2015), *Frontline Ukraine: Crisis in the Borderlands*. London: I.B. Tauris.

Subtelny, O. (2009), *Ukraine: A History*. Toronto: University of Toronto Press.

Van Dijk, T. A. (2001), 'Critical Discourse Analysis', in Deborah Schiffrin, Deborah Tannen and Heidi E. Hamilton (eds), *Handbook of Discourse Analysis*. Malden, MA: Blackwell Publishers.

Van Dijk, T. A. (2006), 'Discourse and Manipulation', *Discourse & Society*, 17 (3), 359–83.

Wilson, A. (2014), *Ukraine Crisis: What It Means for the West*. New Haven: Yale University Press.

Yekelchyk, S. (2015), *The Conflict in Ukraine: What Everyone Needs to Know*. Oxford: Oxford University Press.

1

Discourses of conflict

Cross-linguistic corpus-assisted comparative discourse study of Russian and Ukrainian parliamentary debates of 2014

Tatyana Karpenko-Seccombe

1 Introduction

The year 2014 was undeniably one of the most dramatic years in the history of Ukraine. It saw the annexation of Crimea by Russia; the proclamation of two pro-Russian republics – the Donetsk People's Republic (DPR) and the Luhansk People's Republic (LPR) – leading to full-scale armed conflict between Ukrainian government troops and pro-Russian forces; the failed attempt of a truce and a ceasefire; and continuing disputes between Russia and Ukraine over gas supplies and prices.

Against the backdrop of these events, this study focuses on the parliamentary debates of the two countries in conflict, examining discourses surrounding these contentious events. The aim of this paper is to investigate how these events are framed in debates in the Russian and Ukrainian parliaments. In particular, the following questions are addressed:

(1) How different are linguistic features used in the parliamentary debates of countries in conflict when representing the same events?
(2) What implications do language differences have for constructing the same events in two different discourses?

The methodological framework used in this research is a combination of the following:

- A comparative cross-linguistic approach
- Discourse analysis; analysis of transitivity features
- Corpus analysis

1.1 Cross-linguistic corpus studies

Unlike previous studies in political discourse, most of which focused on one discourse in one country and in one language, this study explores the data of two corpora in two languages, with the aim of providing a comparison between two discourses covering one and the same period of unrest from two opposing points of view. However, up to now, far too little attention has been paid to the combination of corpus and discourse analysis with cross-linguistic research; corpus-assisted discourse studies have so far focused mainly on monolingual corpora (Vessey 2013: 3).

1.2 Discourse analysis and transitivity

Even though corpus studies of discourse have grown into a major area of modern research, there have been comparatively few empirical investigations into parliamentary debates (see Baker 2004, Baker 2009, Findlay 2017, Huysmans and Buonfino 2008). In this study, I provide a new perspective on discourse analysis of parliamentary debate, suggesting a *comparative cross-linguistic* approach to study of conflict discourse.

Halliday's concept of transitivity provides the framework for corpus data analysis.

Vocabulary analysis is informed by Fairclough's suggestion that different ways of wording the same idea would lead to differences in 'ideological representation of the reality' ([1989]1996: 115). In terms of grammar, discourse analysis in this paper draws on Halliday's idea of transitivity (1967), and specifically on the use of active and passive voice and its implications for activization and passivization of the participants.

1.3 Corpus analysis

This study employs a productive combination of discourse and corpus methods in order to suggest 'a possible interpretation of the corpus', and can be described as corpus-assisted (Tognini-Bonelli 2001: 10–11); it 'is grounded in making sense of the frequency patterns provided by computer software' (McEnery, and Baker 2015: 246). Corpus studies are now commonly seen as the first step in linguistic enquiry (see Baker 2006, Gabrielatos and Baker 2008; Mautner, 2009), and they are supplemented by qualitative research offering interpretation of the quantitative data.

2 Corpora and methods

To answer the research questions, two corpora were built, covering the sessions of the Ukrainian parliament, the Rada (February–August 2014), and the Russian parliament, the Duma (January–July 2014) using the transcripts on official sites of both parliaments (Oficialnyj sajt gosudarstvennoj Dumy; Oficijnyj portal Verhovnoji Rady Ukrajiny). The chosen period covers the initial crisis in relations between Russia and Ukraine, followed by fully fledged armed conflict and ending with the Minsk I agreement

(September 2014) – the first attempt at negotiating a peaceful resolution. Corpora were compiled from the official websites containing complete openly available transcripts of parliamentary sessions. Both corpora contain transcripts of all the sessions for the chosen period and thus constitute representative samples of language (see Sinclair 2004) used in the period of conflict. Corpora contain references to the same events, which is essential for answering the research questions. The size of the Ukrainian Rada corpus is 713,507 tokens and of Russian Duma corpus is 1,469,502 tokens. The corpora are different in size because of differences in the number of sessions and in the length of transcribed discussions.

In order to identify differences between corpora, a comparison of keywords was carried out because keywords are 'a useful tool for directing researchers to significant lexical differences between texts' (Baker 2009:126); they 'express important evaluative social meanings' (Stubbs 2010 :21); keywords are characterized by statistically significant frequencies which are not necessarily high, but 'unusual... by comparison with a reference corpus of some kind' (Scott 1997:236).

Thus, two reference corpora were constructed observing the principles of size and similarity (Brezina 2018: 81). Each reference corpus contains the transcripts of one parliamentary session of 2011 from each country, a period of relative stability and peace before the unrest of 2013– 4. This allowed comparisons between parliamentary language used in the debates of both parliaments before and during the military conflict.

The Ukrainian Rada reference corpus covers the period from 1 February 2011 to 8 July 2011 (the complete eighth parliamentary session of the sixth convocation). The size of the Rada reference corpus is 1,227,829 tokens. The Russian Duma reference corpus has 1,703,596 tokens and covers a period from 11 January to 8 July 2011 (the complete seventh session of the fifth convocation) (see Table 1.1).

The first step in the research was to extract and analyse the keywords by comparing target corpora with reference corpora looking for unusual frequencies of particular words, which indicate the significance of this word.

Another line of enquiry was provided by the study of collocates that are indicative of common associations, evaluative overtones and stereotypical attitudes 'widely shared within a speech community' (Stubbs, 2001, p. 35). Statistically significant collocates were derived from both corpora using the AntConc Collocates Tool (Anthony 2018) and applying the Mutual Information (MI) statistical test to establish the strength of association between the words (Baker 2006; McEnery and Wilson 2001) within a five-word span (Baker 2006; Gabreilatos and Baker 2008), with an MI score of 3.0 or higher

Table 1.1 Summary of Corpus Sizes

Corpora	Tokens
Rada (Ukrainian parliament) corpus 2014	713,507
Rada reference corpus 2011	1,227,829
Duma (Russian parliament) corpus 2014	1,469,502
Duma reference corpus 2011	1,703,596

that, according to Hunston (2002) and Stubbs (1995), can be taken as evidence that the two items have a strong collocation.

3 Corpus analysis and findings

Two keyword lists were compiled, one for each corpus in each language, in order to conduct cross-linguistic examination of lists and, subsequently, of the concordance lines. The corpora were analysed with AntConc text analysis tools (Anthony, 2018) that allow for the manipulation of data in the Cyrillic alphabet. In measuring statistical significance, Log-Likelihood (LL) scores were used. Log Likelihood establishes whether there are differences in word frequencies between a target and a reference corpus, and whether the differences are accidental or statistically significant. In this study a cut-off point of LL = 10.83 was applied, providing a certainty of 99.9% that the statistical significance of the keywords was not accidental ($p < 0.001$). However, LL scores do not show the size of the difference in frequencies, or *effect size*. For the effect size, Hardie's Log Ratio (LR) statistic was used. These settings resulted in obtaining 813 keyword types (309,135 keyword tokens) from the Duma corpus and 1,284 keyword types (263,404 keyword tokens) from the Rada corpus.

A higher LR number points to a bigger effect size or difference in frequencies. I used a LR of 3 as a cut-off point, which means that the frequency in the target corpora is at least six times higher than in reference corpus. The keywords in both corpora (with a LL of 10.83 or over) were sorted by LR, and then all the keywords with an effect size below 3 were disregarded. Next, all the proper names (except place names directly related to the conflict, like Crimea, Luhansk, Donbass) were discounted. This left me with 200 keywords for the Russian Duma corpus and 466 keywords for the Ukrainian Rada corpus. All the results discussed further are given on the basis of the analysis of the complete list of keywords; however, due to the space limitations, only first 100 keywords from each corpus are listed in Tables 1.2 and 1.3 of the Appendix.

In forming thematic groups, some keywords had to be disambiguated by examining concordance lines or larger contexts. For example, concordances of the lemma *teritor*/ territory* showed that in the Ukrainian Rada corpus, 820 out of 934 tokens of this lemma, were connected with the conflict and used in collocations such as *teritorìâ Krimu /territory of Crimea, na okupovanij teritorìï/on the occupied territories* and *teritorìal'noï cìlostnostì Ukraïni /territorial integrity of Ukraine.*

Keywords connected with government, state institutions, elections, parliament, parliamentary parties and procedures were not considered in this study. Some groups of keywords are indirectly connected to various aspects of conflict – most notably truce and peace (10 keywords), followed by semantic groups connected with Ukrainian revolution of 2014 (6), gas (5) and language (2) (see Table 1.4 in the Appendix).

The keywords of the Russian Duma corpus provide a somewhat different outline of 'aboutness'. Out of 200 keywords in the Russian Duma corpus, twenty-nine, or 14.5 per cent, are connected with the theme of war and conflict, in comparison with 35 per

Table 1.5 Equivalent Keywords Shared between Two Corpora

Lemmas	Keywords Rada	Keywords Duma
Krim*/Krym*/Crimea	12	9
peremir/peremirie/ truce	1	1
majdan/majdan/maidan	3	3
zahid /zapad /West	1	2

cent in the Rada corpus, which shows that the debates in the Ukrainian parliament are more focused on the topics of aggression and war. As keywords are 'most unusually frequent' words (Scott, 2015: 235), the larger number of keywords in the smaller corpus of Ukrainian Rada may indicate that the language of parliamentary debates in the Ukrainian parliament at a time of conflict is much more uncharacteristic and divergent from the 'norm' of pre-conflict debates than the equivalent language of the Russian parliament.

Other thematic groups in the Russian Duma corpus are comparable with those of the Ukrainian corpus (see Table 1.4) and are also significantly smaller. As with the Rada corpus, in order to group keywords thematically, concordance lines had to be examined more closely. For example, the noun *Kiev* was added to the group of conflict because it is used as a modifier in collocations *kievskaâ hunta/Kiev Junta, kievskie marionetki/Kiev puppets* and is related to conflict.

Close manual comparison of keywords further revealed four shared equivalent keywords in both corpora: *Krim*/Krym*/Crimea, peremir/peremirie/truce, majdan/majdan/maidan* and *zahid/zapad /West* with their derivatives (see Table 1.5), three of which – *Crimea, maidan* and *truce* – are directly related to the conflict.

Distribution of keywords connected with war, aggression and conflict between two corpora is shown in Table 1.6 of the Appendix.

Even though the keywords point to common themes in both corpora, there are crucial differences in the meaning, connotation, co-text and context of the apparently equivalent keywords and themes. The sections given further provide such an analysis, focusing in more detail on specific keywords that are representative of particular discoursal themes.

4 Discourse of separatism

The Ukrainian words *separatist, separatizm* and their Russian translation equivalents *separatist, separatizm* mean *separatist, separatism*. Even though they are very similar in their dictionary denotative meanings, they have different contextual connotative meanings, which are apparent in the corpora and can be explained through the lens of the events of 2014. Connotative meaning is understood in this study as 'the communicative value an expression has by virtue of what it *refers to*, over and above its purely conceptual content' (Leech, [1974]1990:12; emphasis as in the original). Connotation can vary even between members of the same speech community,

Table 1.7 Frequencies of Lemma *Separat*/ Separat** in the Rada Corpus and *Separat*/Separat** in the Duma Corpus

	Rada corpus		Duma corpus	
word	Raw freq	Relative freq wpm	Raw freq	Relative freq wpm
separat*	267	374	13	9

depending on 'real world experience' associated with the word or expression ([1974]1990, 12–13).

In May 2014, the Ukrainian government declared the territories of Crimea and the self-proclaimed Donetsk and Luhansk republics 'temporarily occupied' (Zakon [Law] № 1207-VII). Separatism was condemned in several acts of the Ukrainian parliament as criminal and subversive activity fuelled by the Russian Federation and directed at undermining the territorial integrity of Ukraine.

In the Ukrainian Rada corpus, the lemma *separat*/separat** (thirteen keywords) occurs 267 times, all of them referring to Donetsk, Luhansk, Russian or pro-Russian separatists. In the Russian Duma corpus, there are thirteen lemmas *separat*/separat**, nine of which are related to Ukraine.

Close analysis of the co-text shows that in the Ukrainian Rada corpus, all but four occurrences of the lemma *separat*/separat** (263 out of 267 words) are distinctly negatively marked. It can be argued that this is an acquired negative contextual connotation that developed within the political situation of 2014.

To trace the development of negative connotation, consider the meaning of the word *separatizm/separatism* in the Ukrainian online dictionary of borrowed words 'Slovopedia' (*slovopedia.org.ua/36/53409/247899.html*) dating back to 2007, the pre-conflict era:

separatism
(1) Desire to separate
(2) In multinational states, the desire of ethnic minorities to separate and create their own state or autonomous region (*translation TKS*)

This definition is neutral in tone, without evaluative or emotional connotations, which can be attributed with some confidence to the fact that the dictionary was created prior to the conflict between Ukrainian forces and the breakaway eastern regions of Luhansk and Donetsk supported by Russia. In the Rada corpus of 2014, however, the lemma *separat*/separat** consistently co-occurs with words of negative semantics, for example:

ekstremìzmu ta separatizmu / extremism and separatism,

teroristami, okupantami i separatictami / by terrorists, occupiers and separatists

Close reading of concordances showed that the words surrounding the lemma *separat*/separat** in the Rada corpus are also highly emotional, appearing in the contexts of killing and unrest. Such acquired affective negative meaning is defined by Leech as communicating 'the feelings and attitudes of the speaker/writer' ([1974]1990: 23):

*Це **злочини** проти територіальної цілісності України. Це **тероризм, сепаратизм**. І це **злочини** проти фактично людей, які стосуються **масових вбивств** (Ukrainian)*

These are **crimes** against the territorial integrity of Ukraine. This is **terrorism, separatism**. These are **crimes** in fact against people, they concern **mass murders**

Connotative and affective meanings are 'unstable' and may vary depending on 'culture, historical period, and the experience of the individual' ([1974]1990: 13). Negative connotations of the word *separat*/separat** throughout the corpus testify to an almost unanimous negative discourse position towards separatism in Rada debates with very few exceptions. Those exceptions are, however, interesting to consider. In four cases out of 267 in the Rada corpus, the evaluative meaning is different; *separat*/separat** is not used negatively, in effect, opposition speakers try to 'reclaim' the neutral connotation of the word or question its negative connotation:

Почему когда в Ровно, Полтаве вооруженные захваты администрации вы называете революцией, в Крыму вы называете сепаратистским переворотом? (Russian)

Why when it is an armed invasion of city administrations in Rovno, Poltava – you call it a revolution, and in Crimea you call it a separatist coup?

Contextual meaning of *separat*/separat** in Russian corpus is also different. Out of thirteen instances in the Duma corpus, nine are related to separatism in Ukraine, and in all nine cases, speakers are taking exception to rebels in Eastern Ukraine being called *separatists*:

*Геноцид против мирного населения эти СМИ называют антитеррористической операцией, граждан, вставших на защиту своей жизни, чести и достоинства, -- **сепаратистами**, боевиками (Russian)*

The media call genocide against civilians an antiterrorist operation and citizens who are protecting their lives, honour and dignity – **separatists**, militants

In this example from Duma corpus, the Russian Duma speakers reject the term *separatist* exactly because of the negative affective connotation it has in Ukrainian discourse when used with reference to pro-Russian rebels. In the discourse of the Russian parliament the lemma *separat*/separat** is not used with reference to the rebels in the Eastern regions of Ukraine, and such use is condemned.

всё ещё можно изменить, если киевские власти изменят свою риторику, изменят своё отношение к волеизъявлению граждан на юго-востоке

> *Украины, **если они прекратят называть их сепаратистами, прекратят называть их террористами*** (Russian)
>
> everything can still be changed if the Kiev authorities change their rhetoric, change their attitude to the will of the citizens living in the south-east of Ukraine, **if they stop calling them separatists, stop calling them terrorists**

Separatist in the Duma corpus has negative connotation only when it refers to those who attempt to separate from Russia; there are three cases of such use, two of which refer to 'Chechen separatism' (in the 1990s Chechnya declared independence from Russian Federation, which led to a series of armed conflicts).

> *и даже чеченские сепаратисты … не смогли добить Россию!* (Russian)
>
> and even Chechen separatists … could not finish off Russia!

Interestingly, one of the Duma speakers is vehemently objecting to the parallels between separatism of the Donetsk and Luhansk People's Republics and of Chechnya:

> *Я недавно слышал от отдельных наших политических умников, которые считают себя оппозицией, такие заявления в связи с ситуацией в Украине: почему, мол, российская власть не поддерживает киевские власти, ведь точно такая же ситуация была в Чечне, когда армия пыталась подавить очаги сепаратизма?* (Russian)
>
> I have recently heard from some of our political smart alecs who consider themselves an opposition such statements in relation to the situation in Ukraine: why do Russian authorities not support Ukrainian authorities, because the situation in Chechnya was exactly the same, when the army tried to suppress the outbreaks of separatism?

These examples illustrate complicated contextual, connotative and affective meanings of the translation equivalents of *separatist/separatism* and of the variations of these meanings in two different discourses, reflecting differences in the ideologies between different groups of language users who seem to negotiate and re-negotiate these diverse meanings. *Separatists* appear to denote different referents: in the Ukrainian context, only pro-Russian rebels, and in the Russian context, Chechen rebels, but not pro-Russian rebels. These meanings seem to be negotiated and agreed between the members of each community. Cohen, writing on conflict resolution, notes that '[a] cross languages and societies, seemingly functionally equivalent words may depict variant versions of reality' (2001: 29).

5 Discourse of truce

In the Rada corpus, the keyword *peremir/truce* has a statistical significance of 37.86 and an MI effect of 6.0206, and in the Duma corpus, the translation equivalent – keyword *peremirie/truce* – has a statistical significance of 18.15 and an MI effect of 4.762.

This keyword stands out in both corpora for several reasons. First, it is one of four equivalent keywords that are common in keyword lists of the Rada and Duma corpora. Second, it is particularly noticeable against the background of the lexis of war and aggression. Therefore, this item deserved a special concordance-based scrutiny. In the Rada corpus, *truce* was used twenty-four times and only in a negative context – to state that the truce did not work:

> За последние 40 дней только военнослужащих погибло около 500, что в 10 раз больше периода, который был до перемирия (speaking in Russian)
>
> About 500 of military personnel only were killed in the past 40 days, which is 10 times more than before the truce

In five cases, it was preceded by the adjective *tak zvane (so called)*:

> Ми протестуємо проти того, щоб в Україні було введено **так зване** 'перемирье', бо це перемирье ні до чого не призвело заручники не були звільнені, удари військові проти України не були припинені (Ukrainian)
>
> We protest against introducing the **so-called 'truce'** in Ukraine, because this truce hasn't led to anything; hostages haven't been released, military strikes against Ukraine haven't stopped

In the Russian Duma corpus, *peremiri*/truce* was used twenty times; however, its usage is less indicative of the discourse as a whole, because seventeen out of twenty instances were concentrated in only one debate that was not relevant to the truce with Ukraine. It was used in a brief discussion on 24 January 2014 to promote the 'Olympic truce' for the duration of the Winter Olympics and Paralympics in Sochi, which shows that truce was not particularly high on the agenda of Duma debates. There are only three instances related to the truce between Ukrainian and pro-Russian forces, all three dating to July 2014 and referring to the end of the truce and to the alleged violation of it by Ukrainian forces. These three instances, similar to Ukrainian usage, also collocate with negative lexemes and are similarly modified by *âkoby /so-called*:

> является геноцид на земле Новороссии, эта земля кровавыми, жестокими способами, в том числе с использованием запрещённых вооружений, даже в период **якобы** перемирия и прекращения огня зачищается от людей (Russian)
>
> [There] is genocide on the land of Novorossia, this land is being cleansed of people in a bloody and cruel way, including using banned weaponry, even during the **so-called truce** and ceasefire

6 Crimea: Discourse of annexation versus reunification

The annexation of Crimea constitutes one of the major themes of the discourse of conflict in both parliaments: *Krym/Crimea* is the top keyword in the Russian Duma

Table 1.8 Frequencies of the Word *Krim*/ Crimea* in the Rada Corpus and *Krym*/ Crimea* in the Duma Corpus

word	Rada corpus *Krim*/ Crimea*		Duma Corpus *Krym*/ Crimea*	
	Raw freq	Relative freq wpm	Raw freq	Relative freq wpm
Crimea	943	1319	1070	728

corpus; eight other derivatives of it are in top 100 keywords. In the Ukrainian corpus, keyword *Krim/Crimea* comes thirty-eighth (other eleven derivatives are here considered as one term). There are 943 word forms of the lemma *Krim*/Crimea* in the Ukrainian Rada corpus and 1,070 in the Russian Duma corpus (see Table 1.8).

Both corpora were queried for collocates of *Krim*/Krym/Crimea* in order to identify the discourse themes (see Table 1.9 of the Appendix for the top fifty collocates in the Rada corpus). Two major themes in the Rada corpus are the following: the occupation/annexation of Crimea and ethnic minorities. The collocational profile indicates preoccupation with Tatars and Karaims (ethnic groups native to the Crimean peninsula). Apart from the names of ethnic groups (*tatar*/Tatar, karaïm*/ Karaims*), there are also the words *deportacii/deportation* and words for the representative bodies of Crimean Tatars: *medžlis /Mejlis* and *kurultaj /Qurultay*. Examination of concordance lines showed that the word *tatar*/Tatar* is associated with the words of negative connotation (*deportation, problem, genocide, under threat* and *testing times*), and it appears in two contexts: Stalin's 1944 deportation of Tatars from Crimea and the present-day human rights of minorities in the annexed Crimea:

> кримські татари пережили **геноцид** від Сталіна (Ukrainian)
> Crimean Tatars lived through Stalin's **genocide**
>
> кримські татари **під великою загрозою** (Ukrainian)
> Crimean Tatars are **under great threat**

Krim*/Crimea also collocates with words indicating violent and unlawful invasion, for example, with the lemma *okup*/occup** (in bold in Table 1.9). There are thirteen collocates of different word forms of lemma *okup*/occup**, the strongest ranking eleven (MI 16.5377) and twelve (16.4446) on the list of collocates sorted by collocational strength. *Krim*/Crimea* also collocates with the word *aneks*/annex** twice, both words are on the Rada corpus keyword list with MI of 15.5021 and 15.38567 respectively. There is an obvious reason for strong collocations between Crimea and occupation/annexation in the Rada corpus. The collocates *okup*/occup** and *aneks*/annex** point to the main theme of the Rada discourse: annexation of Crimea is consistently seen as occupation. This view is supported by the international community. Three United Nations General Assembly Resolutions (68/262, 2014; 71/205, 2016 and 72/190, 2017) used the terms 'annexation' and 'temporary occupation' with reference to the situation in Crimea.

The collocations of *Krym*/Crimea* in Duma corpus show a different picture: the Russian lemma *anneks*/annex** (translation equivalent of Ukrainian *aneks**) does

Table 1.11 Frequencies of Lemma *Aneks*/Annex** in the Rada Corpus and *Anneks*/Annex** in the Duma Corpus

word	Rada Corpus *Aneks*/Annex**		Duma Corpus *Anneks*/Annex**	
	Raw freq	Relative freq	Raw freq	Relative freq
annex*	54	75.7	4	2.7

not appear either on the keyword list or on the list of collocates for *Krym*/Crimea* (see Table 1.10 of the Appendix). A concordance search on lemma *anneks*/annex** showed that it is used only four times in the whole 1,469,502 word Duma corpus (see Table 1.11), and only on three occasions refers to Crimea.

One instance is the criticism of the Parliamentary Assembly of the Council of Europe, which condemned Russia's actions in Crimea:

> эта сессия, конечно, отличалась просто оголтелой русофобией и оголтелым цинизмом по отношению к нашей стране! **Ассамблея обвинила Россию и в аннексии Крыма**, и в дестабилизации обстановки на юго-востоке Украины (Russian)
>
> *The session was, of course, characterized by rampant Russophobia and unbridled cynicism towards our country!* **The Assembly accused Russia both of annexation of Crimea** *and of destabilizing the situation in the south-east of Ukraine*

Another negative evaluative word is *Anschluss*, which has direct association with the annexation of Austria by Nazi Germany in 1938 and thus draws a parallel between the actions of Russia and Nazi Germany. This word, however, is used to condemn this parallel:

> наша пятая колонна – дошли уже до маразма: **говорят, что это аншлюс**, как Гитлер присоединил Австрию – вот какую они проводят параллель! (Russian)
>
> *our fifth column –* **they** *in their lunacy* **are saying that this is Anschluss**, *like Hitler joined Austria – this is the parallel they are drawing!*

With only three instances of *annex** and one of *Anschluss* being used, and considering high frequency of *Krym*/Crimea* in Duma corpus (728 wpm and the top keyword), further inquiry was needed to understand what lexis was used to describe the annexation and how the situation around Crimea is framed in Duma discourse. The collocational profile of *Crimea* in the Duma corpus is significantly different (see Table 10): instead of negatively coloured *annexation, occupation* and *invasion* of the Rada corpus, neutral or positive words *vossoedinenie /reunification, osvoboždenie /liberation, vhoždenie /joining* were consistently used in Duma debates. The following passage illustrates the co-text around the words *vossoedinenie /reunification, vhoždenje/joining* and *sobiranie /unification* containing rhetorically charged and emotional expressions like *historic event, the day will be written about in history textbooks, call of hearts and* *souls*, and *unification of Russian lands*. In this context, the words used with reference to the annexation of Crimea acquire positive affective connotation.

> *То, что произошло 16 марта в Крыму, когда все народы Крыма ... в большинстве своём проголосовали за **вхождение** в Россию, -- это **историческое событие**. Это день, который действительно войдёт в учебники истории, в нашу с вами историю, ту, которую мы с вами сегодня пишем. Это день начала **собирания земель русских**! Это день **воссоединения разделённого народа**! То, что решено на этом референдуме, -- это действительно **веление души и сердец** тех, кто живёт сегодня в Крыму. (Russian)*
>
> What happened in Crimea on 16 March, when all the peoples of Crimea ... the majority of them voted **to join** Russia – this is **a historic event**. This is the day that will really be written about in history textbooks, in our common history, the history we are writing now. This is the day of the when **unification of Russian lands** began! This is the day of **reunification of separated nation!** The decision of this referendum is **a call from the hearts and souls** of everybody living in Crimea now.

Differences in collocational patterns reveal differences in the way one and the same event is construed in the discourses of the two parliaments. The collocates of *Krim*/Krym*/Crimea* in the two corpora represent 'nodes around which ideological battles are fought' (Stubbs, 2001:188). Table 1.12 in the Appendix summarizes the themes emerging from the comparison of collocates of *Krim*/Krym*/Crimea*.

7   Discourse of 'the other'. *Rosìâ/Russia* and *Ukraina/Ukraine*

Referential strategies of naming and characterizing the participants are pivotal in the representations of 'the other' (Wodak 2001: 72–75). Speakers can choose the way of representing social actors in their discourses (Fairclough [1989]1996, Hart 2014, Van Leeuwen 2013); analysis of such representations can reveal ideologies and attitudes behind them.

This section combines corpus and transitivity analysis to explore the representation of the other country in order to establish semantic roles and processes associated with them in each corpus. I examine the collocates of the nouns *Rosìâ / Russia* in the Ukrainian Rada corpus and *Ukraina / Ukraine* in the Russian Duma corpus in the position of a grammatical subject in the nominative case. The collocates of *Rosìâ / Russia* and *Ukraina /Ukraine* were derived using AntConc within a span of five words on each side of the node; MI score over 3 and a minimum collocational frequency of 3 were applied.

8   *Rosìâ /Russia* in the Ukrainian Rada corpus

In the Rada corpus, the collocates of the node *Rosìâ /Russia* (seventy-one collocates) pointed to several themes that were further explored by using concordances. As the

Table 1.14 Themes Emerging from the Collocates of *Rossiâ/Russia* in the Ukrainian Duma Corpus

Themes	Collocates
War, aggression, conflict	cìlit'sâ/to point at, to level, agresor/aggressor, vìjni/war (2), teroristìv/terrorists, Krim /Crimea
Territorial	kordonì /border, teritorìû /territory
Countries	Rosìâ/Russia (3), ukraïns'ku/Ukrainian (2), Ukraïnu/Ukraine (2)
Gas	gazu/gas

top twenty-five collocates show (Table 1.13), the dominant theme is that of war and aggression, together with the related theme of border integrity. These words constitute eight out of the first twenty-five words collocating with *Rosìâ /Russia*, and additional seven words name the conflicting countries; thus fifteen out of twenty-five collocates (60 per cent) are centred around Russian military aggression (see Table 1.14).

Closer examination of the concordance lines showed that *Rosìâ/Russia* is used 116 times in the debates and is associated with the theme of war, aggression and conflict in seventy-five instances or 65 per cent of cases. Concordances support the first impression of a strong negative collocational profile of *Rosìâ/Russia* in the Ukrainian parliamentary debate, which is hardly surprising in the discourse of a nation at war. Half of the first thirty lines are distinctly negative; a closer analysis of larger context reveals several sub-topics: *Crimea* appears in the same concordance lines or larger context in twenty cases; trade/economic conflict in eight; conflict over gas supplies and prices in twenty-nine instances, for example:

Росія розв'язала цю війну. Росія анексувала українську територію, а саме територію Автономної Республіки Крим. (Ukrainian)

Russia started this war. Russia annexed Ukrainian territory, namely the territory of the Autonomous Republic of Crimea

проти нашої країни ... Росія веде енергетичну війну (Ukrainian)

Russia is conducting an energy war against our country

Thus, the noun *Rosìâ /Russia* is used with additional affective associative meaning developed on the basis of language users' experiences, which is often the case with nationality words (Leech [1974]1990): 19; 43).

Further, I examine the transitivity features of agency and processes associated with the lexeme *Rosìâ/Russia* following the transitivity analytical framework. The value of transitivity analysis in discourse studies has been highlighted by many scholars (Fairclough [1989]1996, Simpson [1993] 2005, Hart, 2014; Goatly, 2000). Simpson's transitivity system, drawing on Halliday's ([1985] 1994:107), distinguishes between *processes*, the *participants* of these processes and the *circumstances* associated with the process (Simpson [1993] 2005: 82). Similar to Halliday, Simpson makes a distinction between *material, verbal* and *mental* processes and a process of being, or a *relational process. Material processes* are further classified into *actions* (intentional and unintentional) and *events*.

To investigate processes associated with Russia as a participant, concordance lines were examined, and sentences where *Rosìâ /Russia* is used as a grammatical subject were analysed. Out of 116 occurrences of *Rosìâ /Russia* in the corpus, it occurred in a position of a subject in the active voice seventy-seven times, showing a stable pattern of performing the role of an actor. In fifty cases, it associated with intentional action material processes (65 per cent), in seven with relational processes, (verbs of being, 9 per cent) and in six with verbs denoting unintentional actions (or, in Simpson's terminology, superventions, 7.8 per cent). This means that the agency of Russia is made unequivocally clear in the parliamentary discourse (verbs in bold):

*Росія ... **цілиться в серце України*** (Ukrainian)
Russia ... **is levelling (a gun) to Ukraine's heart**

*Росія також без оголошення війни **перейшла українські кордони, окупувавши Крим*** (Ukrainian)
Russia without declaring war **crossed Ukrainian borders, having invaded Crimea**

*Росія, – це **відключила всі без винятку українські телеканали*** (Ukrainian)
Russia **switched off all Ukrainian channels without exception**

*Заводи на Донбасі зупинилися! І чому зупинилися? А тому, що **Росія це зробила!*** (Ukrainian)
Plants stopped in Donbass! And why they stopped? Because **Russia did it!**

Other examples of action verbs associated with Russia are: *aneksuvala/annexed, okupuvala/occupied, vede ... ìnformacìjnu vìjnu/is conducting an information war, zaprovadila sankcìï/introduced sanctions* and *zabrala u nas Krim/took Crimea away from us*, making war and aggression a dominant semantic field of verbs associated with Russia.

A strong presence of agency is also felt in sentences with verbs in the passive voice. The search on instrumentative case of *Rosìâ /Russia* (*Rosìêû /by Russia*) showed that all fifteen collocations are connected with the sematic field of aggression: *okupacìâ teroristami âkì finansuût'sâ Rosìêû /occupation by terrorists financed by Russia, z faktičnim progološennâm vìjni Rosìêû/ with factual declaration of war by Russia, teroristami pìdtrimuvanimi Rosìêû/ terrorists supported by Russia* and *Krim zahoplenij Rosìêû/ Crimea invaded by Russia*.

Thus, the majority of processes associated with *Russia* are actional and are negatively viewed by the speakers; *Russia* is presented in the discourse as responsible for these actions.

9 *Ukraina /Ukraine* in the Duma corpus

Collocations of *Ukraina/Ukraine* in Duma corpus did not show any significant patterns that could lead to theme identification. I then examined concordances of *Ukraina/Ukraine* in the nominative case in the function of a subject. Out of 105 sentences, *Ukraina/Ukraine* is a subject in eighty, out of which in forty-four sentences (55 per cent) it is associated with relational processes, or is performing the semantic role of an attribute carrier (Simpson, [1993] 2005: 85).

Украина была *частью Российской Империи (Russian)*
Ukraine was *a part of the Russian Empire*

Украина сегодня - это страшное, но закономерное явление (Russian)
Ukraine today is a frightening, but logical phenomenon

Украина стала разменной монетой в глобальной политической игре (Russian)
Ukraine has become a bargaining chip in a global political game

Украина - это Киев, Житомир, Полтава, Винница, всё! (Russian)
Ukraine is Kiev, Zhitomir, Poltava, Vinnitsa, and that's it!

Украина - это наша историческая родина, *поэтому мы не можем стоять в стороне (Russian)*
Ukraine is our historic motherland, *that is why we cannot stand apart from*

Украина является зоной стратегических интересов Российской Федерации. (Russian)
Ukraine is *a zone of strategic interests of Russian Federation*

Ukraina/Ukraine performs an action process in twenty-four sentences (31 per cent); however, they are mainly non-intentional superventions – 'where the process just happens' (Simpson [1993] 2005: 83) – unlike processes associated with Russia:

*Украина **бурлит** сейчас (Russian)*
*Ukraine **is bubbling** now*

горит Украина (Russian)
*Ukraine **is burning***

*Украина **истекает кровью** (Russian)*
*Ukraine **is bleeding***

*Украина **превращается** в протекторат (Russian)*
*Ukraine **is turning into** a protectorate*

*Украина **раскололась** (Russian)*
*Ukraine **is split***

Considering that 'supervention signal the lack of command' (Simpson [1993] 2005: 95), it can be suggested that in the Duma discourse, Ukraine is presented as a passive entity. Differences in the processes have further implications for power dynamics in discourses. According to Goatly's hierarchy of actions (2000: 288; 2002: 6), material

Table 1.15 Comparison of Processes Associated with *Rosià/Russia* in Rada Corpus and *Ukraina/Ukraine* in Duma Corpus

Participant	Material Action Processes		Relational Processes of Being (%)
	Intentional Action Processes (%)	Non-intentional Processes (Superventions) (%)	
Rosià/Russia in Rada corpus	65	7.8	9
Ukraina/Ukraine in Duma corpus	13.7	17.5	55

actions are the most powerful, and relational are the least powerful. Haig (2012) makes a similar distinction, which may imply that transitivity processes indicate different degrees of agency.

Thus, the analysis shows the over-dominance of material processes in representations of Russia with strongly emphasized agency and material acts of aggression as its dominant characteristics. Representations of Ukraine are mainly relational; Ukraine is framed as a carrier of certain attributes or as an actor in non-intentional processes that 'perform[s] the actions involuntarily' (Simpson [1993] 2005: 83). Both of these categories signal the lack of agency, and that is how *Ukraina/Ukraine* is presented in 72.5 per cent of the cases (see Table 1.15).

10 Participants

Power hierarchies of processes shape the power positioning of participants. Different types of verbs project a different amount of power or powerlessness onto the participants (Goatly 2000, 2002; Haig 2012). The participants performing material intentional actions are the most powerful by virtue of 'doing something to someone' (Goatly 2002 :7), and that is how Russia is presented in the Rada corpus. For the participants in relational processes of being, 'the question of power is less obvious' (Haig 2012 :55). *Ukraine*, as a participant in a relational process, is often is represented in the Duma corpus as less powerful, lacking agency.

The names of the participants – *Russia* and *Ukraine* – in both discourses are mostly used metonymically. Such use was described by Lakoff and Johnson ([1980] 2003: 35–41) in terms of conceptual metonymy INSTITUTION FOR PEOPLE RESPONSIBLE and/or PLACE FOR AN INSTITIUTION; in this study, such metonymy can be reformulated as A COUNTRY FOR PEOPLE RESPONSIBLE or A COUNTRY FOR AN INSTITUTION:

Украина антирусски настроена! *(Russian)*
Ukraine shows *anti-Russian attitudes!*

Росія ще лякає марш-кидком *(Ukrainian)*
Russia is killing *Ukrainian people*

Metonymic usage of *Russia* and *Ukraine* is open-ended: country can stand for the government, the military, political parties or specific sections of population; in other words, the whole country is presented as acting in a particular way or holding one particular view. This way of presenting the participants 'can serve to impersonalize social actors and perpetuate social stereotypes' (Hart 2014: 34). Interestingly, in both corpora there were occasional cases when speakers tried to avoid such stereotyping by using more specific language:

Rada corpus:

Україна воює з Росією, з **путінським режимом** (Ukrainian)
Ukraine is fighting with Russia, **with Putin's regime**

Duma corpus:

Украина воюет, и с кем? С Россией! **Ну, конечно, не сама Украина, конечно, хунта** (Russian)
Ukraine is fighting, and who with? With Russia! **But, of course, not Ukraine itself, junta, of course**

The use of country names in both corpora can also be seen as a form of personification where an inanimate entity – a country – acquires the characteristics of a living being and performs actions that are, in reality, performed by individuals, thus placing responsibility for the actions on the whole country.

11 *Ukrainsk*/Ukrainian* in the Duma corpus and *Rosijs'k */Russian* in Rada corpus

To explore further how the dichotomy of 'self' and 'other' is constructed in parliamentary debates, the two corpora were queried for the nouns associated with the adjectives *Ukrainian* and *Russian* in the Duma and Rada corpora, respectively. Both Russian and Ukrainian adjectives agree with the nouns they modify in gender, number and case. In order to capture these morphological variations, wildcard searches were used: *ukrainsk*/Ukrainian* in the Duma corpus and *rosijs'k */Russian* in the Rada corpus. The search was limited to one word on the right of the node (Adj+N bigrams) using a collocate measure of MI and an MI score of 3 or higher.

The results of queries of *rosijs'k */Russian* bigrams in Ukrainian corpus show 216 collocates, 80 per cent of which fall into semantic groups of aggression and military conflict; government, parliament, state institutions and procedures; media; fascism; language; gas; and business, finance and banking. The eighty-six collocates with the highest statistical value are overwhelmingly negative and connected with war.

The results of the collocates search of *ukrainsk*/Ukrainian* in the Duma corpus show 205 collocates, 71 per cent of which fall into semantic groups similar to those in the Ukrainian Rada corpus, apart from *gas:* not surprisingly, it is absent from the

Duma corpus because it is not associated with the adjective *ukrainsk*/Ukrainian* (see Table 1.16)

However, a detailed concordance analysis showed that words in other groups, such as language, media or business, are also directly or indirectly related to the conflict between Ukraine and Russia. Here, I present a close analysis of two significant collocates. The word *fašist*/fašist*/fascist was chosen because it is used by both sides to refer to each other,* and *brat*/brat*/brother* is interesting because it noticeably differs from the predominantly negative representations.

12 Discourse of fascism

Collocates show that in debates, the opposing side is often associated with fascism. In the Ukrainian Rada corpus, the noun *fašyst*/fascist* collocates with the adjective *Russian:*

> …людей, які захищають країну від **російських фашистів**. *(Ukrainian)*
> people who defend the country from **Russian fascists**.
>
> Судячи з риторики '**російського фюрера**'… *(Ukrainian)*
> Judging from the rhetoric of the '**Russian führer**'…

In the Russian Duma corpus, there are similar collocations of *ukrainsk*/Ukrainian* with *fašyst*/fascist, nacisty/Nazis* and *hunta/junta.*

> **Украинская хунта** делает все для того чтобы было невозможно сесть за стол переговоров *(Russian)*
> **Ukrainian junta** does everything possible to prevent us getting to the negotiation table
>
> Очевидно что США с помощью **украинских фашистов** активизируют выполнение югославского сценария в отношении исторической России *(Russian)*
> It is clear that the USA with the help of **Ukrainian fascists** are actively implementing the Yugoslav scenario in relation to historical Russia

The discourse of fascism is especially notable because for both Russia and Ukraine, it evokes the fascist atrocities and immense human loss of the Second World War; the words *fascism* and *Nazism* have developed intense negative meaning that is both emotional and affective. This is not uncommon in 'words referring to political ideas or movements … Here there seem to be such strong connotations on one side or the other that the dictionary sense of the word can be almost forgotten' (Leech [1974]1990): 43). The use of *fašist*/fašist*/fascist* in the discourse of conflict as a particularly forceful term of condemnation adds to the general negative presentation of the 'other'.

13 Discourse of brotherhood

Against the background of semantically negative collocates of both *ukrainsk*/ Ukrainian* and *posijs'k */Russian* in the two corpora, one collocate is less expected and merits special examination. *Brat*/brother* co-occurs in the Russian Duma corpus with *ukrainsk*/Ukrainian* on four occasions in the collocates list:

> нашей твёрдой приверженности развитию дружеских отношений с **нашими украинскими братьями** (Russian)
>
> our firm commitment to developing friendly relationships with **our Ukrainian brothers**

There are similar collocations of the adjective *bratsk*/fraternal* and the noun *Украин*/ Ukraine*. Out of 109 instances of *brat*/brother* and *bratsk*/fraternal* in the Russian Duma corpus, 68, or 62 per cent, refer to Ukraine or, in some cases, more specifically to the pro-Russian population in the Donbass and Crimea. The rhetoric of a 'brotherly' country is in stark contrast to the mainly negative attitudes reflected in corpus data and represents the discourse of the 'Russian world' (*Russkii mir*) as an attempt of constructing a collective post-Soviet identity with Russia at its heart as a strong unifying force, providing a counterbalance to the West (Feklyunina 2016, O'Loughlin et al. 2016, McDermott 2016). The discourse of the 'Russian world' is characterized, among other things, by the concept of natural closeness of Russians and Ukrainians – cultural, linguistic, historical, religious and territorial. Ukrainians were described by Putin as 'part of our greater Russian, or Russian-Ukrainian world' (cit. in Feklyunina 2016: 784). Within this context, the discourse of 'brotherhood' in the Duma corpus forms part of the 'Russian world' narrative by underlining the original and natural fraternity of the two nations that is demonstrated by concordances of *brat*/brother* and *bratsk*/fraternal*:

> мы с болью в сердце сейчас наблюдаем в **братской Украине** (Russian)
>
> with heartache we are witnessing it in **fraternal Ukraine**

This meaning is further reinforced by frequent collocation with the possessive pronoun *naš*/our*:

> мы болеем всей душой и переживаем за **наших братьев-украинцев**, за **нашу братскую Украину** (Russian)
>
> Our souls are aching and we are concerned for **our brothers-Ukrainians,** for **our fraternal Ukraine**

The 'Russian world' narrative is exemplified by the following examples:

> в идеале мы очень хотели бы территориальной целостности Украины, **независимого сильного братского славянского государства** (Russian)
>
> ideally, we would like to see the territorial integrity of Ukraine, **an independent strong, fraternal Slav state**

*когда мы говорим в своих заявлениях о том, что украинцы -- **братский нам народ**, то это не пустые слова, это на самом деле так, я сказал бы, что **мы -- один народ**! (Russian)*

when we say in our statements that Ukrainians are **our fraternal people**, it is not just empty words, it really is like that, I would say – **we are one nation!**

Concordances of *brat*/brother* and *братск*/fraternal* are revealing also because they demonstrate the process of 'othering' Ukraine in Russian parliamentary discourse. The following examples illustrate the transition from being '*our brother*' and '*one nation*' to an alien:

*Фундамент России – русский народ, а сегодня над ним издеваются в **так называемой братской Украине**! (Russian)*

The foundation of Russia is the Russian people, and today they are being abused in **so-called fraternal Ukraine!**

А вы всё ещё считаете их братским народом! (Russian)

And you still consider them a fraternal nation!

In contrast, in the Ukrainian Rada corpus, there are no statistically significant collocations of *Rosija/Russia* or *російськ*/Russian* with *brat*/brother* and *братськ*/fraternal*; *brother/fraternal* are used in the Rada corpus forty-five times, with thirty (66 per cent) referring to Russia. However, unlike in the Duma corpus, all these instances reject suggestions of brotherhood.

***Нам такого братства не потрібно.** (Оплески) (Ukrainian)*

We do not need brotherhood like that (Applause)

*На Сході знаходиться **ніякий не брат**, а терорист, окупант-країна, яка сьогодні веде цілеспрямовану війну проти України (Ukrainian)*

There is **none such brother** in the East, but a terrorist, a country-occupier, which is conducting targeted warfare against Ukraine

Interestingly, corpus data shows that there is acknowledgement of brotherly relationships in the past that have now ended, expressed in very similar terms as in the Russian Duma corpus.

*захоплювати через військову агресію територію суверенної і незалежної держави, **яку вони раніше називали братською**. (Ukrainian)*

invading by military aggression the territory of a sovereign and independent state, **which they used to call fraternal**

In this paper, I have attempted to show how the discourses of two countries locked in an armed conflict make use of different linguistic and transitivity features to frame the same events from different positions. This paper does not seek to advance any political point of view; however, considering the wider sociopolitical context of discourse about such sensitive issues, some level of unconscious bias might be inevitable. The corpus analysis of the discourses of two parliaments was instrumental in reducing such unconscious bias and in achieving higher degree of objectivity (Baker 2006).

14 Conclusions

The discourses that dominated the parliamentary debates of 2014 can hardly be extrapolated to the variety of discourses existing in Russia and Ukraine at that time, which were obviously much more multivocal. However, the parliamentary discourses represent a snapshot of the ideologies and attitudes of politicians of both parliaments at a time of crisis, and are thus important.

Methodologically, this paper has employed cross-linguistic, corpus-assisted discourse analysis. This methodological framework has allowed me to observe the differences between parliamentary discourses around the same events of two countries in conflict.

A corpus-assisted approach was used to identify keywords that helped in uncovering pivotal points of the debate; it was followed by further qualitative investigation. The study has demonstrated that within different sociopolitical contexts, word connotations are contextualized and re-contextualized by different social actors to reflect their position in the conflict. Changing sociopolitical perspectives have resulted in diverging routes of semantic development of some equivalent words with originally similar meanings.

Even though it was not feasible to accomplish an exhaustive analysis of all the themes and discourse strands suggested by the keywords, this study has identified some significant trends. It has demonstrated that debates in the Ukrainian parliament were strongly focused on discussions of war, aggression and violence. The Russian corpus showed less attention to this theme, even though it was still present in the Duma corpus. The study has also noted strong negative lexicalization in discourses about the 'other side' with intense emotional involvement on both sides. While it is hardly surprising to find that both sides used negative vocabulary, the corpus method has helped quantify these features and establish their prominence in the discourse and their role in developing new connotations. A comparative study of keywords and collocates in context revealed cross-linguistic and, broader, cross-cultural differences in the representation of conflict in the discourses of both parliaments.

To sum up, the study showed that equivalent Ukrainian and Russian words were used to denote different referents in the contexts of different discourses, and different expressions were used co-referentially to denote the same event. The study also revealed movement of some word meanings from neutral to negative and politically-coloured in both corpora, and demonstrated the divergence of the affective, connotative and denotative meanings, depending on the ideologies of the speaking communities. There was an ostensible similarity in language used to describe the 'other side'. Corpus data pointed to particularly revealing transitivity patterns where different linguistic choices signalled different degrees of agency.

The linguistic features identified in this study are at 'the focus of ideological struggle' (Fairclough [1989]1996: 114). Drawing attention to these features may contribute to finding an appropriate language of communication in this conflict, in keeping with recommendation of the first UN resolution on the situation in Ukraine that urged both parties 'to refrain from … inflammatory rhetoric that may increase tensions' (UN Resolution 68/262). More generally, a cross-linguistic, corpus-assisted approach may become a productive tool for studies in conflict resolution.

References

Anthony, L. (2018), AntConc (Version 3.5.7) [Computer Software]. Tokyo, Japan: Waseda University. Available from http://www.laurenceanthony.net/software

Baker, P. (2004), 'Querying Keywords: Questions of Difference, Frequency and Sense in Keywords Analysis', *Journal of English Linguistics*, 32 (4): 346–59.

Baker, P. (2006), *Using Corpora in Discourse Analysis*, Bloomsbury.

Baker, P. (2009), '"The Question Is, How Cruel Is It?" Keywords in Debates on Fox Hunting in the British House of Commons', in D. Archer (ed.), *What's in a Word-List*, 125–36. London: Ashgate.

Brezina, V. (2018), *Statistics in Corpus Linguistics: A Practical Guide*. Cambridge: Cambridge University Press.

Cohen, R. (2001), 'Language and Conflict Resolution: The Limits of English', *International Studies Review*, 3 (1): 25–51.

Fairclough, N. ([1989]1996), *Language and Power*. London, UK: Longman.

Feklyunina, V. (2016), 'Soft Power and Identity: Russia, Ukraine and the "Russian World (s)"', *European Journal of International Relations*, 22 (4): 773–96.

Findlay, J. Y. (2017), 'Unnatural Acts Lead to Unconsummated Marriages', *Journal of Language and Sexuality*, 6 (1): 30–60.

Gabrielatos, C. and Baker, P. (2008), 'Fleeing, Sneaking, Flooding: A Corpus Analysis of Discursive Constructions of Refugees and Asylum Seekers in the UK Press, 1996–2005', *Journal of English Linguistics*, 36 (1): 5–38.

Goatly, A. (2000), *Critical Reading and Writing: An Introductory Coursebook*. London: Routledge.

Goatly, A. (2002), 'The Representation of Nature on the BBC World Service', *Text*, 22: 1–27.

Haig, E. (2012), 'A Critical Discourse Analysis and Systemic Functional Linguistics Approach to Measuring Participant Power in a Radio News Bulletin About Youth Crime', *Studies in Media and Society*, 4: 45–73.

Halliday, M. A. (1967), 'Notes on Transitivity and Theme in English', Part I, *Journal of Linguistics*, 3 (1): 37–81.

Halliday, M. A. ([1985] 1994), *An Introduction to Functional Grammar*. London: Edward Arnold.

Hart, C. (2014), *Discourse, Grammar and Ideology: Functional and Cognitive Perspectives*. London: Bloomsbury Publishing.

Hunston. (2002), *Corpora in Applied Linguistics*. Cambridge: Cambridge University Press.

Huysmans, J. and Buonfino, A. (2008), 'Politics of Exception and Unease: Immigration, Asylum and Terrorism in Parliamentary Debates in the UK', *Political Studies*, 56 (4): 766–88.

Lakoff, G. J. and Johnson, M. [1980] (2003), *Metaphors We Live By*. Chicago and London: University of Chicago Press.

Leech, G. ([1974]1990), *Semantics: The Study of Meaning*. London: Penguin.
Mautner, G. (2009), 'Corpora and Critical Discourse Analysis', in P. Baker (ed.), *Contemporary Corpus Linguistics*, 32–46. London: Continuum.
McDermott, R. N. (2016), 'Brothers Disunited: Russia's Use of Military Power in Ukraine', in *The Return of the Cold War*, 99–129. London: Routledge.
McEnery, A. M. and Wilson, A. (2001), *Corpus Linguistics: An Introduction*. Edinburgh: Edinburgh University Press.
McEnery, A.M. and Baker, P. (eds) (2015), *Corpora and Discourse Studies: Integrating Discourse and Corpora*. London, UK: Palgrave Macmillan.
Oficialnyj sajt gosudarstvennoj Dumy [Official Site of State Duma] (transcripts), http://transcript.duma.gov.ru.
Oficijnyj portal Verhovnoji Rady Ukrajiny [Official portal of the Supreme Rada of Ukraine] (transcripts of the debates), http://iportal.rada.gov.ua/meeting/stenogr.
O'Loughlin, J., Toal, G., and Kolosov, V. (2016), 'Who Identifies with the "Russian World"'? Geopolitical Attitudes in South Eastern Ukraine', *Eurasian Geography and Economics*, 57 (6): 745–78.
Scott, M. (1997), 'PC Analysis of Key Words—And Key Key Words', *System*, 25 (2): 233–45.
Scott, M. (2015), *WordSmith Tools Manual: Version 6.0*, Stroud, Gloucestershire, UK: Lexical Analysis Software Ltd.
Simpson, P. ([1993] 2005), *Language, Ideology and Point of View*. London: Taylor and Francis.
Sinclair, J. (2004), 'Corpus and Text-Basic Principles', *Developing Linguistic Corpora: A Guide to Good Practice*, 1–16. https://ota.ox.ac.uk/documents/creating/dlc/chapter1.htm.
Slovopedia, http://lang.slovopedia.org.ua, Ukrainian, On-line Dictionary Slovopedia.
Stubbs, M. (1995), 'Corpus Evidence for Norms of Lexical Collocation', *Principle and Practice in Applied Linguistics*, 245–56. Oxford: Oxford University Press.
Stubbs, M. (2001), *Words and Phrases: Studies in Lexical Semantics*. London: Blackwell.
Stubbs, M. (2010), 'Three Concepts of Keywords', in M. Bondi and M. Scott (eds), *Keyness in Texts*, 21–42. Amsterdam: Benjamins.
The United Nations General Assembly Resolution 68/262 (27 March 2014), 'Territorial Integrity of Ukraine', https://undocs.org/A/RES/68/262.
The United Nations General Assembly Resolution 71/205 (19 December 2016), 'Situation of Human Rights in the Autonomous Republic of Crimea and the City of Sevastopol (Ukraine)', https://undocs.org/A/RES/71/205.
The United Nations General Assembly Resolution 72/190 (19 January 2018), 'Situation of Human Rights in the Autonomous Republic of Crimea and the City of Sevastopol (Ukraine)', https://undocs.org/A/RES/72/190.
Tognini-Bonelli, E. (2001), *Corpus Linguistics at Work*. Vol. 6. Philadelphia: John Benjamins Publishing.
Tolkovyj slovar Ušakova, https://ushakovdictionary.ru/word.php?wordid=687 [Russian Ushakov dictionary].
Van Leeuwen, T. (2013), 'The Representation of Social Actors', in C. R. Caldas-Coulthard, M. Coulthard (eds), *Texts and Practices: Readings in Critical Discourse Analysis*, 41–79. London: Routledge.
Vessey, R. (2013), 'Challenges in Cross-Linguistic Corpus-Assisted Discourse Studies', *Corpora*, 8(1), 1–26.
Wodak, R. (2001), 'The Discourse-Historical Approach', *Methods of Critical Discourse Analysis*, 1, 63–95.
Zakon № 1207-VII [Law № 1207-VII], http://zakon.rada.gov.ua/laws/show/756-18.

Appendix: Tables

Table 1.2 First 100 Keywords of Rada Corpus

Rank	Freq	Stat.	Significance	Effect	Keyword	Translation
1	418	+	833.13	10.4801	суверенна	sovereign
9	122	+	243.13	8.7034	антитерористичної	antiterrorist
11	98	+	195.3	8.3874	ато	antiterrorist operation
12	196	+	378.97	8.3874	виконуючого	executive
13	70	+	139.5	7.902	сигнальне	signal
15	67	+	133.52	7.8388	люстрацію	lustration (purge)
17	62	+	123.55	7.7269	мобілізації	conscription
19	62	+	123.55	7.7269	сепаратистів	separatists
20	58	+	115.58	7.6307	радикальна	radical
22	115	+	218.6	7.6182	продан	sold
24	54	+	107.61	7.5276	мобілізацію	conscription
25	53	+	105.62	7.5006	терористи	terrorists
27	50	+	99.64	7.4165	гвардію	guard (military)
29	49	+	97.65	7.3874	сепаратизму	separatism
30	47	+	93.66	7.3273	лічильної	counting
31	47	+	93.66	7.3273	терористами	terrorists
32	276	+	519.67	7.2963	всеукраїнське	all-ukrainian
34	44	+	87.68	7.2321	антитерористична	antiterrorist
35	88	+	165.32	7.2321	гвардії	guard
42	76	+	141.7	7.0206	агресії	aggression
43	38	+	75.73	7.0206	люстрації	lustration (purge)
46	37	+	73.73	6.9821	агресора	aggressor
49	71	+	131.87	6.9224	виборчий	electoral
56	65	+	120.09	6.7951	територіальну	territorial
57	32	+	63.77	6.7727	анексії	annexation
59	500	+	921.68	6.7385	включіть	switch on
61	185	+	340.68	6.7191	сісти	sit down
65	29	+	57.79	6.6307	кримських	Crimean
66	29	+	57.79	6.6307	прокоментуйте	commentate
67	678	+	1241.51	6.5929	удар	Strike (political party)
69	28	+	55.8	6.58	мобілізація	conscription
70	28	+	55.8	6.58	сепаратизм	separatism
73	27	+	53.81	6.5276	бюлетені	voting cards
75	27	+	53.81	6.5276	розпуск	dissolution
76	26	+	51.81	6.4731	антитерористичній	antiterrorist
77	26	+	51.81	6.4731	люстрація	lustration (purge)
79	26	+	51.81	6.4731	штабу	headquarters
80	51	+	92.67	6.4451	мов	languages
81	152	+	276.07	6.4357	шановне	esteemed
82	25	+	49.82	6.4165	антитерористичну	antiterrorist
85	49	+	88.76	6.3874	східних	eastern
86	24	+	47.83	6.3577	бюлетень	voting card
88	47	+	84.86	6.3273	спробуємо	let's try
90	23	+	45.83	6.2963	позичальників	borrowers
95	22	+	43.84	6.2321	окупованих	occupied
97	42	+	75.12	6.165	обороноздатності	defence capabilities
98	21	+	41.85	6.165	окупованої	occupied
100	21	+	41.85	6.165	перевибори	re-elections
101	21	+	41.85	6.165	розпочинає	begins
103	950	+	1697.3	6.1409	свобода	Freedom (political party)

Table 1.2 (Continued)

Rank	Freq	Stat.	Significance	Effect	Keyword	Translation
105	40	+	71.23	6.0946	агресію	aggression
106	20	+	39.86	6.0946	вбивали	killed
109	40	+	71.23	6.0946	кримськотатарського	krimean tatar
111	20	+	39.86	6.0946	сепаратистські	separatist
113	19	+	37.86	6.0206	зрадників	traitors
115	19	+	37.86	6.0206	недоторканності	(territorial) integrity
116	19	+	37.86	6.0206	перемир	truce
117	19	+	37.86	6.0206	сепаратисти	separatists
118	19	+	37.86	6.0206	сепаратистських	separatist
119	112	+	198.17	5.9951	цілісності	(territorial) integrity
127	18	+	35.87	5.9426	терористам	terrorists
128	18	+	35.87	5.9426	тури	tours
131	137	+	240.32	5.8707	сідати	sit down
133	17	+	33.88	5.8602	зрадники	traitors
135	17	+	33.88	5.8602	озброєних	armed
137	17	+	33.88	5.8602	фсб	Federal security service
140	33	+	57.66	5.8171	півхвилини	half a minute
141	16	+	31.88	5.7727	бронежилетів	bulletproof vest
142	16	+	31.88	5.7727	ворог	enemy
143	16	+	31.88	5.7727	воює	is engaged in the warfare
144	16	+	31.88	5.7727	дестабілізувати	destabilize
145	16	+	31.88	5.7727	кордонах	borders
146	16	+	31.88	5.7727	кримчан	Crimean residents
148	16	+	31.88	5.7727	лічильна	counting
151	16	+	31.88	5.7727	покарані	punished
152	16	+	31.88	5.7727	татари	tartars
153	16	+	31.88	5.7727	убивають	killing
154	250	+	434.29	5.7385	компартія	communist party
156	15	+	29.89	5.6796	анексію	annexation
157	30	+	51.87	5.6796	гвардія	guard (military)
158	15	+	29.89	5.6796	дострокових	prescheduled
162	15	+	29.89	5.6796	мирне	peaceful
163	15	+	29.89	5.6796	натхнення	inspiration
165	15	+	29.89	5.6796	розпуску	dissolution
167	30	+	51.87	5.6796	списками	lists
168	15	+	29.89	5.6796	сядемо	lets sit down
169	15	+	29.89	5.6796	юго	southern
171	89	+	153.69	5.6635	цілісність	integrity
173	29	+	49.94	5.6307	революція	revolution
176	14	+	27.9	5.58	гтс	gas transportation system
179	14	+	27.9	5.58	окупанта	occupier
181	14	+	27.9	5.58	перейменування	re-naming
184	14	+	27.9	5.58	порадимося	let's discuss
185	14	+	27.9	5.58	республіку	republic
188	221	+	378.43	5.5606	фракціям	parliamentary groups
189	138	+	236.27	5.5593	терористів	terrorists
189	138	+	236.27	5.5593	терористів	terrorists
190	27	+	46.1	5.5276	бюлетенів	voting cards
192	13	+	25.91	5.4731	вторгнення	invasion
193	13	+	25.91	5.4731	газотранспортну	gas transportation
195	13	+	25.91	5.4731	диверсанти	saboteurs
196	13	+	25.91	5.4731	донбас	Donbas
199	13	+	25.91	5.4731	кримської	Crimean
202	13	+	25.91	5.4731	передовій	frontline

Table 1.3 First 100 Keywords of Duma Corpus

Rank	Freq	Stat.	Significance	Effect	Keyword	Translation
9	271	+	398.05	8.2592	крыма	Crimea
14	220	+	321.31	7.9584	севастополя	Sevastopol
16	426	+	621.6	7.9118	крым	Crimea
33	56	+	84.72	6.9844	майдан	maidan
35	221	+	314.04	6.965	крыму	Crimea
40	52	+	78.67	6.8775	севастополе	Sevastopol
44	49	+	74.13	6.7918	устройству	arranging
47	47	+	71.1	6.7317	федеративному	Federal
48	44	+	66.56	6.6365	одессе	Odessa
53	84	+	117.47	6.5694	госпрограмм	Government programmes
62	37	+	55.97	6.3865	найденные	found
68	35	+	52.95	6.3064	фабричный	factory
70	34	+	51.44	6.2645	майдане	maidan
77	31	+	46.9	6.1313	абортов	abortions
80	31	+	46.9	6.1313	севастополь	Sevastopol
82	30	+	45.38	6.084	крымом	Crimea
83	30	+	45.38	6.084	майдана	maidan
84	30	+	45.38	6.084	русгидро	Rusian Hydroelectric
85	58	+	78.87	6.0351	выборный	electoral
86	29	+	43.87	6.0351	графы	column
92	28	+	42.36	5.9844	правого	right
98	26	+	39.33	5.8775	крымчан	Crimeans
99	26	+	39.33	5.8775	показывайте	show
100	26	+	39.33	5.8775	порошенко	Porshenko
105	50	+	67.06	5.8209	чемпионата	championship
107	24	+	36.31	5.762	новороссии	Novorossia
109	24	+	36.31	5.762	эвакуаторов	veihicle remover
116	22	+	33.28	5.6365	киевской	Kiev
117	22	+	33.28	5.6365	концессионного	concessionary
118	22	+	33.28	5.6365	мигрантами	migrants
122	43	+	56.77	5.6033	найдено	found
129	42	+	55.31	5.5694	след	trace
131	21	+	31.77	5.5694	янтаря	amber
133	40	+	52.38	5.499	древесины	timber
136	20	+	30.26	5.499	тайного	secret
142	19	+	28.74	5.425	провоза	freight
145	18	+	27.23	5.347	болотной	marshy
146	18	+	27.23	5.347	голосуются	vote
147	18	+	27.23	5.347	звука	sound
150	18	+	27.23	5.347	натрия	natrum
151	18	+	27.23	5.347	самоопределение	self-determination
154	35	+	45.08	5.3064	генно	genetically
155	17	+	25.72	5.2645	графа	row
156	17	+	25.72	5.2645	кндр	KNDR
158	17	+	25.72	5.2645	кредите	credit
161	17	+	25.72	5.2645	паралимпийские	paralimpic
162	17	+	25.72	5.2645	подконтрольностью	controlled
163	17	+	25.72	5.2645	рекламой	advertisements
164	33	+	42.17	5.2215	общежитии	hostel
165	16	+	24.2	5.1771	авиаперевозок	air traffic
167	16	+	24.2	5.1771	воссоединения	reunification

Discourses of Conflict

Table 1.3 (Continued)

Rank	Freq	Stat.	Significance	Effect	Keyword	Translation
168	16	+	24.2	5.1771	громкости	loudness
169	32	+	40.71	5.1771	евразийской	Eurasian
170	16	+	24.2	5.1771	загс	registry office
173	16	+	24.2	5.1771	корейской	Korean
180	16	+	24.2	5.1771	эвакуаторы	evacuators
181	31	+	39.26	5.1313	гмо	GMO
182	15	+	22.69	5.084	деоффшоризации	to put an end to offshorization
183	30	+	37.82	5.084	досмотр	control
184	15	+	22.69	5.084	западом	West
186	30	+	37.82	5.084	компенсациях	compensations
188	15	+	22.69	5.084	нетрадиционных	not traditional
189	15	+	22.69	5.084	паралимпийцев	paralimpians
190	15	+	22.69	5.084	присоединением	joining
191	15	+	22.69	5.084	смс	message
193	30	+	37.82	5.084	явки	appearance
194	29	+	36.37	5.0351	украинским	Ukrainian
196	14	+	21.18	4.9844	апелляционного	Appellate
200	14	+	21.18	4.9844	квотирования	quota
201	14	+	21.18	4.9844	крымских	Crimean
205	14	+	21.18	4.9844	провоз	freight
207	14	+	21.18	4.9844	разработанный	developed
208	14	+	21.18	4.9844	украинскими	Ukrainian
209	14	+	21.18	4.9844	эвакуатор	recovery vehicle
210	110	+	136.82	4.9584	почтовой	post
213	27	+	33.48	4.932	нко	non-profit organization
214	27	+	33.48	4.932	огонь	fire
215	27	+	33.48	4.932	символики	symbols
216	27	+	33.48	4.932	украинцы	Ukrainians
218	13	+	19.67	4.8775	багаж	luggage
220	13	+	19.67	4.8775	госпрограммах	government programmes
222	13	+	19.67	4.8775	крымский	Crimean
223	13	+	19.67	4.8775	крымчане	Crimean residents
224	13	+	19.67	4.8775	мариуполе	Mariupol
225	13	+	19.67	4.8775	оценщика	valuer
227	13	+	19.67	4.8775	поверки	checks
228	13	+	19.67	4.8775	разнообразия	variety
229	13	+	19.67	4.8775	тамерлан	Tamerlane
231	13	+	19.67	4.8775	хунты	junta
232	12	+	18.15	4.762	fifa	FIFA
234	12	+	18.15	4.762	глутамат	glutamate
235	12	+	18.15	4.762	гринпис	Greenpeace
237	12	+	18.15	4.762	европарламента	Europarliament
238	12	+	18.15	4.762	займе	loan
239	12	+	18.15	4.762	киевские	Kiev
240	12	+	18.15	4.762	концессионера	concessioner
243	12	+	18.15	4.762	мкд	tower block
244	12	+	18.15	4.762	национал	national-
245	12	+	18.15	4.762	неразборчиво	illegible
246	12	+	18.15	4.762	нефрита	Nephrite
247	12	+	18.15	4.762	перемирия	truce

Table 1.4 Thematic Groups of Keywords in Rada and Duma Corpora

Themes	RADA Corpus			DUMA Corpus		
	Total number of keywords 466		Keywords examples	Total number of keywords 200		Keywords examples
	Raw freq	Relative freq (wpm)		Raw freq	Relative freq (wpm)	
War, aggression, conflict	165	231.25	суверенна/sovereign, терористи/terrorist, сепаратисти/separatist, гварðіı/guard, агресії/aggression, мобілізації/conscription, анексію/annexation, окупованих/ occupied, кулемети/machine gun, вбиває/kills, бандитів/bandits, злочинці/criminals, бронежилет/bullet proof vest	29	19.73	Киев/Kiev, Севастополь/Sevastopol, хунта/junta, Новороссия/Novorossia, националисты/nationalist
Government, parliament, elections, parliamentary parties, state institutions and procedures	83	116.3	депутатові/deputies, касаційного/appeal, кандидатура/candidacy алиції/coalition, компартії/communist party, лічильна/vote counting, удар/strike (party)	14	9.5	Выборный/ elected, федеративный/ Federal, апелляционного/ appellate
Truce, peace	10	14.0	перемир/truce, мир/peace, мирні/peaceful	1	0.7	перемирие/truce
Maidan, Ukrainian revolution	6	8.4	майдан/maidan, революція/revolution	3	2.0	майдан/maidan
Gas	5	7.0	Газотранспортний/ gas transportation, газпром/ Gazprom	0	0	
Europe, West	2	2.8	Європейська/European, заnaðе/West	3	2.0	западные/Western, запад/West, европарламент/ Europarliament
Media	3	4.2	Інформаційну /information	3	2.0	Итар/ITAR, дождь/'rain', масс/ TASS (all names of news agencies)
Language	2	2.8		0	0	

Table 1.6 Keywords of War, Aggression and Conflict in Both Corpora

Keywords Rada	Keywords Duma	Keywords Common in Both Corpora
armed forces, military, war, engage in the warfare (13), terrorist (13), occupation (10), peace, peaceful (as in civilians, 9), separatist (9), aggression (7), arms (6), kill (6), conscription (5), defence and security (4), Donbass (4), enemy (4), East (in Ukr, 4), tatars (4), guard (3), traitors (3), annexation (2), battalions (2), borders (2), bulletproof vest (2), defence capabilities (2), East (in Rus, 2), fighters(2), (territorial) integrity(2), invade (2), perish (1), be killed (2), rebels(2), saboteurs (2), shooting (2), Tatars (2), territory(2), wounded (2), armed (1), attacks(1), autonomous (1), bandits (1), bloodshed (1), border guards (1), captivity (1), criminals (1), destabilize (1), disarmament (1), execute(1), Federal Security Service (in Rus, 1), front (1), frontline (1), headquarters (1), hostages (1), machine gun(1), muzzle (1), orders (1), operation (1), provoke (1), punished (1), Russian (1), snipers (1), sovereign (1), split (1), tanks (1), tense (1), violence (1)	Ukraine (8), Kiev (5), Sevastopol (3), junta (1), Novorossia (1), nationalist (1), Odessa (1)	Crimea (12 Rada, 9 Duma) Truce (1 Rada, 1 Duma)

Table 1.9 Top 50 Collocates of Krim*/Crimea in Rada Corpus

Rank	Freq	Freq L	Freq R	Stat.	Collocate	Translation
1	3	1	2	17.70760	займаюся	are engaged
2	4	2	2	17.12264	складами	actus reus
3	4	2	2	17.12264	підслідні	defendants
4	4	2	2	17.12264	провадженнях	proceedings
5	4	2	2	17.12264	кваліфікованими	qualified
6	5	2	3	16.85961	татарин	Tatar
7	3	1	2	16.70760	татарина	Tatar's
8	3	1	2	16.70760	курултая	Kurultay (Crimean Tatar Assembly)
9	3	2	1	16.70760	караїмів	Karaims (ethnic group)
10	3	2	1	16.70760	визнанню	acknowledged
11	4	1	3	16.53768	окупованою	occupied
12	5	0	5	16.44457	окупований	occupied
13	19	5	14	16.37057	татари	Tatars
14	7	3	4	16.34503	півострові	peninsular
15	23	2	21	16.32427	татар	tatars
16	11	10	1	16.26014	автономну	autonomous
17	117	114	3	16.14751	автономної	autonomous
18	4	1	3	16.12264	широкі	broad
19	3	2	1	16.12264	чисток	purges
20	3	0	3	16.12264	татарів	Tatars
21	6	0	6	16.12264	татарам	Tatars
22	3	2	1	16.12264	радио	radio
23	9	2	7	16.12264	півострова	peninsular
24	5	0	5	16.12264	проваджень	proceedings
25	3	2	1	16.12264	представницький	representative
26	3	2	1	16.12264	переселяються	move away
27	3	3	0	16.12264	окупованому	occupied
28	4	4	0	16.12264	меджлісом	Mejlis (Tatar representative body)
29	3	2	1	16.12264	курултай	Qurultay (Crimean Tatar Assembly)
30	10	6	4	16.12264	корінного	native
31	3	3	0	16.12264	депортації	deported
32	35	35	0	16.12264	автономній	autonomous
33	8	5	3	15.95271	окупацію	occupation
34	36	36	0	15.90025	республіці	republic
35	12	11	1	15.90025	республіку	republic
36	5	4	1	15.85961	порушені	violations
37	18	1	17	15.83313	севастополь	Sevastopol
38	9	1	8	15.83313	кодексі	code
39	4	0	4	15.80071	невідворотності	irreversibility
40	8	4	4	15.80071	діяння	actions
41	8	8	0	15.80071	вільній	free
42	124	123	1	15.75491	республіки	republic
43	3	0	3	15.70760	півострів	peninsular
44	3	2	1	15.70760	патріотично	patriotic
45	3	2	1	15.70760	окупувала	occupied
46	3	0	3	15.70760	загальнокримського	pan-Crimean
47	3	1	2	15.70760	вивіз	drove away
48	5	2	3	15.63721	пояснювати	clarify
49	32	2	30	15.63079	провадження	proceedings
50	22	19	3	15.58207	анексії	annexation
51	6	2	4	15.53768	севастополі	Sevastopol

Table 1.10 Top 50 Collocates of Krym*/Crimea in Duma Corpus

Rank	Freq	Freq L	Freq R	Stat.	Collocate	Translation
1	3	0	3	11.75219	севастополю	Sevastopol
2	3	0	3	11.75219	севастопольцев	Sevastopol
3	3	0	3	11.75219	севастополем	Sevastopol
4	5	5	0	11.75219	воссоединением	reunification
5	199	8	191	11.60745	севастополя	Sevastopol
6	25	2	23	11.44185	севастополь	Sevastopol
7	4	4	0	11.43026	воссоединении	reunification
8	3	3	0	11.33715	автономную	autonomous
9	9	9	0	11.22167	создаваемых	created
10	35	3	32	11.18103	севастополе	Sevastopol
11	4	3	1	11.16722	судьбой	destiny
12	6	5	1	11.16722	игорной	gaming
13	10	10	0	11.16722	автономной	autonomous
14	9	9	0	11.11476	судейского	judicial
15	3	3	0	11.01522	потенциале	potential
16	3	3	0	11.01522	посещал	visited
17	3	3	0	11.01522	освобождением	liberation
18	6	4	2	11.01522	вхождении	joining
19	120	1	119	10.95864	значения	significance
20	4	1	3	10.94483	полуостров	peninsular
21	252	249	3	10.92534	республики	republic
22	3	0	3	10.75219	немецко	German
23	3	3	0	10.75219	морю	sea
24	4	4	0	10.75219	вхождения	joining
25	8	8	0	10.75219	воссоединения	reunification
26	44	37	7	10.56776	федерацию	federation
27	152	1	151	10.56132	города	city
28	7	3	4	10.55954	полуострова	peninsular
29	3	0	3	10.52979	фашистских	fascist
30	3	3	0	10.52979	пенсионерами	pensioners
31	3	1	2	10.52979	крымской	Crimean
32	4	3	1	10.43026	порты	ports
33	3	0	3	10.33715	отряды	detachments
34	3	1	2	10.33715	образовательную	educational
35	4	3	1	10.29275	хрущёв	Khrushchev
36	4	2	2	10.29275	северо	Northern
37	4	3	1	10.29275	родиной	motherland
38	47	37	10	10.27335	российскую	Russian
39	3	0	3	10.16722	независимым	independent
40	5	4	1	10.16722	историческое	historical
41	42	2	40	10.14450	составе	included
42	14	13	1	10.10011	особенностях	characteristics
43	4	2	2	10.05175	радость	joy
44	3	1	2	10.01522	наблюдали	witnessed
45	3	2	1	10.01522	донбасс	Donbass
46	3	3	0	10.01522	воссоединение	reunification
47	3	2	1	10.01522	волей	will
48	10	0	10	9.98665	образованием	education
49	3	2	1	9.87772	отдаёт	gives away
50	3	2	1	9.87772	многонационального	multinational

Table 1.12 Themes of Collocates of Krim*/ Crimea in Rada Corpus and Krym*/ Crimea in the Duma Corpus

Rada Corpus		Duma Corpus	
Themes	**Examples of collocates**	**Theme**	**Examples of collocates**
occupation, annexation	окупувала/occupied, анексії/annexation, вільний/ free, порушені/violated	reunification	Воссоединение/reunification, судьбой/by destiny, радость/joy, вхождение/joining, освобождение/liberation, матерью-Родиной/ motherland Russia, историческое решение/ historical decision
ethnic minorities	татарин/Tatar, меджліс/Mejlis курултай/ Qurultay, корінного/ native, караїмів/Karaims, депортаці/ deportation, переселяються/are relocated	ethnic minorities	многонационального/ multinational
political status, geography and infrastructure	автономній/autonomous, республіка/republic, півостріві/ peninsular, кодекс/code, загальнокримського/pan-Crimean, севастополі/Sevastopol	political status, geography and infrastructure	Севастополь//Sevastopol, Федерацию/federation, города/ city, полуострова/ peninsular, республики/ Republic, морю/ sea

Table 1.13 First 25 Collocates of Rosìâ/Russia in Rada Corpus

Rank	Freq	Freq L	Freq R	Stat.	Collocate	Translation
1	4	1	3	13.58659	вставай	get up
2	5	3	2	12.90852	язала	spelling error in processing
3	3	2	1	12.17155	цілиться	to point at, to level *(as in a gun)*
4	4	1	3	11.26466	оголосила	announce
5	3	0	3	10.58659	**агрессор**	**aggressor**
6	3	2	1	9.52769	кордоні	border
7	3	1	2	9.47111	зробила	made
8	7	1	6	8.80898	**війну**	**war**
9	8	4	4	8.72861	росія	Russia
10	5	3	2	8.62311	розв	*(spelling error in processing)*
11	4	4	0	8.45730	росією	Russia
12	4	2	2	7.66772	українську	Ukrainian
13	3	0	3	7.58659	**територію**	**territory**
14	3	2	1	7.51334	україною	by Ukraine
15	5	4	1	7.41666	**війни**	**war**
16	4	2	2	7.17720	газу	gas
17	3	1	2	7.06303	**терористів**	**terrorists**
18	4	3	1	6.94273	українських	Ukrainian
19	3	3	0	6.74528	росії	Russia
20	6	5	1	6.67569	яку	*(function word)*
21	4	3	1	6.46247	само	*(function word)*
22	4	3	1	6.45730	вчора	yesterday
23	4	1	3	6.40668	**крим**	**Crimea**
24	6	2	4	6.17155	**проти**	**against**
25	3	0	3	5.91888	україну	Ukraine

Table 1.16 Themes Emerging from the Right-hand Nominal Collocates of Rosijs'k*/Russian in Rada Corpus and Ukrainsk*/Ukrainian in the Duma Corpus

Themes	Російськ*/Russian Collocates in Rada Corpus		Украинск*/Ukrainian Collocates in the Duma Corpus	
	Total number of collocates	Examples with translations	Total number of collocates	Examples with translations
	216		205	
War, aggression, conflict	86	загарбниками/invaders, бойовиками/militants, найманців/mercenaries, військового/military, окупанти/occupiers, диверсанти/saboteurs, війна/war, терористи/terrorists	44	армии/army, военных/military, границе/border, бмп/armoured personnel carrier, русофобы/Russiophobes пограничниками/border control, самопровозглашённые/self-declared, флоте/fleet
Government parliament, elections, parliamentary parties, state institutions and procedures	45	Федерація/frderation, імперії/empire, держава/state, громадян/citizens, влади/authority	76	руководства/leadership, общество/society, народов/peoples, депутатам/deputes, парламент/parliament, государство/state, законов/laws, граждане/citizens
media	16	телеканалів/tv channels, пропаганду/propaganda, медіа/media, журналістів/journalists	7	сми/media, пропаганды/propaganda, передач/programmes
Fascism	8	шовіністи/chauvinists, фюрер/führer, фашист*/fascist	5	нацисты/Nazis, неонацисти/neonazis, фашист*/fascist, хунта/junta
Language	7	мов*/language	2	язык/language
Business, finance and banking	5	компанія/company, партнерів/partners, банкам/banks	18	предприятий/enterprises, экономики/economy, банками/banks, олигархи/oligarchs
Gas	5	природнй/natural, газ/gas, газпром/Gazprom	0	

2

Metaphor, identity and conflict in political discourse

A case study of President Poroshenko and President Putin's speeches

Liudmila Arcimavičienė

1 Introduction

Recent political tensions across the world cannot go unobserved and unmarked. The rise of negative populism in party politics across Europe, the refugee crisis, the US isolationist foreign policy, the war in Syria and the Ukraine conflict are just a few examples of the political landscape being entrenched in confrontational practices rooted in violence and aggressive rhetoric and actions. As a result, more studies are being devoted to the expression of hate speech and narratives in various contexts of use (Baider and Kopytowska 2018; Kopytowska and Chilton 2018). Linguists from around the world address the issue of hate speech and radicalism in its online representations among internet users in the context of the refugee crisis in the EU (Assimakopoulos, Baider and Millar 2017) or the use of discriminatory language against minorities and their rights in British Parliamentary argumentation (Love and Baker 2015). In addition, it is noted how hostility to the Other is intertwined with the rising hostility towards immigrants' languages in Britain (Musolff 2018). Mobilization against the Other grounded in xenophobic attitudes and hostility across genres is investigated in different social and cultural contexts of Poland and Cyprus (Kopytowska, Grabowski and Woźniak 2017; Baiden and Kopytowska 2018), Malta (Assimakopoulos and Muskat 2017); the UK (Musolff 2018), Germany (Klapp 2018), and so on.

Similarly, political discourse is becoming more polarized, radically populist and conflict-oriented. This kind of political positioning is always realized by a dichotomized hegemonic stance of the *Self* over the *Other*, whereby the *Self* is constructed as the defender of the right and in the fight against the conspiracy of the *Other*. Such political discourse is also referred to as paranoid style in politics (Hofstadter 2008) and has been recently observed in the NRA discourse in American politics (Hodges 2015), or else is also known as right-wing populism being observed in discourses of mainstream and radical parties across Europe (Wodak, KhosraviNik and Mral 2013). Along these lines, populist rhetoric is becoming more prominent among political leaders and how they compete in elections and referendums (e.g. Trump's presidential *America First* campaign, Marine le Pen's presidential *The voice of people, the spirit of France* campaign, Nigel Farage's Brexit *Let's take back control* campaign and nationalist Swedish Democrats as *People's home* election campaign).

This study aims to clarify how conflict scenarios can be re/created in diplomatic discourse in the specific context of Ukraine crisis, being viewed in this study as a cataclysm of rising political tensions both within domestic politics of representative countries (i.e. Ukraine and Russia) and globally. In addition, the significance of the Ukraine crisis and its narrative can be viewed as a turning point in the foreign policy of the Russian Federation and its relationship scenario with the West. If before the Ukraine events, despite its confrontational foreign policy in Georgia, Russia had been represented as a part of Western alliance, after Crimea and Donbas events, the narrative changed to a clear bipolar division into two ideological poles: the West versus. Russia. Both discursively and politically, the ideological conflict between Russia and Ukraine, with the latter being a representative of the West, started to unfold.

This chapter is concerned with how the Ukraine 'crisis' is metaphorically represented by the leaders of the countries in conflict, that is, President Poroshenko and President Putin, in the period of four years starting with 2014 when Crimea events took place and the conflict rose to its heights and ending with President Poroshenko's 2017 UN general assembly address. The analysis of metaphor in this kind of discourse is integrated with identitarian violence categories serving as psychological determinants in political conflict. The chapter consists of four main subdivisions. In the first section, some of the literature on the concept of violence and political metaphor is outlined. The second section provides with the specific characteristics of data and methods, while the third section discusses predominant types of metaphor use and their categorization model. Finally, the ideological patterns and functions of these metaphors within the identitarian approach to politics are reflected on.

1.1 Violence and its complexity

One of the key concepts of this study is violence and its discursive construal. In the psychological realm, violence is viewed as an essential element of conflict caused by psychological factors of Self-perceptions (Fromm 1992). Even more, it has been observed in psychoanalysis how Self-perceptions are recurrent with group identity, especially when individuals are imitating group behaviour to realize oneself (Freud 1975; Brewer 2001). This leads to an assumption that violence as a category is always initiated by individual attempts to oppose the collective Other, by thus giving meaning and legitimacy to the self. In political philosophy, predisposition to violence in relationships has been discussed from the perspective of competitive politics (Hobbes 2016), which today is recognized under the label of 'competitive ethic' in political and economic environments (see Chomsky 2011: 125).

Conflict in politics, differently from its physical counterpart, is carried out discursively; naturally, political conflict is more sophisticated, and less forceful

Figure 2.1 Graphic representation of violence in political discourse.

and abrupt, though more complex in its structure and representation. In addition, political conflict in diplomatic discourse is also relatable with the genre of political performance aiming to create a public image and raise a level of expectations towards the speaker. In this study, political conflict is primarily viewed as a complex, discursive act of ideological violence, which is both identity and performance oriented. In order to understand political conflict, its complexity is analysed via semantic categories of violence that are identity and ideology driven. The concept of violence and how it is perceived within the framework of this study is illustrated in Figure 2.1.

As shown in Figure 2.1, discursive violence in political conflict is based on the relationship between the Self and the Other that is metaphorically realized via semantic categories of violence. The Self and Other relationship in political science and sociology (Ellemers 2012; Malešević 2010; Maynard 2013, 2015) correlates with an ideological positioning or legitimization of the Self in its relationship with the Other in critical discourse studies (van Dijk 1998, 2008, 2011; Fairclough 2001, 2013; Chilton 2004; Wodak and Meyer 2009). Not surprisingly, in political science, conflict is also studied via the deconstruction of a hegemonic myth or storyline (Laclau 2005; Laclau and Mouffe, 2014; Žižek 2008), where a mythical self-representation is given an ideological legitimacy and is positioned in the imaginary realm of ideological truth. In critical discourse analysis, this linguistic representation can be traced via famous Van Dijk's (1993, 1998) 'ideological square' representing semantic macro strategies to positively represent the in-group and misrepresent the out-group. This study hypothesizes that political conflict between Ukraine and Russia is discursively construed via metaphorical violence categories underlying group (Self vs. Other) identity. To test this hypothesis, Maynard's (2015) classification of violence categories has been applied to political metaphor analysis.

1.2 Political metaphor and its implied meaning

The major reason why political metaphor is investigated is its multidimensional functions composition. Political metaphor functions have been researched by scholars from across disciplines, to mention but a few. One of them, specifically important for this study, is an ideological function of political metaphor use. It has been determined how systematic metaphor use helps identify ideological underpinnings in different political contexts such as foreign policy (Lakoff and Chilton 2005); war discourse (Lakoff 1991; Jansen and Sabo 1994); election discourse (Charteris-Black 2006); migration policy (Musolff 2018; Kopytowska and Chilton 2018); EU public discourse (Musolff 2004); populism (Semino and Masci 1996; Arcimavičienė 2019); leadership styles (Charteris-Black 2011; Musolff 2016; Arcimavičienė and Jonaitienė 2015); and so on. Despite these context variations, the ideological dimension of political metaphor is relatable with an idea of framing (Fillmore 1982; Croft and Cruse 2004; Lakoff 1996). As rightly observed by Musolff (2016: 11), metaphorical framing is alike to the integration of two conceptual domains in one semantic field, whereby the target concept is represented via more familiar concepts and assumptions. In politics, framing of reality in certain ways is always leading to consequences. In that regard, political metaphor is self-prophetic (Lakoff and Johnson 1980, 1999) in the sense that new political experiences and changes are always transforming the way linguistic structures are used by discourse participants and how they predict political actions.

Another dimension of metaphor analysis is traced in the intricacy of meaning it can create. Political metaphor has the power to hide certain aspects meaning at the expense of others. For example, Chilton and Lakoff (2005) demonstrate that the US metaphorical foreign policy (e.g. State As Person, State As Container and International Relations As Zero Sum Game) legitimizes the bipolar competitiveness (e.g. nuclear arms *race*), and hides the reality of individual suffering affected by such policies in the long term (i.e. militarization of a state can minimize spending on healthcare and education systems). Along similar lines, Musolff (2016) points out how the discursive conflict between countries can develop into discursive violence. This is shown with the metaphor analysis of Benjamin Netanyahu and Mahmoud Abbas's UN speeches in the period of time between 2011 and 2014, and how the peace-seeking scenario of 'hand-extension' in 2011 gradually developed into 'terrorism' framing in 2014 (2016: 98–102).

In linguistic research, ideological value of metaphor use is generally understood as an implicit construction of a worldview or of a set of beliefs and attitudes underlying a specific fragment of social reality (Goatly 2007). By comparison, in social sciences, ideology is commonly associated with a specific group identity that is seeking or resisting power. In critical discourse studies, ideology and its analysis are carried out by procedurally applying Van Dijk's ideological square (1998), while in critical metaphor analysis, the systematic use of metaphor and its pragmatic functions are determined (Musolff 2016; Charteris-Black 2011).

The current study aims to identify violence categories vis-a-vis metaphorical expressions in order to evaluate the ideological construal of political conflict between Ukraine and Russia represented by their leaders. The following section will give more detail on how the data for this study was collected and analysed.

2 Data and method

The current data consists of two samples: (a) the speeches by President Poroshenko in the time span of four years and (b) the speeches by President Putin in the time span of

Table 2.1 Data Summary

	President Poroshenko (Tokens)	President Putin (Tokens)
Speaking occasions	2014 US Congress address (1,943) 2015 Canadian Congress address (3,898) **2015 UN address (3,192)** 2016 UN address (2,197) 2017 UN address (2,593)	2014 Duma Crimea address (4,638) 2015 UN address (2,350)
Total no. of words	**13,823**	**6,988**

two years. The overview of the collected data, and its time and length characteristics are provided in Table 2.1.

The data was collected by following the criteria of (a) topicality (i.e. Ukraine crisis, or more specifically, the political conflict between Ukraine and Russia), and (b) context (i.e. including the time span and the contextual immediacy of the conflict) with the starting point of Crimea events in 2014 (President Putin's Crimea Duma address and President Poroshenko's Congress speeches in the United States. and Canada) and its development stages (UN speeches).

The collected data samples vary in length, and these variations are caused by external factors. First, it is aimed to analyse only the presidents' speeches at the UN in the time span of 2015–2018 (i.e. President Putin addressed the UN general assembly only in 2015, while President Poroshenko addressed the UN General Assembly annually). Second, the collected samples are content-related (i.e. with the starting point of Crimea events in 2014, and subsequent leaders' international responses to them). The choice of leaders' diplomatic talk was guided by an assumption that both leaders will ideologically construe conflict on behalf of their countries to the international audience via political group identity (friends vs. allies) by thus legitimizing their self-stance and delegitimizing their opponent. Finally, data samples vary in their linguistic form, that is President Poroshenko's speeches were delivered only in English, while President Putin spoke only in Russian. For the purpose of objectivity, officially provided translations for President Putin's speeches were also taken into account.

The collected data was analysed in the framework of two empirically grounded theories: Critical Metaphor Theory in discourse (Cameron 2003; Goatly 2007; Charteris-Black 2004, 2006, 2011; Musolff 2006, 2015) and Conceptual Metaphor Theory (Fillmore 1982; Gibbs 1992; Johnson 1994; Lakoff 1991, 1996; Lakoff and Johnson 1980, 1999; Kövecses 2003, 2004). Within both of these approaches to metaphor analysis, it is attempted to trace how political violence is construed metaphorically in the context of polarized identities (Self vs. Other), and how metaphor analysis can help make sense of the political conflict between Ukraine and the Russian Federation from the perspective of their representative leaders.

Procedurally, metaphor analysis in the collected speeches was carried out at three levels: (a) metaphor identification by procedurally applying Pragglejaz group's Metaphor Identification Procedure (MIP, Pragglejaz Group 2007); (b) deconstruction of source domains; () coding of metaphorical expressions into subcategories of violence (i.e. targeting, mobilization, values, obligation hierarchies and victimhood). During the first step, contextual and basic meanings were compared by using as a point of reference three dictionaries for the English data set (Macmillan, Oxford and Online Dictionary of Etymology) and the online database of Russian dictionaries Slovar. cc (where the first three in the list were accessed to establish the basic meanings). Subsequently, the identified metaphorical expressions were tagged according to their representative source domains derived from basic meanings (e.g. war, nature, person, structure and object). Finally, the source domains were assigned a violence category by using Maynard's classification (2015). Each violence category is viewed here as a basic level concept with the following semantic references:

- *Targeting* as delegitimization of the Other;
- *Mobilization* as a call for collective action against the Other;
- *Values* as normative codes of Self-representation;
- *Obligation hierarchies* as moral and other kinds of responsibilities on behalf of the in-group allies and supporters;
- *Victimhood* as a scenario of the oppressed.

The following two sections demonstrate how President Poroshenko and President Putin's metaphor use can create violence in the context of Ukraine–Russia political conflict and what their individualized styles of that conflict are.

3 Research findings: Overview

The analysis clearly indicates a correlation between the contextual factors of the speech such as time, relevance and immediacy of the occasion, and higher intensity in metaphorical violence style. A more specific account is President Poroshenko's metaphor use in his five speeches, which is summarized in Table 2.2:

The most frequent metaphor use is found in the US Congress address of 2014, that is, with around thirty-four relevant metaphorical expressions per 1,000 words. This is determined by the time factor, it being the first Poroshenko's speech after Crimea events, and the significance of the addressee. By comparison, the subsequent Canada

Table 2.2 Metaphor Frequencies in President Poroshenko's Speeches

	President Poroshenko		
Data samples	Total no. of words	No. of relevant metaphorical expressions	Relevant metaphorical expressions per 1000 words
US 2014	3,898	132	33.9
Canada 2014	1,943	40	20.6
UN 2015	3,195	83	25.9
UN 2016	2,171	56	25.7
UN 2017	2,523	63	24.9
Total	**13,700**	**374**	

Table 2.3 Metaphor Frequencies in President Putin's Speeches

Data samples	President Putin		
	Total no. of words	No. of relevant metaphorical expressions	Relevant metaphorical expressions per 1000 words
Crimea 2014	5,208	165	31.7
UN 2015	2,970	63	21.2
Total	**8,178**	**228**	

speech of 2014 is the least frequent in violence-related metaphor use. Finally, it is seen how the UN addresses have a very similar distribution of metaphor frequency, with the 2015 address as the most metaphorical.

A similar pattern is observed with President Putin, where his metaphor frequency is also determined by the factors of time proximity (i.e. Crimea address is chronologically the first speech) and the significance of his audience (i.e. the Russian Duma, the domestic viewers and the world audience).

The Crimea address has higher metaphor frequency (almost thirty-two relevant metaphorical expressions per 1,000 words) in comparison to the UN speech of 2015 with twenty-one metaphorical expressions per 1,000 words. Finally, a similar semantic pattern of metaphorical violence between the two speakers is found in their first speeches, where they seem to be more aggressive in their rhetoric. It has also been determined that both speakers consistently evoke two violence categories – (a) targeting the other, and (b) expressing values and ideal self-images. Each speaker's conflict identity will be discussed in more detail in the Subsections 3.1 and 3.2.

3.1 President Poroshenko's 'Pro-Values conflict identity'

In President Poroshenko's case, political conflict is mainly construed by the categories of targeting, mobilization and values. The percentage for all violence categories is provided in relation to the total distribution of metaphors of 100% in the collected speeches (i.e. US Congress in the blue bar, Canada speech in orange, UN 2015 in grey, UN 2016 in yellow and UN 2017 in blue).

The speaker's perception of conflict is construed mainly by targeting, mobilization and values, while the categories of obligation hierarchies and victimhood are evoked only occasionally. It can be argued that the category of **value systems** is essential to President Poroshenko's ideological positioning. The emphatic use of self-values helps the speaker establish a moral order and self-legitimacy, within which he is ideologically positioning group relations. Here are a few typical examples of how the speaker appeals to the normative codes within his established political identity:

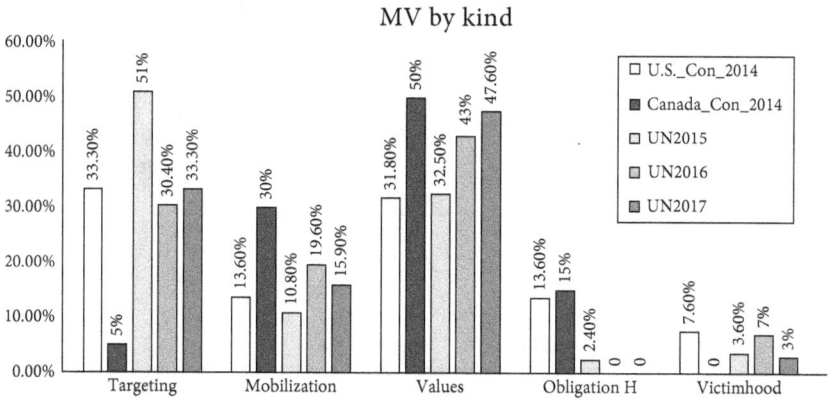

Figure 2.2 Metaphorical violence by kind in President Poroshenko's sample.

The category of values

(1) By **supporting Ukraine**, you **support a nation** that has **chosen freedom** in the most cynical of times. (US Congress, 2014) [PERSON metaphor]
(2) However, it is not only history that **bonds us**, but also the **shared values** that make Canada and Ukraine **integral parts**. (Canada, 2014) [POLITICAL SPACE IS PHSYCAL SPACE metaphors]
(3) Today Ukraine **pays a very high price** for **defending** what we **believe in** – democracy and freedom to **choose our own future**. (Canada, 2014) [WAR, PERSON metaphors]
(4) **Freedom, peace, respect** for the sovereignty and territorial integrity – **Ukraine doesn't demand more**. However, it will **not settle for less**. (UN 2015) [PERSON metaphor]
(5) However, **Ukraine as a responsible international actor** has always been and remains a **committed advocate** of nuclear non-proliferation and disarmament. (UN 2016) [PERSON metaphor]
(6) The world is **divided** again – between those **who believe that freedom** is indispensable and those who believe freedom is expendable. One group wants **to reach a better future**. The other one **drags us into the past**. (OBJECT, JOURNEY metaphors)

These examples illustrate how the speaker is using variations of self-ideals such as responsibility in (5) or commitment in (4) to approximate appeals to loyalty and respect as in (1) and (2) via personifying the entire nation as a high value person whose political space is integrated with the so-called democratic landscape of freedom and democracy, which is linguistically realized via the metaphor of Physical Space, as in (2). The value systems also inhere moral systems that define the in-group and are used as a source of legitimization, as in (6) where the in-group is demonstrated as the one heading towards 'a better future', while the out-group is associated with the past. In that context, the JOURNEY metaphor is playing an ideological role associated with positive changes and hope, whereby forwarded movement blended with the temporal scale of the future is seen as a positive change in contrast to the backward movement.

It can be observed how President Poroshenko refers to values in all of his speeches with the purpose to highlight the significance of representing the in-group identity of the West associated with democracy, freedom and hope. Although values do not provoke and express violence directly, they do project political group identity, on the basis of which conflict is articulated. By contrast, direct confrontation is explicitly generated by targeting and mobilization, and these are some of their most typical realizations.

Violence categories of targeting and mobilization

(7) I think that war in the East of Ukraine is **war against terrorism**. It is **our common war**. I am confident of that. (Canada 2014) [WAR metaphor]

(8) By imposing its **disgraceful** veto on this draft resolution, **Russia clearly demonstrated** to the whole world its **defiance in establishing the truth**. (UN 2015) [PERSON metaphor]

(9) The judicial and penitentiary systems in Crimea have been **converted by Russia into a tool of repressions**. (UN 2016) [PERSON/CRIMINAL metaphor]

(10) The death of the MH17 victims is **on Russia's conscience**. (UN 2017) [PERSON metaphor]

(11) **With your support**, with the support of global community we will **win this struggle**. (Canada 2014) [WAR metaphor]

Despite different occasions, the enemy is clearly defined either with direct reference to it as in (8, 9 and 10) or implicitly as in (7 and 11). This kind of rhetoric is serving ideological purposes of both legitimizing of the Self and delegitimizing of the Other. The shift in representing the Other as an implicit enemy as in (9, 10) or an amoral criminalized person in (7 and 8) ideologically produces major causal links between political identity and violence. The Other, as an ideological enemy causing destruction and war, must be stopped and defeated; thus is mobilized against in the sense of the collectivist logics as in (7) with 'our common war'. It is also implied that the violence against the identity of the Other is becoming a moral agenda and an inevitable response.

The least two frequent categories semantically evoked by President Poroshenko are obligation hierarchies and victimhood. It is also interesting to observe how these two coordinates are at its peak of use in the US Congress Speech, with eighteen instances for Obligations and ten for Victimhood. By contrast, in subsequent speeches, their representation is getting much less expressed in frequency (i.e. from two to four instances of use). Such political performance is necessitated by the proximity of the situation, as Poroshenko's US Congress speech is his first international address after Crimea events in March of 2014 and not surprisingly the frequency of metaphor use with reference to obligations is the highest in that particular speech, for example:

Violence category of obligation hierarchies

(12) I urge **America and the world not to be silent** about these crimes. (U.S. Congress 2014) [PERSON metaphor]
(13) 'Values come first' – this is **the truth the West would remind Ukraine** of over the last years. Now it is Ukraine's turn **to remind the West of this truth!** (U.S. Congress 2014) [PERSON metaphor]

In the given example, it can be seen how obligation hierarchies are recreated via the Country As a Person metaphor. The political conflict is ideologically established while emphasizing obligations of the political identity of Western values paralleled with the truth. This also implies the collective identity of Ukraine with the West and America and with the world by thus creating a moral space of order threatened by the enemy and its crimes. Overall, the use of obligation hierarchies emphasizes the needs and values of the collective in-group (i.e. America as an in-group representing Western values and the truth and Ukraine as its complementary part). Despite the fact that the category of obligations is overlapping with the category of values, there a semantic difference between these two. The former refers to the collective group identity where the obligations are distributed hierarchically (e.g. the United States and Ukraine as one collective whole, where the United States is the leader that has to protect its followers); while the latter is more self-centred (e.g. the values of Ukraine are positively represented).

Victimhood category is another form of in-group identity that is most commonly realized via personification, whereby Ukraine is personified and positioned as a victim, for example:

Violence category of victimhood

(14) Therefore, I urge you not to let **Ukraine stand alone in the face of this aggression.** (U.S. Congress 2014) [PERSON metaphor]
(15) **Ukraine has paid and continues to pay an extremely high price for its freedom**, and the right to live in a free country – **the price of human lives.** (UN 2015) [PERSON metaphor]
(16) **A three-year-long war with Russia** has resulted in 10 thousand people killed, 7% of Ukrainian territory occupied, 20% of Ukrainian economy and industrial output is **seized, destroyed or simply stolen.** (UN 2017) [PERSON metaphor]

With the use of Ukraine As A Person metaphor, President Poroshenko asserts the crimes committed by Russia against the in-group by drawing on another personification metaphor of Russia As An Enemy/Criminal. This kind of discourse incites ideological violence in the sense that the division between political identities of an in-group and out-group is only deepening, and embodies the out-group as a guilty party, violence against which is seen as morally necessary and legitimate.

To summarize, President Poroshenko creates an in-group political identity represented via the ideological conflict with an out-group. This is linguistically achieved by blending the personification of Country Is A Person with the metonymic representation of Nation As A Leader. Ideological conflict is thus articulated by

Metaphor, Identity and Conflict in Political Discourse   55

semantic representation of self-values, mobilization against the Other and targeting the Other. This is how the speaker creates a legitimate space within which his in-group is given characteristics of moral stance and righteousness, being targeted by the out-group and thus legitimately mobilized against.

3.2 President Putin's 'anti-oppression conflict identity' via metaphorical violence categories

President Putin's conflict discourse has its own pattern of ideological representation, which is reflected in the fact that the speaker, differently from his opponent, primarily employs the conceptual schemas of values, targeting, victimhood and obligation hierarchies in the Crimea address, with the mobilization category being the least recurrent. Similarly, in the UN address, his conflict narrative is based on the two main categories, values and targeting, while the remaining three (mobilization, hierarchies and victimhood) are very low in frequency of systematic use. Also, the significance of the Crimea speech for President Putin's political identity and its legitimacy is undoubtedly crucial, and this is reflected in the fact that all five violence categories are linguistically enacted, with his particular emphasis on self-values. The comparison of metaphorical violence (i.e. the percentage of the specific metaphor kind in relation to the total number of metaphorical expressions) in his two speeches (Crimea speech labelled as blue, while the UN address represented by the red bar) is provided in Figure 2.3.

Targeting as a conceptual schema is a recurrent pattern in both of the speeches, though it is almost as half as more prominent in the UN address. By comparison, values play a significant role in both speeches, and this category is realized at a similar frequency rate with the difference of 4 per cent. Also, it is noted how all the conceptual categories inciting an ideological conflict and legitimizing violence are evoked in the Crimea address, with an exception of mobilization being at 7 per cent. By contrast, the UN address is centred around the categories of targeting and values, with the former being the most representative at 52 per cent.

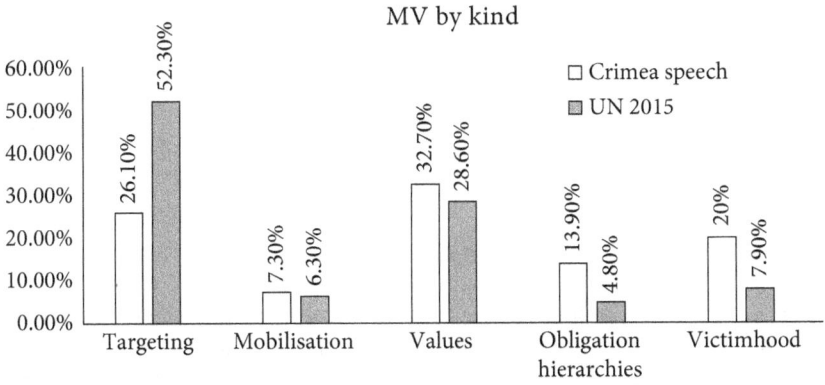

Figure 2.3 Metaphorical violence by kind in President Putin's sample.

The conceptual schema of targeting, differently from President Poroshenko, is more essential to the identity of the in-group in President Putin's rhetoric[1]. In the Crimea address, the main out-group is the government of Ukraine (as in 18), while in the UN address, it is the West and particularly the United States (as in 17 and 19), for example:

Violence category of targeting

(17) We all know that after the end of the Cold War the world was left with ***one center of dominance***, and those who found themselves **at the top of the pyramid** were tempted to think that, since they are so powerful and exceptional, they know best what needs to be done and thus they don't need to reckon with the UN, which, instead of ***rubber-stamping the decisions*** they need, often ***stands in their way***. (UN 2015) [PHSYICAL SPACE, JOURNEY metaphors]

(18) Ponimaû, počemu lûdi na Ukraine hoteli peremen. Za gody «samostijnosti», nezavisimosti, **vlast', čto nazyvaetsâ, ih «dostala», opostylela prosto**. Menâlis' prezidenty, prem'ery, deputaty Rady, no **ne menâlos' ih otnošenie k svoej strane i k svoemu narodu**. Oni «doili» **Ukrainu, dralis' meždu soboj** za polnomočiâ, aktivy i finansovje potoki. (Crimea 2014) [PERSON, ANIMAL metaphors]

I understand why Ukrainian people wanted change. They had had enough of the authorities in power during the years of Ukraine's independence. Presidents, prime ministers and parliamentarians changed, but their attitude to the country and its people remained the same. They **milked the country, fought among themselves** for power, assets and cash flows and did not care much about the ordinary people.

(19) Nevertheless, **NATO has kept on expanding**, together with its military infrastructure. Next, the post-Soviet states were forced **to face a false choice between joining the West and carrying on with the East**. Sooner or later, this logic of confrontation was bound to spark off a major geopolitical crisis. (UN 2015) [PHYSICAL SPACE, JOURNEY]

The way targeting is expressed metaphorically is more varied than in President Poroshenko's case, who evoked a lot of personification to assert a single collective actor for 'good' in its conflict with 'evil'. By contrast, President Putin elaborates his conflict scheme on specifically targeting the out-group by using the metaphors of Physical Space and Journey (i.e. 17 and 19). The metaphor of Physical Space creates a narrative of political habitus dominated or exploited by the out-group (i.e. the use of such metaphorical noun phrases as 'one ***centre*** of dominance, the ***top of the pyramid***' or metaphorically used verbs as '***expand***' or '***stand in their way***' etc.).

The concept of physical space and motion within it are metaphorized in the context of political sphere of influence aiming to imply the necessity for the in-group (i.e. Russia in this case) to defend its own space against the so-called oppressive expansionism. In addition, the targeting category always has a directly expressed moral evaluation of the out-group, as in his reference to 'a false choice' (in 19). The speaker creates antagonism towards the government of Ukraine on behalf of the Ukrainian people (in 18), who, as he argues, 'got fed up with its government'. This example also shows how President Putin identifies himself with the oppressed Ukrainian people by using such slang expressions as 'vlast ih «dostala», opostylela prosto' (these expletives cannot be literally translated into English, but they generally mean 'being fed up with' or 'getting tired of'). In the same example, the personification of the Ukrainian government as an active agent committing crimes against its own people is effectively combined with the objectification of the country, for example, the Country Is an Animal metaphor, as in 'They *milked* a country'.

The second metaphorically represented category of violence is that of value systems. In the Crimea address, the conceptual schema of value systems evokes the emotional appeal to such self-ideals as 'spiritual bondage', 'neighbourly and brotherly relationship', 'homeland and common ancestry', for example:

The category of values

(20) Vse èti gody i graždane, i mnogie obŝestvennye deâteli neodnokratno podnimali ètu temu, govorili, čto Krym – **èto iskonno russkaâ zemlâ**, a Sevastopol' – **russkij gorod**. Da, vsë èto my horošo ponimali, **čuvstvovali i serdcem, i dušoj**, no nado bylo ishodit' iz složivšihsâ realij i uže **na novoj baze stroit' dobrososedskie otnošeniâ** s nezavisimoj Ukrainoj. A **otnošeniâ s Ukrainoj, s bratskim ukrainskim narodom** byli i ostaûtsâ i vsegda budut dlâ nas važnejšimi, klûčevymi, bez vsâkogo preuveličeniâ. (Crimea 2014) [PERSON, RELATIONSHIP metaphors]

All these years, citizens and many public figures came back to this issue, saying that Crimea is **historically Russian land** and Sevastopol is **a Russian city**. Yes, we all knew this **in our hearts and minds**, but we had to proceed from the existing reality and build our **good-neighbourly relations** with independent Ukraine on a new basis. Meanwhile, our relations with Ukraine, with the **fraternal** Ukrainian people have always been and will remain of foremost importance for us.

(21) I naša obespokoennost' ponâtna, ved' **my ne prosto blizkie sosedi**, my faktičeski, kak â uže mnogo raz govoril, **odin narod. Kiev – mat' gorodov russkih. Drevnââ Rus' – èto naš obŝij istok, my vsë ravno ne smožem drug bez druga**. [PERSON, RELATIONSHIP metaphors]

Our concerns are understandable because we are **not simply close neighbours** but, as I have said many times already, we are **one people**. Kiev is **the mother** of Russian cities. Ancient Rus is **our common source** and we **cannot live without each other.**

The value system expressed by President Putin semantically goes beyond the self-ideal of emotional bondage between Ukraine and Russia, which is linguistically realized by personification and relationship metaphors ('fraternal', 'neighbourly', and 'close neighbours'); it extends to the discourses of 'the people' and the 'heartland' known as essential features of populism (Mudde 2004; Mudde and Kaltwasser 2013; Arcimavičienė 2019). By evoking them, the speaker creates a homogenous collective identity that is emotionally valorized. In that context, Crimea events are represented as an act of deep emotional bondage and patriotism. The in-group is clearly represented by the self-deals of nationalism and patriotism that effectively contribute to self-legitimization and high moral apprehension.

The third in frequency and intensity is a metaphorical category of victimhood, which, similarly to values, is another semantic group of the in-group identity. In President Putin's case, its construal captures a range of ways in which he asserts the political identity of Russia as being a target of violence. Consider how it can be realized linguistically via the Russia Is a Victim metaphor, for example:

The violence category of victimhood

(22) Dear colleagues, I must note that such **an honest and frank approach on Russia's part** has been recently used **as a pretext for accusing it of its growing ambitions** — as if those who say that have no ambitions at all. However, **it is not about Russia's ambitions**, dear colleagues, but about the recognition of the fact that **we can no longer tolerate** the current state of affairs in the world. (UN 2015) [PERSON metaphor]

(23) I kogda Krym vdrug okazalsâ uže v drugom gosudarstve, vot togda uže **Rossiâ počuvstvovala, čto eë daže ne prosto obokrali, a ograbili**. (Crimea 2014) [PERSON, OBJECT metaphors]

It was only when Crimea **ended up as part of a** different country that **Russia realized that it was not simply robbed, it was plundered.**

In both instances, though on different occasions, the speaker is using accusations of violence as an implicit projection of Russia' victimhood (especially in 23). It is also interesting to observe how two opposite metaphors correlate in the same frame – Person and Object. The former is used in the representation of the in-group or Russia that is criminally assaulted (i.e. 'robbed, plundered'), while Crimea is objectified and is represented as an object of transfer and an implicitly Russian possession. Crimea is thus represented as a constituent element of Russia's political identity, and its disownment is becoming an act of robbery that provokes a defensive response, which also explains why more aggressive victimhood sounds defensive in (23). A more implicit and less provoking victimhood is represented (in 22) where President Putin addresses an international community and how unfairly Russia is being treated. The personification of Russia in 'Russia's ambitions' points to the salience of the dominant political violence from others (i.e. 'we can no longer tolerate the current state affairs in the world').

Finally, the last recurrent conceptual schema in projecting political violence against an in-group (i.e. Russia) is that of obligation hierarchies. By evoking this metaphorical category, he implicitly defines a boundary of morally regulated behaviour that also necessitates the in-group to legitimately project violence. Not surprisingly, this is enacted through the relationship metaphor whereby both Russia and Crimea are personified, for example:

The violence category of obligations

(24) V svâzi s ètim žiteli Kryma i Sevastopolâ obratilis' k Rossii s prizyvom zaŝitit' ih prava i samu žizn', ne dopustit' togo, čto proishodilo, da i sejčas eŝë proishodit

i v Kieve, i v Donecke, v Har'kove, v nekotoryh gorodah Ukrainy. Razumeetsâ, my **ne mogli ne otkliknut'sâ na ètu pros'bu, ne mogli ostavit' Krym i ego žitelej v bede,** inače èto bylo by prosto predatel'stvom. (Crimea 2014) [PERSON, RELATIONSHIP metaphors]

In view of this, the residents of Crimea and Sevastopol **turned to Russia for help in defending their rights and lives, in preventing the events** that were unfolding and are still underway in Kiev, Donetsk, Kharkov and other Ukrainian cities. Naturally, **we could not leave this plea unheeded; we could not abandon Crimea and its residents in distress**. This would have been **betrayal** on our part.

In this example, the obligation hierarchy is based on the regulated moral behaviour featuring brotherhood and humanity, and those cannot be questioned and are juxtaposed with betrayal. As a moral agent, Russia responds to the victim's pleas, thus becomes a protector of the oppressed. This heroic myth can also be paralleled with the populist scenario of the 'pure people' that have to be heroically protected against a corrupt oppressor (see Mudde 2004; Laclau 2005). By using Laclau's concept of 'an empty signifier' (2005), it can be seen how an act of political violence can be projected as a heroic stance in the name of the oppressed. To summarize, President Putin projects political identity by integrating a range of violence categories; the most recurrent patterns are relatable with the conceptual schemas of values, targeting and victimhood. A less recurrent, but still effective, coordinate that is essential to the political identity of Russia in the speaker's rhetoric, especially in the context of the Crimea events, is that of obligation hierarchies.

4 Conclusions

This study aimed to clarify how political identity and political violence can be communicated by the leaders of countries in conflict. The analysis of President Poroshenko and President Putin's speeches has demonstrated two different approaches to political violence, and how it can be metaphorically instigated vis-a-vis such categories as values, targeting, mobilization, obligation hierarchies and victimhood.

In President Poroshenko's case, this is done by targeting and value systems via such metaphors as Ukraine and as the West Are Moral Agents and Russia Is an Enemy/Criminal. In addition to that, the speaker evokes the metaphor of Ukraine Is a Victim that necessitates obligation hierarchies on the part of the West to protect a member of its in-group. This is also achieved by mobilizing the in-group members (the United States, Canada, the West and the world) against the out-group represented by Russia. In the context of values, the speaker positions the in-group within a moral spectrum of such concepts as freedom, democracy and the truth. The speaker uses a very aggressive tone to reproach the out-group, and incites a direct confrontation with it. Specifically, President Poroshenko's rhetoric is a values-oriented narrative, allowing the speaker to create a political habitus of two confrontational realities: the Self vs. the Other. The Self-representation is legitimized via its positioning in the realm of Western values that give order and stability to the world. The Other-representation is criminalized and paralleled with chaos, instability and disruption.

By contrast, President Putin creates a political habitus where Russia is metaphorically construed as either a Victim or a Protector of the Oppressed (i.e. Crimea and Russian people). His composition of political identity is aggressively defensive, as reflected in the use of person and relationship metaphors. It is also interesting to observe how the same referent can have an opposite positioning: Crimea as an Object in the context of the values (the object that belongs to Russia), and Crimea is as an oppressed person whose protection becomes an unwavering act of morale and justice. The speaker represents the in-group via such self-ideals as empathy, self-denial, strength, discipline and spirituality. Finally, differently from President Poroshenko, President Putin is also using populist arguments to incite political violence with his reference to patriotism, nationalism and an empty signifier of the oppressed. Both leaders' violence styles with the sequenced violence categories across all their speeches are summarized in Figure 2.4.

Both speakers position themselves differently though with a few recurrent features. On the basis of Western values represented by an ideological in-group (i.e. the West: the United States, the EU and Ukraine), President Poroshenko targets an out-group (i.e. Russia), and mobilizes against it by criminalization and delegitimization. As Ukraine is positioned in the realm of democratic values, its victimhood is not highlighted, while the obligation hierarchies of stronger moral agents (namely the United States) towards weaker moral agents (Ukraine) take over a victim scenario in his political performance. By contrast, President Putin's political violence is centred on the idea of anti-oppressive self-defence. The speaker targets an ideological oppressor (Ukraine and the West, the United States in particular) by giving legitimacy to Russia's stance on defending oppressors' victims, and thus raising one's own values and credibility. The scenario of obligation hierarchies is mainly evoked in the context of nationhood and patriotism; mobilization is thus linked to the narrative of 'united we stand' against an oppressor, and in the name of nationhood and common heritage.

Despite certain differences in conflict scenarios between the two speakers, one common pattern of time relevance can be observed. The closer the speakers are in time to the conflicting event, the more violent their rhetoric and political performance become. This is easily observed with President Poroshenko, who was the most violent in his expression in US Congress address in 2014 (35 per cent) and subsequent UN address in 2015 (22 per cent). By comparison, his further addresses are becoming more balanced and show lesser degree of direct confrontation (i.e. UN 2016 with 15 per cent, and UN 2017 with 17 per cent).

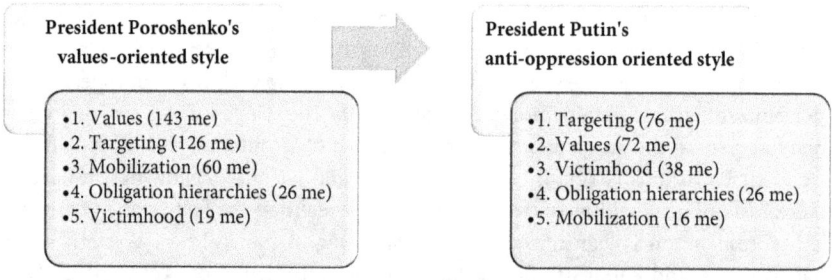

Figure 2.4 Both leaders' conflict metaphorical styles.

A similar pattern can be traced with President Putin's performance, though it can also be determined by the addressee factor. His two prominent speeches aim to address two different kinds of audience: the Crimea speech is mainly delivered to the domestic audience, and only then Ukraine and the world community; while his UN address is primarily targeting the world community. As a result, a noticeable difference in the degree of violence (e.g. Crimea 2014 address with 72 per cent and UN 2015 with 28 per cent) can be observed. Another important similarity lies in the intersection across both leaders' rhetoric of two violence categories – values and targeting. To clarify, it seems that political conflict revolves around these two schemas, which can point out to a possible definition of political conflict as a kind of discursive political performance, whereby political leaders *target* their opponents in the context of their own *values-based identity*.

Finally, this kind of analysis has revealed that various representations of violence in political discourse can help to understand a political conflict better. The metaphorical content of identities, including such specific categories as values, obligation hierarchies, mobilization, targeting and victimhood, can be variant and context-dependent. It is also important to observe how the deployment of such identities results in different centres of power and contribute to creating a subjective narrative of political identity and its role in political leadership.

Note

1 It should be noted that President Putin's examples are provided either in English (i.e. the synchronic translation during the delivery) or Russian (i.e. with its transliteration and its official translation provided at Kremlin.ru). Thus, the examples from the UN speech are provided in English, while the Crimea speech is illustrated in both formats.

References

Arcimavičienė, L. (2019), 'Self and Other Metaphors as Facilitating Features of Populist Style in Diplomatic Discourse: A Case Study of Obama and Putin's Speeches', in *Populist Discourse*, 89–123. Cham: Palgrave Macmillan.

Arcimavičienė, L. and Jonaitienė, V. (2015), 'Metaphor Evaluation of Leadership Styles: A Case Study of Presidential New Year Greetings', *Open Linguistics*, 1 (1): 345–60.

Assimakopoulos, S. and Muskat, R. V. (2017), 'Exploring Xenophobic and Homophobic Attitudes in Malta: Linking the Perception of Social Practice with Textual Analysis', *Lodz Papers in Pragmatics*, 13 (2): 179–202.

Assimakopoulos, S., Baider, F. H. and Millar, S. (2017), *Online Hate Speech in the European Union: A Discourse-Analytic Perspective*. Springer. SpringerBriefs in Linguistics, https://doi.org/10.1007/978-3-319-72604-5.

Baider, F. and Kopytowska, M. (2018), 'Narrating Hostility, Challenging Hostile Narratives', *Lodz Papers in Pragmatics*, 14 (1): 1–24.

Brewer, M. B. (2001), *Ingroup Identification and Intergroup Conflict. Social Identity, Intergroup Conflict, and Conflict Reduction*, 3, 17–41. Oxford: Oxford University Press.

Cameron, L. (2003), *Metaphor in Educational Discourse*. London: A&C Black.
Charteris-Black, J. (2004), *Corpus Approaches to Critical Metaphor Analysis*. London and New York: Palgrave Macmillan.
Charteris-Black, J. (2006), 'Britain as a Container: Immigration Metaphors in the 2005 Election Campaign', *Discourse & Society*, 17 (5): 563–81.
Charteris-Black, J. (2011), *Politicians and Rhetoric: The Persuasive Power of Metaphor*. London and New York: Palgrave Macmillan.
Chilton, P. (2004), *Analysing Political Discourse: Theory and Practice*. London and New York: Routledge.
Croft, W. and Cruse, D. A. (2004), *Cognitive Linguistics*. Cambridge: Cambridge University Press.
Chomsky, N. (2011), *9-11: Was There an Alternative?*. New York: Seven Stories Press.
Ellemers, N. (2012), 'The Group Self', *Science*, 336 (6083), 848–52.
Fairclough, N. (2001), *Language and Power*. Harlow: Pearson Education Limited.
Fairclough, N. (2013), *Critical Discourse Analysis: The Critical Study of Language*. Abingdon and New York: Routledge.
Fillmore, C. J. (1982), *Frame Semantics. Cognitive Linguistics: Basic Readings*, 373–400. Berlin and New York: Mouton de Gruyter.
Freud, S. (1975), *Group Psychology and the Analysis of the Ego*. New York and London: W.W. Norton & Company.
Fromm, E. (1992), *The Anatomy of Human Destructiveness*. London and New York: Palgrave Macmillan.
Gibbs, Raymond W. (1992), 'Categorization and Metaphor Understanding', *Psychological Review*, 99, 572–7. American Psychological Association.
Goatly, A. (2007), *Washing the Brain: Metaphor and Hidden Ideology*. Amsterdam: John Benjamins.
Hobbes, T. (2016), *Thomas Hobbes: Leviathan* (Longman Library of Primary Sources in Philosophy). New York: Routledge.
Hodges, A. (2015), 'The Paranoid Style in Politics: Ideological Underpinnings of the Discourse of Second Amendment Absolutism', *Journal of Language Aggression and Conflict*, 3 (1), 87–106.
Hofstadter, R. (2008), *The Paranoid Style in American Politics, 1952*. New York: Vintage.
Jansen, S. C. and Sabo D. (1994), 'The Sport/War Metaphor: Hegemonic Masculinity, the Persian Gulf War, and the New World Order', *Sociology of Sport Journal*, 11 (1): 1–17.
Johnson, M. (1994), *Moral Imagination: Implications of Cognitive Science for Ethics*. London: University of Chicago Press.
Klapp, M. (2018), 'Salam-Online: Preventive Measures against Extreme Online Messages among Muslims in Germany. Insights into a Pilot Project at the Center for Islamic Theology, Münster', *Lodz Papers in Pragmatics*, 14 (1): 181–201.
Kövecses, Z. (2003), *Metaphor and Emotion: Language, Culture, and Body in Human Feeling*. Cambridge: Cambridge University Press.
Kövecses, Z. (2004), 'Introduction: Cultural Variation in Metaphor', *European Journal of English Studies*, 8 (3): 263–74.
Kopytowska, M. and Chilton P. (2018), '"Rivers of Blood": Migration, Fear and Threat Construction', *Lodz Papers in Pragmatics*, 14 (1): 133–61.
Kopytowska, M., Grabowski, Ł. and Woźniak, J. (2017), 'Mobilizing against the Other', *Contemporary Discourses of Hate and Radicalism Across Space and Genres*, 93: 57.
Laclau, E. (2005), *On Populist Reason*. New York: Verso.

Laclau, E. and Mouffe, C. (2014), *Hegemony and Socialist Strategy: Towards a Radical Democratic Politics*. London: Verso.

Lakoff, G. (1991), 'Metaphor and War: The Metaphor System Used to Justify War in the Gulf'. *Peace Research*, 23 (2/3): 25–32. Retrieved from https://escholarship.org/uc/item/9sm131vj.

Lakoff, G. (1996), *Moral Politics: How Liberals and Conservatives Think*. Chicago and London: University of Chicago Press.

Lakoff, G. and Chilton, P. (2005), 'Foreign Policy by Metaphor', in *Language & Peace*, 61–84. New York: Routledge.

Lakoff, G. and Johnson, M. (1980), 'The Metaphorical Structure of the Human Conceptual System', *Cognitive Science*, 4 (2): 195–208. doi.org/10.1207/s15516709cog0402_4.

Lakoff, G. and Johnson, M. (1999), *Philosophy in the Flesh: The Embodied Mind and Its Challenge to Western Thought*. New York: Basic books.

Love, R. and Baker, P. (2015), 'The Hate That Dare Not Speak Its Name?', *Journal of Language Aggression and Conflict*, 3 (1): 57–86. Amsterdam: Benjamins Publishing.

Malešević, S. (2010), *The Sociology of War and Violence*. Cambridge: Cambridge University Press.

Maynard, J. L. (2013). 'A Map of the Field of Ideological Analysis', *Journal of Political Ideologies*, 18 (3): 299–327.

Maynard, J. L. (2015), 'Identity and Ideology in Political Violence and Conflict', *St Antony's International Review*, 10 (2): 18–52.

Mudde, C. (2004), 'The Populist Zeitgeist', *Government and Opposition*, 39 (4): 542–63.

Mudde, C. and Rovira Kaltwasser, C. (2013), 'Exclusionary vs Inclusionary Populism: Comparing Contemporary Europe and Latin America', *Government and Opposition*, 48 (2): 147–74. Cambridge: Cambridge University Press.

Musolff, A. (2004), *Metaphor and Political Discourse: Analogical Reasoning in Debates about Europe*. London: Palgrave Macmillan.

Musolff, A. (2006), 'Metaphor Scenarios in Public Discourse', *Metaphor and Symbol*, 21 (1): 23–38.

Musolff, A. (2015), 'Dehumanizing Metaphors in UK Immigrant Debates in Press and Online Media', *Journal of Language Aggression and Conflict*, 3 (1): 41–56.

Musolff, A. (2016), *Political Metaphor Analysis: Discourse and Scenarios*. London, New York, Sydney and Delhi: Bloomsbury Publishing.

Musolff, A. (2018), 'Hostility Towards Immigrants' Languages in Britain: A Backlash Against "Super-diversity"?' *Journal of Multilingual and Multicultural Development*, 40 (3): 257–66.

Pragglejaz Group. (2007), 'MIP: A Method for Identifying Metaphorically Used Words in Discourse', *Metaphor and Symbol*, 22 (1): 1–39. Research, 23 (2/3): 1–39.

Semino, E. and M. Masci (1996), 'Politics Is Football: Metaphor in the Discourse of Silvio Berlusconi in Italy', *Discourse & Society*, 7 (2): 243–69.

Van Dijk, T. A. (1993), 'Principles of Critical Discourse Analysis', *Discourse & Society*, 4 (2): 249–83.

Van Dijk, T. A. (1998), *Ideology: A Multidisciplinary Approach*. Thousand Oaks, CA: Sage Publications.

Van Dijk, T. A. (2008), *Discourse and Context: A Socio-Cognitive Approach*. Cambridge: Cambridge University Press.

Van Dijk, T. A. (ed.) (2011), *Discourse Studies: A Multidisciplinary Introduction*. Thousand Oaks, CA: Sage Publications.

Wodak, R. and Meyer, M. (eds.) (2009), *Methods for Critical Discourse Analysis*. Thousand Oaks, CA: Sage Publications.

Wodak, R., KhosraviNik, M. and Mral B. (eds) (2013), *Right-Wing Populism in Europe: Politics and Discourse*. London and New York: Bloomsbury Academic.

Žižek, S. (2008), *Violence: Six Sideways Reflections*. New York: Picador.

ized by these measures that at the same time contribute to the

3

The image of the Ukrainian crisis in the Polish-language media in Ukraine

Ewa Szkudlarek-Śmiechowicz and Izabela Błaszczyk

The objective of the analysis summarized in the main part of this chapter is to describe the image of the Ukrainian crisis in the media. This image is examined from the perspective of the type of discourse from which it emerges. Therefore, the analysis focuses on the discursive image of the crisis in the Polish media operating in Ukraine, represented by three periodicals addressed to the Polish minority in this country: *Kurier Galicyjski*, *Monitor Wołyński* and *Słowo Polskie* (in quotations henceforth *KG*, *MW* and *SP*). The study encompasses editions of these periodicals for the period of five years from October 2013 to October 2018. The periodicals constituting the research material share three important characteristics: First, they are among the most important Polish periodicals in Ukraine; second, they all have their internet versions (kuriergalicyjski. com; slowopolskie.org; and monitor-press.com), which makes it much easier to create the text corpus and search for language data; and third, all receive financial support from the Senate of the Republic of Poland and the Polish Foundation Freedom and Democracy, which suggests that they represent a similar point of view and type of discourse.

The entire study consists of four parts: the first part presents the basic data on the Polish diaspora in Ukraine; the second, the theoretical basis for research; the third, a description of the research procedure; and the fourth part, which is the main and the most extensive part, will be dedicated to semantic and axiological analysis of discursively significant lexical measures, focused around the term Maidan, which is profiled and conceptualized by these measures that at the same time contribute to the development of the image of the Ukrainian crisis in Polish-language press in 2013–2018.

1 The Polish diaspora in Ukraine

According to statistical data available in the *Demoskop Weekly* bulletin, Poles constituted the fourth largest language and ethnic group in the Ukrainian Soviet Socialist Republic before the Second World War (476 thousand people; *Demoskop Weekly* 2019a), and the seventh largest in 1989 (219 thousand; *Demoskop Weekly* 2019b). Despite a visible decrease in the number of Poles in Ukraine since the 1930s, there are still large Polish communities in the country. According to various estimates, the Polish minority in Ukraine comprises from 144,000 (Ukrainian general census of 2001) to 2 million people (Furmaniak 2011). Most of them live in Eastern Volhynia, Podolia, Galicia and Bukovina. However, Poles are dispersed throughout the entire territory of Ukraine, with a visible concentration in Kiev and in the area of Kherson (Kowalski 2015: 22). In many communes of the Lviv, Khmelnytskyi, Chernivtsi and Zhytomyr Oblasts, Poles declaring Polish to be their mother tongue constitute from 25 per cent to 98 per cent of all inhabitants (Ukrainian general census of 2001). Official results of the general census of 2001, however, do not include those Poles who declared any other language to be their mother tongue, constituting 87 per cent on the scale of the entire country, or the population of Polish origin who declared being of Ukrainian nationality, despite their emotional ties to Poland still being strong (Kowalski 2015: 22).

The number of Poles in Ukraine is dropping systematically, mainly due to mixed marriages and dispersion of Polish settlements, which contributes to assimilation (Kowalski 2015: 23). According to Czyżewski, Dworczyk and Kowalski (2015), the number of Poles in individual administrative districts of Ukraine is now much smaller in comparison to 2001 (that is, less than 144,000). However, no accurate data is available in this regard. In the *Atlas polskiej obecności za granicą* ['Atlas of the Polish presence abroad'] (2012) and in the *Rządowy program współpracy z Polonią i Polakami za granicą w latach 2015–2020* ['Governmental programme for cooperation with the Polish communities and Poles living abroad in 2015–2020'] (2015), the Polish Ministry of Foreign Affairs refers only to the data from the last Ukrainian general census.

Although the Polish diaspora in Ukraine is much less populous in comparison with Germany (1.5 million people), Great Britain (800 thousand) or the United States of America (10 million) (*Rządowy program współpracy z Polonią* ... 2015), it has the highest number of institutions that popularize the Polish language and knowledge of Poland – as many as 410 (cf. Germany, 260' Great Britain, 169; USA, 154; *Atlas polskiej obecności* ... 2012). There are about a dozen newspapers and publications in Polish (published in 500 to 10,000 copies) receiving funds from the Polish budget through consulates and non-governmental organizations. The most important periodicals are: *KG, Dziennik Kijowski, Krynica, MW, Mozaika Berdyczowska* and *SP* (*Atlas polskiej obecności* ... 2012). Three of the periodicals listed serve as a basis for research presented in the further part of this chapter.

KG and *SP* are published entirely in Polish, while *MW* has two language versions: Polish and Ukrainian. The biweekly *KG* has been published since 2007. It has a nationwide periodical status in Ukraine. According to the data of the publishing house, the printed version is available in 6,000 copies. Moreover, there is a YouTube video channel ('TV Kurier Galicyjski') connected to the periodical. The printed version and the online version of this periodical, as well as the audiovisual channel, are co-financed by the Foundation Freedom and Democracy on the basis of responsibility of the Senate of the Republic of Poland for care of the Polish communities and Poles abroad. The biweekly *MW* also receives financial support from the Foundation Freedom and Democracy. The printed version is available in 5,000 copies. *MW* is a bilingual

Polish-Ukrainian periodical. It is distributed on a regional scale (Volyn, Rivne and Ternopil Oblast). It has been published since 2009. The most recently established periodical, which nevertheless declares to be linked to the historical Polish press,[1] is *SP*, published monthly since 2012. It is also supported by the Foundation Freedom and Democracy. The printed version of the monthly is distributed in three oblasts, Zhytomyr, Khmelnytskyi and Vinnytsia, inhabited by more than 50 per cent of all Poles living in Ukraine (Wójcicki 2012).

2 Theoretical basis for research

The further part of the study is based on analysis of such terms as discursive image of the world, point of view, profiling of concepts, which determine the theoretical and methodological base for the analysis, and the associated semantic and axiological processes that shape the linguistic measures used in text and discourse. The discursive image of the world is defined as:

> a profiled interpretation of reality, which can be grasped as a set of judgments of the world, people, things and events ... the DIW [discursive image of the world] is constructed linguistically, negotiated on the basis of emotional or rational arguments, which are distributed through the media (Warnke 2009). Linguistic and media-based construction of the DIW means that facts are negotiated under the banner of struggle for the truth, and the truth here is not an ontological phenomenon, but a discursively negotiated one. Following Kloch (2006: 36), we state that the media 'construct the criteria of a judgment of what is the truth and how it is verified.' Meaning and sense of all processes, things, etc. are constructed in this manner. Facts are negotiated through application of techniques and strategies that either justify or negate knowledge, which has been constructed linguistically. Therefore, DIW is a dynamic, open and flexible entity, resulting from a clash of different strategies, disputes, antagonisms, authority, and the power of interpretation. (Czachur 2011: 87)

The analysis of the discursive image of the world defined in this manner implies the concept of profiling (Langacker 1987, 1995, 2008). According to the ethnolinguist and cognitivist Jerzy Bartmiński (2006), who contributed to the development of the work of Ronald Langacker in Poland, we understand it as 'a subjective ... linguistic-conceptual operation, consisting of a specific shaping of the image of an object by placing it in the context of its chosen aspects (subcategories, facets), such as origin, features, appearance, functions, events, experiences etc. within the framework of a specific type of knowledge and in accordance with requirements of the adapted point of view' (Bartmiński, Niebrzegowska 1998; Bartmiński 2006: 99). Profiling results in the emergence of subjectively relativized variants of the image of an object (that is, a phenomenon or an object of non-linguistic reality); the subject chooses specific information concerning the object, its features, characteristics, attributes and structures them in a specific manner, being guided not only by their knowledge of the object but also by the type of discourse and values that are associated with it (Bartmiński 2006: 94–99).

Profiling of concepts depends on the point of view, which is a subjective-cultural factor:

> determining the mode of speaking of the object, including its categorization, selection of the onomasiological base for the creation of its name, selection of features that are attributed to the object in specific statements and fixed in meaning. The point of view assumed by the subject thus functions as a set of directions that shape the content and structure of words and entire statements. (Bartmiński 2006: 78)

In the most expressive manner, the point of view is contained in the evaluation of words and expressions, because the axiological parameter constitutes an important determinant of information processes and structure of concepts (Lakoff and Johnson 1980; Krzeszowski 1997), while values are the factor that controls the process of constructing of the vision of reality by the subject experiencing this reality and conceptualizing its components in language, text and discourse (Bartmiński 2006: 131–48). Knowledge of the world, type of rationality, system of values and point of view of the object create the interpretation framework (Fillmore 1985: 222–54).

The situation of viewing, as well as the associated interpretation and categorization, thus consists of three components: the subject that views the object, viewing as an act (process or condition) and the object being viewed. Most importantly, language data makes it possible to describe the image of the object (phenomenon). The basic modes of profiling, regardless of whether we assume the semasiological perspective (in which the starting point is made of names, words and their use in text) or the onomasiological perspective (where the starting point is an object in the real world and its presentation in language, text or discourse), consist of a description of terms within the framework of specific semantic-lexical relations. The most important of these include hyponymous and hyperonemous, synonymous and antonymous relations, including metaphoric relations that can be used in text to express equivalence or quasi-equivalence, opposition, collection, and relations of superiority and subordination, as well as evaluations, expressed directly or indirectly using lexical measures (Zinken 2004; Bartmiński 2006). The significance of these relations for the analysis of discourse has been pointed out in sociological works (Czyżewski et al. 2017), as well as in studies on text and discourse linguistics (van Dijk 1998; Spützmiller and Warnke 2011).

Profiling of concepts in text and discourse applies to appellatives and proper nouns. Both types of lexical units can be subjected not only to semantization, that is, various semantic transformations, but also to the process of symbolization, which means that some selected characteristics of the object 'gain greater importance in comparison with other characteristics of the same object ... so that the entire unit starts to represent (symbolize) not as much itself as the selected characteristic' (Tołstaja 2004). The process of symbolization, known as symbolic semantization (Tołstaja 2004; Bińczyk 2004), is strictly related to valuation – thus, symbolic semantization is always of axiological nature.

3 Description of the research procedure

For the purpose of the study, an initial text corpus was created, using the software AntConc and Korpusomat – a Polish web-based application – for the creation of inflectionally marked corpora of texts (Kieraś, Kobyliński and Ogrodniczuk 2018). In total, the corpus contained 309 editions of periodicals (*KG*: 118; *MW*: 126; *SP*: 65) and 8,034,587 tokens (*KG*: 5,365,212; *MW*: 1,469,521; *SP*: 1,199,851). Using the terminology describing the mode of selection of the material sample in corpus research, we can speak of targeted selection (Gabrielatos and Baker 2008), and not random sampling or selection based on the availability of data.

As the basic keyword for the discourse on the Ukrainian crisis of the second decade of the twenty-first century, justifying a periodization of the materials for research purposes, we chose the proper name *Majdan* as an abbreviation of the main square in Kiev, that is, the Independence Square (Майдан Незалежності), which was the place of the Ukrainian protests that took place from November 2013 to February 2014. At the starting point of our analysis, we assumed the onomasiological perspective. The keywords referred to as 'nodes around which ideological battles are fought' (Stubbs 2001: 188), can be determined using two basic methods: on the basis of knowledge of the issue discussed (Mautner 2005; Degano 2007) or on the basis of comparison of the frequency list of words in a given corpus, with a frequency list of a reference corpus (Scott 2013). In both cases, further analysis of keywords is the task of the researcher; nevertheless, thanks to computer software, the scholar's attention can be focused on phenomena that are typical for the discourse being analysed. During the first phase of research, we adapted the first approach. We decided that events that took place in 2013/2014 on the Maidan in Kiev were a significant moment in the most recent history of Ukraine, and the onym *Majdan* became our starting point to the gathering of data (Kamasa 2014). During the further stage of the study, we compared the two corpora: the reference corpus (RC), consisting of 309 editions of periodicals addressed to the Polish minority in Ukraine, and the context corpus (CC), developed on the basis of the reference base consisting of around 1,500 contexts of use of word *Majdan* in the periodicals examined. In total, the CC consisted of 507,645 tokens. In the RC, the stem *majdan-*[2] appeared 1,786 times (222 words per million), including 1,543 times (192 words per million) as the noun *majdan/Majdan*. The use of two corpora prepared specifically for the purpose of this research study made it possible to focus the analysis on expressions that were typical for the discourse being examined.

Synonymous and hyperonymous expressions, as well as names of values connoted by lexeme *Majdan/majdan*, were excerpted from the frequency lists for RC and CC. This made it possible to analyse the process of profiling and axiological semantization of the term *Majdan*, which goes from the locative, through the temporal to the event-based aspect. The text equivalents of the term *Majdan* in its event-based profile subjected to analysis were the following words: *demonstracja, protest* and *rewolucja* [*demonstration, protest* and *revolution*]. A comparison of the frequency of these words in the RC and the CC proves their significant role in profiling of the event-based aspect of the concept of *Majdan* (cf. Table 3.1). We also paid particular attention to the expression Rewolucja Godności [Revolution of Dignity], which also constituted

Table 3.1 The Word Frequency: *Majdan, Demonstracja, Protest, Rewolucja, Rewolucja Godności, Euromajdan, Godność, Solidarność, Wolność* in the RC and the CC (per Million Words)

Word	RC	CC
Majdan	192	3040
protest	102	1452
rewolucja	99	1243
euromajdan	22	351
rewolucja godności	18	280
demonstracja	17	142
godność	52	541
wolność	261	504
solidarność	64	366

text equivalents of the term Maidan, but associated with its axiological profile. The names of values occurring in the source material in such numbers that justify their recognition as being important for the discourse are: godność [dignity], solidarność [solidarity] and wolność [freedom], cf. Table 3.1.

A proper description of the discursive image of the Ukrainian crisis in the selected periodicals addressed to the Polish minority in Ukraine should thus focus on two basic issues: the discourse profiles of the lexeme/term *Majdan*, and the associated hyperonyms and contextual synonyms (text equivalents) and values that are connoted by them.

4 The discursive image of the Ukrainian crisis in selected periodicals for the Polish minority in Ukraine

In the press addressed to the Polish minority in Ukraine, particular emphasis is put on the ties between Poland and Ukraine, which are connected to the fact that the two countries are neighbours, as well as to the similarity of their sociopolitical processes. The common 'Soviet experience' of Poland and Ukraine, that is, the political and economic dependency on the USSR after the Second World War, the complicated Polish-Ukrainian relations, determined by history and politics, are the main factors that legitimize the statements, comments and opinions of Polish broadcasters on current Ukrainian affairs. It is recognized that these issues exert a direct impact on the Polish diaspora in Ukraine, at the same time influencing Poland and Poles indirectly. Therefore, statements published in the periodicals underline such aspects as participation of the Polish authorities in the mediation process and attempts to solve the Ukrainian conflict, the involvement of Poles in the protests at the Maidan, the organization of pro-Ukrainian manifestations in Poland, the presence of the Polish minority in Ukraine and the growing number of Ukrainians migrating to Poland.

The word frequency list developed on the basis of the reference corpus, the lexemes *polski/Polska/Polak/RP* [*Polish/ Poland/ Pole/RP* (abbreviation for: *Republic of Poland*)] in various inflectional forms and forms of the lexemes *Ukraina* [*Ukraine*] and *Lwów*

[*Lviv*], occupied the top ten positions (the frequency lists did not include conjunctions, prepositions, pronouns) (cf. Table 3.2).

On the frequency list of the CC, the top three places were occupied by inflectional forms of the words: (1) *Ukraina*, (2) *Majdan* and (3) *Polska/polski*. Such a high frequency of words with morpheme *pol-* confirms the thesis of the Polish (official and governmental) perspective of Ukrainian affairs being dominant in the periodicals analysed. This is indicated, for instance, by comparisons made between the events in Ukraine and the turning points in the history of Poland, such as a comparison of the Euromaidan with the activity of the Solidarity Movement in the 1970s and the 1980s in Poland, and its real and symbolical impact on the process of systemic transformation in Poland in 1989, or the annexation of Crimea by Russia in 2014 with aggression of the Soviet Union against Poland in September of 1939 (cf. examples in the further part of the study).

The content presented in the periodicals is, on the one hand, pro-Ukrainian (with reference to Ukrainian-Russian relations) and, on the other hand, pro-Polish (with reference to Polish-Ukrainian relations). In the analysed periodicals there is no pro-Russian or anti-Ukrainian perspective. This does not mean, however, that there are no opinions critical towards Ukraine, pertaining to historically difficult Polish-Ukrainian relations and the current policy of the Ukrainian authorities. The discourse addressed to Poles in Ukraine by the Polish community is based on values that are important for the development of a sense of attachment to the homeland of the ancestors. It is aimed at delivering and strengthening the knowledge of Polish national heritage: culture, language, history and religion of the society of the receivers of this discourse.[3] A standard in press discourse addressed to the Polish minority in Ukraine, co-financed by the Polish Ministry of Foreign Affairs and the Foundation Freedom and Democracy, is a reference to the Polish tradition, the past, to historic events that are of significance for Poland, to religion and Catholic values. The events taking place in Ukraine are presented and evaluated from this perspective.

Table 3.2 The Word Frequency List Developed on the Basis of the Reference Corpus (Places 1 to 10)

Place	Word	In Total	Per Million Words
1.	polski/Polski [Polish-NOM.M.SG/Poland-GEN.SG]	13038	1623
2.	*Ukrainy* [Ukraine-GEN.SG]	12503	1556
3.	*Ukrainie* [Ukraine-DAT.SG/INS.SG]	10654	1326
4.	*polskiej* [Polish-GEN.F.SG/DAT.F.SG/LOC.F.SG]	9823	1223
5.	*polskiego* [Polish-GEN.M.SG/GEN.N.SG/ACC.M.AN.SG]	9291	1156
6.	*Lwowie* [Lviv-LOC.SG]	8940	1113
7.	*polskich* [Polish-DAT.PL/ACC.M.PERS.PL/LOC.PL]	7919	986
8.	*Polska/polska* [Poland-NOM.SG/Polish-NOM.F.SG]	7647	952
9.	*RP* [*Republic of Poland*]	6874	856
10.	*Polak* [Pole-NOM.SG]	6861	854

4.1 Profiling of the term *Maidan*

The basic meaning of the lexeme *majdan* is a locative one. As a common name *maidan* means 'a square, a market', and as a *nomen proprium* it is a toponym or an anthroponym. In the meaning, which is interesting to us, *Maidan* is an urbanonym – an abbreviated name of the main square in Kiev, that is, the Square of Independence (Ukrainian: Майдан Незалежності), a place, where important cultural for Ukraine and the Ukrainians and state ceremonies are held.

Toponymic proper names, while they mostly play an identifying role, are often subject to profiling: the unit locative name is enriched with an event-based profile, which means it starts to name events that are associated with a given place. Further on, the name becomes a term that symbolizes a certain feature of the event, which usually is not axiologically neutral – it is used as a symbolical reference to other events that are in some way similar to the original event. Semantic extensions of this kind are conditioned culturally – they do not apply to the same lexical units or the same symbolical value in all languages.[4] Similar changes can be observed in profiling of the term *Majdan*: the basic locative meaning ('square' or 'square in Kiev'), has been enriched by an event-based aspect ('protests in Maidan of Kiev') and a temporal aspect ('protests in Maidan of Kiev in years 2013/2014'), which was then assigned a metonymic meaning ('protests in other cities') and a symbolical meaning ('revolution of dignity' or 'Euromaidan').

4.1.1 *The locative profile*

In the examined material, the collocation of the lexeme *majdan/Majdan* associated with its locative meaning ('square', 'square in Kiev' or 'place of protest') with the highest frequency is the combination with the prepositions *na* [*to* and *at*]: *na Majdan* (ACC. SG.) [*to Maidan*]; *na Majdanie* (LOC.SG.) [*at Maidan*], *na majdanch* (LOC.PL.) [*at maidans*] (cf. Table 3.3).

The prepositional phrases *na Majdan/na Majdanie/na majdanach* are connoted by verbs or verbal nouns expressing movement (*na Majdan*) or being, staying in a place (*na Majdanie/na majdanach*). The highest frequency in the examined material was observed for the following verbs, underlining the locative aspect of the term *Majdan* (cf. Table 3.4).

Other verbal phrases with the prepositional phrase *na Majdanie* are, for example, *odbywać się; oddać życie; polec; postrzelić; spędzać czas; spotkać się; stracić życie; strzelać; walczyć; wieźć/przywieźć; zabić;* and *zbierać się* [*take place; sacrifice life; die; shoot; spend time; meet; lose life; shoot to death; fight; drive/bring; kill;* and *gather*]. The

Table 3.3 The Frequency of the Prepositional Phrases: *na Majdanie, na Majdan, na majdanach* (Per Million Words)

Phrase	RC	CC
na Majdanie	34	544
na Majdan	13	205
na majdanach	2	33

Table 3.4 Verbs Underlining the Locative Aspect of the Term *Majdan* (Per Million Words)

Verb/Phrase	RC	CC
być na Majdanie/na majdanach [be at Maidan/at maidans]	8	122
jechać na Majdan [go to Maidan] (pojechać, przyjechać, wjechać, zjechać [go, come, arrive, leave])	4	65
iść/chodzić na Majdan [go/walk to Maidan] (wyjść/wychodzić, przyjść/przychodzić [go out, arrive])	3	45
stać na Majdanie/na majdanach [stand at Maidan/at maidans]	2	34
zginąć na Majdanie [die at Maidan])	2	34

prepositional phrase *na Majdanie* is also combined with nouns that name events or actions: *demonstracje na Majdanie; protesty na Majdanie; wiece na Majdanie; rewolucja na Majdanie; wydarzenia na Majdanie;* and *uroczystości na Majdanie* [*demonstrations at Maidan; protests at Maidan; rallies at Maidan; revolution at Maidan; events at Maidan;* and *celebrations at Maidan*], as well as struggle and death: *masakra na Majdanie; śmierć na Majdanie; starcia na Majdanie; walki na Majdanie;* and *zabójstwa na Majdanie* [*massacre at Maidan; death at Maidan; fights at Maidan; heat at Maidan;* and *killings at Maidan*].

4.1.2 The event-based profile

The locative profile ('square') and the event-based profile ('protest') are combined in the expression *kijowski Majdan* [the *Maidan of Kiev*] (RC: 8 words per million; CC: 124 words per million – comparison of numerical data from sub-chapter 4.1.2 – cf. Table 3.5), and most of all in the following expressions: *barski Majdan, charkowski Majdan, doniecki Majdan, lwowski Majdan, łucki Majdan, ługański Majdan* and *wołyński Majdan* [*Maidan: of Bar, of Kharkiv, of Donetsk, of Lviv, of Lutsk, of Luhansk* and *of Volhynia*], which the lexeme *majdan* has the exclusive meaning of a 'protest, demonstration', and the locative function is taken over in Polish by the substantival adjective (*barski, charkowski, lwowski,* etc.) created on the basis of the local name.

Lexemes *demonstracja* and *protest* are contextual synonyms of the term *Majdan*, rooted in its event-based profile. As we have already stated, these terms are characterized by a high frequency of occurrence in our CC, and thus they often appear next to the lexeme *majdan*. Collocations of the lexeme *protest* indicate several features of *maidans-protests*. They are referred to in the examined material as: *masowe* [*mass*] (RC: 2; CC: 37); *antyrządowe* [*anti-governmental*] (RC: 0,5; CC: 6); *studenckie* [*student*] (RC: 0,5; CC: 6); *społeczne* [*social*] (RC: 0,5; CC: 6); *ogólnonarodowe* [*nationwide*]; *prounijne* [*pro-EU*]; and *demokratyczne* [*democratic*]. Another collocation, which emerges more frequently than others, is the combination *protest/protesty studentów* [*protest/protests of students*] (RC: 1; CC: 14). The lexeme *demonstracja* [*demonstration*] (*majdan-demonstracja* [*maidan-demonstration*]) is most often connected with the adjective *antyrządowy* [*anti-governmental*] (*antyrządowa demonstracja* [*anti-governmental demonstration*] –

Table 3.5 The Frequency of Collocations Important for the Event-based Profile of the Term *Majdan* (Per Million Words)

Collocation	RC	CC
kijowski Majdan	8,0	124,0
masowe protesty	2,0	37,0
antyrządowa demonstracja	1,5	22,0
protest/protesty studentów	1,0	14,0
Antymajdan	<1,0	12
studenckie protesty	0,5	6,0
społeczne protesty	0,5	6,0
antyrządowe protesty	0,5	6,0

RC: 1,5; CC: 22), and it is also a term used to refer to the so-called *antymajdan* [*anti-maidan*], cf. *prorządowa demonstracja* [*pro-governmental demonstration*] (SP-2013/17), *antymajdanowa demonstracja* [*anti-maidan demonstration*] (KG-2015/4).

The event-based aspect of the term *Majdan* is emphasized particularly clearly in those collocations in which one of the elements of the expression is the participant's name, such as *aktywista/aktywiści Majdanu; bohater/bohaterowie Majdanu; przywódcy Majdanu; działacze Majdanu; uczestnik/uczestnicy Majdanu;* and *ludzie Majdanu* [*activist/activists of Maidan; hero/heroes of Maidan; leaders of Maidan; protesters of Maidan; participant/participants of Maidan;* and *people of Maidan*], and in combinations, in which another profile of the term emerges, that is, a social profile – the name of the event replaces the names of participants of the events: *duch Majdanu, fenomen Majdanu, głos Majdanu, pomoc dla Majdanu* and *poparcie dla Majdanu* [*spirit of Maidan, phenomenon of Maidan, voice of Maidan, help for Maidan* and *support for Maidan*].

Apart from words *protest* and *demonstracja*, defining the lexeme *Majdan* in its event-based profile, there are many singular, occasional expressions in the materials gathered. Presentation of all of these would go beyond the scope of this study; however, worth noting is at least one quotation, in which we are dealing with a number of comparisons and metaphorical expressions to describe events at the Maidan of Kiev in 2013/2014:

> *In the last few days, the central square of Kiev has been compared ... to the Zaporozhian Sich. 'The territory of will', 'a state within a state', 'center of Europe', 'central square of the world' – these names have been used in the media and by those, who make up the Maidan. I would compare the Maidan to an allergic rash on the body of our society. But this rash has a very positive meaning. It is a symptom of something bad going on in the organism. It's an appeal to stop poisoning the body from within and from the outside. ... It's an appeal to fight to survive ... to purify ... the changes can be seen not only in the squares but also in the minds of Ukrainians.*
> (MW-2013/12)

The denominations used here draw attention because of their multitude and their hyperbolic meaning (cf. *Maidan* is *the centre of Europe* and *the central square of the world*), as well as due to the particular nature of the series of metaphors, such as *allergic rash; symptom; poisoning of the body;* and *purification*, which result from the conceptualization of Ukraine (the Ukrainian society) as a person. This makes it possible to assign to this person such characteristics as 'being sick', and at the same time connoting the need for a change of this state – 'healing and treatment'.

In the process of profiling of terms, an important place is occupied by antonyms. Although the lexeme *Antymajdan* [*Anti-Maidan*] appears in the corpus only six times (less than one word per million in RC; CC: 12), its contextual uses are worth noting, as they indirectly profile the term *Majdan* as well. *Antymajdan* is referred to as *prorządowa* (SP-2013/17) and *prorosyjska demonstracja* [*a pro-governmental* and *pro-Russian demonstration*] (SP-2015/30) organized by workers (in opposition to Maidan as a *student protest*), cf.:

> *300 m from the barricades, the workers are building an Anti-Maidan scene. (KG-2013/23-24)*
>
> *in Kharkiv, we also had a place, where both the Maidan and the Anti-Maidan gathered. The latter was attended by pro-Russian people, whole buses coming from Russia. The people were also beaten, they tried to present Maidan as an anti-constitutional activity. ... The situation changed after the Maidan. Earlier, on the television ... members of the Municipal Council, representatives of culture openly supported the Berkut beating up people in Kiev and the Anti-Maidan. With time, people understood they didn't want to go back to Yanukovych's regime. Here, in Kharkiv, we appreciate freedom, we don't want to be guided by foreigners, we are an independent state and that's why we want Ukraine to be free. (SP-2015/30)*

The opposition of terms *Majdan* – *Antymajdan* in the analysed discourse is an opposition of such characteristics as *anti-governmental* – *pro-governmental; anti-Russian* – *pro-Russian;* and *sovereign* – *dependent on foreign influence.*

4.1.3 The temporal profile

In the quotation given earlier, particular attention should be paid to the expression *after Maidan*, which combines the event-based profile and the temporal profile. Events at the Maidan of Kiev of 2013/2014 constitute a turning point, which is often underlined in the periodicals examined. There are three types of reference to time here: *przed Majdanem* [*before the Maidan*], *w czasie Majdanu/podczas Majdanu* [*during the Maidan/at the time of the Maidan*] and *po Majdanie* [*after the Maidan*]. While the expression *przed Majdanem* is not frequently found in the analysed texts (RC:1; CC:14) and does not bring significant meanings into the discourse examined, and the terms *w czasie Majdanu/podczas Majdanu* (RC: a bit more than 1; CC: 18) are connected mainly to the event-based profile of the term, the expression *po Majdanie* not only appears quite frequently in the reference corpus (RC: 3; CC: 53) but also plays a significant role in the creation of the image of the Ukrainian crisis (cf. Table 3.6). These contexts present a diagnosis of the situation of Ukraine after 2013/2014, as a result of which the concept of Maidan as a turning point in the most recent history of Ukraine acquired symbolical meanings.

Table 3.6 The frequency of collocations important for the temporal profile of the term *Majdan* (per million words)

Collocation	RC	CC
przed Majdanem	1	14
w czasie Majdanu/podczas Majdanu	>1	18
po Majdanie	3	53

In the contexts, in which the expression *after the Maidan* appears, the emphasis is put on economic, social and military effects of the Ukrainian crisis, cf.:

> *a lot could have happened after the Maidan, but nobody expected such a turn of events: a bad economic and social situation, struggle of politicians to get influence, corruption, dissatisfaction of the society and lack of trust in politicians, an armed intervention of Russia and its active support for separatists in eastern Ukraine ... Everyone must realize that nobody will help Ukraine if it does not start to help itself! Well-fed Europe is slowly becoming indifferent to Ukrainian affairs. (KG-2014-2015/23–24)*

The context of the Ukrainian-Russian war is one of the most significant frameworks, in which the Polish-language press in Ukraine is placing the events of 2013/2014 in the discourse, and the Maidan is becoming a symbolical starting point for the Russian armed action against Ukraine, cf.:

> *The nation is fighting against evil. Particularly now, when, after the Maidan, Russia as the aggressor has temporarily taken away the Crimea from us, and now has got into Donbass, the people have risen against this aggressor, against Russia, to defend their land and willing to sacrifice their lives. (KG-2015/14–15)*

> **The revolution** *of dignity has been punished with a bloody war that has taken lives of 10 thousand people and making more than 2 million homeless. (SP-2016/47)*

> *The Maidan revolution, the Russian annexation of the Crimea and the war in the Donbass, which has been going on for more than three years, have taken their toll. (KG-2017/19)*

However, the time *after the Maidan* has two dimensions. Not only the real one, which is associated with the economic condition of Ukraine and the war in the eastern part of the country but also the ideological one. The axiological profile of the term *Majdan* is an outcome of its event-based and temporal profiles – the events of 2013/2014 are presented as a symbolical start of a change in the Ukrainian society, or even an emergence of the Ukrainian civic society:

> *after the second Maidan, nobody will say there is no civil society in Ukraine. (KG-2014/18)*

> *during the revolution* **of the Euromaidan** *and during the war with Russia, the Ukrainian nation was transformed. As a civic nation and not an ethnic nation. (KG-2015/4)*

> How has this way of thinking changed now, after the Maidan? [The revolution] gave
> rise to thinking of the state as something that is ours, civic. (KG 2015/11)

Events of such social importance, which become symbols, require special names – not axiologically neutral, but grandiose, referring to the values that are attached to them. Such names are *The Revolution of Dignity* and the *Euromaidan*.

4.2 Symbolical names and values

The expression *rewolucja godności* [Revolution of Dignity] and the neologism *euromajdan* [Euromaidan] are terms serving as symbolical names of events in the Maidan of Kiev of 2013/2014, and which have been popularized and widely used in periodicals for the Polish minority in Ukraine. These names create the ideological, symbolical profile of the term *Majdan*.

The lexeme *euromajdan* as a text equivalent of the *Majdan* has been functioning in all profiles that are typical for it: locative – *manifestacja na Euromajdanie w Kijowie* [*a manifestation at the Euromaidan in Kiev*] (MW-2014/2); event-based – *młodzież wyszła na euromajdany* [*the youth has gone out to join the Euromaidans*] (MW-2014/11); social – *pokojowy protest Euromajdanu* [*a peaceful protest of the Euromaidan*] (KG-2014/4; MW-2014/4, MW-2014/24); and temporal – *relacje polsko-ukraińskie po Euromajdanie* [*Polish-Ukrainian relations after the Euromaidan*] (KG-2014/10). In the symbolic dimension, however, it is richer; the meanings and senses implied by the word-formative base (*majdan*) are accompanied by the meaning contained in the morpheme *euro-* [*Euro-*], which in this neologism means not only 'associated with Europe' but also 'pro-European', 'consistent with European values; and democratic, opting for freedom'; cf.: *Euromajdan – świadectwem walki o europejskie wartości* [*Euromaidan – a testimony to struggle for European values*] (KG-2016/7); and *Droga do wolności – Euromajdan* [*The road to freedom– Euromaidan*] (MW-2014/7).

The expression *revolution of dignity* refers to the name of the first Maidan, called the *orange revolution*, but unlike the events of 2004/2005, it transfers the discourse directly to the axiological perspective. The name given to the events of 2013/2014 emphasizes the fundamental value for personalistically viewed ethics (Dróżdż 2005, 2015) – dignity, understood as awareness of own value and sense of self-respect. The concept contained in the expression revolution of dignity, defined in this manner, connects it with the social and symbolic profile of the term *Majdan*, cf. *Majdan: obudził Ukrainę* [*Maidan: was a wake-up call for Ukraine*] (KG-2014/22), *zmienił Ukrainę* [*changed Ukraine*] (KG-2014/22), *wywołał pragnienie wolności, chęć walki z korupcją i walki o demokrację* [*was evoking desire for freedom, willingness to fight corruption and to fight for democracy*] (KG-2016/11) and *dotyczył walki o suwerenność narodu, wolność wyborów politycznych i niepodległość kraju* [*was about a fight for sovereignty of the nation, freedom of political choices and independence of the country*] (MW-2014/13).

The names of values connoted by the word *godność* [*dignity*], particularly with regard to social relations, which are most emphasized in the press discourse are *wolność* [*freedom*], which has been proven by quotations provided earlier, and *solidarność* [*solidarity*]. The events associated with the Maidan of 2013/2014 are metaphorically

Table 3.7 The most frequent collocations of the lexeme *solidarność* (per million words)

Collocation	RC	CC
solidarność z ... [solidarity with ...]	8,0	124,0
gest solidarności [gesture of solidarity]	2,0	28,0
znak solidarności [sign of solidarity]	1,5	24,0
akt solidarności [act of solidarity]	0,5	10,0

referred to not only as *rewolucja godności* but also as *wyspa wolności* [*an island of freedom*] (SP-2014/25) – a reference to the locative profile of the term; *epoka wolności* [*the era of freedom*] (KG-2014/ 22) – a reference to the temporal profile; or *rewolucja wolności* [*a revolution of freedom*] (KG-2014/22) – a reference to the event-based profile.

Solidarity, understood as a sense of community based on shared views and aims, takes the form of declarative and symbolical actions, which is reflected by the most frequent collocations of the lexeme, cf. Table 3.7.

The entities that are assigned the characteristic of 'being loyal' are Europe, Poland and the Ukrainian society; cf. *Bruksela pokazała **solidarność** z Ukrainą ...* [*Brussels has shown **solidarity** with Ukraine ...*] (KG-2016/13); *... podpisana umowa jest wyrazem **solidarności** polskich uczonych z ukraińskimi kolegami ...* [*the agreement signed is an expression of **solidarity** of Polish scholars with their Ukrainian colleagues ...*] (KG-2015/23–24); *Na znak solidarności z Majdanem uczestnicy protestu [we Lwowie] wspólnie zaśpiewali narodowy hymn ...* [*As a sign of their solidarity with the Maidan, participants of the protest [in Lviv] sang the national anthem together...*] (KG-2014/3). The combination of words: *solidarność z ...* [solidarity with ...], which has a high frequency in the CC, shows that beneficiaries of this support include *kijowski Majdan, naród ukraiński, naród walczący o niepodległość, mieszkańcy regionów objętych wojną, rodziny ofiar, Tatarzy Krymscy, naród krymski*, itp. [*the Maidan of Kiev, the Ukrainian nation, the nation fighting for independence of Ukraine, inhabitants of regions affected by the war, families of victims, the Crimean Tatars, the Crimean nation, etc.*].

Almost one-half of all occurrences of the lexeme *solidarity* in the RC pertained to the establishment of the 'Solidarity' Trade Union in Poland in 1980. The 'Solidarity' Trade Union was an enormous anti-communist social movement, thanks to which Poland and then other countries under political and military domination of the Soviet Union regained sovereignty. References in the discourse examined to the Polish movement 'Solidarity' are related to events in the Maidan of Kiev, but at the same time they are a symbolical identification of the fate of Ukrainians and Poles, typical for the Polish point of view, reflected by the press for the Polish minority.

5 Conclusion

In creation of the discursive image of the Ukrainian crisis present in the press for the Polish minority in Ukraine, the Polish perspective and point of view is assumed when involvement of the Poles and the Polish authorities in events at the Maidan of Kiev is underlined, as well as the organization of various actions of support for the protesters, and when the most recent history of Ukraine is compared with the past of Poland, cf.:

> Is the Maidan movement going to become Ukrainian Solidarity? (KG-2014/1);
>
> When you walk through the Maidan ... when we try to get past the governmental district, I am reminded of the martial law in Poland (KG-2014/3).
>
> Russian occupation of the Crimea and the alleged protection of the Russian minority **against the Maidan** is strikingly similar to the Soviet aggression in 1939 on the eastern parts of the pre-war Republic of Poland (SP-2014/20).
>
> The atmosphere of the Maidan was compared by Jankowski to that of the early days of the Warsaw Uprising. (KG-2015/12)

Such constant references to the history of Poland to the Ukrainian crisis are the most typical features of the discursive image created in the texts examined.

The process of profiling of the term *Majdan*, which can be traced from the press for the Polish minority in Ukraine, from its locative through the event-based and the temporal aspect to the symbolical dimension, has not only deep linguistic-cultural but also social-discursive roots, which are indirectly pointed out in the periodicals analysed:

> after the Maidan, new figures emerged [in the Ukrainian national pantheon] ... [Ukrainians] are searching for such components of their history that would help them construct a view of the world and a foundation myth for the new Ukraine. Banderism has remained in the sphere of notions and myths .... These myths are supported by such as the Heavenly Hundred (KG-2015/2)

Symbolical semantization of the term *Majdan* in the press of the Polish minority is based on two overlapping images created in the texts: the image of the war, defence of the country against a foreign aggressor in the name of sovereignty, freedom, democracy, and the associated motif of sacrificing one's life for the homeland, and the image of a rebellion, refusal to accept coercion and humiliation, which lead to a rebirth of the society or constitute its symbolical beginning. The symbolism that idealizes the events, used by authors of the press for the Polish minority, which identifies the *Majdan* with the *Rewolucja Godności*, is rooted in the mental processing of reality – categorization and conceptualization (Rutkowski 2007: 273). The onym *Majdan*, which has been assigned a high rank of a carrier of specific content, has been used on its own, as a name-symbol, for conceptualization of other fragments of reality. Syntheticism, shortness, ambiguity have become advantages of the symbolical name especially in the media discourse, in which recategorization and transformation of reality take place, turning it into a mental being separate from the objective world.

Notes

1 'Słowo Polskie' is the name of Polish periodical published in Lviv (1895–1945) and in Wrocław (1945–2004) (Harasimowicz 2000).
2 Apart from the noun *Majdan/majdan*, the database contained derivatives: personal nouns *majdanowiec, antymajdanowiec, majdanczanin, majdanczyk* [*maidan activist, anti-maidan activist*] and adjectives *majdanowy, postmajdanowy* [*maidan, post-maidan*]. Such a great number of derivatives confirms the thesis of substantial topicality and importance of the word *Majdan/majdan* in the texts examined.
3 Cf. selected permanent sections in the examined periodicals: KG – *The Polish press about Ukraine; Review of the Polish press in Ukraine; Poles in Ukraine; Churches in Lviv*; MW – *Save from oblivion; Memories; ABC of Polish culture*; SP – *History of the Borderlands and the Republic of Poland; Memory; From the life of the Catholic Church*.
4 Cf. the symbolic meanings of selected toponyms in Polish culture: Termopile [Thermopylae] – (1) 'in the ancient times, a narrow strip of land in the eastern coast of Greece'; (2) 'battle of Thermopylae'; (3) 'a symbol of unequal struggle in defense, ending with defeat', for example *Warszawskie Termopile* – Warsaw Uprising 1944, *Polskie Termopile* – the Polish defence war of September 1939; Jałta [Yalta] – (1) 'city in Crimea'; (2) 'conference in Yalta in 1945'; (3) 'a symbol of concessions made by superpowers at the expense of a weaker state' (Rutkowski 2007: 255–259).

References

Atlas polskiej obecności za granicą [*Atlas of the Polish Presence Abroad*]. (2012). Available online: https://www.msz.gov.pl/pl/ministerstwo/publikacje/atlas_polskiej_obecnosci_za_granica (accessed 11 February 2019).

Bartmiński, J. (2006), *Językowe podstawy obrazu świata* [*Linguistic Basics of the Image of the World*]. Lublin: Uniwersytet Marii Curie-Skłodowskiej.

Bartmiński, J. and Niebrzegowska-Bartmińska, S. (1998), 'Profile a podmiotowa interpretacja świata', ['Profiles and Subjective Interpretation of the World'], in J. Bartmiński and R. Tokarski (eds), *Profilowanie w języku i tekście* [*Profiling in Language and Text*], 211–24. Lublin: Wydawnictwo Uniwersytetu Marii Curie-Skłodowskiej.

Bińczyk, E. (2004), 'Mowa magiczna a referencja' ['Magic Speech and Reference'], in. A. Pałubicka, Dobosz, A. (eds), *Umysł i kultura* [*Mind and Culture*], 175–86. Bydgoszcz: Oficyna Wydawnicza Epigram.

Czachur, W. (2011), 'Dyskursywny obraz świata. Kilka refleksji' ['The Discursive Image of the World. Some Reflections'], *Tekst i Dyskurs – Text und Diskurs*, 4: 79–97.

Czyżewski, R., Dworczyk, M. and Kowalski, M. (eds) (2015), *Placówki oświatowe na Ukrainie. Informator* [*Educational Institutions in Ukraine. A Guidebook*]. Warszawa: Fundacja Wolność i Demokracja.

Czyżewski, M., Otrocki, M., Piekot, T. and Stachowiak, J. (eds) (2017), *Analiza dyskursu publicznego. Przegląd metod i perspektyw badawczych* [*Analysis of Public Discourse. Review of Research Methods and Perspectives*]. Warszawa: Wydawnictwo Akademickie SEDNO.

Degano, Ch. (2007), 'Dissociation and Presupposition in Discourse: A Corpus Study', *Argumentation*, 21 (4): 361–78.

Demoskop Weekly. (2019a). Available online: http://www.demoscope.ru/weekly/ssp/sng_n ac_26.php?reg=1752 (accessed 15 February 2019).
Demoskop Weekly. (2019b). Available online: http://www.demoscope.ru/weekly/ssp/sng_n ac_89.php?reg=2 (accessed 15 February 2019).
Dróżdż, M. (2005), *Osoba i media: personalistyczny paradygmat etyki i mediów* [*Person and Media: A Personalistic Paradigm of Ethics and Media*]. Tarnów: Wydawnictwo Diecezji Tarnowskiej Biblos.
Dróżdż, M. (2015), 'Dialog jako doświadczenie etyczne' ['Dialogue as an Ethical Experience']. *Studia Socialia Cracoviensia*, 7 (1): 9–21. Available online: http://dx.doi.org/10.15633/ssc.973 (accessed 10 November 2018).
Fillmore, Ch. (1985), 'Frames and the Semantics of Under Standing', *Quaderni di Semantica*, 6 (2): 222–54.
Furmaniak, P. (2011), 'Polacy na Ukrainie - sytuacja polskiej mniejszości' ['Poles in Ukraine - The Situation of the Polish Minority']. Available online: http://www.psz.pl/168-archiwum/piotr-furmaniak-polacy-na-ukrainie-sytuacja-polskiej-mniejszosci (accessed 10 March 2019).
Gabrielatos, C. and Baker, P. (2008), 'Fleeing, Sneaking, Flooding: A Corpus Analysis of Discursive Constructions of Refugees and Asylum Seekers in the UK Press, 1996–2005', *Journal of English Linguistics*, 36 (1): 5–38.
Harasimowicz, J. (ed.) (2000), *Encyklopedia Wrocławia* [*Encyclopedia of Wroclaw*]. Wrocław: Wydawnictwo Dolnośląskie.
Kamasa, V. (2014), 'Techniki językoznawstwa korpusowego wykorzystywane w krytycznej analizie dyskursu. Przegląd' ['Corpus Linguistics Techniques Used in Critical Discourse Analysis. Overview'], *Przegląd Socjologii Jakościowej*, 10 (2): 100–17
Kieraś, W., Kobyliński, Ł. and Ogrodniczuk, M. (2018), 'Korpusomat — A Tool for Creating Searchable Morphosyntactically Tagged Corpora', *Computational Methods in Science and Technology*, 24 (1): 21–27. Available online: http://cmst.eu/articles/korpusomat-a-tool-for-creating-searchable-morphosyntactically-tagged-corpora/ (accessed 15 April 2019).
Kloch, Z. (2006), *Odmiany dyskursu. Semiotyka życia publicznego w Polsce po 1989 roku* [*Kinds of Discourse. Semiotics of Public Life in Poland after 1989*]. Wrocław: Wydawnictwo Uniwersytetu Wrocławskiego.
Kowalski, M. (2015), 'Raport na temat szkolnictwa polskiego na Ukrainie' ['Report on Polish Education in Ukraine'], in R. Czyżewski, M. Dworczyk and M. Kowalski (eds), *Placówki oświatowe na Ukrainie* [*Educational Institutions in Ukraine*], 11–80. Warszawa: Fundacja Wolność i Demokracja. Available online: http://wid.org.pl/wp-content/uploads/Informator-Placwki-owiatowe-na-Ukrainie.pdf (accessed 15 February 2019).
Krzeszowski, T. (1997), *Angels and Devils in Hell. Elements of Axiology in Semantics*. Warszawa: Wydawnictwo Energeia.
Lakoff, G. and M. Johnson (1980), *Metaphors We Live By*. Chicago: University of Chicago Press.
Langacker, R. (1987), *Foundations of Cognitive Grammar. Volume 1. Theoretical Prerequisities*. Stanford: Stanford University Press.
Langacker, R. (1995), *Wykłady z gramatyki kognitywnej: Kazimierz nad Wisłą, grudzień 1993* [*Lectures on Cognitive Grammar: Kazimierz nad Wisłą, December 1993*]. Lublin: Wydawnictwo Uniwersytetu Marii Curie-Skłodowskiej.
Langacker, R. W. (2008), *Cognitive Grammar: A Basic Introduction*. New York: Oxford University Press.

Mautner, G. (2005), 'The Entrepreneurial University', *Critical Discourse Studies*, 2 (2): 95–120.

Rutkowski, M. (2007), *Nazwy własne w strukturze metafory i metonimii. Proces deonimizacji* [*Names in the Structure of Metaphor and Metonymy. The Process of De-onymization*]. Olsztyn: Wydawnictwo Uniwersytetu Warmińsko-Mazurskiego.

Rządowy program współpracy z Polonią i Polakami za granicą w latach 2015–2020 [*Governmental Programme for Cooperation with the Polish Communities and Poles Living Abroad in 2015–2020*], (2015), Ministerstwo Spraw Zagranicznych RP. Available online: https://www.gov.pl/web/dyplomacja/rzadowy-program-wspolprac-z-polonia-i-polakami-za-granica-w-latach-2015-2020 (accessed 20 April 2019).

Scott, M. (2013), *WordSmith Tools*. Liverpool: Lexical Analysis Software.

Spitzmüller, J. and Warnke, J. H. (2011), *Diskurslinguistik. Eine Einführung in Theorien und Methoden der transtextuellen Sprachanalyse* [*Discourse Linguistics. An Introduction to Theories and Methods of Transtextual Speech Analysis*]. Berlin and Boston: De Gruyter.

Stubbs, M. (2001), *Words and Phrases: Corpus Studies of Lexical Semantics*. Oxford and Malden: Blackwell Publishers.

Tołstaja, S. M. (2004), 'Znaczenie symboliczne a punkt widzenia: motywacja znaczeń symbolicznych (kulturowych)' ['Symbolic Meaning and Point of View: Motivation of Symbolic (Cultural) Meanings'], in J. Bartmiński, S. Niebrzegowska-Bartmińska and R. Nycz (eds), *Punkt widzenia w języku i w kulturze* [*Point of View in Language and Culture*], 177–84. Lublin: Uniwersytet Marii Curie-Skłodowskiej.

van Dijk, T. A. (1998), *Discourse as Structure and Process*. London, Thousand Oaks and New Delhi: Sage Publications.

Warnke I. H. (2009), 'Die sprachliche Konstituierung von geteiltem Wissen in Diskursen' ['The Linguistic Constitution of Shared Knowledge in Discourses'], in E. Felder and M. Müller (eds), *Wissen durch Sprache. Theorie, Praxis und Erkenntnisinteresse des Forschungsnetzwerks ›Sprache und Wissen‹* [*Knowledge through Language. Theory, Practice, and Interest of the Research Network 'Language and Knowledge'*], 113–40. Berlin and New York: De Gruyter.

Wójcicki, J. (2012), 'Semper Fidelis – nie tylko Lwów…' ['Semper Fidelis - Not Only Lviv…'], *Słowo Polskie*, Sierpień: 1.

Zinken, J. (2004), 'Punkt widzenia jako kategoria w porównawczych badaniach dyskursów publicznych' ['Point of View as a Category in Comparative Studies of Public Discourses'], in J. Bartmiński, S. Niebrzegowska-Bartmińska and R. Nycz (eds), *Punkt widzenia w języku i w kulturze* [*Point of View in Language and Culture*], 65–78. Lublin: Uniwersytet Marii Curie-Skłodowskiej.

4

Blended names in the discussions of the Ukrainian crisis

Natalia Beliaeva and Natalia Knoblock

Blended names such as *Merkozy* < [*Angela*] *Merkel* + [*Nicolas*] *Sarkozy* and *Billary* < *Bill* [*Klinton*] + *Hillary* [*Klinton*] have become an important part of contemporary media discourse, particularly because of their attention-catching and punning nature. The semantic functions of blends can vary from providing a taxonomical label, for example, in hybrid names such as *tigon* < *tiger* + *lion* to adding humorous and/or derogatory connotations, as is often the case with blended proper names. Blended names such as *Putinburg* < *Putin* + Peterburg (St. Petersburg') and *Bandûkovič* < *bandûk* (bandit) + *Yanukovich* are often used in Russian and Ukrainian media to add derogatory connotations, to express the speaker's (often negative) attitude to the named entity or person or to discredit the political opponent. This chapter focusses on novel blends exploiting the surnames of Vladimir Putin and Petro Poroshenko used in the discussions of war in Ukraine and related political events. In particular, the use of blended names such as *Putler* < *Putin* + *Hitler* and *Parashenko* < *paraša* (piss can) + *Poroshenko* and their functions in political discourse are investigated. To achieve this aim, the contexts surrounding blended names in Russian and Ukrainian news posts, blog posts and forums are analysed, and the relations between the semantics of blended names and their role in political discourse are explored.

1 Introduction

The punning function of blended names conforms to the overall characteristics of blending as a type of word formation that evokes greater creativity than other word-formation processes, as pointed out, for example, in Gries (2012), López Rúa (2007, 2012) and Renner (2015). The attention-catching effect of blends is, in its turn, related to the fact that, to understand a blend, the language user has to make additional cognitive effort in order to recognize its constituent words. For example, the processing of a blend such as *stagflation* involves more cognitive effort than the processing of a compound such as *food inflation* since the former requires recognition of the constituents *stagnation* and *inflation* (see also Arndt-Lappe and Plag (2013), Beliaeva (2015, 2016) and Gries (2012) for experimental evidence and discussion).

Blending is established in many typologically diverse languages, including Russian (Hrushcheva 2017) and Ukrainian (Borgwaldt, Kulish and Bose 2012; Gut, Panchenko and Zabolotna 2015). In Slavic languages, the increase in the popularity of blending is seen to be largely due to the influence of English (Konieczna 2012). Indeed, some blended names such as *reiganomika* are loans from English (calque of *reaganomics* < *Reagan* + *economics*), which in some instances trigger the coinage of later formations with native constituents, for example, *putinomika* < *Putin* + *ekonomika* (economics) in Russian and *kuchmonomika* < *Kuchma* + *ekonomika* in Ukrainian. In addition to loans and cross-linguistic blends, a number of blends coined by merging together native source words has been established in Russian and Ukrainian languages in late twentieth–early twenty-first century, for example, Ukrainian *smrada* < *smrad* (stink) + *rada* (council), with some examples dated as early as nineteenth century (Kornienko 2016: 223), for example, Russian *guvernân'ka* < *guvernantka* (governess) + *nân'ka* (nanny). Blended names discussed in this chapter belong to the latter category of native Russian and Ukrainian blends.

The emergence of multiple neologisms in the antagonistic discourse of the Ukrainian conflict has been noted by several researchers. For example, in an onomasiology study, Lyashenko (2014) and Lyashenko and Fedyunina (2017) collected novel ethnonyms, including blends, from web forums of the neighbouring cities of Belgorod (Russia) and Kharkov (Ukraine), and analysed the word-formation processes involved in their creation. Kostromicheva and Polyakov (2014) discussed the novel pejorative lexis emerging during the Ukrainian crisis from a typological point of view. A thesaurus of Russian-Ukrainian conflict compiled by Zhabotinskaya (2015) catalogued a large number of novel lexical and phraseological units that appeared in Russian and Ukrainian in 2014–2015, according to van Dijk's (1998) 'ideological square'.

The present research zooms in on the aspects of novel blends produced in the discourse of conflict and specifically focuses on the names of the Russian and Ukrainian presidents, *Putin* and *Poroshenko*, and on the blends involving parts of their names, in particular, *Putler*, *Kaputin* and *Haputin*, and *Parashenko*, *Potroshenko* and *Poproshenko*, respectively. These blends were repeatedly mentioned as neologisms in both journalistic and academic writing dedicated to the Ukrainian conflict, and they allowed for a comparison of verbal attacks on the official representatives on Russia and Ukraine.

2 Lexical data: Formal and semantic characteristics

All blends included in the present analysis combine chunks of the surnames of the respective presidents with chunks of different lexical items with negative connotations. The blend *Putler* suggests that Putin is similar to Hitler; *Haputin* combines Putin's name with the beginning of the verb *hapat'* (grab), thus suggesting that he is greedy or sticky-fingered; and *Kaputin* alludes to Putin's similarity to Hitler again by combining his surname with a part of the word *kaput* most commonly used in the idiom *Hitler kaput*, a relic of the Second World War. The blends coined using the surname of the

Ukrainian president combine the second part of his name (*shenko*) with initial parts coming from the words *paraša* (piss can) in *Parashenko*, *potrošit'* (to gut/disembowel) or *potrošitel'* (alluding to Jack the Ripper) in *Potroshenko*, and *poprošajničat'* (to beg / panhandle) or *poprošajka* (beggar) in *Poproshenko*.

It is worth noting that among the blends selected for the present study, the ones exploiting the surname *Poroshenko* exhibit greater overall similarity between the source words, compared to blends with the surname *Putin*. In the blend *Putler*, the source words *Putin* and *Hitler* share one grapheme and one phoneme, respectively. Similarly, one grapheme in the blend *Haputin* belongs to both source words, *hapat'* and *Putin*. A higher degree of similarity can be observed in *Kaputin*, where both constituent words (*Kaput* and ***Putin***) are present in their entirety due to the overlap (the overlapping segments in all examples are in bold type). In contrast, the source words of blends with the surname *Poroshenko* share greater proportion of their graphemes and phonemes: cf. ***Parashenko*** < *paraša* + *Poroshenko*, ***Potroshenko*** < ***potrošit'*** + ***Poroshenko*** and ***Poproshenko*** < *poprošajka* + *Poroshenko*. Moreover, all source words of these blends start with the same letter, which increases the recognizability of the source words in the blends (see, for example, Whitney (2001) and White et al. (2008) for experimental findings illustrating the role of word beginnings in recognition).

In sum, the small sample of blended names under investigation demonstrates remarkable diversity in terms of origin of the source words (the constituents of the blends include colloquial words, a vulgarism, a loan word and a literary allusion), grammatical structure (verbs or nouns as source words) and the degree of similarity between the source words. On the other hand, a regularity that can be observed on the semantic level is that in all blends, surnames of politically significant persons are blended with words having negative connotations. Further analysis investigates whether this semantic characteristic of the blended names resonates with the characteristics of the contexts in which they are used in political discussions.

3 Hypotheses

The main purpose of this chapter is to study the meaning and functions of blended names in political texts and discussions related to the events in Ukraine in 2013–2018. In line with this goal, we study immediate contexts of blended names and their unblended counterparts in Russian and Ukrainian web-media texts and forum discussions in order to find out (a) whether the contexts of blended names in Russian and Ukrainian political discussions differ from those of their unblended counterparts, and (b) whether the patterns of use of blended names in Russian media sources differ from the patterns of use of the same names in Ukrainian sources.

As discussed in the Introduction, the findings in literature to date suggest that blended names in political discourse are mainly used with derogatory connotations, or as means of expressing (often negative) attitude to the names' referents. With regard to this, it was hypothesized that blended names in the discussions of Ukrainian crisis should be used in (a) more informal register and (b) more emotional ways than their unblended counterparts. This can be evidenced by the presence of colloquial lexical elements, emotionally (in particular, negatively) coloured words, obscene words and similar lexical elements in the context of blended names.

Another aspect of the use of blended names is related to the components of their meaning. Research on the semantics of blends (e.g. Algeo (1977), Gries (2006) and Renner (2015), to name just a few) shows that the constituents of blends are often in paradigmatic relations, for example, are synonyms, as in *needcessity* < *need* + *necessity*, or are hyponyms of the same concept, as in hybrid names such as *zorse* < *zebra* + *horse* and *cronut* < *croissant* + *doughnut*. In case of the blended names under investigation, the semantic relations of synonymy or co-hyponymy between the source words of the blends may not be reflecting real facts but, rather, are implied by the speaker. That is, the supposed synonymy of *Putin* and *Hitler*, the source words of *Putler*, is based on some similarities between the two political figures, or their actions, that may be intentionally brought to attention by the user of the blend. Likewise, such blends as *Potroshenko* and *Poproshenko* imply some associations between Poroshenko and Jack the Ripper or beggar, intentionally drawn by the speaker. Due to this, the semantic relations established between the constituents of the blended names may need to rely upon additional explanatory elements or associations in the context. Therefore, it was hypothesized that the source words of blended names, their synonyms or other semantic associates should be present in the context.

4 Methodology

The analysis was conducted on two mid-sized corpora that were compiled for this project. Text collection was done with the help of a tool called WebBootCat, provided by the corpus management system Sketch Engine (Kilgarriff et al. 2004). WebBootCat creates custom corpora by searching the internet for the keywords supplied by the user and downloading relevant texts containing those keywords. Keyword identification was determined by the focus of our project: we used *Putin, Putler, Kaputin, Haputin, Poroshenko, Parashenko, Potroshenko* and *Poproshenko*, that is, the surnames of the two countries' presidents and three of the most commonly used insulting blends based on each of their names. Scraping the web for these words, WebBootCat identified and downloaded texts from dozens of sites. The Russian Poroshenko-Putin corpus (henceforth labelled as RPP) resulted from the search on Russian websites, that is, the websites in the *.ru* web domain, and other media sites, blogs and forums where Russian is used as a dominant language (e.g. politikus.ru, reactor.com and others). The web scraping for this corpus was performed with the target words in Cyrillic spelled according to Russian conventions. The Ukrainian Poroshenko-Putin corpus (henceforth UPP) resulted from the search on the websites in the Ukrainian domain and other Ukrainian websites (daykiev.ua, ukrpress.info and others), with the target words spelled in Cyrillic according to Ukrainian conventions. These abbreviations will be used throughout the chapter while referring to the corpora under investigation. The RPP measures approximately 800,000 words and the UPP approximately 380,000 words.

It is important to note that the data in either of the corpora analysed for this study are not homogeneous in terms of the language used. In particular, RPP contains texts primarily in Russian, but also includes examples of code-switching into Ukrainian or borrowings from Ukrainian, which is predictable, given that using the name of Ukrainian president in the text suggests discussing Ukrainian realia. Moreover, UPP contains not only texts in Ukrainian but also texts in Russian, bilingual Russian-Ukrainian texts or texts in the so-called Surzhyk, a language variety combining Ukrainian and Russian (Bilaniyk 2004). In addition, a large part of both corpora is compiled from forum discussions, which contain comment entries both in Russian and in Ukrainian, which is especially typical for Ukrainian websites. This is due to the fact that Ukrainian web media are largely multilingual, which, in turn, is related to the complex situation of language contact in Ukraine, as discussed, for example, in Bilaniyk (2004, 2005) and Nedashkivska (2010). Therefore, the comparison between the two corpora in the analysis presented here implies comparing the patterns of use of the target words in different linguistic and social contexts (that is, in Russian vs. in Ukrainian web media), rather than in Russian and Ukrainian languages. Juxtaposing the use of the target words in two different languages is outside the scope of this study as it would require a different approach to collecting data.

The patterns of use of the target words in the texts were first investigated by means of automatic identification of the collocates of the target words by Sketch Engine using various statistical measures (T-score, MI, MI3, Dice or log likelihood) and setting the minimum co-occurrence count at three. The Word Sketch feature of Sketch Engine normally provides a summary of a word's grammatical and collocational behaviour by showing the word's collocates categorized by grammatical relations, such as words that serve as an object of the verb, words that serve as a subject of the verb, or words that modify the word, etc. However, the software produced too many errors, such as confusion about which noun modified which, while analysing Russian texts. Among 212 frequent collocates of the target words *Putin, Putler, Poroshenko* and *Parashenko* that were identified by Word Sketch, ninety-seven were grammar words, which did not reveal any meaningful information about differences in use from one keyword to the other. Moreover, the Word Sketch feature was not available for the Ukrainian language. Thus, the corpus-analytic software available to us did not appear to process Russian and Ukrainian texts well in analysing grammatical relations of the target words, which is one of the key purposes of this study. Therefore, we turned to manual coding of the data for the content analysis of grammatical constructions that target words were part of. For content analysis, we used a random sample of 100 concordance lines containing the target words *Putin* and *Poroshenko*, and all concordance lines containing the blended names. In these contexts, we identified (a) verbal predicates in sentences where target words served as subjects, and (b) modifiers of the target words, most commonly adjectives or nouns. The words thus identified were then rated by two researchers independently as being emotionally negative neutral, or positive, with 95.5 per cent initial agreement on the ratings. The final rates were assigned after discussing differences and achieving agreement. A three-way contingency table analysis (presented graphically as a mosaic plot) was then used to estimate whether there is a relation between the emotional evaluation of the collocates and their presence in the context of either blended or unblended names.

Finally, a conditional inference tree (decision tree) analysis was performed to figure out if (a) the contexts of blended names differ from those of non-blended names, and (b) the contexts of the target words in RPP differ from those in UPP. This method involves estimating a regression relationship between the variables by binary recursive partitioning in a conditional inference framework. The dependent variable (in our case, the target word) is analysed in relation to one or several independent variables. First, the algorithm tests the null hypothesis of independence between the dependent variable and any of the independent variables. If the null hypothesis is rejected, the independent variable that has the strongest association with the dependent variable is selected. At this stage, the data set is split into two groups (branches of the decision tree) if the difference between the value of the outcome variable in two branches 'growing' from one node is statistically significant at the 5 per cent level (that is, the p-value must be smaller than 0.05 in order to split the node). Then this process is recursively repeated until further splits are no longer justified. Each time, the full set of independent variables is taken into consideration for a potential node split, so that the same variable can cause more than one split (see Hothorn, Hornik and Zeileis, 2006) for a detailed description of the method). In accordance with our research questions, the decision tree predicted which of the four target words were used in the contexts as an outcome of the influences of the following independent variables:

- Whether or not the name was a blend
- The corpus (RPP or UPP)
- The number of obscene words in the concordance line
- The number of derogatory terms in the concordance line
- The number of blend source words
- The number of the associates of blend source words in the concordance line
- The number of other blends in the concordance line

The conditional tree analysis was carried out using a random sample of 100 concordance lines containing *Putin* and 100 concordance lines containing *Poroshenko*, as well as all concordance lines containing the most frequent blended name of each, that is, *Putler* and *Parashenko*. Each concordance line included seven words before the target word and seven words after. The concordance lines were manually coded for the presence of the following:

- Obscene words, categorized as such in Akhmetova (1996), for example, *bl'at'* (fucking bitch), *suka* (bitch) and their derivatives;
- Colloquialisms and vulgarisms with derogatory collocations, categorized as such in Ozhegov and Shvedova (2006) or listed in the dictionary of contemporary slang (Slovar' sovremennoi leksiki, žargona i slenga 2018), for example, *sdohnut'* (kick off), *debil* (moron), *žopa* (ass) and their derivatives;
- The words that were merged with the names Putin and Poroshenko to form the keyword blends Putler and Parashenko, that is, *Gitler* (Hitler), the source word of *Putler*, and *paraša* (piss can), the source word of the blend *Parashenko*;

- The words closely associated with the source words of blends, that is, their synonyms or frequent collocates, for example, *fûrer* (Führer), which is often used as synonym of *Hitler*, its frequent collocate *kaput* or *unitaz* (toilet), a synonym of *paraša*;
- Blended words other than keyword blends, for example, *Pidro*, which is a blend of *pidar* (faggot) and the name *Petro*, *Yajtsenyuk*, a blend of *jajca* (balls) and the surname of the thirteenth prime minister of Ukraine Yatsenyuk, or keyword blends used in the context of other keywords.

5 Results and discussion

Two corpora collected for the present study are very different in size, RPP being more than twice the size of UPP because Russian political media sources and forums are in general more numerous than Ukrainian ones. Due to the different sizes of the corpora, both raw frequencies and normalized as words-per-million (wpm) will be reported here. Table 4.1 presents the frequencies of the target words in RPP and UPP. They are arranged to demonstrate the frequency of usage of the non-blended names and blends.

The first impression one gets after checking out the frequency data is that the blends are used quite rarely: the names *Poroshenko* and (especially) *Putin* were used several times more than any of the blends in both RPP and UPP, which is not a surprising finding in itself, given that blends are comparatively rare in the language. In this respect, the observed lower frequency of blended names such as *Putler* and *Potroshenko*, compared to the surnames *Putin* and *Poroshenko* conforms to the fact that blends such as *brunch* are much be less frequent than unblended nouns such as *breakfast* (see, e.g. Plag (2003) and Bauer, Lieber and Plag (2013) for a discussion of blending in morphology).

The sentiment analysis of the data revealed some tendencies in the use of different target words. Among 412 verbs in the sentences where target words were identified as subjects, only eight (1.9 per cent) were evaluated as emotionally positive, 317 (76.9 per cent) as neutral and eighty-six (20.9 per cent) as negative. Similar tendency is observed for modifiers: among the 143 modifiers of the target words: three (2.1 per cent) were

Table 4.1 Frequencies of Use of the Target Words in RPP and UPP

RPP		UPP	
Target Word	**Frequency**	**Target Word**	**Frequency**
Putin	5,253 (4,846 wpm)	Putin	416 (852 wpm)
Putler	165 (152 wpm)	Putler	32 (66 wpm)
Haputin	61 (56 wpm)	Haputin	0
Kaputin	64 (59 wpm)	Kaputin	0
Poroshenko	1,635 (1,508 wpm)	Poroshenko	370 (758 wpm)
Parashenko	119 (110 wpm)	Parashenko	22 (45 wpm)
Potroshenko	88 (81 wpm)	Potroshenko	30 (61 wpm)
Poproshenko	68 (63 wpm)	Poproshenko	3 (6 wpm)

evaluated as emotionally positive, seventy-seven (53.8 per cent) as neutral, and sixty-two (4.34 per cent) as negative. It has to be noted that an unusually large proportion of the negative tokens is present in the data, in particular, some of the words associated with each of the keywords are derogatory terms, for example, *prezik*; a derogatory clipping of *prezident* (president); obscene words, for example, *hujlo* (dickhead); or vulgarisms, for example, *dročil* (jerked off). Many of the negatively evaluated verbs and modifiers had semantic associations with death, as in *zdohnet* (will kick the bucket), or with crime, as in *razvoroval* (plundered). The distribution of negative verbs and modifiers used with different target words is shown in Table 4.2.

In the RPP corpus, *Putin* as a subject was used with negative verbs 6 per cent of the time: three negatives, such as *zanimajetsâ onanizmom* (masturbates) or *budet otgrebat'* (will scoop up/grab), out of forty-two verbs were found in the sample of 100 concordance lines. On the other hand, negative verbs associated with *Putler*, such as *prigrozil* (threatened), *uničtožit* (will destroy) or *ubivajet* (kills), were used twenty times out of sixty-two. There were few uses of *Kaputin* in a complete sentence with a lexical verb, but out of the three cases that were identified, two were negative: *zdohnet* (will kick the bucket) and *razvoroval* (plundered). *Haputin* was not used as a subject, so there were no lines to evaluate verbs for negativity.

In the UPP corpus, the non-blended surname *Putin* was used as a subject of a negative verb only three times out of fifty-eight. *Putler*, again, is used in much more negative contexts. There were sixteen negative verbs, such as *napadat'* (attack) or *srët* (shits), that were used with *Putler* out of twenty-one total uses. No lexical verbs were used with either *Kaputin* or *Haputin* in the collection of Ukrainian texts.

The non-blended name *Poroshenko* in the RPP corpus associated with negative verbs, such as *zdohnet* (will kick the bucket) or *obosralsâ* (shit himself), more often than in the UPP, with ten verbs out of forty-eight falling in this category. Among the verbs that were found in sentences with the blend *Parashenko* as the subject, fifteen out of forty-three were negative, for example, *gavkajet* (barks) or *obmanul* (deceived). However, the blend *Potroshenko* combined with negative verbs such as *morit* (starves) or *zastrelitsâ* (will shoot himself) seven out of forty-seven times, and the blend *Poproshenko* linked with negative verbs such as *razrušil* (destroyed) or *primazyvajetsâ*

Table 4.2 The Percentage of Negative Verbs and Modifiers Used with Target Words in RPP and UPP

Target Word	RPP		UPP	
	verbs	modifiers	verbs	modifiers
Putin	6%	-	5%	4%
Putler	32%	100%	76%	67%
Kaputin	67%	33%	-	-
Haputin	-	100%	-	-
Poroshenko	21%	16%	8%	16%
Parashenko	35%	59%	37%	59%
Potroshenko	19%	90%	25%	90%
Poproshenko	11%	81%	-	81%

(clings to) two times out of eighteen, which is less frequent that the non-blended name *Poroshenko,* if taken as a percentage of all analysed uses.

In the UPP corpus, *Poroshenko* was used as a subject of a sentence with a negative verb, such as *vral* (lied) or *razrušil* (destroyed), in 8 percent of the lines out of 100 randomly picked lines from the corpus (five negatives out of fifty-nine), and it was used with a verb of a positive connotation 3 per cent of the time (two positives out of fifty-nine). However, *Parashenko* was used with negative verbs such as *hoče razvâzaty vijnu* (wants to wage war) three times out of eight. Negative verbs, such as *istreblât'* (exterminate), served with the subject *Potroshenko* three times out of twelve, and *Poproshenko* was used as a subject only once and with a neutral verb.

Similar tendencies are observed in the use of modifiers with target words. In the RPP corpus, modifiers of the non-blended surname *Poroshenko* were mostly neutral, but three uses out of nineteen were negative, for example, *p'ânyj* (drunk) or *hišnyj konditer* (predatory pastry chef). Negative modifiers of *Parashenko* were much more frequent, and words such as *žulik* (swindler) or *svinorylyj alkogolik* (pig-faced alcoholic) constituted ten out of seventeen cases. The blend *Poproshenko* was modified by a negative word such as *cyničnyj* (cynical) or *Graf Dâkula* (a Ukrainized variation of the name Count Drakula) nine out of ten times; and a similar trend was observed in the uses of *Potroshenko,* which was modified by such nouns as *sliznâk* (slug), *svinorylo* (pigface), or a fictional first name and patronymic *Lûdojed Krovopijevich* 'Ogre, son of Bloodsucker', thirteen times out of sixteen.

There were no negative modifiers of *Putin* in the RPP corpus; all ten of them were neutral. There were two cases when Putin's surname was used with a diminutive of his first name, which might be considered disrespectful, but for the purposes of this study we decided to assess words at their face value while gauging their emotional values, so we treated diminutives as variants of the names and, as such, neutral. However, *Putler* was modified exclusively by negative nouns such as *zver'* (beast) or *man'jak* (maniac), or negative adjectives such as *krovavyj* (bloody) or *umališonnyj* (insane): all eighteen modifiers were clearly negative. One out of three modifiers of *Kaputin* was negative, and the blend *Haputin* was used with a negative modifier.

In the UPP corpus, the surname Putin was mostly used with neutral modifiers, most of the time *President of RF* or *Volodymyr.* There was only one sarcastic use of *zavklub* (club manager) that could be considered negative out of the twenty-five uses. The blend *Putler,* similarly to the RPP corpus, was used with negative modifiers, such as *vyrodok* (degenerate) or *dyktator* (dictator); however, it was much less frequent than in the RPP corpus, and there were only three cases where *Putler* was used with a noun or adjective as a modifier. The blends *Kaputin* and *Haputin* did not appear in the UPP at all.

The data suggest that the distribution of the verbs and modifiers associated with target words is different with respect to both the corpus (RPP or UPP) and whether or not the name is blended. A quantitative analysis of all data merged into one corpus supports this hypothesis. A mosaic plot for the distribution of emotionally neutral, positive and negative verbs used in sentences with keywords as subjects is shown in Figure 4.1. In a mosaic plot, larger areas represent greater number of observations in the corresponding subset of the data, and smaller areas represent smaller numbers of observations, respectively. In Figure 4.1, the left part of the plot represents RPP (subcorpus: rus), and the right part of the plot represents UPP (subcorpus: ukr). The x-axis gives the emotional value of the collocates (neg = negative, neu = neutral and pos = positive), and the y-axis gives the morphological structure of the target word (yes = blended and no = unblended). The numeric data for the mosaic plot are provided in Table 4.3.

As shown in Figure 4.1 and Table 4.3, most verbs that are used in the sentences with target words as subjects are classified as neutral in all cases (both with unblended names and with blended names in RPP and in UPP). Among the remaining verbs, there are more negative than positive ones in all groups of data (with no positive verbs at all used in sentences with blended names as subjects in UPP). While this is an overall tendency for the whole data set, there is a clear relation between the emotional evaluation of the verbs and their presence in the sentence with either blended or unblended names, both in RPP and in UPP (p-value <0.001), as shown in Figure 4.1. In both corpora, the number of emotionally negative verbs used with blended names was significantly higher than the number of emotionally negative verbs with unblended

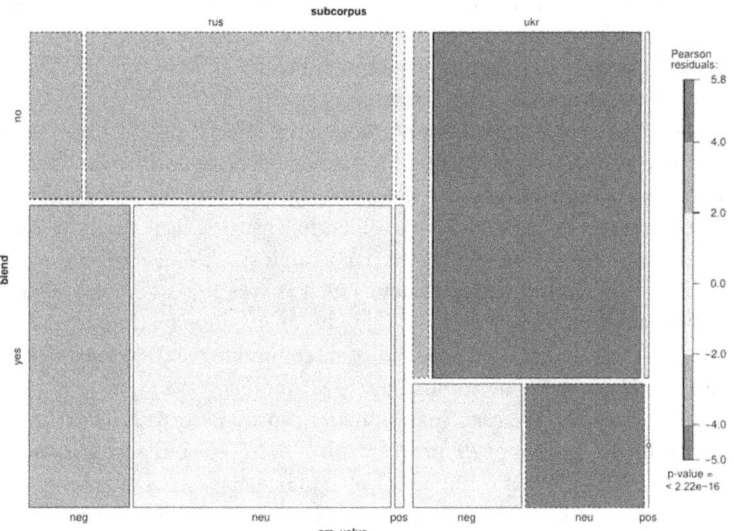

Figure 4.1 Emotional value of verbs used in the sentences with target words as subjects, by corpus and the structure of target words.

Table 4.3 The Distribution of Verbs Used in Sentences with the Target Words as Subjects in RPP and UPP

Subcorpus	RPP			UPP		
Emotional value	Negative	Neutral	Positive	Negative	Neutral	Positive
Unblended names	13	75	2	8	107	2
Blended names	45	114	4	20	22	0

names. In the RPP corpus, negative verbs comprise 14.4 per cent of all the verbs used with unblended target words (thirteen out of ninety verbs), while 27.6 per cent verbs used with blended names (forty-five verbs out of 116) are negative. The difference, however, is more dramatic in the UPP corpus, where only eight out of 117 (6.8 per cent) negative verbs are used with unblended names, while nearly half of the verbs used with blended names (twenty out of forty-two, or 47.6 per cent) are classified as negative.

Similar analysis was performed for the modifiers of target words. In the mosaic plot in Figure 4.2, the left part of the plot represents RPP (subcorpus: rus), and the right part of the plot represents UPP (subcorpus: ukr). The x-axis gives the emotional value of the modifiers (neg = negative, neu = neutral and pos = positive), and the y-axis gives the morphological structure of the target word (yes = blended and no = unblended). The numeric data for the mosaic plot are provided in Table 4.4.

Again, the analysis confirmed that there is a relation between the emotional evaluation of the modifiers and their presence in the sentence with either blended or unblended names, which is true both for RPP and for UPP (p-value <0.001). In particular, the number of emotionally negative modifiers used with blended names was significantly higher than the number of emotionally negative modifiers with unblended names. In fact, for more than a half of observations in our data set, if a blended name has a modifier, this modifier is negative (fifty out of sixty-two, or 80.6 per cent of observations in RPP, and seven out of ten observations in UPP). The statistical significance of this result is especially prominent for the RPP data, due to the scarcity of the UPP data (only ten observations of blended names with modifiers). However, the UPP data demonstrate the same tendency, as is evident from the right part of the plot in Figure 4.2.

The results of the contingency table analysis were further substantiated by the analysis of the contexts of the target words (the unblended names *Putin* and *Poroshenko*, as well as their most frequent blended counterparts *Putler* and *Parashenko*) using decision tree method. The conditional inference tree estimating the relations between the form of the target word and a set of independent predictors is shown in Figure 4.3. The data set is split into two groups (branches of the decision tree); each time, a statistically significant difference between two subsets is indicated. Each node of the tree where a split takes place is labelled by the variable that works as the best predictor for it. In particular, the following predictors turned out to be significant in the analysis, from top to bottom: blend (whether or not the keyword is a blend), obscene_n (the number of obscene words in the context) and sw_assoc_n (the number of associates of the blend source words in the context). The branches coming from each node of

Table 4.4 The Distribution of Modifiers of Target Words in RPP and UPP

Subcorpus	RPP			UPP		
Emotional value	Negative	Neutral	Positive	Negative	Neutral	Positive
Unblended names	3	25	1	2	39	1
Blended names	50	12	0	7	2	1

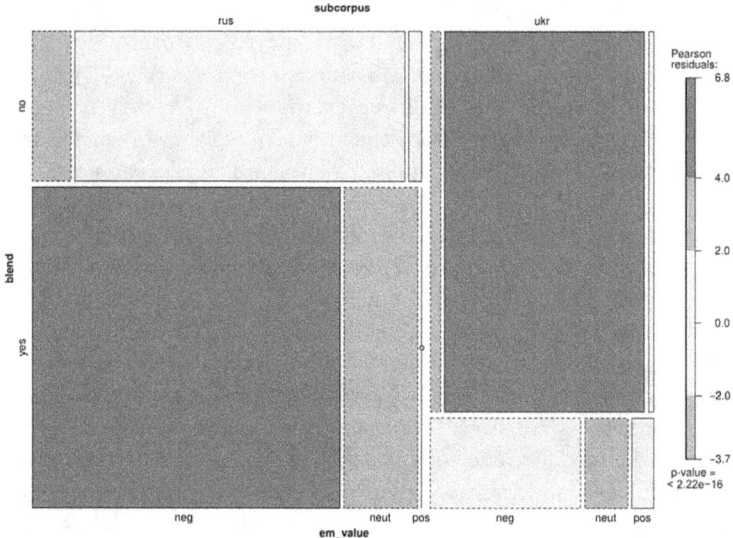

Figure 4.2 Emotional value of modifiers of target words, by corpus and the structure of target words.

the decision tree are labelled by the values of the relevant factors for which the split is significant, with the valid p-value for the node. The number of concordance lines in each of the resulting nodes (n) is displayed on top of the nodes. The resulting nodes are visualized as bar charts showing the proportion of concordance lines containing each of the four target words (coded as follows: 1– Parashenko, 2–Poroshenko, 3–Putin and 4–Putler).

The results of the decision tree analysis have demonstrated that blended names differ significantly from non-blended names in terms of the content of their contexts, as is evident from Figure 4.3, where the data set is split into two 'branches', the left branch representing all cases of the use of unblended names (the variable 'blend' equals 'no'), and the right branch all cases of the use of blended names, respectively (the variable 'blend' equals 'yes'). The fact that the variable 'blend' designates the top node split in the decision tree indicates that this factor (i.e. whether or not the target word is blended) has the strongest predictive value of the outcome of the decision tree (that is, the given concordance line containing the target word 'Putin', 'Poroshenko', 'Putler' or 'Parashenko') This result is not surprising in itself, since it necessarily follows the classification of the target words into blended and unblended ones. What is more interesting for the present analysis is that different contextual factors turned out to be significant predictors for blended names, as compared to unblended ones.

Among blended names (the right branch of the decision tree), there are further significant differences between *Putler* and *Parashenko* in terms of the number of the associates of the blend source words in the context (coded in the tree as sw_assoc_n). In particular, such words as *fûrer* (Fürher), *fašizm* (fashism) and *kaput* that can be found in the context of the name Hitler and are semantically associated with it, tend

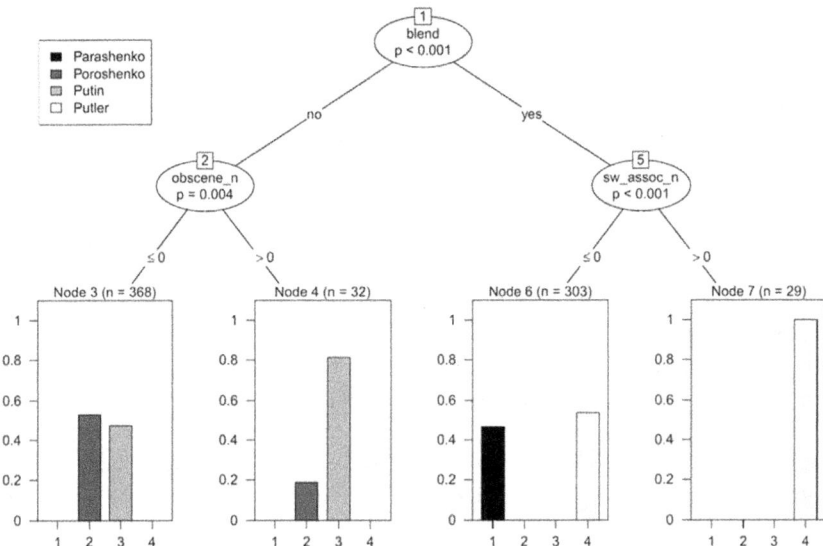

Figure 4.3 A decision tree analysis of the contexts of the keywords in RPP and UPP.

to be used in the immediate context of *Putler* in our data set. In twenty-nine contexts of the blend *Putler,* one or more associates of the source word of the blend are present (Node 7 of the decision tree). In contrast, no synonyms or other associates of the source word *paraša* (piss can) could be found in the context of *Parashenko*, as can be seen in Node 6 of the decision tree. With regard to the hypothesis about the presence of the associates of the blends' source words in context for substantiating the purported similarity between the referents of these words, it turns out that this substantiation is present for *Putler,* but not for *Parashenko.* This can be explained by greater possibility for factual grounding of the semantic association between Putin and Hitler (both are people, both are political leaders, not to mention negative semantic associations regarding dictatorship that could motivate the speakers to use the blend), but not between Poroshenko and *paraša* (a piss can, which is an inanimate object). On the other hand, the formation of the blend *Parashenko* could be motivated by phonological similarity between its source words to a greater extent than by their semantic relations, as pointed out in Section 2.

For unblended names (the left branch of the decision tree), significant differences are observed in terms of the use of obscene words in the context. In general, the majority of the contexts of unblended names (368 out of 400, that is Node 3) do not contain obscene words, but among those thirty-two which do, the contexts of *Putin* prevail, as shown by greater height of the corresponding bar in Node 4. Note also that the most frequent obscene word in the context of *Putin* is *hujlo* (dickhead). The origin of this obscene collocation is likely to be related to the slogan '*Putin hujlo!*' ('Putin is a dickhead ') popular in Ukrainian media, which originated in Ukraine in 2014 from a football chant first performed by football fans in March 2014 on the onset of the Russian annexation of Crimea (Taylor 2014).

It is also interesting to look at differences between RPP and UPP in terms of the characteristics of the contexts. The analysis in Figure 4.3 does not reveal any significant differences. However, the influence of this variable may be masked by the effect of the main predictor (that is, the 'blend' variable in Figure 4.3). Therefore, additional analysis was performed, with the 'blend' variable removed from the model. The results are displayed in Figure 4.4. As in the previous analysis, each node of the conditional inference tree in Figure 4.4 is labelled by the variable that works as the best predictor for it. With the main predictor removed from the analysis, the best predictor turned out to be the variable 'subcorpus', that is, whether or not the context is from the RPP (rus) or the UPP (ukr) subcorpus. Further significant predictors are (from top to bottom) the following: sw_assoc_n (the number of associates of the blend source words in the context), derog_n (the number of derogatory terms in the context), obscene_n (the number of obscene words in the context) and blends_n (the number of blends, other than the target word, in the context). The branches coming from each node are labelled by the values of the relevant factors for which the split is significant, with the valid p-value for the node provided, and n is the number of contexts in each node.

The decision tree in Figure 4.4 shows significant differences between RPP and UPP in terms of the contexts of the target words. For UPP (the right branches of the decision tree), the predictors that have significant effect are the number of derogatory terms (derog_n) and the number of obscene words (obscene_n). The node with the highest number of derogatory terms (Node 13) contains predominantly contexts of the blended name *Putler*. The node with the highest number of obscene words (Node 12) contains about 80 per cent of contexts of the unblended name *Putin*. Interestingly,

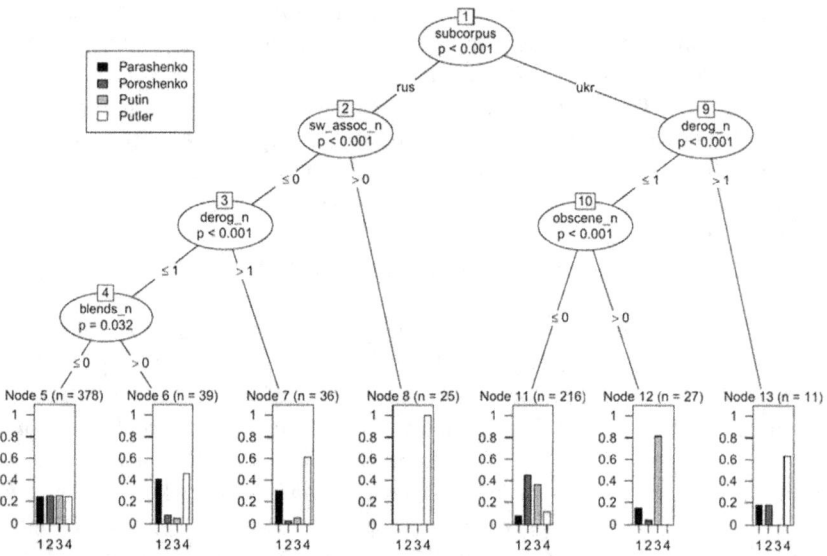

Figure 4.4 A decision tree analysis of the content of the contexts of the keywords in RPP and UPP, with the main predictor (blend) removed from the model.

it appears that for Ukrainian community the amount of negative lexical content in the context is generally higher for *Putin* than for *Poroshenko*, whether the names are blended or not.

A different tendency can be observed for RPP data (the left branches of the decision tree). The number of the associates of the word *Hitler* is significantly higher in the contexts of *Putler* (Node 8), as compared to other names, whether blended or unblended. This result can be explained by different motivation of the blended names. That is, the high degree of similarity between the surname *Poroshenko* and the source words of blends *Poroshenko, Potroshenko* and *Parashenko* implies that the coinage of these blends could be motivated by phonological associations alongside semantic value, which is in line with the findings reported in Gries (2012), where the phonological and graphical similarity between the source words is named among the key factors of well-formedness of blends. However, in the blend *Putler*, the semantic association, that is, the suggested similarity between Putin and Hitler, could have been a stronger factor than phonological similarity between the source words. The reasons underlying the observed differences are yet to be explored.

The number of derogatory terms in the contexts is higher for blended names than for non-blended names in RPP. In addition, the contexts of the blended names *Putler* and *Parashenko* tend to contain other blend words more often than the contexts of non-blended names, as shown in Node 6. This can be explained by the phenomenon of analogy: the presence of blended names increases the probability of using other blends in the immediate context by analogy (see, for example, Mattiello (2017) on the discussion of analogy in word formation).

Overall, the results of the conditional inference tree analysis are in line with the findings of the contingency table analysis, since they show clear differences between the patterns of use of the target words depending on their morphological form (blended or unblended), as well as clear differences between RPP and UPP.

The scarce number of blended names in UPP provides a serious shortcoming of the present analysis, and can be one of the reasons underlying the differences between RPP and UPP. However, the tendencies that are revealed regarding the use of blended names conform to the overall patterns of the use of blends outlined in earlier literature. Moreover, the observed results signify important extralinguistic factors that may underlie the differences between RPP and UPP, and therefore should be regarded as beacons for future investigations.

6 Conclusions

This study has shown that blended names that are used in the discussions of Ukrainian crisis differ significantly from their unblended counterparts in terms of the patterns of their use. The contexts of blended names contain more colloquial elements and more negatively coloured lexical content than the contexts of unblended names. This confirms the hypothesis that blended names are used in a more informal way and bear more emotional value than their unblended counterparts.

The content analysis of the target words' contexts of use has revealed significant differences between the RPP and the UPP corpus. A comparatively higher percentage of words evaluated as emotionally negative were found among the collocates of *Putin* in the UPP corpus and *Poroshenko* in the RPP corpus. Thus, negative evaluations are more likely to be directed to the president of another country (cf. a slogan *Putin hujlo* (Putin is a dickhead) in Ukrainian media), but not to the president of the purported country of origin of the speaker. This difference does not refer, however, to the blended names such as *Putler* or *Potroshenko*, which generally associate with negatively evaluated lexical elements in both corpora.

Another important tendency that characterizes the use of blended names in our data is the presence of the source words, their synonyms and collocates in the context. As pointed out in Konieczna (2012: 70), the interpretation of many blends in the media 'is possible only in the context in which they appear, as they require knowledge of the extra-linguistic world and its socio-political reality'. The results presented in this chapter further substantiate this claim as the interpretation of blended names such as *Putler, Haputin, Parashenko* and *Poproshenko* requires not only recognition of their source words but also extralinguistic knowledge, for example, about the reasons for comparing Putin to Hitler or Poroshenko to a beggar. The use of synonyms or collocates of the source words in the context of blends can, therefore, be explained by the need to establish stronger associations between the referent of the blend (e.g. Putin) and the extralinguistic facts the language user relates to this referent in the discussed situation (e.g. aggressive external policy).

References

Akhmetova, T. V. (1996), 'Russkij mat. Tolkovyj slovar' [*Russian Obscenities. Explanatory Dictionary*]. Moscow: Kolokol-Press.
Algeo, J. (1977), 'Blends, a Structural and Systemic View', *American Speech*, 52: 47–64.
Arndt-Lappe, S. and Plag, I. (2013), 'The Role of Prosodic Structure in the Formation of English Blends', *English Language and Linguistics*, 17 (3): 357–563.
Bauer, L., Lieber, R. and Plag, I. (2013), *The Oxford Reference Guide to English Morphology*. Oxford: Oxford University Press.
Beliaeva, N. (2015), 'Blends at the Interface between Compounding and Clipping: Evidence from Readers' Evaluations', *Neologica*, 9: 205–19.
Beliaeva, N. (2016), 'Blends at the Intersection of Addition and Subtraction: Evidence from Processing', *SKASE Journal of Theoretical Linguistics*, 13 (2): 23–45.
Bilaniuk, L. (2004), 'A Typology of Surzhyk: Mixed Ukrainian-Russian Language', *International Journal of Bilingualism*, 8 (4): 409–25.
Bilaniuk, L. (2005), *Contested Tongues: Language Politics and Cultural Correction in Ukraine*. Ithaca: Cornell University Press.
Borgwaldt, S. R., Kulish, T. and Bose, A. (2012), 'Ukrainian Blends: Elicitation Paradigm and Structural Analysis', in V. Renner, F. Maniez and P. J. L. Arnaud (eds), *Cross-disciplinary Perspectives on Lexical Blending*, 75–92. Berlin: De Gruyter Mouton.
Gries, S. T. (2006), 'Cognitive Determinants of Subtractive Word-Formation Processes: A Corpus-Based Perspective', *Linguistics*, 17 (4): 535–58.

Gries, S. T. (2012), 'Quantitative Corpus Data on Blend Formation: Psycho- and Cognitive-Linguistic Perspectives', in V. Renner, F. Maniez and P. J. L. Arnaud (eds), *Cross-Disciplinary Perspectives on Lexical Blending*, 145–67. Berlin: De Gruyter Mouton.

Gut, N., Panchenko, I. and Zabolotna, O. (2015), 'Ukrainian Blends-Neologisms as the Reflection of Current Social and Political Situation: A Splendid Prophecy or a 20-Years' Collapse', *Studia Slavica Academiae Scientiarum Hungaricae*, 60 (2): 389–403.

Hothorn, T., Hornik, K. and Zeileis, A. (2006), 'Unbiased Recursive Partitioning: A Conditional Inference Framework', *Journal of Computational and Graphical Statistics*, 15 (3): 651–74.

Hrushcheva, O. A. (2017), 'Blendy sovremennogo russkogo jazyka kak zerkalo kultury' ['Blends of Contemporary Russian Language as a Culture Mirror'], *Vestnik Orenburgskogo Gosudarstvennogo Universiteta*, 202: 66–70.

Kilgarriff, A., Rychly, P., Smrz, P. and Tugwell, D. (2004), 'The Sketch Engine', in G. Williams and S. Vessier (eds.), *Proceedings of the 11th EURALEX International Congress*, 105–15. Retrieved from http://www.euralex.org/elx_proceedings/Euralex2004/011_ 2004_V1_ Adam%20KILGARRIFF,%20Pavel%20RYCHLY,%20Pavel%20SMRZ,%20 David%20TUGWELL _The%20%20Sketch%20Engine.pdf

Konieczna, E. (2012), 'Lexical Blending in Polish', in V. Renner, F. Maniez and P. J. L. Arnaud (eds), *Cross-Disciplinary Perspectives on Lexical Blending*, 51–73. Berlin: De Gruyter Mouton.

Kornienko, O. (2016), 'Social and Economic Background of Blending', in L. E. Grinin, I. V. Ilyin, P. Herrmann and A. V. Korotayev (eds), *Globalistics and Globalization Studies: Global Transformations and Global Future*, 220–25. Volgograd: 'Uchitel' Publishing House.

Kostromicheva, M. V. and Polyakov, A. S. (2014), 'Rossiysko-ukrainskij konflikt: Invektivnyje novoobrazovanija', in A. P. Chudinov (ed.), *Politicheskaja kommunikacija: Perspektivy razvitija nauchnogo napravlenija: Materialy meždunarodnoj naučnoj konferencii*, 129–31. Ekaterinburg: Ural'skij Gosudarstvennyj Pedagogicheskij Universitet.

López Rúa, P. (2007), 'Keeping Up with the Times: Lexical Creativity in Electronic Communication', in J. Munat (ed.), *Lexical Creativity, Texts and Contexts*, 137–59. Amsterdam and Philadelfia: Benjamins.

López Rúa, P. (2012), 'Beyond All Reasonable Transgression: Lexical Blending in Alternative Music', in V. Renner, F. Maniez and P. J. L. Arnaud (eds), *Cross-Disciplinary Perspectives on Lexical Blending*, 23–34. Berlin: De Gruyter Mouton.

Lyashenko, I. V. (2014), 'Etnicheskije prozviša ukraincev v rossiyskoj i ukrainskoj blogosferah', *Nauchnyj resul'tat. Voprosy teoretičeskoj i prikladnoj lingvistiki*, 1 (2): 110–19. Retrieved from http://cyberleninka.ru/article/n/etnicheskie-prozvischa-ukra intsev-v-rossiyskoy-i-ukrainskoy-blogosferah#ixzz3mTfQNQ4b.

Lyashenko, I. V. and Fedyunina, I. E. (2017), 'Etnicheskije prozviša russkih v ukrainskoj i rossiyskoj blogosferah', *Nauchniy resul'tat. Voprosy teoreticheskoy i prikladnoy lingvistiki*, 3 (1): 42–8.

Mattiello, E. (2017), *Analogy in Word-Formation*. Berlin and Boston: De Gruyter Mouton.

Nedashkivska, A. (2010), 'Symbolic Bilingualism in Contemporary Ukrainian Media', *Canadian Slavonic Papers*, 52 (3/4): 351–72.

Ozhegov, S. I. and Shvedova, N. Y. (2006), *Tolkovyj slovar' russkogo jazyka: 80 000 slov i frazeologičeskih vyraženij [Explanatory Dictionary of Russian: 80 000 Words and Phraseologisms]*, 4th edn. Moscow: OOO A Temp.

Plag, I. (2003), *Word-Formation in English*. Cambridge: Cambridge University Press.
Renner, V. (2015), 'Lexical Blending as Wordplay', in A. Zirker and E. Winter-Froemel (eds), *Wordplay and Metalinguistic / Metadiscursive Reflection: Authors, Contexts, Techniques, and Meta-reflection*, 119–33. Berlin: De Gruyter Mouton.
Slovar' sovremennoj leksiki, žargona i slenga [Dictionary of Contemporary Lexis, Jargon, and Slang] (2018). Retrieved from https://argo.academic.ru/
Taylor, A. (2014), '"Khuilo": The Offensive Term That Has Attached Itself to Putin', *The Washington Post*, 16 June 2014. Retrieved from https://www.washingtonpost.com/news/worldviews/wp/2014/06/16/khuilo-the-offensive-term-that-has-attached-itself-to-putin/?arc404=true
White, S. J., Johnson, R. L., Liversedge, S. P. and Rayner, K. (2008), 'Eye Movements When Reading Transposed Text: The Importance of Word-Beginning Letters', *Journal of Experimental Psychology. Human Perception and Performance*, 34 (5): 1261–76.
Whitney, C. (2001), 'How the Brain Encodes the Order of Letters in a Printed Word: The SERIOL Model and Selective Literature Review', *Psychonomic Bulletin and Review*, 8 (2): 221–43.
Zhabotinskaya, S. A. (2015), *Jazyk kak oružije v vojne mirovozzrenij Majdan-Antimajdan: Slovar'-tezaurus leksičeskih innovatsij. Ukraina dekabr' 2013–dekabr' 2014* [*Language as a Weapon in the War of Ideologies Maidan-Antimaidan: A Thesaurus of Lexical Innovations. Ukraine December 2013–December 2014*]. Retrieved from http://uaclip.at.ua/zhabotinskaja-jazyk_kak_oruzhie.pdf

5

The antagonistic discourses of the Euromaidan

Kolorady, *Sovki* and *Vatniki* versus *Jumpers*, *Maidowns* and *Panheads*

Olga Baysha

It has been increasingly recognized that social media, instead of fostering a democratic exchange of opinions – a hope many scholars had shared – may only deepen social antagonisms and cause new tensions among culturally and politically alienated groups. Because it is so easy in the digital world to ignore and shun dissonant voices, it has been recognized that online public spaces, with the various social media filters through which people are segregated and shielded from one another, can result in much greater homogeneity in terms of political opinion than offline public spheres (Noel and Nyhan 2011; Pariser 2011; Schwarz and Shani 2016). It has been argued that by allowing users to unfriend, unfollow and block others, social media facilitates the exclusion of dissonant voices and thereby discourages dialogue between those holding different views on political issues (Garrett et al. 2014; Himelboim, McCreery and Smith 2013; Stroud 2010). As Zhu and her colleagues suggest, 'selective avoidance is likely to deepen the existing social divisions and diminish the possibilities for deliberation and reconciliation between different sides' (2017: 126), reducing the possibility of democratic communication. Such developments are most likely during political turbulence and wars – the times when deliberation and negotiations are most needed for peace-building.

However, as this chapter demonstrates, social networking may exacerbate conflicts not only by allowing users to shield themselves from the 'other' but also by creating unlimited opportunities to disseminate conflict-instigating memes – 'particular idea[s] presented as a written text, image, language "move," or some other unit of cultural "stuff"' (Knobel and Lankshear 2007: 202). Transmitted virally, memes can ruin communication in a different sense – through closing discourse and establishing solid frontiers between compatriots divided over social, cultural and political issues (Shomova 2019). This is what researchers call the 'non-intended' effects of internet memes that refer 'to (non-propositional) feelings, emotions, impressions, etc. which are not overtly intended by the sender user, but are generated from the act of communication' (Yus 2018: 3). Drawing on Nico Carpentier's conceptualization of antagonistic discourse and using the case study of the Ukrainian Euromaidan, this chapter discusses how some popular memes, which had been created or activated during the Euromaidan revolution (hereafter, 'the Maidan') and in its aftermath, contributed to the intensification of the conflict in Ukraine. In what follows, I present the findings of my analysis after briefly discussing (a) Nico Carpentier's (2017) theory of antagonistic discourse, (b) the context of this study and (c) its research method, which draws on the discourse theory of Ernesto Laclau and Chantal Mouffe (1985).

1 Nico Carpentier's antagonistic discourse

In his recent book *The Discursive-Material Knot*, Carpentier (2017) identifies three nodal points of antagonistic discourse: homogenization of the self as opposed to the enemy, the radical difference of the enemy and the need for destruction of the enemy. *Homogenization* appears when the diversity of the self is made invisible; all differences are obliterated to the extent that anybody who dares problematize total homogenization is branded a 'traitor'. This is what is often referred to as a 'Jacobin imaginary', juxtaposing the imagined homogeneity of 'us' against 'them'. The *radical difference* between self and enemy, as presupposed by antagonistic discourse, appears when there is no symbolic space that the self and other can be imagined to share, as the two are thought to be irreconcilably at odds. As Carpentier puts it:

> The construction of this radical other is supported by the logic of dichotomy, whereas the idea of the absence of a common space produces distance. In the more extreme cases, this radical othering leads to a dehumanization and demonization of the other, denying even the most basic features of humanity to that other, which makes its destruction easier and even necessary. (2017: 12)

Moreover, 'the dichotomy that defines the enemy and the self is not considered neutral, but it supports a hierarchy that positions the enemy as inferior, and the self as superior' (Carpentier 2017: 172).

To transform antagonism into agonism – that is, to stop seeing opponents as enemies and instead begin to view them as adversaries whose differences matter – it is necessary to re-articulate the nodal points of antagonistic discourse and to re-create a common symbolic space among the conflicting participants in a political process. To re-establish 'conflictual togetherness', as Carpentier (2017: 178) puts it, the structural balance needs to be restored so that those involved are no longer positioned hierarchically. It is also necessary to move away from dichotomization by making the solid, impermeable frontiers between the self and the opponent more porous, so as to activate a diversity of positions and allow pluralism to flourish – a precondition for agonism to emerge.

Introducing greater permeability between the identities of self and other as well as pluralizing the positions within each camp enables connections between former enemies, which can lead to alliances across borders and the creation of symbolic spaces of sharing. 'If adversaries belong to the same political space, and do not attempt to destroy (or annihilate) each other, then the reflection on the nature of this interaction becomes unavoidable' (Carpentier 2017: 179), paving the way towards mutually acceptable terms of coexistence and reducing the chance of violence – physical, material, structural or symbolic.

The transformation of antagonism into agonism is important for preserving societal peace. This task requires the establishment of political mechanisms through which collective passions over the issue at stake are channelled and expressed without opponents being seen as enemies, but rather as 'friendly adversaries'. Pluralistic democracy presupposes the clash of different political positions and makes room for dissent; disagreement is considered legitimate and welcome. If this is missing, there is danger of replacing democratic contestation with violence. Moreover, an all-inclusive democratic project cannot be successful without incorporating a wide variety of social groups into the political process. An unwillingness and/or inability to make alliances with 'others' will have detrimental results for democratic struggles: The revolutionary minority either cannot succeed or it grasps power by violent means and keeps it through totalitarian methods of government, repressing 'underdeveloped' compatriots who oppose the reforms.

In what follows, I trace how antagonistic discourse as discussed by Carpentier has manifested itself through each side's usage of memes to represent their opponents in the internal Ukrainian conflict, which, in parallel to the conflict between Ukraine and Russia, has been unfolding since the beginning of the Revolution of Dignity in November 2013.

2 Context

As this volume is devoted exclusively to the Ukrainian crisis and its linguistic representations, there is no need to go into detail regarding all the developments of the Maidan that led not only to the conflict between Russia and Ukraine but also to the intensification of the internal Ukrainian confrontation. However, with respect to the topic of this chapter, it is important to highlight one critical aspect that is often ignored in academic accounts of the revolution: the revolt against President Yanukovych and his system of power was not unanimously supported across the whole of Ukraine. Before and after the revolution, several polls were conducted by different research institutes asking respondents to choose between joining the EU or joining the Eurasian Customs Union led by Russia; all such polling showed that regional differences were very sharp.

The farther east one looked, the stronger and more unified a rejection of the Maidan with its European agenda one would find (KIIS 2014). Starting in late February of 2014, demonstrations protesting the 'coup d'état' took place in Ukraine's eastern and some southern regions. Many of these gatherings were held under Russian national banners, although, according to the Kiev International Institute of Sociology (KIIS), only about 12 per cent of people living in the 'separatist' regions of Donetsk and Luhansk 'definitely agreed' in April 2014 that their regions 'should secede from Ukraine and join Russia' (KIIS 2014).

April of 2014 was when the protests escalated into an armed insurgency backed by Russia. Russia not only provided the rebels with weapons but also supported them with Russian troops (Sutyagin 2015) – which is why the insurgency is usually referred to as 'the Russian invasion'. However, what is often lost in representing the Ukrainian crisis exclusively through this frame is that 45.3 per cent of the people living in Donetsk and 55.1 per cent living in Luhansk justified the armed resistance against the new Kyiv government on the grounds that 'during the revolution, the protesters in Kyiv and western regions did the same' and 'there was no other means to attract the centre's attention to the problems of the regions' (ZN, UA 2014). In other words, what is usually left without attention is that the roots of the insurgency were local, despite its co-opting by Russia for its own geopolitical interests.

Although, as mentioned earlier, the vast majority of people living in the territories controlled by the rebels were against the 'coup d'état' but not in favour of joining Russia, the new Kyiv government labelled the whole of the anti-Maidan movement 'separatist' and later as 'terrorists' (Baysha 2017). In April 2014, an 'anti-terrorist' military operation (ATO) was launched; from its onset until 15 May 2017, a total of 10,090 combatants and civilians were killed, while at least 23,966 were wounded (UN News 2017). Hundreds of thousands have been internally displaced or have fled the country.

Today, five years after the Maidan, Ukraine is still split into two conflicting camps – the supporters and opponents of the Maidan and the ATO that followed – and this split goes across all Ukraine, not only its south-eastern regions. It is still normal for the citizens of Ukraine on opposite sides of the Maidan to hurl insults at each other such as 'jumpers' (*skakuny* in Ukrainian; *skakuny* in Russian), panheads (*kastrûlegolovi* in Ukrainian; *kastrûlegolovyje* in Russian), 'maidowns' (*majdauni* in Ukrainian; *majdauny* in Russian), 'sovki' (*sovky* in Ukrainian; *sovki* in Russian) and 'vatniki' (*vatnyky* in Ukrainian; *vatniki* in Russian) (Korrespondent 2014) – derogatory memes that ascribe an inferior mental, intellectual and/or civilizational condition to the opposing camp. Of the memes I discuss in this paper, and whose etymologies are presented below, only one signifier has gone out of usage – 'kolorady' (*kolorady* in Ukrainian; *kolorady* in Russian) – following a horrendous act of violence in Odessa on 2 May 2014. I will discuss the term and this in more detail in the 'Findings' section.

Here is a brief description of the memes in alphabetical order:

'Jumper' is a word that traces its origin to late November 2013, when the students protesting on the Maidan created an action of jumping while chanting, 'If you are not jumping, you are a Moskal [a derogatory term for Russians]' (Radio Liberty 2013). Opponents of the Maidan have called its activists 'jumpers' as a way to infantilize them and suggest they are unable to foresee the consequences of their actions.

'Panhead' is a compound word uniting *kastrûlâ* (kitchen pan) and *golova* (head). This term was created after Maidan participants were seen wearing pots and pans on their heads to counter a law of 16 January 2014 that prohibited helmets at protests. The term is used to imply that Maidan supporters are 'brainless'.

'Kolorad' (*kolorady* in plural) is a word originally denoting Colorado potato-eating insects distinctive for their bright orange and black stripes. Because their colours are reminiscent of the orange-and-black St. George ribbon, a symbol of Russian military glory, which many anti-Maidan protesters have worn, the term came to denote Maidan opponents who favoured the Russia-led Customs Union over the European Union advocated by the Maidan.

'Maidown' (*maidowny* in plural) is a compound word uniting 'Maidan' and 'Down', as in Down syndrome; it has been used to ascribe Maidan support to an 'abnormal' mental condition. This condition was projected onto Maidan supporters as an accusation that they were unable to foresee the consequences of their revolutionary actions.

'Sovok' (*sovki* in plural) – a derivative of 'Soviet' whose homonym *sovok* means 'shovel' – is a term used to assign an 'unworthy' social condition to those holding anti-Maidan views. Imagined as having a 'Soviet' mentality manifesting itself in resisting Westernization and progressive historical changes, 'sovki' are presented as underdeveloped and uncivilized.

'Vatnik' (*vatniki* in plural) originally referred to a warm Russian jacket filled with cotton (*vata*). In Maidan-related discourse, the term came to denote those opposing the Maidan due to stupidity, as if their heads were filled with cotton. Because a 'vatnik' is a traditional Russian article of clothing popular among rural populations, this signifier also came to suggest an outdated/pre-modern civilizational condition.

As early as August 2014, the BBC observed that these and similar derogatory internet memes were 'firmly established in everyday language' (Karpyak 2014). 'It is impossible to imagine any discussion on politics without them', *Komsomolskaya Pravda* echoed, noting also that 'the majority of these words have derogatory shades' (Lyabina 2014). These demeaning terms became 'ingrained in mass media, social networks, and people's heads', Channel 24 (2015) asserted a year later, counting more than thirty such linguistic creations. Media outlets covered the Maidan's many neologisms, including those listed here, in 2014 and 2015; however, as my research shows, many of these terms are still actively used today, five years after the revolution and the announcement of the ATO.

The purpose of my analysis was to trace the usage of these terms online to gain insight into their role in Maidan-related discourse. My research question was this: How did these terms, as deployed in Facebook exchanges among and between the two sides of the Maidan in 2014 and 2017, sustain the type of antagonistic discourse described by Carpentier?

3 Research design

To answer my research question, I analysed discussions of the Maidan and its developments by Ukrainian users of Facebook (hereafter, FB-users). By 'Ukrainian', I mean Ukrainian- and Russian-speaking FB-users whose 'place of living' was identified as a city or village in Ukraine. The posts of those who did not identify their place of living or whose places of living were outside Ukraine were not analysed.

I collected my data using Facebook searches. The following search parameters were set: (a) Posted by: 'anyone'; (b) Tagged location: 'Ukraine'; (c) Date posted: '2014' (the year of the victory of the Maidan and ATO announcement) and '2017' (to check if the memes are still in use); and (d) Subject: 'kolorad', 'maidown', 'panhead', 'skakun', 'sovok' and 'vatnik' (in Ukrainian and in Russian, consecutively). Searching with these criteria, I identified 1,730 public posts in Russian and Ukrainian. Taking this number as my data universe, I employed a 'cyclical process' (Mautner 2008: 35): I first selected a small corpus of posts within each of the categories, analysed it, and then used my findings to inform the next round of selections. In such a fashion, more and more material was included into my analysis in a process continuing until new data no longer brought new insights. I considered the point of 'saturation' to be reached when it became evident that new findings only reinforced previous ones.

The links between the signs 'jumper', 'kolorad', 'maidown', 'panhead', 'sovok', 'vatnik' and other elements of the discursive field were identified through a qualitative discourse analysis informed by Laclau's theory of discourse, which he developed in partnership with Chantal Mouffe (1985). According to this theory, discourse appears to be 'a real force which contributes to the moulding and constitution of social relations' (Laclau and Mouffe 1985: 110). Since social relations are seen as discursively constructed, the classical 'thought/reality' dichotomy no longer appears relevant, and 'the categories which have until now been considered exclusively of one or another' are reconsidered (Laclau and Mouffe 1985: 110).

Synonymy, metonymy, metaphor and other rhetorical devices are understood not as 'forms of thought that add a second sense to a primary', but as 'part of the primary terrain itself in which the social is constructed' (Laclau and Mouffe 1985: 110). Insisting on the ontological generality of rhetoric and on the tropological character of any articulation, Laclau asserts that hegemony is realized through a passage from metonymy to metaphor, from a 'contiguous' starting point to its consolidation in 'analogy' (Laclau 2014: 22). The culmination of this tropological movement is the moment of synecdoche, when one particular sector represents the new collective identity – when a part stands in for the whole. All the elements of this new collective identity are equivalentially united, but only one of them represents the whole.

When signs displaced each other metonymically (i.e. as a contingent substitution), metaphorically (i.e. as an unquestioned analogy) and, finally, synecdochically (i.e. when the most frequently used sign was asserted as a new collective identity), they were assumed to organize a chain of equivalence forming a hegemonic discourse.

All the posts under my analysis were done either in Ukrainian or in Russian. Since I am a native Ukrainian- and Russian- speaker, I analysed and translated all of the posts discussed in this chapter.

4 Findings

4.1 Homogenization

As explained in the introductory part of the chapter, homogenization, according to Carpentier (2017), appears when the diversity of the self is made invisible, and when all differences are obliterated to the extent that anybody who dares problematize total homogenization is branded a 'traitor'. This has been readily apparent in the online usage of all the terms discussed in this paper, regardless of whether the individuals posting were for or against the Maidan.

Anti-Maidan articulations. In posts by FB-users opposing the Maidan, its proponents appeared as 'jumpers', 'panheads' and 'maidowns'. An impossible unity of mentally sick, stupid, infantile and brainwashed Euromaidan protesters was discursively formed. Wearing weird implements and behaving in an inconceivable fashion, the 'panhead' 'jumpers' appeared to anti-Maidan FB-users as a homogenized mob of brainless half-people unaware of the consequences of their deeds. Here are some examples:

> Uncle Vasya [a collective image of working people] knows: previously, he had 500 dollars and electricity. Then, jumpers came. They jumped, and now he has only 235 dollars and no light. (FB-user 1, Odessa)
>
> If only we could charge higher utility costs only for panheads … (FB-user 2, Chernivtsi)
>
> How could these morons know what would be the outcome of their schizoid panhead Maidan? (FB-user 3, Kyiv)
>
> Maidown is not an insult; it's their real psychological state. (FB-user 4, Donetsk)

The pathological condition ascribed to the protesters, imagined to be an undifferentiated mass of morons, did not presuppose much possibility for meaningful communication. Instead, this antagonistic presentation of the protest encouraged people to spurn or ignore the demands of the 'abnormal' mass of Maidan supporters, who were uniformly in need of 'treatment'.

Pro-Maidan articulations. The antagonistic impossibility of dialogue between anti-Maidan and pro-Maidan FB-users was equally conditioned by the fact that the latter also imagined their opponents in terms of a homogeneous mass of undeserving creatures in need of treatment, correction and even eradication. What enabled such a totalization was the linking of the signifiers 'kolorad', 'sovok' and 'vatnik' in an equivalential chain united by a hegemonic idea of cultural backwardness, mental underdevelopment, a pre-modern condition (in the cases of 'sovok' and 'vatnik') or a simple lack of humanity (in the case of 'kolorad'). Here are some examples:

> 'Vatnik-land' – this is how I call our local lads and grannies brainwashed by Dima Kiselyov [a well-known Russian propagandist]. (FB-user 5, Donetsk)
>
> These hominoids resemble humans only on the surface … They are typical representatives of the species Homo Sovetikus Vulgaris [sovki]. (FB-user 6. Kyiv)
>
> How is it possible to transform a vatnik into a person? (FB-user 7, Kyiv)
>
> Exterminate Colorado bugs from Ukrainian soil! (FB-user 8, Dnipro)

As is evident from these and similar constructions, not only did pro-Maidan FB-users imagine their opponents in homogeneous terms, as an undifferentiated mob of mentally deficient creatures, but there was also a clear tendency to dehumanize them. I will address this tendency in more detail in one of the following sections.

Discursive closures of anti- and pro-Maidan antagonistic discourses. In both pro-Maidan and anti-Maidan articulations, each of the signifiers discussed came to represent synecdochically imagined homogeneous unities standing in for all who sympathized with the other side – not only those who jumped, wore cookware on their heads or attended pro-Maidan gatherings (on the Maidan side), and not only those who felt nostalgia for the Soviet Union, wanted to join Russia or wore St. George ribbons (on the anti-Maidan side). Used interchangeably, these and similar signifiers created chains of equivalence in which the political demands of both the Maidan and anti-Maidan were deactivated or made completely invisible. As a result of these tropological substitutions, for millions of Ukrainians the empty signifiers 'Maidan' and 'anti-Maidan' assumed hegemonic representations not of various political demands, but of second-order hegemonic constructions that excluded from the field of representation any meaningful political concerns.

4.2 Radical difference between self and enemy

The second nodal point of antagonistic discourse as discussed by Carpentier (2017) is the radical difference between self and enemy, which appears when the two are thought to be irreconcilably at odds, and this dichotomy is constructed not as neutral, but in hierarchical terms: the enemy is presented as inferior, the self as superior. Again, this trend is readily apparent in both of the cases discussed in this paper, both pro- and anti-Maidan.

Anti-Maidan articulations. As mentioned earlier, the mental conditions associated with 'jumping' or being a 'panhead' or 'maidown' who supported the uprising primarily suggested an inability to foresee the Maidan's consequences: the annexation of Crimea, the war in Donbas, a dramatic increase in utility costs and so forth. All of these signifiers were linked to ideas of childishness or mental sickness, implying the anti-Maidan writers saw themselves as comparable to 'adults' or 'doctors' capable of rational observation and accurate diagnosis of their opponents. In other words, they saw themselves as 'normal', in contrast to 'abnormal' pro-Maidan 'others'; the latter were imagined to be 'psychos' (FB-user 9, Kyiv) representing a 'panhead species' with 'low IQ' (FB-user 10, Donetsk) that could be 'brainwashed easily and firmly' (FB-user 11, Kyiv). Interestingly, some previous Maidan supporters who became opponents after the revolution adopted this 'Maidan-as-sickness' construction, presenting the Maidan as a state of abnormality: 'I am not a panhead any longer!! I've come back to myself after getting sucked into that terrible stupor!" (FB-user 12, Kyiv). In this and similar cases, the 'awakening' of the mind was equated to a renunciation of the Maidan.

Such constructions positioned the self and the other as opposites (children vs. adults, and patients vs. doctors). The imagined difference between the two sides was especially radical in the case of 'maidown', which implied that the pro-Maidan 'patients' linked to this signifier were stricken with cognitive impairment and thus wholly incapable of rational judgement. The signifiers 'jumper' and 'panhead' were not as harsh, since they implied – especially at the beginning of the confrontation – that pro-Maidan 'others' were able to think, albeit not always 'adequately'. But in spite of the depiction of radical difference between the anti-Maidan self and the pro-Maidan other, linking the latter to such signifiers as 'jumpers', 'maidowns' and 'panheads' nonetheless implied that the two sides had something in common – their shared humanity. Because both 'doctors' and their 'patients' were imagined to be humans, dehumanization and extreme antagonism had not yet appeared; some symbolic space for potential communication remained. As further examples show, this was not always the case in Maidan-related antagonistic discourse.

Pro-Maidan articulations. Radical 'othering' of the opponent was even more prominent in the case of pro-Maidan discourse. As in the earlier constructions by anti-Maidan users, pro-Maidan FB-users also imagined themselves to be intelligent and independent in their judgements. They considered themselves a radical outside as compared to their 'sovok' and 'vatnik' opponents: 'You do not think as others. You look independent. You are not a vatnik' (FB-user 13, Kyiv); 'How to rehabilitate this army of sovoks dragging us into the past?' (FB-user 14, Kherson). Whereas linking 'pro-Maidan' to the signifiers 'maidown' and 'panhead' thrust upon the former a meaning of mental disease, connecting the signifiers 'sovok' and 'vatnik' to 'anti-Maidan' made the latter seem like an historical abnormality. Against this 'backward' historical condition, many pro-Maidan FB-users whose posts I analysed saw themselves as nothing less than the standard-bearers of civilization: 'The work on vatniks requires huge effort, but this is what distinguishes civilization from barbarism' (FB-user 15, Kyiv). As the proponents of the Maidan considered themselves superior to their 'backward' counterparts, they felt they were up to the historical challenge of carrying 'barbarians' along towards the apex of civilization. I will discuss this in more detail in the following section.

At any rate, despite all the antagonism and implied lack of possibility for democratic (all-inclusive) communication carried by the terms discussed so far – 'jumpers', 'maidowns', 'panheads', 'sovoks' and 'vatniks' – the radical othering enacted by them has not led to dehumanization per se. Dehumanization of opponents occurred when they came to be imagined not as humans who happened to be 'sick' or 'backward', but as harmful insects in need of eradication. This is exactly what happened when anti-Maidan 'others' were linked to the signifier 'kolorad' – potato-eating beetles that are a scourge for Ukrainian farmers and can only be dealt with through extermination. The extreme level of othering implied by linkage to this signifier, with its wholly negative relation to 'the human condition', suggested the complete destruction of the shared symbolic space necessary for communication, and thus heralded the extreme case of 'radical difference' as discussed by Carpentier. In line with the main postulate of discourse theory whereupon 'discourse' is understood as a social force, shaping social relations and establishing the horizons of the social imaginary (Laclau and Mouffe 1985), this radical discursive othering found its material consequences during the Odessa tragedy of 2 May 2014, discussed in the following section.

4.3 The need for destruction of the enemy

'Kill Kolorady!' In April 2014, it was popular among FB-users to share posts warning of the presence of 'kolorady' in the cities of South-Eastern Ukraine and advocating for

their extermination. This 'information campaign' was not limited only to Facebook; it was widespread:

> A current insecticide ad running on Channel 5, the station owned by Ukrainian presidential candidate Petro Poroshenko, has even raised chuckles among some Ukrainians with its promise to kill Colorado beetles 'on the spot' – although in this case, the enemies in question are the actual bugs. (Radio Liberty 2014)

This piece, describing the TV campaign against 'kolorady' and its promise 'to kill Colorado beetles on the spot' appeared on the Radio Liberty website on 28 April 2014. Five days later, on 2 May, a fire during street clashes between pro-Maidan and anti-Maidan forces in Odessa killed forty-eight 'kolorady' and left more than 200 with burns and other injuries.

The tragedy happened when protesters against the Maidan were chased by radicals and sought shelter in the House of Trade Unions. There, they were attacked with Molotov cocktails, which caused the fire. According to many sources (e.g. UN OHCHR 2014), the clashes on that day were provoked by anti-Maidan activists who started shooting at a pro-Maidan gathering in the centre of Odessa. Many argue that the purpose of those throwing the 'cocktails' at the Trade Union building was not to kill people hiding there and definitely not to burn them alive (StopFake 2015). For those holding anti-Maidan views, however, this argument had little validity. Many of them have been confident that the mass killing was done on purpose, prompted by and in line with promises to 'kill kolorady' spread by pro-Maidan media and social networks on the eve of the tragedy. Indeed, it is quite difficult to believe it a coincidence if one follows the discussion of the tragedy by pro-Maidan FB-users on the day it occurred: 'Well done, Odessa! Let all kolorady be extinguished!' (FB-user 16, Mykolayiv); 'Exterminate Colorado bugs from Ukrainian soil!' (FB-user 17, Lutsk); 'To burn all kolorady!' (FB-user 18, Brovary); 'We need to roast kolorady cockroaches with Molotov cocktails!' (FB-user 19, Kyiv) and so forth. The number of such postings that are still publicly visible on Facebook is impressive.

As my analysis shows, the sign 'kolorady' was usually linked to such signifiers as 'terrorists', 'katsapi' (a derogatory term to refer to Russians), '(pro-Russian) separatists', 'traitors' and the like. 'Great job! A hot welcome to katsapi kolorady. The same fate is awaiting all Russian terrorists!' – this is how a male from Kyiv (FB-user 20) hailed the gruesome deaths of four dozen people. 'Death to kolorady! Death to traitors!', echoed a female writer from Dnipro (FB-user 21). What united these and numerous similar constructions was the empty signifier 'kolorady' that came to denote the impossible unity of the anti-Maidan, imagined not only as against the Maidan but also as against the Ukrainian condition, constituting its radical outside. Among those who supported the Maidan, the link between 'kolorady' and an anti-Ukrainian stance was sedimented to such an extent by May 2014 that some FB-users were absolutely confident that the majority of those who had been trapped in the burning Odessa building were not Ukrainians. 'Among those who died in Odessa, there were fifteen from Russia, ten from Transnistria, and nobody from Odessa' – this statement was shared by numerous FB-users on the day of the tragedy and shortly after. Later, it became clear that all the victims held Ukrainian citizenship, and all but two lived in the city of Odessa or its region. But this discovery did not ultimately make much of a difference: the hegemonic pro-Maidan discourse continued to present these people as harmful 'anti-Ukrainian' insects in need of extermination.

Correcting abnormality. The sign 'kolorady' was an outlier in its radical othering, going further than other such insults to suggest, unequivocally, the physical annihilation of political opponents imagined in non-political terms. In contrast, all the signs discussed earlier in this chapter invited a gentler method of defeating 'others', through 'healing' or 'correcting' their 'abnormality'. What was easily distinguishable in the calls of pro-Maidan FB-users to 'work on vatniks/sovoks' was the motif of the 'white man's burden' – the responsibility of European civilizers to modernize non-European barbarians. In the context of the Europeanization agenda of the Maidan, this motif was hegemonic (Baysha 2015). 'How is it possible to transform the vatnik into a person?' (a male FB-user 22, Kyiv) – this was one of the most actively discussed questions by some pro-Maidan FB-users whose posts I analysed. In line with the progressive historical imaginary that equates 'progress' with 'Westernization' (Baysha 2018; Taylor 1992; McCarthy 2010), anyone who challenged this normalized historical outlook (anti-Maidan 'others') came to be seen as an 'abnormal otherness' to be subjected to correction, discipline and modernization. The possibility of seeing them not as 'barbarians' but as people holding alternative opinions worthy of respect was not considered.

Interestingly, anti-Maidan articulations involving the signifiers 'jumpers', 'maidowns' and 'panheads', which linked the Maidan with the meaning of mental sickness, did not entail discussion of how to 'cure' those imagined in these terms: Nowhere in the online discussions I analysed did I find such considerations. However, the potentiality of such a conversation – to 'cure' political others instead of listening to their arguments and concerns – was obviously present in these cases as well. In both the pro-Maidan and anti-Maidan articulations discussed in this chapter, the tendency to ignore the concerns of political opponents by re-articulating them in non-political terms was a dominant trend.

4.4 Three nodal points of pro- and counter-Maidan antagonistic discourses

As discussed in the introductory part of this paper, Carpentier (2017) identifies three nodal points that, in his view, constitute antagonistic discourse: (a) the radical difference of the enemy, who is kept at a distance; (b) the homogenization of the self in opposition to the enemy; and (c) the need to destroy the enemy (172). All three points were evident in 'anti-other' discourses of both pro-Maidan and anti-Maidan FB-users organized through activation of the signifiers 'jumper', 'kolorad', 'maidown', 'panhead', 'sovok' and 'vatnik'.

Homogenization manifested itself when one of the protesting camps was imagined as uniformly sick and outdated or, in contrast, as uniformly healthy and modern. However, unlike Carpentier's conceptualization of antagonistic discourse, which presupposes the homogenization of one side of the conflict ('homogenization of the self as opposed to the enemy'), the antagonistic discourses of the Maidan (on both sides) rendered invisible the diversity within the opposing camps. The differences within each of them were obliterated to such an extent that the two sides came to be seen as totally internally homogeneous and mutually exclusive.

Depiction of political 'others' as radically different from the self was a dominant trend in posts by both anti-Maidan and pro-Maidan FB-users. From the articulations that I analysed, FB-users on both sides presented themselves as fundamentally different from those considered the enemy because of opposing political views. The former was always what the latter was not – and vice versa – as the latter became an outside against which the inside was constituted. In both cases, opponents were portrayed as incapable of rational thought; moreover, when the sign 'kolorady' was activated, those linked to it were presented as an existential threat to Ukrainian society as a whole. Both sides constructed the radical difference between pro-Maidan and anti-Maidan forces not in neutral terms, but in a hierarchical manner, with the 'self' always put forward as superior in comparison to the 'enemy'. In the discourse of pro-Maidan FB-users, this superiority was imagined in historical civilizational terms: The activation of the signifiers 'sovok' and 'vatnik' allowed pro-Maidan users to paint their opponents as 'barbarians' needing instruction and correction.

In sum, by depicting each other as unified 'masses' that were essentially sick, amoral or pre-modern, both pro-Maidan FB-users and their anti-Maidan counterparts created the conditions for 'maximum separation', to put it in Laclau and Mouffe's terms, where 'no element in the system of equivalences enters into relations other than those of opposition to the elements of the other system' (1985: 129). When this condition is reached, 'two societies' appear in place of one, and the confrontation between these 'societies' becomes 'fierce, total and indiscriminate: there exist no discourses capable of establishing differences within an equivalential chain in which each and every one of its elements symbolizes evil' (Laclau and Mouffe 1985: 129). In the cases I analysed, this 'fierce' confrontation manifested itself in the symbolic annihilation of 'others' through denigration and dehumanization, or through suggestions to 'correct' their 'abnormality' or even kill them. It is here that we find the third nodal point of antagonistic discourse as discussed by Carpentier (2017) – the need to destroy the enemy. Though it takes on various forms, this destruction is always about annihilation of the enemy in its present form: either through changing it beyond recognition or getting rid of it by other means.

5 Discussion

As is evident from my analysis, the discourses of both pro-Maidan and anti-Maidan FB-users organized through the employment of derogatory memes about each other possessed all the qualities of antagonistic discourse as conceptualized by Carpentier (2017). Instead of targeting the differences between their preferred democratic projects in political terms through the discussion of ideological, economic and political aspects of the situation, this discourse appealed to morality and constructed a dichotomy of good versus evil that could not possibly have led to a political resolution. By imagining themselves as 'the forces of good' fighting against 'the forces of evil', the FB-users whose posts I analysed showed themselves unaware of the antagonisms, contradictions and tensions existing within each of the two imagined unities. Their insistence on seeing the opposing side as a homogeneous entity instead of a complex web of relations prevented them from seeing multiple possibilities for engaging with social reality for the sake of positive change, envisioned in inclusive, pluralistic terms. To use Mouffe's words (2013), they were 'trapped' by their closed social imaginary, which convinced them they could bring about positive change through mere negativity. A social imaginary of this kind simply fails to acknowledge the intricacy of hegemonic struggles and the complexity of identity construction.

As stated in the theoretical section of this chapter, in order to transform antagonism into agonism, it is necessary to re-articulate the nodal points of antagonistic discourse, re-create a common symbolic space, and re-establish 'conflictual togetherness'. One can hardly expect, however, that any re-articulation of antagonistic into agonistic discourse can take place as long as opinion leaders, whose judgements matter for their followers, are engaged in the discursive games of dehumanizing political others. Here are some typical instances of such dehumanization of political others by the most charismatic activists of the Maidan whose victory brought them to the top of Ukraine's political Olympus:

On 13 April 2014, the newly appointed Minister of Internal Affairs of Ukraine Arsen Avakov made a FB-post announcing the beginning of the anti-terrorist operation and called those opposing this decision 'mean kolorady'. More than 8,000 FB-users liked this post; and more than 2,000 of them shared it.

On 21 August 2017, the Attorney General of Ukraine Yuri Lutsenko made a FB-post devoted to an anniversary of Ukraine's independence; addressing the difficulties of building the post-Maidan Ukraine, he claimed that its political elites were fighting against not only Russia's aggression but also internal 'vata'. More than 3,000 FB-users liked the post, and more than 1,000 shared it.

An exhaustive list of such extreme othering of Ukrainian citizens by post-Maidan Ukrainian public figures could go on indefinitely, but these examples are very telling as they represent the opinions of the heads of the most important law-enforcement agencies of Ukraine, who are responsible for national security. As is evident from their posts, they interpreted 'national security' to include defence not only against the external enemy (Russia) but also against the internal one – 'kolorady' and 'vatniki' living in Ukraine.

To be sure, the dehumanization of the enemy by opinion leaders has been taking place on both sides of the conflict – not only by pro-Maidan forces as in the examples given earlier. However, given that after the victory of the revolution, many Maidan activists became Ministers, Parliament members and other high-ranking officials, the political and social consequences of their discourses are clearly evident. Proof of the interrelation between symbolic and physical violence in post-Maidan Ukraine can be found in UN reports that have regularly expressed concerns about 'increasing manifestations of intolerance' towards alternative opinions in Ukraine, and legal prosecution of Ukrainian journalists based on 'the broad interpretation and application of terrorism-related provisions' (UN OHCHR 2017). It is these 'broad interpretations' that have allowed post-Maidan authorities in Ukraine to accuse opposition journalists, bloggers, and media organizations of aiding 'separatists' and/or 'terrorists', and of being guilty of 'parricide'.

'With the passage of time', the most recent UN report claims, 'divisions in Ukrainian society resulting from the conflict will continue to deepen and take root' (UN OHCHR 2017: 40). In order to stop this tendency, the UN advises the law-enforcement agencies of Ukraine to 'ensure investigation of violence against those holding alternative political opinions, including the cases of enforced disappearance, incommunicado detention, and torture in which Ukrainian forces and right-wing groups have allegedly been involved' (UN OHCHR 2017: 41). However, recognition is also needed – and this aspect is missing from UN reports – that physical violence is highly probable when the radical othering of political opponents is taking place on the level of discourse. Without addressing the issue of symbolic violence, one can hardly put an end to its physical manifestations.

6 Conclusion

The Ukrainian conflict has many facets, all of which must be understood for the situation to be effectively addressed. This chapter has concentrated on one aspect in the development of the confrontation: the role of internet memes, which become viral through Facebook, in promoting and intensifying radicalization. It is noteworthy that both pro-Maidan and anti-Maidan activists used this platform actively to disseminate their antagonistic visions of the situation; the sharing options provided by Facebook made it very convenient for this purpose. While working on this chapter, I was astonished to discover that posts from 2014 calling to 'kill kolorady' were still up on Facebook, with little or no visible objection from the 'kolorady' side. This can be explained, at least partially, by the fact that Facebook's functions of 'unfriending', 'unfollowing' and 'blocking' allow its users to filter out dissonant voices, create more homophilic digital spaces and easily avoid dialogue with those holding different views – a problem discussed in the introductory part of the chapter. With respect to the subject of this study, by allowing FB-users to shield their discussions from political 'others', Facebook seems to have also contributed to the radicalization of the antagonistic discourses separating 'vatniki' from 'panheads' and making the prospects for peaceful dialogue between them unlikely. More research is needed in this respect.

As this research also suggests, Facebook provides fertile soil for radicalizing antagonisms, allowing the barrier between self and other to become solid and impermeable. It is this stabilization of discursive closures that prevents any re-articulation of antagonism into agonism, and thus decreases the likelihood of finding a peaceful solution for the internal conflict in Ukraine. As the discourse theory suggests, physical violence is highly probable when the radical othering of political opponents is taking place on the level of discourse. Without addressing this issue, peace can hardly be achieved – something the UN and other international intermediaries would do well to acknowledge.

References

Baysha, O. (2015), 'Ukrainian Euromaidan: The Exclusion of Otherness in the Name of Progress', *European Journal of Cultural Studies*, 18 (1): 3–18.

Baysha, O. (2017), 'In the Name of National Security: Articulating Ethno-Political Struggles as Terrorism', *Journal of Multicultural Discourses*, 14 (4): 332–48.

Baysha, O. (2018), *Miscommunicating Social Change: Lessons from Russia and Ukraine*. Lanham, MD: Lexington.

Carpentier, N. (2017), *The Discursive-Material Knot: Cyprus in Conflict and Community Media Participation*. New York: Peter Lang.

Channel 24 (2015), 'Ukropy', 'vatniki' i ešë 30 novejših slov [Ukropi, Vatniki, and 30 Neologisms More], *Channel 24*, 11 April. Available online: https://24tv.ua/ru/ukropy_vatniki_i_eshhe_30_novejshih_slov_n564050 (accessed 22 October 2018).

Garrett, R. K., Dvir-Gvirsman, S., Jognson, B. K., Tsfati, Y., Neo, R. and Dal, A. (2014), 'Implications of Pro- and Counterattitudinal Information Exposure for Affective Polarization', *Human Communication Research*, 40 (3): 309–32.

Himelboim, I., McCreery, S. and Smith, M. (2013), 'Birds of a Feature Tweet Together: Integrating Network and Content Analysis to Examine Cross' Ideology Exposure on Twitter', *Journal of Computer-Mediated Communication*, 18 (2): 40–60.

Karpyak, O. (2014), 'Vata s ukropom: jazyk političeskih memov' [Vata and Ukrop: The Language of Political Memes], *BBC.com*, 8 August. Available online: http://www.bbc.com/ukrainen/ukraine_in_russian/2014/08/140808_ru_s_new:words (accessed 22 October 2018).

KIIS (2014), 'The Views and Opinions of South-Eastern Regions Residents of Ukraine', *Kiev International Institute of Sociology*, 14 April. http://www.kiis.com.ua/?lang=eng&cat=reports&id=302&y=2014&page=9 (accessed 22 October 2018).

Knobel, M. and Lankshear, C. (2007), *A New Literacies Sampler*. New York: Peter Lang.

Korrespondent, (2014, June 6), 'Kolorady vs Ukropy. Kakie slova podarili Ukraine Maidan I vojna' ['Kolorady and Ukropy: The Words Ukraine Has Been Presented by the Maidan and War'], *Ukraineindent.net. Korrespondent.net*, 6 June. Available online: https://korrespondent.net/ukraine/politics/3374179-kolorady-vs-ukropy-kakye-slova-podaryly-ukrayne-maidan-y-voina (accessed 22 October 2018).

Laclau, E. (2014), *The Rhetorical Foundations of Society*. New York: Verso.

Laclau, E. and Mouffe, C. (1985), *Hegemony and Socialist Strategy: Towards a Radical Democratic Politics*. London, UK: Verso.

Lyabina, A. (2014), 'Novyj russko-ukrainskij clovar': 10 neologizmov Postmajdana' ['New Russian-Ukrainian Dictionary: 10 Neologisms of the Post-Maidan'], *Kp.ru*, 21 July. Available online: https://www.kp.ru/daily/26258.5/3137433/ (accessed 22 October 2018).

Mautner, G. (2008), 'Analyzing Newspaper, Magazines and Other Print Media', in R. Wodak and M. Krzyzanowski (eds), *Qualitative Discourse Analysis in the Social Sciences*, 30–53. New York, NY: Palgrave Macmillan.

McCarthy, T. (2010), *Race, Empire, and the Idea of Human Development*. Cambridge, MA: Cambridge University Press.

Mouffe, C. (2013), *Agonistics: Thinking the World Politically*. London and New York: Verso.

Noel, H. and Nyhan, B. (2011), 'The "Unfriending" Problem: The Consequences of Homophily in Friendship Retention for Causal Estimates of Social Influence', *Social Networks*, 33 (3): 211–18.

Pariser, E. (2011). *The Filter Bubble: What the Internet Is Hiding from You*. New York: Penguin Press.
Radio Liberty. (2013). 'From Maidan to Berkut: A Ukraine Protest Glossary', *Radio Liberty*, 4 December. Available online: https://www.rferl.org/a/ukraine-protest-glossary-euromaydan/25190085.html (accessed 22 October 2018).
Radio Liberty (2014), 'What's Orange and Black and Bugging Ukraine?' *Radio Liberty*, 28 April. Available online: https://www.rferl.org/a/ukraine-colorado-beetle-separatists/25365793.html (accessed 22 October 2018).
Schwarz, O. and Shani, G. (2016), 'Culture in Mediated Interaction: Political Defriending on Facebook and the Limits of Networked Individualism', *American Journal of Cultural Sociology*, 4 (3): 385–421.
Shomova, S. (2019), 'Vybory prezidenta RF – 2018 v zerkale memov: novyje realii političeskoj kommunikativistiki' ['Russia's Presidential Elections 2018 in the Mirror of Mems: New Realities of Political Communication'], *Polis: Journal of Political Studies*, 1 (3): 157–73.
StopFake. (2015), 'The Chronology of Events in Odessa, May2', *StopFake.org*, 4 May. Available online: https://www.stopfake.org/hronologiya-sobytij-2-maya-v-odesse-chast-2/ (accessed 22 October 2018).
Stroud, N. J. (2010), 'Polarization and Partisan Selective Exposure', *Journal of Communication*, 60 (3): 536–76.
Sutyagin, I. (2015), 'Russian Forces in Ukraine', Royal United Services Institute, March. Available online: https://rusi.org/sites/default/files/201503_bp_russian_forces_in_ukraine.pdf (accessed 22 October 2018).
Taylor, C. (1992), *Sources of the Self: The Making of the Modern Identity*. Cambridge, MA: Harvard University Press.
UN News. (2017), 'Conflict in Ukraine Enters Fourth Year "with No End in Sight" – UN Report', *News.un.org*, 13 June. Available online: https://news.un.org/en/story/2017/06/559322-conflict-ukraine-enters-fourth-year-no-end-sight-un-report (accessed 22 October 2018).
UN OHCHR (2014), 'Report on the Human Rights Situation in Ukraine', Office of the United Nations High Commissioner for Human Rights, 15 June. Available online: https://www.ohchr.org/Documents/Countries/UA/HRMMUReport15June2014.pdf (accessed 22 October 2018).
UN OHCHR (2017), 'Report on the Human Rights Situation in Ukraine. 16 August to 15 November 2017', Office of the United Nations High Commissioner for Human Rights, 12 December. Available online: http://www.ohchr.org/Documents/Countries/UA/UAReport20th_EN.pdf (accessed 22 October 2018).
Yus, F. (2018), 'Identity-Related Issues in Meme Communication', *Internet Pragmatics*, 1 (1): 113–33.
ZN, UA (2014), 'Mneni â I vzglâdy ž itelej Ûgo-Vostoka Ukrainy' [Opinions and Views of the Citizens of the Southeastern Regions of Ukraine], *ZN, UA*, 18 April. Available online: http://zn.ua/UKRAINE/mneniya-i-vzglyady-zhiteley-yugo-vostoka-ukrainy-aprel-2014-143598_.html (accessed 22 October 2018).

6

The Ukrainian nation – stepmother, younger sister or stillborn baby?

Evidence from Russian TV debates and related political sources (2013–15)

Daniel Weiss

1 Introduction

The present study is part of a larger research project entitled 'The Ukraine conflict as a battlefield of conflicting legitimization discourses' (Ukraine conflict 2014), which analysed data from four languages (Ukrainian, Russian, Polish and Czech) and four discourse types (government statements, parliamentary and TV debates, and selected newspaper articles). [The background was provided by the main political events that framed the beginning of the conflict: the uprising on the Maidan in Kiev (21 November 2013 – 21 February2014), Ukraine's president Yanukovich's flight to Russia, the seize of power by a transitional government (26 February), ensued by the Russian infiltration and final annexation of the Crimea (18 March), and the outburst of the separatist war in the south-eastern Donbass region.] The Ukrainian data encompassed excerpts in Ukrainian and Russian, irrespective of the speaker's political affiliation.

In terms of methodology, data coverage, object languages and research goals, the present study has a much more limited scope than the larger research project: it discusses the various metaphorical mappings of forty-six tokens (occurrences) of family metaphors referring to Ukraine, stemming from Russian TV debates and including six examples from government statements, parliamentary debates and the press, and relates them to eighteen other (mainly Ukrainian) metaphors revealing a similar cognitive frame. Taken together, the examples to be analysed represent but a small fraction of the sample of metaphors extracted from all types of data, which numbered approximately 600.

Section 2 discusses methodological aspects, especially those related to the distinction of fresh (novel) and conventional metaphors. To demonstrate this, one family metaphor out of the sample will be presented that illustrates the functioning of a novel metaphorical blend in context. This is intended to provide a better assessment of the discursive embedding of different types of metaphors. Section 3 is devoted to the conceptualization of Ukraine by conventional family metaphors, which play a prominent role in the conflict and reveal an especially inconsistent pattern of mappings. This is a predominantly Russian issue, which sheds new light on the impact of a deeply entrenched frame (Section 4). The Ukrainian side is represented by voices anticipating or resuming elements of this frame (Section 5).

2 Methodology

The present study adopts the Conceptual Metaphor Theory in its discourse-centred (Kövecses 2009, 2014, 2015; Musolff 2000, 2004, 2017) version; the latter also includes Critical Metaphor Analysis (Charteris-Black 2004, 2011, 2014). The use of metaphors in natural discourse also calls for a systematic account of contextual factors (Kövecses 2015). In this chapter, I will focus on the impact of the immediate linguistic context (2015: 110 ff.); the broader cultural context will only be exemplified by historical reminiscences, mainly Soviet propagandist imagery.

Since my examples also include overt comparisons and similes (see 2, 4, 8, 9 and 14) introduced by markers like *as, similar to, reminiscent of* and so on, the relation between comparisons and metaphors calls for a more thorough account. The traditional, but debatable, understanding of metaphors as abbreviated comparisons initiated by Quintilian has been somewhat downgraded in Conceptual Metaphor Theory. Still, the terms *similarity* and *analogy* have not been banned from its metalanguage. To mention but a few key formulations: the subtitle of Musolff 2004 is 'Analogical Reasoning in Debates about Europe', Kövecses (2005: 265) states that 'The phenomenon of analogy is a crucial part of our Metaphorical thinking', and the same author opposes the 'as if-connection' for metaphors to the 'through-connection' for metonymies (cf. Kövecses 2014: 20). More precisely, Charteris-Black (2014: 171) writes: 'There is some psycholinguistic evidence that when metaphors are first introduced they are processed by means of comparison.' This refers to Bowdle and Gentner (2007), who posit 'a shift in mode of mapping from comparison to categorization'. Therefore, metaphors were included into a new hyper-category under the umbrella term 'analogical reasoning'. This hyper-category (for details see Weiss 2017: 471–84; 2018: 332–41) embraces explicit comparisons, metaphors based on analogy and analogies conveyed indirectly by quotations (Weiss 2016).

My investigation was based on a sample of about 600 metaphors from all four languages related to the Ukraine conflict and dating from November 2013 to November 2015.[1] The automatic 'MIP' developed by the *Pragglejaz* group was not employed since it had no Ukrainian and Czech application, and it provided rather poor results even in its Russian version (Zaychenko 2011): due to its wide scope, it yields too many trivial or even dead metaphors and at the same time it cannot cope with innovative metaphors. Thus, it did not prove appropriate for the specific purpose of my project, and all metaphors were extracted manually. Establishing their exact number seemed rather contestable since, as Charteris-Black 2015: 170 puts it, 'If one were to ask ten metaphor scholars to count the metaphors in a text, they would probably arrive at ten different answers'. The examples were mainly collected according to their *degree of conventionality*: the more innovative they looked, the easier they found their way into the collection. This does, however, not hold for family metaphors, which were collected because of their mutual inconsistency rather than their novelty.

Although my approach to metaphors was not quantitative, it was tempting to test the procedure proposed by Charteris-Black (2015: 179), which runs as follows:

> 'if a metaphor occurs fewer than five times in a sample of 100 corpus entries it is a candidate for being a novel metaphor; when more than the half of the entries have a metaphoric sense it is an entrenched metaphor. Conventional metaphors are likely to be those that occur somewhere between 5 and 50 times in a sample of 100 corpus entries.[2]

My sample of Russian TV excerpts yields all three types distinguished by Charteris-Black. However, the main topic of the present study is more specific in that all family metaphors except one in my sample are conventional. How to assess the degree of novelty of a fresh metaphorical collocation will therefore be illustrated by this unique example. It stems from one of the most popular Russian TV debates:[3]

(1) Да Тимошенко из того же клана. Они все из одного клана. Они все были вот такие *ласковые дидяти, присосавшиеся к материнской газовой сиське*.

But [Julija] Timoshenko is from the same clan. They are all from the same clan. They were such tender *little babies, suckling mother's gas boob*.

V. Solovyov, *Poedinok*, 12 December 2013[4]

The economic dependency on the Russian mother is captured in a highly creative ironic blend (Fauconnier and Turner 2002) of source (*babies, suckling* and *mother's boob*) and target (*gas*) components. The string *gazovaâ sis'ka* or 'gas boob' is not attested in the Basic corpus of the Russian National Corpus (RNC), which currently encompasses more than 209 Mio tokens, nor in the Press subcorpus (over 113 Mio tokens); its novelty is thus beyond any doubt, and it seems a fair guess that even if there was a special corpus of Russian political texts available, as was the case in Charteris-Black 2015 (see earlier), this would not change the picture.

Example 1 serves to illustrate the creative use of metaphors in Russian televised debates. Against this background, most family metaphors to be analysed now look considerably less impressive. Yet as will be shown, they are intriguing in other respects.

3 Family metaphors: the inventory

In Weiss (2019), I investigated one target domain ('approaching danger') by mapping it on different source domains. This section follows the reverse procedure: it is devoted to the single source domain 'family' mapped on different target meanings.[5] The concept of 'family' as a model for nation states is a particularly well-explored field.

Besides Lakoff's often-questioned distinction of the Strict Father model and Nurturant Parent model characterizing the US Republicans and Democrats, respectively (cf. Cienki 2008), a rich source of family metaphors is offered in the debate on the EU (Musolff 2000, 2004). Many of the findings to be formulated here will coincide with the findings of these previous studies, whereas others will only hold for the Ukrainian case. Moreover, unlike in Musolff's research, this is a one-sided affair: it is all about how Russian sources conceptualize Ukraine, and not vice versa. The explanation is evident: Ukraine simply no longer wants to belong to this family, those to whom the family ties were dear having split off and created the separatist People Republics of Donetsk and Luhansk.

As will be shown in this section, the family metaphors in my sample do by no means follow a consistent pattern of kinship relations; this is perfectly in line with said studies. In particular, in a sample of thirty-five metaphorical expressions (lexemes-types and collocations) and forty-six tokens (occurences), I have come across no less than seventeen different roles assigned to Ukraine or Ukrainians within the family concept. The list contains the following items: *marital couple, spouse, family, relative, mother, stepmother, child, younger sister, elder sister, younger brother, brother, grandchild, stepchild, baby, embryo, foetus* and *stillborn baby*.[6] To this list may be added the *wife*, which was involved in the divorce metaphor related to the collapse of Soviet Union in 1991.[7] As can easily be seen, the first two roles are 'self-sufficient' in that they only target Ukraine, whereas the remaining ones are relational terms that presuppose the existence of at least one other member of the same family, thus opposing Ukraine to political entities such as Russia, EU or separatists. Another general observation concerns the distribution of sexes: the (*younger*) *brother* is the only metaphor marked as male.

3.1 Siblings

The first item from the aforementioned list to be analysed is the *younger sister*. The attribute *younger* is historically motivated: the rarely used term *Ukraina* had come to denote the own steppe frontier in Polish and Russian sources from the Middle Ages on, but as a formally autonomous and stable political and geographical entity, Ukraine came into being only with the formation of the Soviet Union. But there is more to the *younger sister*: this role is usually associated with smaller and presumably weaker female beings, as the following fragment of a newspaper report shows:

(2) 'В представлении наших сограждан отношения Росии и Украины не равновесны, последняя воспринимается как младшая сестра', – отметил Григорий Кертман.

'In the view of our fellow citizens, the Russian-Ukrainian relations are not of equal weight, the latter is perceived *as the younger sister*', G. Kertman said.

Komersant, Rossiânam ne nravitsâ evropejskij vybor Ukrainy,
10 December 2014

The connotation of smallness is reminiscent of the term *Malorossija* 'Little Russia',[8] which served as the official denotation of Ukraine under the Tsarist rule, when the existence of a separate Ukrainian nation and language were denied. Even today, this former discrimination plays an important role in Ukrainian political discourse.

On the other hand, the weakness of the *younger sister* may also trigger protective feelings. The same holds true for the *elder sister* (one occurrence), as the following quotation from the Russian TV show *Poedinok* shows:

> (3) Украина для России – *это старшая сестра*. Сейчас она в очень трудном состоянии. Мы не можем не думать и не переживать о том, что сейчас происходит в Киеве. (01:44) Я считаю, что Россия и Украина – это *разделённая нация, разделённый народ*. Мы – одно целое ... И для нас Киев и Украина – это больше, чем Косово для Сербии. (39:30)
>
> For Russia, Ukraine is *the elder sister*. Right now, she is in a difficult condition. We cannot but think about and suffer from what is going on in Kiev [....] I think that Russia and Ukraine are *a divided nation, a divided people. We are one whole* ... . And to us, Kiev and Ukraine mean more than Kosovo to Serbia.
>
> D. Kiseliov, *Poedinok. Maidan!* (Kiseliov and Gudkov), 24 January 2014

What seems noteworthy here is the idea of compassion with the suffering elder sister. But how can the same entity sometimes be conceived as the younger and sometimes as the elder sister? Again, history offers a plausible explanation. The Serbian parallel at the end helps motivate the choice of the metaphor at the beginning of the quote: historically, the Kievan *Rus'* was the cradle of Russian statehood in the Middle Ages – hence Russia's *elder sister*. The parallel to Kosovo alludes to the current diplomatic conflict about the status of this former Serbian province, which is still considered part of the Serbian territory by Serbian authorities. However, the majority of the Russian audience was presumably aware of the historical background: similar to the Kievan Rus' in relation to Russia, Kosovo was (one of) the medieval centre(s) of the Serbian empire, and the defeat on the Kosovo Pole against the Ottoman forces is closely associated with the loss of Serbian independence in 1389.

To be precise, this family metaphor does not point to Ukrainian history, but to the origins of Russia.[9] In view of this genealogy, one would therefore rather expect the *mother* metaphor. This would be perfectly in line with the legend of the foundation of Kiev in 882 in the first Russian chronicle, where we read: 'And Oleg sat down, ruling in Kiev, and Oleg said: "Let it be the mother of Russian cities"'. Not accidentally, Putin in his address to the Federal Assembly after the annexation of the Crimea on 18 March 2014[10] refers to this source: '*Kiev – mat' gorodov russkih. Drevnââ Rus' – èto naš obšij istok*' ('Kiev is the mother of the Russian towns. The old Rus' is our common origin'). As for Kiseliov's claim that Russians and Ukrainians are one nation, this is unique in my TV corpus, but in Putin's aforementioned address we find a similar formulation: '*my faktičeski odin narod [...] my vse ravno ne smožem drug bez druga*' (In fact, we are one nation [...] we cannot do without each other). The ominous political conclusions to be drawn from this formulation cannot be discussed here.

The *younger brother* could actually evoke similar feelings. In reality, this term seems to carry contradictory connotations, as is attested in the next two examples. In the first one, a political scientist participating in a TV show ironically characterizes the Russian attitude towards Ukraine as a demand for unconditioned obedience:

(4) Украина *как младший брат* должна сдаться: немедленно отступить и *поднять лапки*, а этого не произошло, потому что работает совершенно другая логика.

Ukraine has to surrender like a *smaller brother*: retreat right on the spot and *give paw*, but this did not happen since there is a completely different logic at work.

D. Oreshkin, *Licom k Sobytiû*, 5 September 2014[11]

Interestingly, this younger brother behaves more like a well-educated dog – a hint that in the speaker's view Russia's stance towards Ukraine is morally doubtful. According to the other view, the younger brother strives to get rid of the family pressure:

(5) Я должен сказать, что история показывает, что на Украине всегда был этот *комплекс младшего брата* и им всегда нужно было отталкиваться, как бы, от России, противостоять ей, чтобы достичь собственной идентичности. Это было в 17 году, и они немцев принимали с радостью, лишь бы избавиться от Москвы.

I must say that history shows that in Ukraine there always existed that *complex of the younger brother* and they always wanted to take their distance from Russia, oppose it, to achieve an own identity. This was the case in 1917, and they were happy when the Germans came, just to get rid of Moscow. (43:24)

Ju. Petrov, *Voskresnyj večer s Vl. Solov'evym: Pravyj sektor idet v nastuplenie*, 20 March 2014

The behaviour ascribed to this male youth contrasts sharply with the allegedly expected behaviour in Example 4. The attitude described in Example 5 fits better into the general cultural model of male adolescents. This seems to be the reason for the choice of the metaphor in Example 5 and explains the deviation from the rule that family metaphors referring to Ukraine exclude male sex.

There was another tradition that held the *brother* metaphor in great esteem: in Soviet rhetoric, all countries belonging to the Soviet camp carried the epithet *brotherly*. After the implosion of the communist system, this terminology ceased to work, but Ukraine was still conceived of as a brotherly nation. This is illustrated by the Russian UN representative V. Churkin's utterance on 4 March 2014:

(6) Если для отдельных западных политиков Украина – территория геополитической игры, то для нас она *братская страна*, с которой мы связаны общей многовековой историей.

If for some western politicians Ukraine is [only] a territory for a geopolitical game, for us it is a *brotherly country*, with which we are linked by a common century-old history.

This time, the *brother* stands for emotional closeness. Unlike real family relations, this relation is not symmetric: in our corpus, Ukrainians never refer to Russians as their brothers.[12] If such utterances do occur, they express the feelings of separatists. The participants of a spontaneous meeting on the Nakhimov Square in Sevastopol' on 28 February 2014 are reported to have chanted: *My ne ânki, my slavâne, naši brat'â –Rossiâne* 'we are not Yankees, we are Slavs,[13] *our brothers* are the Russians'. Loyal Ukrainian politicians react to this imagery with repulsion. V. Ulyachenko commented on Putin's statement that Ukraine remains a *brotherly nation* sarcastically: 'all this is similar to a spectacle of the type "coercion to love" [allusion to a book title, DW] – "coercion to brothership" [...] when an armed military convoy enters the scene' (20 October 2014). What comes to mind here is the intervention of the *brotherly* socialist countries in Czechoslovakia in August 1968. *Brotherly* is the only family metaphor that is resumed by Ukrainian sources in my sample.

3.2 Motherhood and birth models

Expanding the childhood frame, we eventually end up with Ukraine as a baby. Such was the role of today's Ukrainian elite in a non-distant past according to Example 1. Among the different concepts of motherhood (Lakoff 1987: 74–6), it is the birth model that was represented there. Another participant of a *Poyedinok* debate gives preference to the nurturance model by rendering the idea of economic dependency with the more abstract 'food' metaphor:

(7) Слушайте, мы 15 лет *кормили* Украину [....] Мы *кормили* эту страну, чтобы она не провалилась в тартары. и именно на наших деньгах выросла вся современная политическая элита Украины.

Listen, we *fed* Ukraine for fifteen years [....] We *fed* this country to prevent it from falling into Tartarus, and Ukraine's whole contemporary political elite has grown up with our money.

S. Mikheyev, *Poedinok*, 5 December 2013[14]

The general code of conduct, one is to infer, would require a more grateful behaviour of those who benefited from Russia's material support. The grown-up Ukraine commits an even more outrageous moral crime:

(8) То что я щас вижу, это для меня – это всё равно, что *предать* свою *родную мать и выбрать мачеху*, которая более богата и более успешна, возможно. Но *мать* останется всегда *матерью*.

What I see now is the same thing as if I *betrayed my own mother* und *chose a stepmother* who is perhaps *better off and more successful*. But a mother will always remain a mother.

A. Khirurg, *Poedinok*, 5 December 2013[15]

If we take it for granted that Russia still is the own mother, who could be the wealthy stepmother? This role is obviously assigned to the EU. Note that the negative connotation of the *stepmother* inherited from the folklore does not work here, since the (grown-up) stepchild selects her on its own. This child has presumably spent its whole childhood with its biological mother and then left her for purely financial reasons.

Leaving the Ukrainian subject for a while, it may be added that V. Zhirinovsky accuses the former Soviet satellite countries of the same immoral conduct in the following comparison (State Duma, 16 September 2014):

(9) а мы им ещё последние копейки отдавали, всех их подняли – и Будапешт, и Варшаву, и Берлин, и они же, *как неблагодарные дети, бросают своих, так сказать, престарелых родителей*!

and we gave them our last kopecks, we propped them all up: Budapest, Warsaw, Berlin, and [now] *they so to say abandon their aged parents like ungrateful children*!

Note the marker of figurative speech *so to say*; such markers are usually missing in my TV data.

Back to Ukraine, one wonders what the birth of this child may have looked like. The following quotation gives a merciless answer:

(10) Украина – это по сути искуственно созданное государство [....] в 17-м году зародился *зародыш* украинской государственности [....] этот *зародыш, эмбрион* развивался в Советской империи, в 91-м родилось на свет *мёртворождённое дитя*. И вот сейчас Америка пытается реанимировать долларовыми вливаниями, госпереворотами и так далее. Но ничего не помогает. Вот сейчас даже применили электрошок: войну на Донбассе. Но всё равно *дитя не дышит*. Запад рождает *выкидыши*. Но тем не менее на Украине *родился один крепкий, здоровый ребёнок*. И имя ему: *Новороссия*. У него: *русская мать, русский отец* и непременно счастливое русское будущее [...].

Ukraine is actually an artificially created state. [....] In 1917 the *embryo* of Ukrainian statehood was engendered. [....] This *foetus, embryo* developed in the Soviet empire. In 1991 the *stillborn child* entered the world. And now the US attempts to reanimate this child with dollar infusions and coups d'état. But nothing helps. Right now they even applied an electric shock therapy. Yet, the child does not breathe. The West produces only *miscarriages*. Nevertheless, a *healthy and strong baby* has been born in the Ukraine. Its name is *Novorossija*. It has *a Russian mother, a Russian father* and no doubt a happy Russian future. G. Kornilov

A. Gordon i G. Kornilov, *Politika s* Petrom *Tolstym*, 9 April 2015[16]

As can be seen, we are dealing with an extremely lengthy birth process. The embryo Ukraine originated in the October Revolution, but remained in the womb for the whole Soviet period. Obviously, this points to Ukraine's only apparent autonomy in Soviet times. Only after the breakdown of Soviet Union did Ukraine gain full independence, but it turned out to be non-viable despite all American attempts to reanimate it. Contrary to this, the new separatist *baby*, which is covered by the controversial label *Novorossia*,[17] is healthy because it was engendered by healthy Russian parents. Historically, this Russian genealogy is motivated insofar as the majority of the settlers in *Novorossia* were of Russian origin. Consequently, the Russian motherhood is now narrowed down to Eastern and Southern Ukraine, whereas the real biological mother of the rest turns out to be the Soviet Union. It may be noted that the family metaphors interact with disease/health imagery, and that the opposition 'healthy Russia vs. sick West' is lively reminiscent of Soviet propaganda.

In Ukrainian sources, the only trace of the birth metaphor points back to the Soviet past: '*23 roki pidrâd mi tâgnemo za soboû pupovinu Radâns'kogo Soûzu*' ['for twenty-three years we have been dragging behind us the umbilical cord of the Soviet Union'] (I. Eremeev, Verkhovna Rada, 16 September 2014).

The conviction that the independent Ukraine was doomed to failure right from the beginning is widespread in my data. Even the *miscarriage* metaphor may be found with other speakers, be it the political 'enfant terrible' V. Zhirinovsky, who intentionally embeds it in a paradox (Ukraine is dying but has never existed):

(11) Украина гибнет – мы сожалеем. Мы можем организовать поминки. Я заплачу за поминки. По случаю гибели 20-летнего государства «Украина», которого никогда не было. *Родился урод, выкидыш. Выкидыш – на помойку!*

Ukraine is dying – we are sorry. We can organize a funeral dinner. I'll pay for the funeral dinner on the occasion of the death of the twenty years old state 'Ukraine', which never existed. [instead] A *monster was born, a miscarriage.* [Let's throw] the *miscarriage* in the dump!

V. Zhirinovsky, *Poedinok*, 31 January 2014

Instead of being the new-born baby, Ukraine in other contexts gives birth herself, the outcome being a new political system. In Russian eyes, this is again a long-lasting and agonizing process:

(12) Ведь в сущности, если посмотреть на всё что происходит с некоторой дистанции, то это – *мучительный процесс родов*. 22 года Украина не может *родить* полноценное государство.

After all, if we watch on all this from a certain distance, this is an *agonizing birth process*. For 22 years, Ukraine *has not been able to give birth* to a full-fledged state.

L. Radzikhovsky, *U Korzuna*, 27 February 2014[18]

To complete this picture, Ukraine can even take the mother role and simultaneously act as a stepmother. As O. Caryov puts it: 'Ukraine must not be the mother for one part [of the population] and the stepmother for the other' (*Poedinok*, 27 February 2014).[19] The solution to this riddle lies in the identity of the speaker, who is one of the leaders of the separatist movement in Donetsk. From his perspective, Ukraine treats her children in the southeast as *stepchildren*.

What could be a possible common semantic denominator for the family metaphors encountered so far? To say the least, Ukraine is conceived of as a small, weak and passive or non-autonomous, if not inexistent, being; these features are shared by the concepts *younger sister, elder sister, younger brother (1), baby, embryo, foetus* and *stillborn baby*. In the remaining cases, Ukraine tries to act autonomously, but does so in a morally doubtful way as the ungrateful children betraying their mother, or its behaviour is evaluated with condescendence (*younger brother 2*).

3.3 Ukraine as a whole family

From Caryov's perspective (see earlier), Ukraine treats her children in the southeast as *stepchildren*. This manifests itself in an unfair distribution of goods and a disrespectful behaviour, cf.

> (13) Украина – это *семья*, в которой оказались рядом люди, в том числе не имеющие своей исторической близости, не являющиеся *прямыми родственниками*. […] В 91-м году все согласились с тем, что так как *семья* живёт, пусть она и живёт. Но затем прошло время и выяснилось, что какая-то часть живущих в *этой семье* людей ощущают себя не *родными людьми или внуками, а пасынками*, которым не достаётся еда, одежда, которых *мачеха* тиранит как *Золушку*, гоняет батогами. И тогда эти *дети* пришли за помощью к своим *кровным предкам*, к своим *родственникам*, являющимся по *крови*.
>
> Ukraine is a *family* that gathered people who historically had nothing in common, who were not *direct relatives* […] In 1991 all agreed that *this family* should continue to live this way. But then time passed and a part of those living in this family did not feel like *relatives* or *grandchildren* but *stepchildren* who had not enough food and clothes, whom the *stepmother* tyrannized like *Cinderella* and chased away with rods. And now these children asked their real *ancestors* for help, their *blood relatives*.
>
> Khinshteyn A., *Politika s* Petrom *Tolstym*,
4 September 2015[20]

This whole excerpt fits into the setting of 'government as parents' and 'citizens as children'. The first sentences seem to describe a sort of patchwork family. This is a fairly faithful picture of today's Ukraine, which is composed of six historically and culturally heterogeneous parts still in search of a common denominator. In other words, what is at stake here is the Ukrainian *nation-building*. But over the years, some of the family members become aware of their inferior status: they are treated unfairly by their *stepmother* (cf. Caryov's statement given earlier; presumably, they do not have a real mother). Obviously, these *stepchildren* refer to the inhabitants of the *Donbass* area with Russian roots. Not surprisingly, they address their *blood relatives* (however, probably not their ancestors!) living in Russia. Within this whole family conflict, one wonders whether there are any male parents around.

My last example repeats the mapping family <—> Ukraine, but focuses on the marital couple:

(14) Украина как государственный проект неуспешна. По одной причине: нация – разные граждане, разных регионов [....] Это *очень похоже на семью*, в которой *супруги* не договорились на старте: по каким принципам они живут и сейчас, грубо говоря, *один из супругов* говорит: ты будешь смотреть по телеку те программы, которые мне интересны, ты будешь делать то, что мне интересно и ты будешь жить так как я хочу. А *второй супруг* возмущается и говорит: стоп стоп стоп. если мы с тобой создаём союз, у нас должны быть равные права. […] только в том случае союз будет успешен.

Ukraine as a state project is not successful. For one reason: a nation – different citizens, of different regions [....] This is very *similar to a family*, in which the *spouses* have not made an agreement right from the start what will be the principles they will comply with, and now *one spouse* says: you will watch the TV shows I am interested in, you will do what I am interested in and you will live the way I want to. And the *other spouse* gets upset and says: stop, stop, stop! If we unite we should have equal rights […] Only in that case will our union succeed.

Bondarenko E., *Politika s* Petrom *Tolstym*, 4 September 2015

This simile is unique in that it carefully avoids the sex-specification of the grown-ups involved. Moreover, it is the only one to describe the conflict as a marital and not an intergenerational problem.

It may be noted that the annexation of Crimea is sometimes described as a new wedding. Thus, on the eve of the official ceremony, V. Zhirinovsky labels the referendum on the Crimea as *pomolvka* or 'betrothal', and the final act as *registraciâ v zagse* 'civil or registration at the registry office' (State Duma, 16 March 2014).

3.4 Family metaphors: discussion

It is not easy to summarize the findings of this section – the different mappings are too inconsistent, and the targets are too divergent: besides Ukraine or parts of it, both Russia and the EU are involved. Moreover, the family metaphors that were found target either human beings or personified nations, parts of nations, states and a supranational unity (EU).[21] At first glance, the overall impression seems to be: 'everything goes'. More precisely, the thirty-five metaphorical expressions types and the forty-six tokens show: 'A particular source domain may have several targets and a particular target domain may have several sources' (Kövecses 2009: 14). Thus, even reverse terms can denote the same entity, as in the case of *stepchild* and *stepmother,* which may both refer to Ukraine. Moreover, inconsistent metaphors may also be used in the same debate (cf. examples 10 and 13). In one case (the *younger brother,* Examples 4 and 5) the implications of the term were not self-evident and had to be spelled out in the context. In another case, the *older sister* replaced the expectable *mother* concept (Example 3). As for the different scenarios, they are almost never fully filled in. For instance, with relational terms such as *brother (of X)* or *stepchild (of X)*, the second argument X of the relation is often missing. This is completely in line with A. Musolff's (2004) observations on family metaphors.

On second glance, however, there is a systematic gap in this grid of metaphors: *male grown-ups do not exist*. In a number of empty slots, Russia could fill in this gap, but it is never explicitly mentioned as a father, brother or husband. As in the case of *Ukraina*, this may be partly due to the female grammatical gender of *Rossija* and *Rus'*, but more importantly, the deeply entrenched stereotype of *matuška Rus'* 'mother Russia' points to female sex. This has the undesirable implication that Ukraine and Russia would form a lesbian couple, which in the current climate of official homophobia creates an even more outrageous scenario than the former Soviet polygamy.

A second deviation from the usual patterns found in family metaphors concerns the emotional values: some metaphors, such as *still-born child, miscarriage, stepmother* or *Cinderella*, carry an inherent negative load; others occur in contexts that point to a disordered script, as in the case of the ungrateful children who betray their mother or the younger brother who should behave himself. All in all, what is most often missing or explicitly denied is the conceptual element of *love* characterizing the ideal family. Instead, we find the almost all-pervading frame of 'Ukraine is an inferior, weak and non-autonomous being'. The only two exceptions are Examples 13 and 14, where Ukraine herself is conceptualized as a whole family, but this family is torn apart by dissent and injustice.

4 The overarching cognitive frame

How does all this fit into the general picture of metaphorically expressed Russian attitudes towards Ukraine? If we leave aside those metaphors whose source domain is the family itself (Examples 13 and 14), we find many other metaphors pointing to the same direction as the family metaphors illustrated in Section 3, notably those expressing weakness and lack of autonomy. In Russian televised debates, Ukraine is described as a *marionette*, a *pawn offer*, *cannon fodder* and a *bargaining chip*, the active part always being played by the United States.[22] There are also voices that denounce Ukraine as a *phantom* or simply *inexistent*, which is compatible with the *miscarriage* metaphors cited earlier. According to former Ukrainian president L. Kravchuk (28 February 2014), Putin himself once pronounced the statement that Ukraine is not 'a natural state and has no historical future (*sic*!)'. In the same vein, Ukraine together with its economy is described as a zero and a phantom in the following extract, the reason being its unstable borders and governments:

(15) Мы говорим о том, что Украинское Государство собирается реформировать экономику. Здесь есть сразу два 'ноля': первый – это Украинское Государство, а второй – это украинская экономика [....] Украинское Государство с политической точки зрения является *фантомом*: мы не знаем, где пройдёт линия фронта завтра, где она пройдёт послезавтра и кто в Киеве кого начнет свергать через неделю.

We are talking about the Ukrainian preparations to reform its economy. Here there are two '*zeroes*': the first is the Ukrainian state, the second the Ukrainian economy [....] From a political perspective, the Ukrainian state is a *phantom*: we don't know where the front line will lie tomorrow, where the day after tomorrow and who will subvert whom in Kiev in a week.

P. Ishchenko, *Pravo golosa*, 10 October 2014[23]

Thus, there is sufficient evidence that we have come across a general *frame* (in the sense of Critical Discourse Theory; cf. Wehling 2016 and Musolff 2019): the dominant Russian perception of Ukraine is that of an inferior, weak and passive entity that either needs help or may be freely bent to one's own will. This frame seriously aggravates the conflict, since it prevents Russia from taking a fresh view of recent developments. How powerful such a frame may be is convincingly shown in A. Musolff's analysis of the impact of the negatively connotated metaphor 'at the heart of Europe' and its derivatives in the Brexit campaign (Musolff 2017).

5 Ukrainian voices

It comes as no surprise that this frame is echoed by Ukrainian stakeholders. Among the pro-Russian orientation under Yanukovich's's rule, we find replicas of Russian metaphors with the same political interpretation: for example, the *bargaining chip* also appears in a statement by the Ukrainian Minister of Foreign Affairs.

(16) Впрочем, как минимум одна делегация была готова подписаться почти под каждым словом господина Лаврова – ее возглавлял и. о. министра иностранных дел Украины Леонид Кожара. Он [...] сказал, что Киев не хочет быть '*разменной монетой* в геополитических играх'.

At least one delegation was ready to sign almost every word said by Mr. Lavrov: it was headed by the Ukrainian minister of foreign Affairs Leonid Kožara. He said that Kiev doesn't want to be the '*bargaining* chip in geopolitical games'.

Komersant, *Ukraincev potoropili v budušee*, 3 February 2014

The opponents of the pro-Russian orientation utilize the same imagery in two ways: on the one hand, they re-direct the metaphors at pro-Russian Ukrainian politicians by denouncing the 'terrorists' in the Donbass region, for example, as Russian *marionettes*:

(17) Перебіг антитерористичної операції підтверджує, що з терористами ні про що домовлятися не можна, тим більше, вони – *шестерки*, вони *маріонетки російські*.

The development of the antiterrorist operation[24] confirms that you can't find an agreement with terrorists, all the more so as they are *gofers*, they are *Russian marionettes*.

O. Lyashko, Verkhovna Rada, 4 July 2014

P. Poroshenko also associates this group with Russia: '*najmanci ta jihnij "**staršij brat**"* ('hirelings and their "*elder brother*"'). Here, the *younger brother* is not only obedient (Example 4) but also a will-less tool in the hands of his elder sibling.

On the other hand, anti-Russian politicians also describe Ukraine's treatment by Russia in similar terms. Especially after Yanukovich's decline to sign the Association Treaty with the EU, Ukrainian right-wing politicians coined new metaphors stressing Ukraine's inferior status towards Russia. For instance, O. Tyahnybok comments on Ukraine's refusal to sign the Association Treaty with the EU as follows:

(18) Всі в Європі шоковані пропозицією української влади, що виявляється тепер всі перемови з європейськими країнами будуть вестися виключно разом з Росією. Україна не стає, виявляється, вже суверенною державою, бо ми йдемо на будь-які перемовини з Європою тільки з *нашим суфлером*, з *хазяїном*, який тепер буде управляти і керувати ...

Everybody in Europe is shocked by the Ukrainian authorities' proposal; as it turns out now, all negotiations with European countries will be carried out only together with Russia. Ukraine is no longer a sovereign state, from now on we will negotiate with Europe only together with *our prompter, our boss*, who will now rule and direct ...

O. Tyahnybok, *ShusterLive*, 29 November 2013

The *prompter* relates to the same source domain 'theatre' as the *marionette* metaphor, the main difference being that this time it is not the Americans but the Russians that pull the strings. The marionette metaphor itself is activated from the retrospective by another right-wing politician and targeted at the former president:

(19) Действительно, россияне рассматривали власть Януковича как *марионеточную*, призванную обеспечить все их «*хотелки*», но все равно к захвату Крыма они готовились заранее.

Indeed, the Russians considered Yanukovich's government a *marionette* government that should satisfy their whole '*wishlist*' but nevertheless they prepared themselves for the occupation of the Crimea in advance.

O. Turchinov, *Livij bereg*, 27 June 2014[25]

In the next example, Yanukovich's loss of importance for Putin engenders two new metaphors related to the source domain 'play':

(20) Янукович сегодня никто. И для Владимира Владимировича Путина. Потому что *отыграна карта*. Это уже проблема Владимира Ввладимировича, куда ж его девать, ту *игрушку, которую он придумал* ...

Yanukovich is a nobody today. Also for Vladimir Vladimirovich Putin. Because he is a *card placed*. It is Vladimir Vladimirovich's problem where to put him, that *toy which he created*.

D. Zhvaniya, *ShusterLive*, 28 February 2014

Ukraine's subordination is also rendered by metaphors expressing the idea more directly in spatial terms ('up' is the lord, 'down' is the servant). Thus, Ukraine may be conceptualized as a doormat on which Russians clean their shoes (Weiss 2020: 20); the same metaphor targets president Yanukovich's (then still on duty) treatment by the Russian government (L. Kravchuk, *ShusterLive*, January 20, 2014). A no less humiliating posture is depicted in Russia's alleged wish to make Ukraine crawl on its knees to the enemy (Weiss 2020: 20). This imagery is refuted as illusionary in the next quotation:

(21) В тоталитарных режимах всегда так: кого-то уничтожить, кого-то – *поставить на колени*. Но Украину они *поставить на колени* не смогли.

Totalitarian regimes always act like this: to destroy some people and *bring others to their knees*. But Ukraine they *could not bring to its knees*.

O. Turchinov, *Lìvij béreg*, 27 June 2014

Note that the same posture verb *kneel* (*stoât' na kolenâh*) has also been applied to Russia itself: after the annexation of the Crimea, Putin was praised because he *podnâl Rossiû s kolen* 'raised Russia up [lit. from its knees]', a phrase which soon went viral in the social media.

In sum, in my data, Ukrainian politicians use a similar imagery to their Russian counterparts (except family metaphors) to conceptualize the idea of passive stance and subordination. Their targets depend on their political affiliation. Pro-Russian partisans share the official Russian view that Ukraine is manipulated by the West. In contrast, anti-Russian politicians see the separatists as Russian marionettes, and they replace the West by Russia when accusing the latter of manipulating Yanukovich's government and still adhering to the same dominant attitude after his fall. This political repartition does not come as a surprise, but the use of the same stock of conventional metaphors on both sides seems remarkable. However, the phenomenon that metaphors may mirror each other in an argument between two conflicting parties is also attested elsewhere: A. Musolff's (2000) contrastive analysis of metaphors in the debate about the future of the EU offers ample evidence. The lack of mirrored family metaphors on the Ukrainian side thus remains an exception.

This said, it seems striking that there does not emerge any powerful competing frame that would emphasize Ukraine's independence and self-reliance. This one-sided situation is reminiscent of the Brexit campaign in the United Kingdom as described in Musolff (2019), where only the Brexiteers succeeded in framing their objective in an efficient imagery. By contrast, the contrast of the Strict Father model vs the Nurturant Parent model in US politics provides two (equally?) powerful metaphorical frames that 'represent diametrically opposed worldviews that inform the fundamental divide in US political cultures' (2019: 2).

6 Concluding remarks

To my knowledge, the inconsistent mappings found in family metaphors have never been commented upon by the participants of TV shows or other recipients, although some of them occurred in the same debate. Even if the audience were aware of different conceptualizations, they felt no need to intervene. Yet there is also a deeper lying reason that licenses such a tolerant stance: unlike explicit argumentation, metaphorical argumentation does not have to be logically consistent. The concept of similarity, on which metaphors are finally based, is so all-embracing that with sufficient imagination we will nearly always find a common aspect linking a source X and a target Y. This is why Ukraine may be considered a stepmother in one respect and a stillborn baby in another.

Nevertheless, the question arises, what determines the *persuasive force* of the given metaphor in the given context? There seem to be two contradicting answers to this. For one part of the audience, it should fit into some widely accepted general frame, such as the one illustrated in Section 4. The other part will appreciate the unexpected effects of fresh and innovative metaphors that challenge our mind by launching new ideas, opening new perspectives, shedding new light on established truths or at least denigrating the opponent in a new way, as was the case of Example 1.

Taken all in all, Ukraine's relation to Russia is a thread that permeates the whole Ukrainian conflict. Due to Russia's unwillingness to accept Ukraine as a full-fledged independent nation, Ukraine has to define its national identity predominantly in terms of its relation to Russia, much more so as to the West. The Ukrainian stance is thus rather reactive than proactive: instead of describing themselves metaphorically, Ukrainians refer to or anticipate the Russian view on them. Moreover, the new-born state is now forced to defend its territorial integrity against its former dominator, with whom it is linked with numerous historical and ethnic ties, and who has not yet wholeheartedly accepted the separation.

Ukraine's own nation-building is addressed only in one simile on Russian TV (14) but never in my Ukrainian data. This stance seems comprehensible, since when facing an existential threat, one attaches more importance to one's unity than to one's diversity. However, it should be born in mind that this study covers only the initial period of the conflict. After five years of an enduring impasse, the Ukrainian debate on the roots and perspectives of the conflict has most likely become more differentiated and the figurative language more diversified. Yet the idea of Ukraine's inferiority still seems to be deeply entrenched, and it recurs in other domains: in a study devoted to the conceptualization of Ukraine-EU relations in the Ukrainian press of the first half of 2016 (Zhabotynska 2018), the author presents evidence that Ukraine is far more frequently seen as a subordinate of the EU (seventy-nine metaphors), whereas the view of the EU and Ukraine as politically and economically equal partners is represented by only seventeen metaphors (their political affiliation is not specified).

Notes

1 Out of this set, 190 examples taken from Russian TV debates stem from an unpublished MA thesis (Brunner 2015), which covers the period up to November 2015 and hence does not fully coincide with the temporal limit (spring 2015) of the project.
2 The problems related to the selection of a reference corpus in Charteris-Black's quantitative approach are discussed in Weiss 2019.

3   For an overview of the relevant political talk shows on the most influential TV channels and their ratings in the period under discussion, see Dolgova 2015.
4   http://russia.tv/video/show/brand_id/3963/episode_id/933610/video_id/931964.
5   For a general overview of possible metaphorizations of Slavic family terms, see Hill 2013.
6   This list is by no means exhaustive. A presentation given by H. B. Meyer at a conference in Dresden on January 25, 2019 comprised the following additional items: *prijomnaja mat'* 'adoptive mother', *bludnyj syn* 'lost son', *bludnaja mat'* 'lost mother' (a wordplay), *čado* 'offspring, (beloved) child'.
7   Nobody seems to have taken notice of the morally doubtful implications of this image: since fourteen republics split off from Russia, the Soviet Union must have been based on an extremely polygamous family.
8   The corresponding ethnonym *malorossy* is opposed to *velikorossy* (great Russians), which in Lenin's writings came to denigrate Russian great-power chauvinists.
9   This narrative is currently questioned by Ukrainian historians, who treat this period as the beginning of Ukrainian statehood despite the anachronistic use of the geographic term *Ukraina*.
10 http://kremlin.ru/events/president/news/20603.
11 https://www.youtube.com/watch?v=sgXVnwyFvLU.
12 For a thorough scrutiny of the brother metaphor and its diverse interpretations in different Russian and Ukrainian genres (but excluding TV data), see A'Beckett (2017).
13 As our quantitative contrastive analysis of keywords has shown, the root *slavân-* appears exclusively in Russian sources.
14 http://russia.tv/video/show/brand_id/3963/episode_id/933610/video_id/931964.
15 http://russia.tv/video/show/brand_id/3963/episode_id/933610/video_id/931964.
16 http://www.1tv.ru/video_archive/projects/tolstoy/p91294.
17 This term can be traced back to the time of the Russian seizure of the Ukrainian steppe at the end of the 18th century and in 2014 became a non-official designation of all Ukrainian territories claimed by separatists.
18 http://www.1tv.ru/video_archive/projects/tolstoy/p91294.
19 http://russia.tv/video/show/brand_id/3963/episode_id/970423/.
20 http://www.1tv.ru/video_archive/projects/tolstoy/p91294.
21 Metaphors such as *umbilical cord*, which only entail a family relation, were not included in the count.
22 These examples are taken from Brunner 2015. Due to the lack of space, they are not presented in context here.
23 https://www.youtube.com/watch?v=a3UdxG2ruPU.
24 This was the official Ukrainian term for what the Russian side described as civil war ongoing in the Donbass, see Weiss (2018: 342–4).
25 http://lb.ua/news/2014/06/27/271204_aleksandr_turchinov_pri_vtorzhenii.html.

References

A'Beckett, L. (2017), 'Fragmentation of the Discourse Community through the Lens of Metaphor Analysis: A Case Study of RUSSIANS AND UKRAINIANS ARE BROTHERS', in K. Broś and G. Kowalski (eds), *Discourse Studies – Ways and Crossroads*, 365–86. Frankfurt-Bern: Peter Lang.

Bowdle, B. and Gentner, D. (2005), 'The Career of Metaphor', *Psychological Review*, 112 (1): 193–216.

Brunner, G. (2015), *Metapherngebrauch in russischen Fernseh-Debatten zur Ukraine-Krise* Master thesis, Universität Zürich, unpubl.

Charteris-Black, J. (2004), *Corpus Approaches to Critical Metaphor Analysis*. Basingstoke: Palgrave Macmillan.

Charteris-Black, J. (2011), *Politicians and Rhetoric. The Persuasive Power of Metaphor*. Basingstoke: Palgrave Macmillan.

Charteris-Black, J. (2014), *Analysing Political Speeches: Rhetoric, Discourse and Metaphor*. Basingstoke: Palgrave Macmillan.

Cienki, A. (2008), 'The Application of Conceptual Metaphor Theory to Political Discourse: Methodological Questions and Some Possible Solution', in T. Carver and J. Pikalo (eds), *Political Language and Metaphor. Interpreting and Changing the World*, 241–56. London: Routledge.

Dolgova, J. I. (2015), 'Fenomen populârnosti obŝestvenno-političeskih tok-šou na rossijskom TV osen'û 2015 goda – vesnoj 2015 goda', *Vestnik Moskovskogo universiteta, ser. 10, žurnalistika*, 6: 160–75.

Fauconnier, G. and M. Turner (2002), *The Way We Think. Conceptual Blending and the Mind's Hidden Complexities*. New York: Basic Books.

Hill, P. (2013), 'Dzâdz′ka ni bac′ka, a cëtka ni matka. Len' – mat' vseh porokov. Verwandtschaftstermini als Ausdruck stereotypischer Bezeichnungen', in S. Kempgen, M. Wingender and N. Franz (eds), *Deutsche Beiträge zum Internationalen Slavistenkongress Minsk*, 151–60. München: Sagner.

Kövecses, Z. (2005), *Metaphor in Culture. Universality and Variation*. Cambridge: Cambridge University Press.

Kövecses, Z. (2009), 'Metaphor, Culture, and Discourse: The Pressure of Coherence', in A. Musolff and J. Zinken (eds), *Metaphor and Discourse*, 11–24. Basingstoke: Palgrave Macmillan.

Kövecses, Z. (2014), 'Metaphor and Metonymy in the Conceptual System', in F. Polzenhagen, Z. Kövecses, S. Vogelbacher and S. Kleinke (eds), *Cognitive Explorations into Metaphor and Metonymy*, 15–34. Frankfurt am Main and Bern: Peter Lang.

Kövecses, Z. (2015), *Where Metaphors Come From: Reconsidering Context in Metaphor*. Oxford: University Press.

Lakoff, G. (1987), *Women, Fire, and Dangerous Things. What Categories Reveal about the Mind*. Chicago: University of Chicago Press.

Musolff, A. (2000), *Mirror Images of Europe: Metaphors in the Public Debate about Europe in Britain and Germany*. München: Iudicium, 2000.

Musolff, A. (2004), *Metaphor and Political Discourse: Analogical Reasoning in Debates about Europe*. Basingstoke: Palgrave Macmillan.

Musolff, A. (2017), 'Truths, Lies and Figurative Scenarios – Metaphors at the Heart of Brexit', *Journal of Language and Politics*, 16 (5), 641–57.

Musolff, A. (2019), 'Metaphor Framing in Political Discourse', *Mythos-Magazin: Politisches Framing*, 1, 1–10.

Pragglejaz Group (2007), 'MIP: A Method for Identifying Metaphorically Used Words in Discourse'. *Metaphor and Symbol*, 22 (1): 1–39.

Ukraine Conflict 2014. *The Ukraine Conflict as a Battlefield of Competing Legitimisation Discourses*. www.research-projects.uzh.ch/p21358.htm

Wehling, E. (2016), *Politisches Framing. Wie eine Nation sich ihr Denken einredet – und daraus Politik macht*. Köln: Halem.

Weiss, D. (2016), 'Quotations in the Russian State Duma: Types and Functions', in D. Weiss (guest ed.), *Contemporary Eastern European Political Discourse, Zeitschrift für Slawistik 1/2016*, Special issue: 184–214.

Weiss, D. (2017), 'Implizite Argumentation im politischen Diskurs: Metaphern, Vergleiche, intertextuelle Verweise', in A. Mayer and L. Reinkowski (eds), *Im Rhythmus der Linguistik. Festschrift für S. Kempgen*, 465–83. Bamberg: University of Bamberg Press.

Weiss, D. (2018), 'Украинский конфликт в зеркале корпусной лингвистики', in E. Velmezova (ed.), *Schweizerische Beiträge zum Belgrader Slavistenkongress*, 321–48. Bern and Frankfurt: Peter Lang.

Weiss, D. (2019), 'Threat Scenarios in the Ukraine Conflict', to appear in *International Journal of Cross-Cultural Studies and Environmental Communication (IJCCSEC)*.

Weiss, D. (2020), 'Der Ukraine-Konflikt im Spiegel einer kontrastiv-quantitativen Diskursanalyse: methodologische Grundlagen', to appear in M. Scharlaj (ed.), *Argumentation und Aggression. Ukraine-Diskurse nach dem Euromajdan*. Leipzig: BiblionMedia.

Zaychenko, N. (2011), *Comparative Analysis of Metaphor in English-Russian Translation*, Master thesis, VU Amsterdam.

Zhabotynska, S. (2018), 'Images of Ukraine–EU Relations in Conceptual Metaphors of Ukrainian Mass Media', *Cognition, Communication, Discourse*, 17, 118–40.

Last retrieval of all internet sources: 28 September 2018.

Who are 'they' for Ukrainians in Ukraine and in the diaspora?

Othering in political discourse

Natalia Beliaeva and Corinne A. Seals

1 Introduction to the research

Discussions of the events in Ukraine from 2013 onwards, including the Maidan protests, the annexation of Crimea, the self-manifestation of the Donetsk and Luhansk republics and other related events offer a wealth of valuable material for research on language and identity, given that the national, ethnic, linguistic and other identities of many Ukrainians have undergone dramatic transformation under the influence of these events (cf. Seals 2019). Discursive choices that the speakers make in discussions of this sensitive subject matter can provide valuable insights into the nature of identity negotiation.

Investigating the identity negotiation of contemporary Ukrainians is particularly important because of the peculiarities of the political situation. As pointed out by Kuzio (2007), the national identity of Ukrainians since declaring independence in 1991 has been 'an identity in transition'. This transition became even more relevant with the development of Euromaidan and the war with Russia, which involved, for many Ukrainians, an othering of Russia and Russians.

One type of such discursive choice that is particularly interesting in this respect is the choice between the pronouns *we/our/us* and *they/their/them*. The use of such pronouns is related to the formation of imaginary 'in-groups' and 'out-groups' (Taifel and Turner 1986), which is closely intertwined with identity negotiation. These in-groups and out-groups reflect speakers' conceptualizations of imagined communities (Anderson 1991 [1983]). Defining the features of these imagined communities and drawing their borders is often done by distinguishing the members of this imaginary group ('us') from members of other groups ('them'). Furthermore, understanding who the 'others' are and what they represent is essential for constructing one's own identity (Chebel d'Appollonia 2011), through negative identity practices (i.e. 'I am not that') (cf. Bucholtz 1999; Seals 2017). Creating imaginary boundaries between in-groups and out-groups, insiders and outsiders, is known in social, philosophical and psychological studies as the phenomenon of 'othering'. The focus of linguistic research related to othering lies in drawing ideological borders through discourse (Van Leeuwen and Wodak, 1999; Wodak and Boukala 2015). The current chapter analyses Ukrainian participants' negotiation of in-groups and out-groups (a) in relation to the changing social and political situation in Ukraine, (b) in relation to their own ideological principles and attitudes, (c) in relation to the degree of involvement in the events, including physical distance from the events and (d) in relation to their current residence either in Ukraine or in the diaspora.

1.1 Review of related literature

The distinction between 'us' and 'them' has become one of the key sociopolitical issues in contemporary Ukraine, especially after the crucial changes in political life of the country since Euromaidan, and with the raising of political turmoil in Donbas and Crimea. This is due to the fact that national identity has been renegotiated by many Ukrainians over the past few years in response to the war (Seals 2019). Following the poststructuralist tradition, identity, including national identity, is viewed as a dynamic construct, and an essential part of this socially constructed collective identity is uncovered when asking who is constructed as part of 'us' versus who is part of the 'other' (Fligstein 2008; Wodak and Boukala 2015).

As previously mentioned, national identity is directly tied to the notion of imagined identity (Anderson 1991[1983]), as it encompasses ideologies of shared languages, cultural practices, and often ethnicity. As such, individuals of a shared national identity may effectively eliminate borders if coming together as an imagined community (Roberts 2004), or they may create borders that are ideologically defended through language (Dolgova Jacobsen 2008; Sharma 2005; Zhang 2005). Additionally, imagined communities exist in the mind – it is only because people believe they share commonalities that they act on such presupposed commonalities. Even when discussing the discursive construction of 'nationhood', there is no singular national identity. Rather, what national identity looks like and how it is conceived of is multiple and depends upon the ideologies, experiences and social networks (Milroy 2008; Milroy and Milroy 1985) of the individuals asked (cf. De Cillia, Reisigl and Wodak, 1999). During a time of war, this sense of national identity is consciously revisited and renegotiated, again drawing into question – who is part of 'us' and who is part of 'them'?

Finally, for Ukrainians living outside Ukraine, the situation is even more complicated. First, they live in a situation of constant identity negotiation between self-identification as part of the host society and self-identification as part of a diaspora community, or identifying oneself as different from either (Wodak and Boukala 2015). For Ukrainians in diaspora communities, the current issues with national identity negotiation, including self-identification as different from Russians, are intertwined with what it means to be a resident of a new host country. In some cases, this can also be further complicated by negative identity practices in an effort to discursively identify as different from other diaspora communities (such as the Russian diaspora). All of these issues will be discussed throughout this chapter.

2 Method of the study

The data for the current study come from interviews conducted with thirty-eight Ukrainian young adults (18–40 years old) during 2014 and 2015. The second author recruited all participants by posting information in social media groups on Facebook related to Ukrainian interests, or through the New Zealand diaspora community of which she is a part. The participants needed to be between 18 and 40 years old at the time of the interview; to either live in Ukraine or have moved to the United States, Canada, or New Zealand after the age of 16; and to be speakers of Ukrainian, English and Russian to some degree[1].

From those interested in participating, thirty-eight individuals were identified: twelve in Ukraine, twelve in North America and fourteen in New Zealand. Within each cohort, one-fourth were originally from Eastern Ukraine, one-fourth from Western Ukraine, one-fourth from Central Ukraine, and one-fourth from the Black Sea region, in an effort to get a fairly even sample (for more details on participant recruitment, see Seals 2019).

Interviews were semi-structured, participant driven and conducted by the second author. Each interview took place at a time and via a method most convenient for each participant. Each interview lasted between 45 and 150 minutes, depending on how long each participant wanted to speak. All interviews covered topics such as growing up in Ukraine, school and university experiences, perceptions towards language acquisition and use, and the war in Ukraine.

All interviews were coded and analysed via the Grounded Theory approach to emergent coding (cf. Charmaz 2014). Topic trends within and across interviews were identified, and representative samples were transcribed. These transcribed portions were then subjected to an interactional sociolinguistics discourse analysis (cf. Gumperz 2005), to analyse how people create meaning moment-to-moment across the course of the interviews, through semantic inference, contextualization cues and repetition, among other strategies. The portion of results presented in the current chapter corresponds to the question of how in-groups and out-groups are discursively constructed by participants, and how this relates to place of residence, connections to Ukraine and emotional involvement with the war.

3 Findings

3.1 'Us' and 'them' in Ukraine

Perceived socio-cultural differences between different regions in Ukraine (in particular, South-Eastern, Western, Central, and the Black Sea regions) are recognized by many Ukrainians, as discussed, for example in Seals (2010, 2019). It is not surprising then that this distinction is reflected in the speech of participants who live in Ukraine, in particular, in the way they associate with or dissociate from different ethnic or social groups perceived as being tied to various socio-cultural regions. Consistent with the findings reported in Bilaniuk (2005), this social identity is intertwined with language choice and use in the regions as well as language(s) used by participants themselves. Thus, in the interview with Artem (lives in L'viv, Western Ukraine; identifies as Ukrainian), his association with people in Western Ukraine emerges when he discusses the language policy of recent years and the political movement towards promoting the Ukrainian language:

(1) Artem

(1) Umph, [1] yeah, this, this, thing with language, right now it's- it's very,
(2) er, hard to judge, hard to comment in case,
(3) er, [1] [smacks lips twice] I guess, the- the country is,
(4) er very, like, wide?
(5) er in- geographically and uh, er,
(6) information is really er,
(7) er, distributed not, not er correctly, not evenly, so we have no idea, how it is for people,
(8) er, on the East, and they have no idea how it is for us.
(9) Er, so that's why we don't [1]
(10) pretty much don't understand, er,
(11) each other.

Artem realizes that people in different regions may have different attitudes towards language policy in Ukraine. Explaining the possible misunderstanding between the population of different regions, he dissociates from people 'on the East', talking about the rest of Ukraine (or, presumably, Western Ukraine) as 'us' ('they have no idea how it is for us'). Thus while acknowledging that Ukraine is a relatively large country and that not everyone will understand each other, Artem still utilizes discourses of 'them' and 'us' to explain this geographical, and perceived socio-cultural, divide between Eastern and Western Ukraine.

In the example given earlier, the speaker's primary language is Ukrainian, and othering is directed to regions with prevailing Russian language. However, othering takes a different direction in the speech of Milena (lives in Dnepropetrovsk, Eastern-Central Ukraine; identifies as Ukrainian), who does not use Ukrainian as her primary language. Although Milena was born in Ukraine, most of her family is Russian, and her native language is also Russian. It is not surprising, therefore, that she uses 'they' to refer to Ukrainians, in particular, people speaking Ukrainian. Although Milena comments in the interview that she cannot call herself Ukrainian, she does not explicitly identify as Russian either. Moreover, some of the in-group markers in her discourse refer to Ukrainians:

(2) Milena

(1) and ... this terrible situation here, but ...
(2) and ... also M- Maidan ... was ...
(3) er, v- was appeared.
(4) Um, it's sort of, it's like not so... not so good
(5) er according to the ... political and economical situation in Ukraine,
(6) however, they raise really great patriotism in Ukraine ...
(7) So, I think that er ... we are ...
(8) mm mmm we are moving in the right direction.

Milena has mixed feelings about Maidan and the events that followed it, which makes sense, given her own mixed identity presentation. Her dissociation with a strong Ukrainian identity is likely one of the reasons why she uses 'they' to refer to people who participated in Maidan and 'raise really great patriotism in Ukraine'. However, the use of 'we' in 'we are moving in the right direction' can be attributed to Ukraine as a country, and further shows complex identity negotiation. Additionally, long pauses and hesitation markers around 'we' indicate high emotional involvement in the discourse.

The in-group markers 'we' or 'us' are most evident across the interviews in discussions of political events in Ukraine, including Maidan and the war in the South-Eastern regions. Specific ethnic groups or regional communities within Ukraine cease functioning as in-groups in a situation when some external force appears to threaten Ukraine as a whole. Such a threat seems to trigger a sense of belonging to an in-group that can be broadly defined as 'the country of Ukraine or Ukrainian nation'. This tendency is summarized here by one of the participants, Klara (lives in Kyiv, Central Ukraine; identifies as Ukrainian).

(3) Klara

(1) And the society is becoming ... more grown-up.
(2) In terms of ... f- ...
(3) in terms of first of all,
(4) defining ourselves as Ukrainians.
(5) Not ... former Soviet-Unions-ners,
(6) not ... Russian friends, or not friends, but actually Ukrainians who have their own path ...
(7) And ... we finally, we- ... Ukraine ... wanted to have good relationships in- with Russia for so long,..
(8) And ...
(9) w- were- w-was willing to give up ...
(10) n- little and big things to stay friends ...
(11) is finally willing to: ...
(12) to not stay friends and not give up anything, because ...
(13) because the ... stocks ... are ... our lives already.
(14) You can't give up your life to stay friends.

This is a crucial point in the interview, and one of the most prominent examples of verbalizing the speaker's identity in political discourse. Klara defines her in-group by naming it ('defining ourselves as Ukrainians') and then by providing a description of what this identity means for her. As in the previous example, hesitation markers (e.g. false starts, pauses and repetitions) indicate the highly emotional state of the speaker. Note also the interchangeability of Ukraine with 'we', which is accompanied by personification of Ukraine in lines 7–13. This personification, alongside multiple uses of 'we' shows that Ukrainian national identity is deeply meaningful for Klara.

Similarly, Marina (from the Black Sea region of Ukraine; lives in Kyiv, Central Ukraine; identifies as Ukrainian) identifies with the in-group 'we' that means 'Ukraine as a country'. For Marina, the 'others' are those who threaten this perceived national unity. While Marina identifies herself as Ukrainian, she acknowledges her mixed background as well. In Example 4 given further, the conflation of in-groups occurs in the discourse related to the status of Russian language in Ukraine, in particular, an attempt to cancel the law regulating the status of Russian as regional language, which triggered the separatist movement in the Donetsk and Luhansk regions. An example of this discourse shows othering of Ukrainian government in the discussion of language policy.

(4) Marina

(1) It will be very hard to make Russian as a mmm, second language,
(2) er although a lot of people speak it and understand it,
(3) just because, they- people,
(4) will always associate Russian with Russia who is now an aggressor?
(5) And if we, you know make Russian language second official language we're sort of,
(6) kind of,
(7) I don't know what the right word is um,
(8) we're in favor of the aggressor or something?
<...>
(9) that's why they will never do it, at least not in the near future.

This excerpt also displays a shift in the direction of othering. At line 3, 'they-' (although self-corrected to 'people') outlines the group that associates 'Russian with Russia', which is not the case for Marina, a Russian-speaking Ukrainian. Later, at line 9, 'they' refers to the Ukrainian government. In-group markers here refer to Ukraine as a country, rather than the government (cf. 'in our country', and also several uses of 'we' at line 5 and further). Interestingly, when discussing the reasons why it is not possible, in her opinion, to make Russian the second official language in Ukraine, Marina uses 'we', 'if we, you know make ...', but later she concludes using 'they', 'they will never do it', thus othering the group of people responsible for the final decision.

The discursive construction of a strong Ukrainian nation identity is also salient in the interviews with Ukrainians who have emigrated, as discussed further.

3.2 Identity negotiation and othering in the Ukrainian diaspora

As mentioned in Section 3.2, the present data come from Ukrainian immigrants living in the United States, Canada and New Zealand. Having moved to another country, they preserve (to a greater or lesser extent) personal and social connections to their homeland, and continue identifying themselves as Ukrainians nationally and/or ethnically. However, their investment in the host society yields a sense of belonging and thus triggers the formation of new in-groups. In addition to investment in the host society, immigrants often invest in diaspora communities, which may bring them back to associating themselves with their homeland and culture, but may also become a trigger for othering in their homeland.

Furthermore, as discussed in Seals (2019: Chapter 4), the cycles of identity negotiation are continuous, and during each one, the borderlines of in-groups and out-groups are re-evaluated and redefined. Each individual pathway is unique, and among the factors that influence identity negotiation are age, gender, occupation, place of residence, period of immigration, degree of investment into the host society, and so on. A prominent example of this complex negotiation can be found in the interview with Fedir (from Volyn, Western Ukraine; lives in New Zealand; identifies as Ukrainian).

(5) Fedir

(1)   C- er I said something I can't remember what word it was and he said,
(2)   Oh, I haven't heard that for so many years ago.
(3)   I guess in- in English in New Zealand it'd be like using word 'choice'.
(4)   Nobody uses that anymore.
(5)   Um, used to be you know used to mean 'great', you know, now a little bit, um,
(6)   hardly ever heard anybody say that anymore, you know?
(7)   So, so the same thing happens but,
(8)   we don't know it.
(9)   They pick up on it but they can't really ...
(10) ((smacks lips)) they can't pick up on it, a hundred percent because,
(11) it's familiar but yeah, slightly off ...

Prompted to recollect unusual incidents related to the use of language in Ukraine, Fedir explains that the Ukrainian language has changed since the time he lived in Ukraine. By saying 'we don't know it' in line 8, Fedir acknowledges that he was not aware of the language change, while simultaneously associating himself with others living outside of Ukraine. This association with an imaginary community of Ukrainian emigrants is followed by othering of people living in Ukraine in line 9. As shown earlier, language (or varieties of language) is a crucial factor affecting the sense of belonging to a certain group. Therefore, unexpected changes within the language results in othering of self and various dialectal groups.

Furthermore, examples from the interview with Lilia (from L'viv, Western Ukraine; lives in Canada; identifies as Ukrainian) demonstrate how language use contributes to attitudes towards members of the diaspora community as well as towards family members. In Lilia's family, Russian is not usually spoken. She has relatives in Russia, and explicitly differentiates between family members speaking Ukrainian and those speaking Russian. In Lilia's interview, she includes herself in the in-group of family using Ukrainian by othering family members who speak Russian: 'When they visit us, they speak Russian, we speak Ukrainian, and everyone's ... everyone's happy'. Thus, Lilia considers dual non-accommodation a situation that is acceptable for everyone.

At the time of the interview, Lilia was living in Canada. Upon her arrival there, Lilia discovered that the Ukrainian diaspora community in Canada spoke a different variety of Ukrainian from the one she was used to in Ukraine. This is because the Canadian diaspora's language developed outside of Ukraine from the nineteenth century. It became so different from the Ukrainian spoken in Ukraine that Lilia expressed not being able to effectively communicate with the diaspora community in Ukrainian (e.g. 'I was really surprised that my Ukrainian really differs from- from their Ukrainian'). Another possible explanation of Lilia's othering the diaspora community relates to language attitudes:

(6) Lilia

(1) That's- that's- the- that's the bad phenomenon here,
(2) that, er, people don't really distinguish between
(3) ethnicity and, er, citizenship.
(4) For them everyone Ukrainian is supposed to speak Ukrainian,
(5) which is not the case,
(6) in- in Ukraine.
(7) You can be a Ukrainian citizen, but-speak- but speak Russian, or Polish, or ...
(8) I don't know, Kazak,
(9) whatever your ... a- ancestral language is.

Lilia disagrees with the opinion that every Ukrainian 'is supposed to speak Ukrainian'. Ukrainian is Lilia's native language, but she acknowledges different ethnic groups within Ukraine, which sets her apart from the Canadian Ukrainian diaspora in her view. She also feels set apart from the new directions of social development in Ukraine:

(7) Lilia

(1) It looks like we were in a big, big, big, big, big hole,
(2) and ... maybe ...
(3) this is when Ukraine starts ...
(4) slowly getting out of it.
[...]
(5) there is a new generation
(6) of people that are, well, ten-fifteen years younger than- than I am,
(7) that ... weren't really even born in Soviet Union,
(8) and they have a totally different ... outlook ... on a ...
(9) on ... how the country ... should develop, and where it should go.

Lilia closely follows the events in Ukraine, and she sincerely believes that the situation in Ukraine will improve in the future, which she discusses metaphorically (lines 1–4). At the same time, she does not count herself among the people who are going to shape the country's future. Interestingly, she also draws an ideological line between those born in the Soviet Union and those born afterwards (line 11). The only 'we' in the earlier excerpt refers to Ukraine's past leading up to this point (line 1). When discussing the future of Ukraine, Lilia mentally distances herself from the events in Ukraine both in time (perceiving herself as belonging to a different generation) and in space (being a distant observer of the events).

The examples show how the emigration/immigration experience can transform the imagined communities a person perceives as in-groups or out-groups. Sometimes, the borders of the in-groups may become less clear-cut, or, as is often the case with the participants of the present study, immigrants do not identify with any particular in-group in the host country. At the same time, their connections to the in-groups inside Ukraine can weaken when they move out of the country. This experience is revealed in discourse where we encounter 'I' versus 'them', rather than 'us' versus 'them'. However, not all emigrants from Ukraine experience isolation. For example,

Raisa and Lev (a married couple from Zaporizhia, South-Eastern Ukraine; live in New Zealand; both identify as Ukrainian) appear to have preserved a strong sense of belonging to Ukraine during the seven years they have lived in New Zealand. The in-group markers 'we/us/our' referring to Ukraine can be found in their interview, both when they discuss political events in Ukraine and when they talk about their life outside of Ukraine. Instead, markers of othering (e.g. 'they') occur in relation to Russia, the Soviet Union and political aggression, like in Excerpt 8:

(8) Raisa

(1) But- but previously, you even... you know, like, er ...
(2) They tried to ... wipe ... everything about our culture ...
(3) In ... language, er ... ffft ..

Raisa is discussing Soviet Russification, when Russian was imposed as the dominant language on the territory of Ukraine. For Raisa, this meant an attempt to extinguish Ukrainian culture. Othering here is directed at the political force behind Russification, not necessarily the Russian people. Raisa associates herself with Ukrainian-speaking people who, in this context, represent Ukrainian culture and nation (cf. 'our culture'). Further elaborating upon the topic of languages spoken in Ukraine, Raisa mentions Russian people who come to the country, but are reluctant to learn and use Ukrainian:

(9) Raisa

(1) Mmm ... they had ... Russian people there ...
(2) Nobody ... ever, like, treated- er, ne- never heard somebody treated them differently.
(3) But what interesting about them, they never, never ... spoke Ukrainian.
(4) They even ... don't try to study Ukrainian.
(5) Like, you know, you-go- we came here, to English speaking country,
(6) so we studied, er ... English, because we ... need to communicate with people,
(7) and we want people to understand us, er, and find job, and everything, you know ...
(8) They don't think like this.

In Excerpt 9, Raisa states that Russian people in Ukraine did not learn Ukrainian and never used it. Intensifiers (e.g. even, never and ever) and repetitions in her discourse show how meaningful this observation is for Raisa. The behaviour of Russian immigrants in Ukraine does not correspond to Raisa's representation of what 'good immigrants' should do (cf. Seals 2019). She antithesizes this behaviour to that of Ukrainian immigrants in New Zealand, which includes her family (lines 5–8).

The examples of othering in the discourses of Ukrainian immigrants in North America and New Zealand demonstrate that moving out of the home country involves a shift in collective identities. First, the identification with geographic regions within Ukraine (i.e. Eastern, Western or Central Ukraine) does not emerge in the discourse of immigrants. Instead, ethnic and national identity is negotiated in various contrasts with ethnic and national groups that they come across in the host countries. Furthermore, an important factor contributing to revision of ethnic and national identity is how national and ethnic groups are seen by members of the host society (e.g. whether or not Ukrainians are confused with Russians or other Slavic people). This is further complicated by investment in the host society or in diaspora communities, depending on how well the beliefs, expectations and attitudes of an immigrant resemble those of the members of the host and/or diaspora communities. Finally, the experience of living outside Ukraine may lead some to a loss of connection with in-groups in Ukraine, but the association with Ukrainian culture and Ukrainian nation remains strong. This seems to occur alongside othering of Russian people and/or Russia as a country, which makes sense given the interviews coincided with the war actions in the Donetsk and Luhansk regions. In what follows, we further explore discourse specifically covering the war in Ukraine and its political context.

3.3 In and out of war discourse in Ukraine

As we have seen in the previous paragraphs, the participants' discursive construction of in-groups is presented in simultaneous juxtaposition of their othering of out-groups. In this section, we will take a closer look at which in-groups and out-groups are evoked in discourse related to the war in Ukraine, and how the focus of othering is connected to the degree of involvement in the war, the geographical distance from the war zone, and other participant-dependent factors.

One of the most important factors is degree of emotional involvement in the war events. For example, the following excerpt from the interview with Marina (from Black Sea region of Ukraine; lives in Kyiv, Central Ukraine; identifies as Ukrainian) contains relatively more in-group markers than the rest of her discourse, and at the same time displays signs of high emotional involvement in the topic:

(10) Marina

(1) Like, the-, the diplomacy, doesn't really work with Russia you know and um,
(2) ((smacks lips)) we don't have much resources and t- t- to fight them back and er,..
(3) it's kind of, it's kind of sad, we just keep losing land,
(4) and people.
(5) You know, and it's just amazing how, in a year, they've progressed like,
(6) they've taken the Crimea,
(7) they've taken two, er regions,
(8) and e:r, they are now moving further South,
(9) and it's just ... really, scary to think of,
(10) what's coming up next, because, I don't think,
(11) we have enough, like ...
(12) I-would- political, maybe, n- not military brain, you know?
(13) To think strategically or tactically about the situation, you know?
(14) We can only fight back,
(15) er, when ... when separatists attack,
[...]
(16) ((sighs)) here is nothing,
(17) right now that we can do to prevent it.

In the aforementioned excerpt, Marina's speech is often interrupted with sighs and other non-verbal signals, long pauses, false starts, repetitions and pause fillers such as 'er' and 'mmm'. Such a high concentration of speech disfluencies signals a high degree of emotional agitation for the speaker (e.g. ,O'Connell and Kowal 2005; Corley and Stewart 2008). Marina follows the war closely and knows people directly involved, which results in her use of many in-group markers, accordingly. In Excerpt 10, the actions assigned to the in-group can only be performed on the level of a whole country ('we just keep losing land'); hence 'we' here consistently refers to the country of Ukraine. Conversely, the referent of the out-group is variable. The referent of 'they' in line 2 may be Russia, which is marked in the discourse by using the geographical name (line 1). However, in other parts of her discourse, the out-group includes the separatists and pro-Russian forces fighting in the war zone (lines 7–8).

A different presentation of the actors in this war can be seen in the discourse of Larysa (from Luhansk, Eastern Ukraine; lives in Kyiv, Central Ukraine; identifies as Ukrainian). Larysa is from Luhansk, the city that became a hearth of the separatists' activity. At the time of the interview, Larysa had been living in Kyiv for fourteen years, but her family still lived in Luhansk, and her father has remained there during the war in order to take care of his property and his business. Therefore, Larysa follows the situation very closely. Interestingly, Larysa others the people participating in the war, alongside the people who have stayed in the region after the war started (though she exempts her father from this):

(11) Larysa

(1) Er, the people who stayed there, er, personally I don't have much compassion for them,
(2) Erm, because the percentage of people like my dad,
(3) Or those old population who can't move because for example they don't have kids,
(4) It's really tiny-tiny percentage, maybe no more than two per cent.
(5) Er, lots of people left the region, er, to ... other places.
(6) ((smacks lips)) Otherwise, those people, er ... er,
(7) for me it's really difficult to call them Ukrainians,
(8) or like citizens of Ukraine, e- either way,
(9) er because o- of ... of what was er done ... by them.
[...]
(10) th- they- they don't want to perceive any other ...
(11) occupation and they just got the guns in their hands,
(12) and they feel like the kings.

Larysa explicitly states that she does not have compassion for people 'who stayed there'. She explains her attitude, estimating that only a very small percentage of the civil population remained living in the region. Larysa's estimate of 'maybe no more than two per cent' is clearly an understatement; according to the UN report, 2.7 million civilians remained in the territories controlled by separatists as of 15 February 2016 (Office of the United Nations High Commissioner for Human Rights 2016). Although Larysa definitely knows of some civilians living in the war zone, she does not perceive the population of the region en masse as peaceful civilians. Furthermore, no in-group markers are used in the discussion, as Larysa talks about her personal attitudes to the participants of the war, distinguishing herself from these people. Moreover, she repeatedly states that she cannot call them Ukrainians. Distancing herself from the people living in the war zone and participating in the war, she also draws a distinction between this group and all other Ukrainians.

The examples given earlier show that discourse related to the war in the Donetsk and Luhansk regions often contains associations with the country of Ukraine as an in-group, rather than particular social groups within the country. At the same time, out-group markers can refer to more narrowly defined groups of actors in the war, as well as an outside opponent (in this case, Russia). Different speakers negotiate their belonging to Ukraine as an in-group depending on their personal investment in the war and their views of various groups participating in it. Personal investment in various groups related to the war also determines the direction and the quality of othering.

3.3.1 War discourse in the diaspora

Those who live outside Ukraine are not likely to be physically involved in the war, although the possibility of emotional involvement or association with groups of people directly involved is still very real.

An example of such discursive group construction in war discourse from within the diaspora comes from Lilia (from L'viv, Western Ukraine; lives in Canada; identifies as Ukrainian). She knows a lot of people who volunteer to support the Ukrainian army, and she follows the news from Ukraine very closely ('as close as I can from here'). Nevertheless, she recognizes her own role as a distant observer, and uses the out-group markers accordingly:

(12) Lilia

(1) The shooting of people on ... in downtown Kyiv, or ....
(2) the downing of the ... plane, or ... er ...
(3) those numerous deaths in the battlefield there, it does? ..,
(4) but you carry on with- with your day life, and ...
(5) because you know there is nothing you can do from- from this end.

Lilia feels that the tragic events such as the mass shooting of people in Maidan and the many deaths in the war affect her daily life, though this influences her emotional state rather than her actual physical circumstances. Lilia is emotionally moved by thinking about the war (see the long silences, false starts and filled pauses). At the same time, she believes that she cannot affect the events in her home country (line 5). Talking about this, she uses generic 'you', thus implying that these thoughts may be shared by other people.

Additionally, although Lilia identifies as Ukrainian both nationally and ethnically, in her discourse related to Maidan and the war, she describes the Ukrainian nation from the position of an outsider:

(13) Lilia

(1) So Ukraine is basically there on- on- on it's own, and ...
(2) will have to ... carry on, I don't think Putin with- just withdraw and ... stop ...

(3) doing what he's- he's been doing.
(4) So it's totally up to ... Ukrainian leaders, and ...
(5) Ukrainian people
(6) to just, phh, carry on, and ...
(7) show that, er ...
(8) they can still prevail.

In this excerpt, Lilia assigns a lot of agency to Putin, outlining the war in Ukraine as a confrontation between Putin and Ukrainian leaders and people. Earlier in the interview, she also mentions that the leaders of other countries do not fully understand the threat to Ukraine and are not willing to interfere, so she concludes that Ukraine is 'on its own'. However, Lilia still expresses hope that Ukrainian leaders and Ukrainian people can 'prevail', although the abundant hesitation markers in this statement show that she is not certain about this outcome. Othering here is consistent with the earlier discourse where Lilia used out-group markers to refer to people who will influence the future of Ukraine. Thus she discursively constructs the present situation and the future of Ukraine as not being part of her life directly, although she feels emotionally connected to Ukraine and its people.

Similarly to the earlier examples, Lana (from Crimea, Black Sea Region; living in New Zealand; identifies as Ukrainian) reports the events related to the war in Ukraine from the position of an outside observer. As she was born in Crimea, her account of her native region becoming part of Russia is especially of interest.

Talking about the war in the Donetsk and Luhansk regions, Lana provides her personal evaluation of the events, while othering all people involved in the war, irrespective of her positive or negative attitude towards them:

(14) Lana

(1) U:m, ((smacks lips)) I- I have really-really big regret that the best, erm,
(2) ((smacks lips)) the best men of Ukraine, they're just dying in that, stupid war?
(3) ((sighs)) And, um,
(4) so, and Ukraine just losing the chance to change, or to become this, um,
(5) swapping to Eu- to Europeah, u:m,
(6) values, to European, erm, w- way of life and they're just losing their, erm,
(7) ((smacks)) all efforts, just, like you know just dying, for nothing?
(8) And, er, and I mean like from, let's say like, er, Russians,
(9) they send not the best people, they send, like prisoners, like former prisoners or,
(10) people who we:re, like, with- have some, erm,
(11) ((smacks lips)) Problems with law?

Lana provides polar characterization of the two sides of the war in South-Eastern Ukraine. On the one hand, she deeply sympathizes with the 'best men of Ukraine' who fight against separatists. On the other hand, she characterizes the latter as criminals, and points out that they come from Russia (lines 8–9). In contrast, Ukraine is described as suffering and losing its best men in the warfare. Revealing her opposite attitudes to the two sides in the war, Lana is nevertheless othering both, referring to all as 'they' and 'them'.

However, as Excerpt 15 shows, when Lana moves from talking about war participants to giving her overall evaluation of the war, she begins using the in-group marker 'we':

(15) Lana

(1) Yeah, uh I mean like now you know we are in twenty-first century,
(2) and now we're facing some,
(3) like, some really big challenges in the, changing climate and,
(4) you know we should stay for our... like big home,
(5) our Earth, our planet, we should, er should-
(6) we sh-should figure out something really quickly how we, can change that.
(7) And, and here we- an- if you're thinking about this just medieval war?
(8) is like, between, Russia and Ukraine like, mostly Russia?
(9) but on Ukrainian territory, I just, like, for me just,..
(10) really, c- controversial situation.

The given excerpt, unlike Excerpt 14, contains abundant in-group markers. As mentioned earlier, Lana discusses the war in an emphatic way, and her emotional involvement is revealed in the high number of parenthetical words ('like' and 'you know'), modal verbs and self-corrections. In this context, repetitive use of 'we' is predictable. However, all cases of 'we' in this excerpt refer to a much wider populace (lines 1–6). For Lana, the facts of the 'medieval war' she pictured seem unthinkable in the contemporary world. Furthermore, when the opposing parties of the war are named, Lana immediately ceases using in-group markers and goes back to reporting her personal account of the situation (lines 8–10). This othering is consistent with her discourse throughout the interview, in which she describes her connection to the Ukrainian diaspora in New Zealand, more so than to people and events in Ukraine.

4 Discussion and conclusions

The aggravation of the political climate in Ukraine, in particular, the annexation of Crimea and the war in the south-eastern region drew the world's attention to Ukraine. The participants who live outside of Ukraine report that as a consequence of these tragic events, people began to distinguish Ukrainians from the nationals they earlier confused them with, in particular, Russians. Thus not only did the war enhance the identification of Ukrainians as different from Russians (reflected in the many examples of othering of Russians discussed in this chapter), but it also highlighted the same distinction in diaspora host countries.

The present analysis has revealed that in-groups and out-groups are constructed differently by participants living in Ukraine from those who emigrated. In particular, Ukrainian residents tend to assign more meaning to perceived regional differences (e.g. Western vs. Eastern or Central Ukraine). Othering of people living in different regions emerges in discussions of language varieties, and also in perceived views of the political situation in Ukraine, as shown in Table 7.1.

Table 7.1 In-groups and Out-groups in the Discourse of Ukrainians from Different Regions of Ukraine (N Refers to the Number of In-group or Out-group Marking Pronouns in the Excerpts Analysed for the Present Study)

Region	In-groups (Us)	N	Out-groups (Them)	N	Speakers
Western Ukraine	people in Western Ukraine	2	people in the Eastern Ukraine	2	Artem
Central Ukraine	Ukrainian nation and Ukraine as a country	3	the Soviet Union	1	Klara
			Russia	2	
Eastern-Central Ukraine	all people in Ukraine	1	people speaking Ukrainian, people identifying themselves as Ukrainians	1	Milena
originally Eastern Ukraine (war zone), moved to Central Ukraine			people currently living in the war zone (as opposed to those who moved out)	7	Larysa
originally Black Sea, moved to Central Ukraine	Ukraine as a country	10	Ukrainian government (in particular, people responsible for language policy)	1	Marina
			Separatists in Donetsk and Luhansk regions	2	
			People in Ukraine who think of Russia as an aggressor	1	
			Russia as an aggressor (when talking about the war)	3	
			Separatists and pro-Russian forces fighting in the war zone	2	

In the discourse of Ukrainians originating from different regions of Ukraine, othering can be related to geographical position and origin (i.e. directed at people living in a different regions). This is especially prominent in the discussions of war (othering of those in the war zone and othering of Russia). In terms of in-groups, there is more unanimity across speakers, with the majority of speakers referring to Ukraine as a whole as an in-group.

Furthermore, in the discourse related specifically to war, the in-group markers referring to Ukraine as a political and social entity often emerge in discourse, co-occurring with othering of the opposing forces (primarily Russia). Furthermore, it is often implied that Russia as Other is connected to particular groups of associated people (e.g., pro-Russian population in Ukraine, separatists, etc.). In some cases, the out-groups are conflated so that it is not always possible to distinguish the exact referent of othering. In juxtaposition to Russia as Other, Ukraine is often discursively presented as victim (cf. Lana), while Russia, on the other hand, is presented as an active agent, with much agency often assigned to Putin (cf. Lilia for an example representative of a general trend across the interviews). This juxtaposition between Ukraine and Russia is frequent in the discourse of the interviewees living in Ukraine.

In contrast, as shown in Table 7.2, individuals living outside Ukraine may juxtapose themselves to people currently in Ukraine, especially when they point out factors that differentiate them, such as language variety (cf. Fedir), attitudes or involvement in political events (cf. Lilia, Raisa). In some cases, alongside othering, the immigrants discursively highlight their association with Ukrainian diaspora communities (cf. Lana). However, this can also be complex, as sometimes the diaspora communities themselves can be discursively constructed as out-groups if an individual disagrees with the views of the community (cf. Lilia) or is not satisfied by its attitude (cf. Raisa).

Table 7.2 shows somewhat different directions of othering, compared to Table 7.1. First of all, a juxtaposition of people in Ukraine and Ukrainians outside Ukraine can be noted. Another feature of discourse here is othering of all participants of the war as a result of positioning of the speaker as a distant observer. Finally, alongside including Ukraine as a whole as an in-group, a wider focus of inclusion (all the people in the world) is present.

Table 7.2 In-groups and out-groups in the discourse of Ukrainians in the diaspora (N refers to the number of in-group or out-group marking pronouns in the excerpts analysed for the present study)

Region of origin	Region of current residence	In-groups (Us)	N	Out-groups (Them)	N	Speakers
Western Ukraine	New Zealand	Ukrainian emigrants outside Ukraine	1	people in Ukraine	3	Fedir
	Canada	Ukraine as a country	1	members of a particular Ukrainian diaspora (in Canada)	2	Lilia
				the generation of Ukrainians who were born after the Soviet Union	2	
				Ukrainian people and Ukrainian leaders (when talking about the war)	1	
South-Eastern Ukraine	New Zealand	Ukraine as a country	1	the Soviet Union	1	Raisa
		Ukrainian immigrants in New Zealand	4	Russian immigrants in Ukraine	5	
Black Sea	New Zealand	people of the world	6	Ukrainian people fighting in Donetsk and Luhansk regions	3	Lana
				Russian or pro-Russian forces fighting in the war	2	

For participants living outside of Ukraine, the construction of empathy with their home country appears despite the effect of geographical distance from the events. Importantly, in-group markers referring to Ukraine as a nation emerge when the speakers are highly emotionally involved in the discourse. Additionally, participants' positive association with Ukraine in the context of war is most prominent if an individual feels personally connected to the events. In general, the participants living in New Zealand express more direct association with the events in Ukraine than those living in North America, which they often attribute to the level of interest that their diaspora community has in Ukrainian events. It is difficult to make inferences on such a small sample, but it is possible that the immigrant communities in New Zealand position themselves as less separated from the home country than the immigrant communities in the United States or Canada. This is an area of interest for future research.

Another important aspect of the present study concerns the role of language in the discursive construction of contemporary Ukrainian identity. While this question is discussed in much more detail in Seals (2019), it is important for the purposes of this paper that language is a key factor in setting the borders of in-groups and out-groups. In a situation when regional boundaries play a much lesser role (i.e. for Ukrainians living outside Ukraine), language allows for the construction of particular in-group and out-group social groups and imaginary communities for the speaker.

Finally, the observed results are consistent with the concept of 'liquid' identity (Bauman 2004), (i.e., the identities of the speakers are re-constructed and co-constructed along with the construction of discourse). This study shows how the construction of identity is reflected in referring to in-groups and out-groups under the influence of such factors as emotional involvement in the discourse, and investment in the diaspora and 'imagined communities'. This further supports the idea of constructing identities in the process of opposing oneself to the Other (or 'macro-Other', cf. Eriksen (1995: 427)). Moreover, the observed cases can be regarded as representing the ongoing process of the construction of Ukrainian national identity, which necessarily includes othering and which becomes even more vivid in political discourse.

Note

1 These requirements were needed for a simultaneous phonological study based on the interviews.

References

Anderson, B. (1991 [1983]), *Imagined Communities: Reflections on the Origin and Spread of Nationalism*. New York: Verso.

Bauman, Z. (2004), *Identity: Conversations with Benedetto Vecchi*. Cambridge: Polity Press.

Bilaniuk, L. (2005), *Contested Tongues: Language Politics and Cultural Correction in Ukraine*. Ithaca: Cornell University Press.

Bucholtz, M. (1999), '"Why Be Normal?": Language and Identity Practices in a Community of Nerd Girls', *Language in Society*, 28 (2): 202–25.

Charmaz, K. (2014), *Constructing Grounded Theory*, 2nd edn. London: Sage Publications.

Chebel d'Appollonia, A. (2011), *Les frontières du racisme [Frontiers of Racism]*. Paris: Presses de Sciences Po.

Corley, M. and Stewart, O. W. (2008), 'Hesitation Disfluencies in Spontaneous Speech: The Meaning of Um', *Language and Linguistics Compass*, 2 (4): 589–602.

De Cillia, R., Reisigl, M. and Wodak, R. (1999), 'The Discursive Construction of National Identities', *Discourse & Society*, 10 (2): 149–73.

Dolgova Jacobsen, N. (2008), '"Identity [iz] a [djifikelt] Question": A Variationist Analysis of the Relationship between L1 Features and Ethnic Identity in the Speech of Russian Learners of English', *EVox: Georgetown Working Papers in Language, Discourse & Society*, 2: 1–28.

Eriksen, T. H. (1995), 'We and Us: Two Modes of Group Identification', *Journal of Peace Research*, 32 (4), 427–36.

Fligstein, N. (2008), *Euroclash: The EU, European Identity, and the Future of Europe*. Oxford: Oxford University Press.

Gumperz, J. J. (2005), 'Interethnic Communication', in S. F. Kiesling and C. B. Paulston (eds), *Intercultural Discourse and Communication: The Essential Readings*, 33–44. Oxford: Blackwell Publishing.

Kuzio, T. (2007), 'National Identity in Independent Ukraine: An Identity in Transition', *Nationalism and Ethnic Politics*, 2 (4): 582–608.

Milroy, J. and Milroy, L. (1985), 'Linguistic Change, Social Network and Speaker Innovation', *Journal of Linguistics*, 21: 339–84.

Milroy, L. (2008), 'Social Networks', in J. K. Chambers, P. Trudgill and N. Schilling-Estes (eds), *The Handbook of Language Variation and Change*, 549–72. Oxford: Blackwell Publishing.

O'Connell, D. C. and Kowal, S. (2005), 'Uh and um Revisited: Are They Interjections for Signaling Delay?' *Journal of Psycholinguistic Research*, 34: 555–76.

Office of the United Nations High Commissioner for Human Rights (2016), *Report on the Human Rights Situation in Ukraine: 16 November 2015 to 15 February 2016*. Accessed from http://www.ohchr.org/Documents/Countries/UA/Ukraine_13th_HRMMU_Report_ 3March2016.pdf (accessed 20 March 2017).

Roberts, S. (2004), 'The Role of Style and Identity in the Development of Hawaiian Creole', in G. Escure and A. Schwegler (eds), *Creoles, Contact, and Language Change: Linguistic and Social Implications*, 331–50. Amsterdam: John Benjamins.

Seals, C. A. (2010), Jazyk kak čast' nacionalnogo samosoznanija: Palatalizacija v tr'ohjazyčnom mežličnostnom vzaimodejstvii Ukraincev' ('Language Is a Part of the National Consciousness: Palatalization in Trilingual Ukrainians' Negotiations of Identity'), in Z. S. Dotmurzieva (ed.), *Materialy 1-oj Meždumarodnoj naučno-praktičeskoj konferencii 'Yazykovaja Ličnost v Sovremennom Mire'* (*Proceedings of the 1st International 'Lingual Identity in the Contemporary World' Conference*). Magas, Ingushetia, Russian Federation: Ingush State University Press.

Seals, C. A. (2017), 'Positive and Negative Identity Practices in Heritage Language Education', *International Journal of Multilingualism*, 15 (4): 329–48.

Seals, C. A. (2019), *'Choosing a Mother Tongue': Positioning, Dialogism, and Identity in Ukrainian Narratives of Conflict*. Bristol: Multilingual Matters.

Sharma, D. (2005), 'Dialect Stabilization and Speaker Awareness in Non-native Varieties of English', *Journal of Sociolinguistics*, 9 (1): 194–224.

Tajfel, H. and Turner, J. C. (1986), 'The Social Identity Theory of Intergroup Behaviour', in S. Worchel and W. G. Austin (eds), *Psychology of Intergroup Relations*, 7–24. Chicago: Nelson-Hall.

Van Leeuwen, T. and Wodak, R. (1999), 'Legitimizing Immigration Control: A Discourse-Historical Analysis', *Discourse Studies*, 1 (1), 83–118.

Wodak, R. and Boukala, S. (2015), '(Supra)national Identity and Language: Rethinking National and European Migration Policies and the Linguistic Integration of Migrants', *Annual Review of Applied Linguistics*, 35: 253–73.

Zhang, Q. (2005), 'A Chinese yuppie in Beijing: Phonological Variation and the Construction of a New Professional Identity', *Language in Society*, 34 (3): 431–66.

8

Discursive practices in online media

Language ideologies in Ukraine in a time of crisis

Alla Nedashkivska

1 Introduction

Ukraine's vibrant linguistic diversity continues to be a source of tensions, conflicts and debates. Its two major languages are Ukrainian and Russian, and they continue to be the subject of lively political, ideological and social debate in Ukrainian society. In the context of the Revolution of Dignity of 2014, Russia's annexation of Crimea and the current Russian war in Eastern Ukraine, public discourse on languages and their roles in society is diverse, particularly acute and, at times, contradictory, demonstrating that issues of linguistic identity, language practices, language attitudes and beliefs continue to be fragile and vulnerable. At the same time, these issues are highly visible and deserving of scholarly discussion.

1.1 A brief overview of the linguistic situation in Ukraine

Since 1989, Ukrainian has been the sole state language of Ukraine. In 1996, the Constitution of an independent Ukraine ratified this language law, securing the status of Ukrainian as a 'state language'. As Bilaniuk notes, 'the status of Ukrainian as the sole state language of Ukraine has stood firm as an emblem of the country's legitimacy since independence [1991]' (2017b: 344). However, in reality, the status of Ukrainian has not been as straightforward or smooth: in Ukraine, Ukrainian is often regarded as the language of ethnic Ukrainians and is relegated to a symbolic role.

Typically, Russian has been more widespread in Ukrainian society, enjoying a status of power and prestige, and is perceived as the language of social and economic mobility. Indeed, Russian remains common in industry, sports, culture and media, although, as discussed further, certain shifts are taking place. The visibility of Russian in Ukraine is the result of imperial Russia's power over Ukraine over centuries, and harsh Soviet language policies of Russification since the late 1920s, with their promotion of Russian as the language of 'inter-ethnic communication' among the peoples of the Soviet Union. The state of Russian in Ukraine is also influenced by the ambiguities of the 1989

Ukrainian language law with respect to language policies in the country and support for minority languages, Russian in particular, as stated in the law.

1.1.1 Language situation and language ideologies in Ukraine since independence

Since gaining independence in 1991, Ukraine has experienced significant tension between Ukrainian and Russian with respect to their status and their actual social, cultural and political functions. Kuchma, president from 1994 to 2004, led a period of ambivalent politics with respect to Ukrainian (Kulyk 2006). He spoke of the importance and preservation of Ukrainian, while still promoting Russian in several spheres (Nedashkivska 2010: 352–3). As Kulyk (2014b: 124) notes, in the initial post-Soviet years, different political and intellectual groups have assessed Ukraine's linguistic situation in various ways that relate to distinct language ideologies. In that period, allies of the Ukrainophone ideology tended to promote the wider use of Ukrainian and defended its national status (2014b: 124). Russian, as a minority language within this ideological position, was perceived as the language of a neighbouring state and the language of the former empire (2014b: 125). Meanwhile, supporters of a more Russophone ideology promoted 'the uninhibited use of Russian in all domains[,] ground[ing] their claim on the perceived role thereof as *the language of (more than) half of Ukraine's population ...*, as a *language which all Ukrainians know well*' (2014b: 125). In public discourse, these two ideologies were marginalized by the centrists, who 'sought to defend the interests not of one particular group but rather of the entire population, whose interests they saw as not determined by linguistic, ethnic or any other group identity' (2014b: 126).

Tensions surrounding language questions gained prominence prior to and during the national presidential campaign of 2004, followed by the Orange Revolution, as proposals to grant Russian the status of Ukraine's second state language entered the debate. During the presidential campaign of 2004, Yanukovych 'advanced the idea of the Russian language as the second state language (official language), using the slogan "two languages, one nation"' (Taranenko 2007: 132). In this same campaign, Yushchenko, president of Ukraine from January 2005 until February 2010, promoted Ukrainian. Since then, linguistic conflict has intensified, though it was not the main issue on the election agenda.[1]

While in power, Yanukovych, president of Ukraine from winter 2010 to February 2014, pursued vague and unclear language policies, with his stance on the status and function of both Ukrainian and Russian oscillating between various positions (Nedashkivska 2010: 353). In 2012, a controversial law 'On the principles of the State Language Policy' was passed. According to this law, in regions of Ukraine in which at least 10 per cent of the population spoke a minority language, this language was to be granted regional and official status. In the east and south of Ukraine, this minority language was Russian, which was thus given extensive rights to be used in official documentation, education, the judiciary system and mass media. In reality, this also meant that in nearly half of Ukraine's regions, the 'state' status of Ukrainian was significantly downgraded.[2]

Following the Orange Revolution, both Ukrainian and Russian speakers embraced the symbolic status of Ukrainian and accepted the coexistence of the two languages in most social domains (Kulyk 2014b: 138–9). The results of the 2012 study of language and identity (Kulyk 2013) demonstrate distinct dynamics in different parts of Ukraine, so that rather than demonstrating a process of Ukrainianization, the study reveals a 'deepening division into two parts with different languages and identities' (2013: 23).

The sociopolitical context of Ukraine's linguistic situation produces an extremely complicated map of language politics in Ukraine in the period leading to the Maidan Revolution of 2014. Studies focusing on the Maidan and post-Maidan periods have shown significant transformations in Ukrainian society, particularly its shift from an ethnically and linguistically divided nation to a civic society that embraces diverse ethnic and individual backgrounds (Onuch 2014: 49, Diuk 2014: 88, Osypian 2014: 180, Kulyk 2014a: 114). In the context of political events of the Maidan Revolution, both print and online media drew attention to the language question.

Most studies of the post-Maidan period demonstrate a transformation in language attitudes and ideologies in Ukraine (Kulyk 2018, Bilaniuk 2015, 2017a). Bilaniuk (2015, 2017a) delineates two main language ideologies: 'language does not matter' or 'it does not matter which language you speak', and 'language matters' or 'language choice matters'. The 'language does not matter' orientation promotes language choice: people are free to choose the language they speak, and this choice is not significant as long as they can understand each other (Bilaniuk 2017a). This trend could neutralize the politicization of language choice, but may also be problematic because in Ukraine, these languages are not treated as socially or politically equal, nor are they equally known by everyone (Bilaniuk 2015: 4). While discussing the 'language matters' ideology, Bilaniuk (2017a) talks about code-switching from Russian to Ukrainian. The 'language matters' trend supports linguistic Ukrainianization, the key idea of which 'is that Ukrainian language is essential in justifying Ukraine's sovereignty and reducing the threat from Russia' (2017a: 5).

Kulyk (2018) also demonstrates the contrasting and conflicting ideologies in the presentation of the national 'self' and the internal 'other', and the crucial role of language in this conflict. While analysing perceptions of Ukraine's Russian speakers, Kulyk outlines the competing language ideologies amidst the continuing conflict in Ukraine: the ideology of identification, which 'prioritizes the role of language as a marker of group identity, first and foremost a national one' (2018: 76); and the ideology of understanding, which is 'a widespread belief seeing language primarily not as a marker of group identity but as a conduit for conveying information' (2018: 79).[3]

In the context of the post-Maidan period, Bilaniuk also discusses the languages of protest and pluralingualism that are being promoted in Ukraine (2017b: 351–7). She notes that whereas purist ideologies remain significant, alternative language ideologies such as nonstandard language use, language mixing, and language playfulness are all visible (2017b: 360). Bilaniuk attributes such ideological shifts towards greater pluralism to Ukraine's confidence in its own sovereignty and the perceived stability of Ukrainian as the state language.

This study continues the discussion of the post-Maidan period of Ukraine, focusing on linguistic matters that became acute following the Revolution of Dignity and that are still pertinent in a time of war. The analysis incorporates the investigation of discursive practices in online media, relating them to the multitude of language ideologies currently being constructed and enacted in Ukraine.

2 Theoretical framework and methodology

2.1 Discursive practices and ideologies

Discursive practices, in Foucauldian terms, are 'places where what is said and what is done, rules imposed and reasons given, the planned and the taken for granted meet and interconnect' (cited in Bacchi and Bonham 2014: 181). For the purposes of this study, online media texts in which discussions about language and language roles, status and image in Ukraine 'meet and interconnect' are considered as 'places'. This study defines discursive practices as both linguistic practices, what social actors do with language; and as metadiscursive practices, what social actors communicate about the language.

Discursive practices are constitutive in both conventional and creative ways, by contributing to the reproduction of extant society, including social identities, social relationships, systems of knowledge and belief, and also by contributing to or facilitating transformations in a society (Fairclough 1992: 65). Discursive practices can have an ideological dimension, or may be 'ideologically invested' (1992: 67, 91). This ideological dimension is at the core of this study; specifically, the distinct discursive practices of online media texts and how these texts and practices contribute to the multiplicity of language ideologies and active social change in post-Maidan Ukraine.

I operate with Fairclough's view that ideologies are 'significations/constructions of reality (the physical world, social relations, social identities), which are built into various dimensions of the forms/meaning of discursive practices, and which contribute to the production, reproduction or transformation of relations of domination' (1992; 88). To this definition, I add relations of contrast, diversity and/or multiplicity. More precisely, I situate my analysis within the framework of language ideologies, 'which problematizes speakers' consciousness of their language and discourse as well as their positionality ... in shaping beliefs, proclamations, and evaluations of linguistic forms and discursive practices' (Kroskrity 2000: 192).

According to Kroskrity, language ideologies have four main overlapping layers of significance that assist in 'identify[ing] and exemplify[ing] language ideologies – both as beliefs about language and as a concept designed to assist in the study of those beliefs' (2000: 195). First, language ideologies are perceptions and discourses that promote, protect and legitimate the interests of a particular social or cultural group (2000: 195). Second, 'language ideologies are profitably conceived as multiple ... [and] are thus grounded in social experience which is never uniformly distributed throughout polities of any scale' (2000: 197). Third, language ideologies may be either explicitly articulated by social actors, or embedded in discursive practices (2000: 198). Fourth, language ideologies mediate between the socio-cultural experiences of social actors and their linguistic and discursive resources (2000: 200). This study also relies on the assumption that 'language ideologies are constantly produced, reproduced, circulated in a variety of discursive arenas, including (but not restricted to) mediated public discourses' (Androutsopoulos 2010: 184).

Drawing on the key concepts presented earlier,[4] the primary aim is to discuss how discursive practices of online media construct, reproduce, present and circulate specific language ideologies in various online spaces and texts.

2.2 Data

The data in this study come from a larger project that addresses how language and linguistic matters are presented in Ukraine in general, and in media and social media in particular. The study focuses on online media devoted to language matters that have emerged since 2012, such as the passing of the Regional language law, but mostly those following the Maidan revolution of 2013–4. I view these texts as socio-cultural constructs, as discursive practices and as 'ideological sites' (Silverstein 1979; Philips 2000) that drive and portray social, linguistic and ideological tendencies in a particular community. In other words, media sites are both sources and results of specific discursive practices that contribute to multiple language ideologies. As Spitulnik (1998: 181) notes, media are 'exceptionally charged arenas' for battles over languages, their use and value 'because of their high prestige, their high visibility, and their inherent publicizing function'.

The original intent of this study was to understand the diversity of stances and beliefs about language(s) in Ukraine at the time of the crisis. The project began with an observation of Facebook posts devoted to language matters, and communication related to those posts. In the course of data collection, the snowball effect proved advantageous, as the Facebook search yielded references to other online media that highlight specific language-related projects that were relevant to this study. Therefore, the satellite texts are also considered in this project.

In order to effectively identify relevant texts, a regular search for Facebook pages was carried out using key words in Ukrainian [U] and Russian [R]: [U] *українська мова* (Ukrainian language), *українська* (Ukrainian), *двомовність* (bilingualism), *Україна двомовна* (Ukraine bilingual), *багатомовність* (multilingualism), *багатомовна Україна* (multilingual Ukraine), *російська в Україні* (Russian in Ukraine), *мова* (language), *діалект* (dialect), *діалекти України* (dialects of Ukraine), *мови меншин* (languages of minorities), *меншини* (minorities), *меншини в Україні* (minorities in Ukraine); and [R] *украинский язык* (Ukrainian language), *русский в Украине* (Russian in Ukraine), *русский язык и Украина* (Russian language and Ukraine). This Facebook search did not yield any results on dialects, language varieties and minority languages, but did references to online media productions (television shows and animations) that relate to dialects, language varieties and minority languages, which are included in this study. Overall, the search generated eleven Facebook pages relating to language matters in Ukraine. From these pages, nineteen satellite pages and sites, not necessarily connected to Facebook, were established as relevant to the purposes of this study. The following main criteria were used to narrow down the corpus: (a) the topic of the page or site relates primarily to language and language matters in Ukraine, as evident from the title of the page or site and from major discussions; (b) the page or site is not produced or managed by a specific institution, establishment or political entity; (c) the site is not produced or managed by scholars; and (d) the creation date is in or after 2012.

After the core selection of eighteen social media pages and eight online media sites were established, the primary units of analysis that 'express or signal the opinions, perspective, position, interests or other properties of groups' (van Dijk 1995: 22) were identified. As van Dijk notes, the representations of ideologies 'are often articulated along an *us* versus *them* dimension' (1995: 22); therefore, a unit that 'expresses, establishes, confirms or emphasizes a self-interested group opinion, perspective or position, especially in a broader socio-political context of social struggle, is a candidate for ... an "ideological" analysis' (1995: 23). Considering these properties of discourse, the analysis was restricted to the following units: profile images, titles and slogans on the profile image and/or the main page, and main description of the project with its aims, if focusing on language matters (the 'about', or 'community' or 'info' sections on a Facebook page or a site). Discussion threads on the Facebook pages, including images, relating to language matters were also studied, with a time span of one month from the date of first access set as the window for data collection. This selection yielded 109 units of analysis. Because the units of analysis are both verbal and visual, the analysis incorporated a multimodal approach that captures how linguistic and visual texts contribute to the representation of language(s) and language matters in online media. The multimodal analysis in this project, as in many other studies in the field, is grounded on Kress and van Leeuwen's seminal work on the grammar of visual design (1996/2006). As Kress and van Leeuwen (2001) demonstrated, visual texts, specifically the juxtaposition of verbal and visual texts, provide a wider range of expression than verbal texts alone. Without claiming any quantitative authority, this study seeks to provide a close reading of these texts as representative of the visible opinions, perspectives, positions and interests of a particular group that produces and reproduces, and is produced and reproduced by, this set of language-ideologically charged texts.

The texts were collected primarily in November 2016, with additional texts added to the corpus in the course of 2017–8.

3 Analysis: Language ideologies in Ukraine in a time of crisis

In the data set, the units of analysis, specified earlier, are all that contain explicit references to, and include arguments about, language(s) and language matters in Ukraine. The analysis of these units paid special attention to how language(s) and language matters are explicitly topicalized, used, presented and discussed, both verbally and visually. Each unit was studied and classified with respect to theme saliency. The verbal analysis relied on identifying key arguments. The visual analysis considered the concepts of (a) the representation of social actors; (b) modality, particularly colour and, to some extent, (c) composition of image (Kress and van Leeuwen 1996/2006). For instance, the salient theme of the site *Мова серце нації* (Language is the Heart of the Nation) was identified as 'language – the national symbol'. The main slogan of the site,

'Language matters', another unit of analysis, was thematized as 'Ukrainian language is important'. This slogan was presented against a background of Ukraine's national colours of blue and yellow, a visual unit of analysis that was classified under the theme of 'language as a national symbol'. The title of another site, *Я спілкуюся українською мовою* (I communicate in Ukrainian), was classified as 'communicating in Ukrainian'. Additionally, the site presents an image of the national symbols of Ukraine, the trident and the national colours, and the visual unit was therefore classified as 'Ukrainian – the national symbol'. In discussion threads, each verbal and visual post, as a unit, was similarly classified.[5] With respect to online media productions, one episode was chosen for analysis to determine its main theme with respect to language matters. For instance, an episode of the online television production *Наші без Раші* (Our [people] without Russia) that was devoted to linguistic matters was classified under the theme of 'Galician dialect'.[6] All units of analysis were similarly classified into a total of 152 themes during the initial process.[7] The texts that were studied produced a number of specific themes that were very generally grouped as follows: (a) Ukrainian – national symbol, Ukrainian – core/foundation of nation, Ukrainian – ethnic and national identity, my language – Ukraine, and Ukrainian national language – under threat and in need of protection; (b) Ukrainian language: language of people, dynamic language, lively language, timely language, modern language, language in need of rejuvenation, cultivating native language, communicating in the native, Ukrainian, language, switching to Ukrainian and Ukrainian a defensive weapon against Russia; (c) Ukraine is bilingual, Russian is equal to Ukrainian and Ukraine with national unity is bilingual; and (d) Surzhyk as a legitimate language variant, regional dialects as legitimate means of communication, diaspora dialect, English influence on Ukrainian, minority languages as visible in Ukraine and multilingual Ukraine. Subsequently, these themes were narrowed into four visible language ideologies: (a) the ideology of language as a national and state symbol (twenty-nine themes); (b) the ideology of 'mother tongue' or native language activism (ninety-six themes); (c) the ideology of 'democratic' linguistic bilingualism (eight themes); (d) the ideology of pluralingualism and internal diversity (seventeen themes).[8] Overall, the analysis of discursive practices of online media shows diverse ideological dimensions and a multiplicity of language ideologies in today's post-Maidan Ukraine, and these are illustrated below with representative examples of the four language ideologies identified in the data set.

This project cannot do justice to all the intricacies of the texts in question, and its aim is not to study the prevalence of specific ideological positions, which would require a more statistically oriented work.[9] Rather, it focuses on those specific aspects of the texts/pages that clearly point towards a specific orientation of the text with respect to language matters, and thus to language ideological positions visible in online media.

3.1 The ideology of language as a national and state symbol

The ideology of language as a national and state symbol, in the sense of 'one nation, one principal language' as a crucial means of achieving national identity, is prominent in the discursive practices discussed in this study. The iconization of Ukrainian as the only language of Ukraine, Ukrainian as the 'heart' of the Ukrainian nation and one language as the foundation of the state, are the threads that are attributed to the ideology of language as a national and state symbol.

The Facebook site *Мова – серце нації* (Language is the Heart of the Nation) constructs the ideology of language as national symbol.[10] It is 'the page of Ukrainian linguistic and cultural identity', and its goal is 'to support Ukrainian ethnicity, contribute to the preservation of the development of the Ukrainian culture in conditions of anti-Ukrainian governmental politics of the so called "state of Ukraine", as well as a call from the world, which is in the process of globalization. The page is supported by Ukrainians of good will'. The profile image features the slogan 'Language matters'.[11] Most discussions on this page relate to Ukrainian as the sole state language of Ukraine, which must be protected, promoted and popularized.

Another example is *Українська мова – код Української Нації* (The Ukrainian language is the code of the Ukrainian Nation),[12] which, according to the moderators, was created to support a movement towards the protection of the Ukrainian language. The discussions here are mostly about the state of Ukrainian in society, language laws and their regulations, including not observing language laws, and calls to preserve and cherish Ukrainian. The site also features poetry and quotations from prominent writers and philosophers regarding language and its central role in nation-building. The overarching theme of the site is that Ukrainian is the core of the Ukrainian state and the Ukrainian nation. The capitalization of the terms *Українська Мова* (Ukrainian language) and *Українська Нація* (Ukrainian nation) in several posts, even though they would not be capitalized in Ukrainian, is noteworthy. This mechanical feature as a linguistic practice signals the prominence and elevation of language in relation to a nation in this discursive and ideological space.

The ideology of language as a national symbol is visible in discursive practices on sites such as *Я спілкуюся українською мовою* (I communicate in Ukrainian).[13]

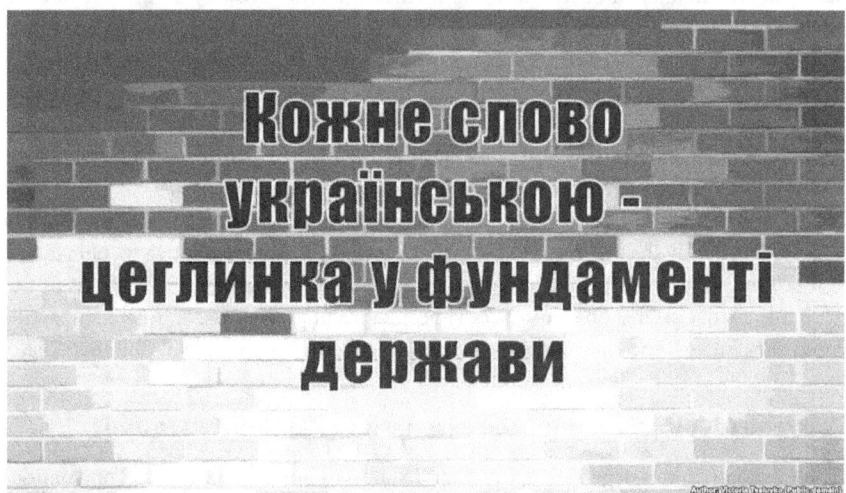

Figure 8.1 Language as a national symbol.[14]
(Every word in Ukrainian – is a small brick in the foundation of the state)

Figure 8.2 One nation – One language.¹⁵
(Ukraine, am – I; a Ukrainian, am – I; my language is – I. please ... do not hassle me...)

Figure 8.1 from this ideological space illustrates the construction of the idea of language as national symbol and an essential element in nation-building:

This particular message was followed by several comments, such as 'let's cherish and preserve our language', 'the state is the language', 'first of all, we need to think in Ukrainian' and 'let's respect our language because the country begins with the language'. The visual text foregrounds the national colours of Ukraine, and all of these comments have a common thread that links language to nation-building.

The same social media community featured another discussion relating to the thread of 'one nation – one language', illustrated in Figure 8.2.

The message in Figure 8.2 links the concepts of Ukraine, its citizens and its language to the personal and national 'self'. This Ukrainian 'self', as depicted in large font at the centre of the image, is being invaded and is in need of protection. In this post, the image of a male in a Ukrainian embroidered shirt, holding a weapon, represents the Ukrainian national 'self' being threatened and compromised.

In all the examples discussed here, language emblematizes the people of Ukraine and is presented at the core of the nation, as the national 'self' and as an essential part of the independent state. These discursive practices promote the ideology of the Ukrainian language as the national and state symbol of Ukraine.

3.2 The ideology of 'mother-tongue' or native language activism

In the corpus of this study, the ideology of 'mother tongue' or native language activism emerges as a process in which Ukrainian, in addition to being promoted as the national symbol of Ukraine, is thematized as the language of its people: dynamic, timely and modern. Ukrainian is presented in these items as the native language of Ukraine and of Ukrainians that should be rejuvenated and cultivated.[16] In addition, this native language activism is visible in the various appeals to communicating in Ukrainian, calls for switching to Ukrainian and portrayals of Ukrainian as a defensive weapon against Russia. The following representative examples illustrate this ideological orientation.

The discursive practices of the Facebook community *Українська мова – жива мова мого народу* (Ukrainian Language – The dynamic language of my people) construct an image of Ukrainian as what the site's title indicates: the language of the people and a dynamic language.[17] As its administrators point out, this social media community 'is created for all of those who want to learn about our Ukrainian language through history, Culture, Traditions as the basis of our nation, in the process of live communication' (capitalization and bold in original). The main goals of this community are to 'learn, acquire, disseminate and popularize the Ukrainian language, language history and simply history of our nation, culture and traditions not only in Ukraine, but also beyond its borders. We are energetic, positive and young Ukrainians'. In its profile picture, the community highlights the cultural traditions of Ukraine (for example, the traditional colourful wreath as a head piece), its literary past (a quotation from the Ukrainian poet Taras Shevchenko, 'Love your own Ukraine') and its vibrancy (the multicoloured palette of the profile picture).

The themes of bringing the Ukrainian language to the minds of the people, creating a positive and trendy image for Ukrainian, and making Ukrainian visible in society are prominent in the material examined here. For instance, the online resource *Словопис* (Wordwriter)[18] popularizes Ukrainian via the following slogans: 'the Ukrainian language – it is contemporary and timely' and 'Enrich yourself with Ukrainian!' Both are powerful statements, suggesting that, regardless of what one's first language is, Ukrainian as the native language will enrich one as a person, as a Ukrainian.

The project *Мова ДНК нації* (The Language is the DNA of a nation),[19] stresses in its very title that language is the core, the DNA, and the main mechanism of a nation. An educational digital project featuring various platforms for interaction, the project exhibits native language activism by encouraging the teaching and learning of Ukrainian, and seeking to create a positive and interactive relationship between Ukrainian and its users. The project popularizes Ukrainian and promotes the 'correct' forms of Ukrainian without unnecessary borrowings.

Calls for language rejuvenation are found in the project *Чиста мова* (Clean Language),[20] whose title suggests a tendency towards purification. The primary goal of this community, as noted by its administrators, is to 'remember our language and to contribute to its richness and its potential'. Their main motto is: 'One can master a foreign language in six years, but a native language needs to be studied over a lifetime'. This quotation, adapted from Voltaire, directly contributes to native language activism by reminding readers of the need for lifelong attention to one's native language.

The crowdsourcing projects *Мислово* (WeWord)[21] and *Словотвір* (Word creator)[22] are young peoples' responses to a lack of language planning initiatives towards the corpus of Ukrainian, by encouraging contributors to send recommendations about which items should be included in the *new* database of Ukrainian.

Figure 8.3 Distancing Ukrainian from Russian.²³
(This is *syr*=cheese. 'Tvoroh=cheese' is in the language of the enemy)

The theme of Ukrainian as a distinct language from Russian is common in these texts, as illustrated in Figure 8.3.

In this image, the Russian word *творог*, commonly used by Ukrainians, is juxtaposed with the 'true' Ukrainian word *сир*, which is presented as much more suitable, correct and better. Additionally, this example further elevates the native language by overtly presenting the Russian language as the language of the enemy, thus constructing an opposition and articulating its ideology along the 'us' and 'them' axis (van Dijk 1995: 22).

The theme of appeals for communication in Ukrainian are visible in the Facebook community *Я спілкуюся українською мовою*,²⁴ whose main objective as stated by its moderators is to protect and preserve the Ukrainian language. Only Ukrainian is allowed in communications on this 'ideological site', which indexes inclusions and exclusions based on the language one uses. Participants of this site display their native language activism by sharing their thoughts about fostering the use of Ukrainian in online space, media, schools and other public spaces.

The topic of language choice in Ukraine is a common theme in discussions in this community. The overt question 'Do you speak Ukrainian?' and lively discussions surrounding this question further illustrate the users' native language activism, presented in Figure 8.4.

In Figure 8.4, the question is presented in a flirtatious manner, supported by the image and the gaze of the participant, which playfully promote the use of the Ukrainian language. The discussions that followed this post display the community's predominant goal of presenting Ukrainian as the native language of all Ukrainians and the language that every Ukrainian should know, use and cherish.

Another site, *Українська мова для всіх* (The Ukrainian language for all),²⁶ is meant for those 'who are not indifferent to Ukrainian. For those who know it and do not

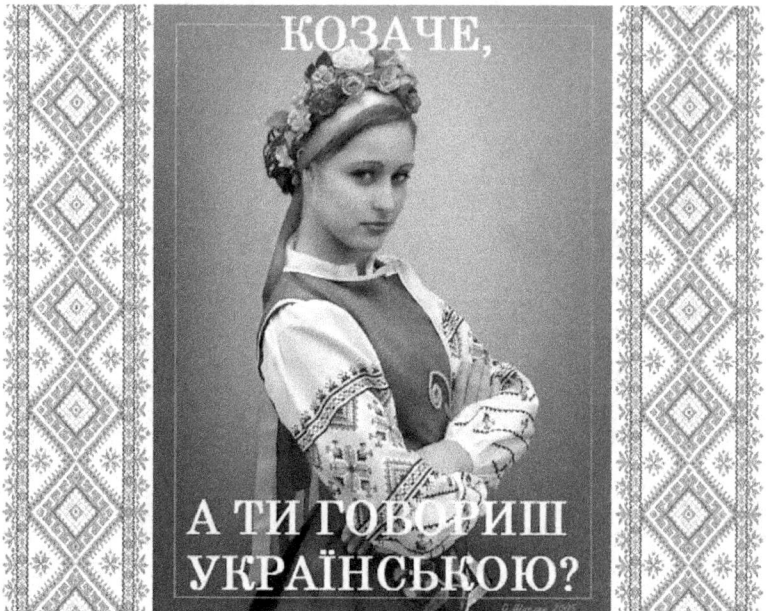

Figure 8.4 Language choice: Do you speak Ukrainian?[25]
(Hey Cossack, do you speak Ukrainian?)

know it. For those who want to learn it, and also for those who can help others learn it'. The profile image stresses the 'softness, fashion and uniqueness' of Ukrainian, with the slogan 'This is your language!' calling for members to communicate in Ukrainian, and for those whose first language is not Ukrainian to learn it.

One particular display of native language activism is the encouragement of Russian-speaking Ukrainians to switch to Ukrainian in everyday communication. The Facebook group *Переходь на українську* (Switch to Ukrainian)[27] announces such an appeal in its name.[28] This group grew out of the social initiative of the same name, which began in 2016.[29] Its profile image showcases a roadway crosswalk painted in blue and yellow, which are the national colours of Ukraine. In the 'about' section, the creators note that this project presents 'stories of people who switched to the Ukrainian language and since then communicate in it constantly'. In their posts, members discuss various topics relating to Ukrainian, its status in society, and some of the intricacies of the language and its structure. One discussion also includes calls to the Ukrainian army to make a switch in their language practices in favour of Ukrainian.

The switch to Ukrainian is further justified by the reality of contemporary Ukraine, especially in a time of political crisis and war with Russia, as Ukrainian is portrayed as a defence weapon against Russian aggression. The site of the pan-Ukrainian association *Рух захисту української мови* (Movement to defend Ukrainian),[30] as illustrated in Figure 8.5, amply demonstrates this call to speak Ukrainian as a defensive weapon in the war against Russia:

Figure 8.5 Switch to Ukrainian: Language as a defense weapon.[31]
(Switch to Ukrainian! Speak the state language and language of the nation! Ukrainian is our weapon in the war with Russia!)

In addition to underlining the importance of Ukrainian in the face of Russian aggression, this text demonstrates the theme of promotion of Ukrainian as 'the state language of the nation', that is, as the national symbol of the Ukrainian state.

The Facebook site *Ініціатива 'Мовна безпека'* (Initiative 'Language Security')[32] is not a sizeable community, but its goal and thematic discussions are meant to withstand Russification in Ukraine, underscore the idea that Ukrainian is in need of protection and emphasize the acuteness of the language situation in Ukraine today.

Multiple discursive practices that focus on the promotion of the 'mother tongue' or native language activism, as in the examples cited earlier, construct Ukrainian as the language of the Ukrainian people that is lively, vibrant, fun and distinct from Russian. A number of these discursive practices also construct Ukrainian as in need of rejuvenation and cleansing from unnecessary borrowings. The practices of language creativity and crowdsourcing are directed towards enhancing the quality of the Ukrainian being used. Native language activism is visible in communities that voice appeals for communications in Ukrainian in Ukraine in both physical and online spaces and to legitimize the use of Ukrainian in everyday communication by calling on Russian-speaking Ukrainians to switch to Ukrainian. These tendencies are also strengthened by the construction of Ukrainian as a means of defence against Russian aggression.

3.3 The ideology of 'democratic' linguistic bilingualism

A distinct ideological orientation from those discussed earlier is visible in sites that portray Ukraine as an inherently bilingual nation in which both Ukrainian and Russian have their respective and well-established spaces. Some of these texts display an orientation towards a presumably democratic bilingualism, aimed at mediating national unity regardless of linguistic diversity.

The promotion of a bilingual Ukraine is seen on [R] *Украинская нация – двуязычная*, or [U] *Українська нація – двомовна* (Ukrainian nation – bilingual) site.[33] Unlike other sites discussed, its profile image is not tied to any Ukrainian national symbols, national colours or narrative about the language. Instead, the image is rather depoliticized or seemingly neutral, showing an image of Odessa as the sea port of Ukraine.

Under its description, the administrators note that this group is created specifically for discussing language questions in Ukraine, 'for those who consider that the Russian language equally to the Ukrainian language, contributes to the richness of Ukraine', with the main focus of the page presented in both Russian and Ukrainian. The discussions are based on the idea that Ukraine is bilingual, with bilingualism projected as non-accommodating, or what Bilaniuk calls the 'language does not matter' ideology (2015, 2017a), in which people speak whichever language they prefer. A closer examination of the discussions reveals that the language of choice on this site is exclusively Russian, and its main theme is that Russian is discriminated against in Ukraine and that it should be given the status of a second state language in Ukraine. One image shows the slogan [R] *Русский язык* [U] *Понад усе!* (The Russian language above all else!),[34] clearly promoting the superiority of Russian and of its status and prestige in this discursive space. Therefore, this site is an example of hybrid ideology construction that projects a misbalanced bilingualism. On the surface, the title and the group description suggest a 'democratic' bilingualism, but the discussions, including those by the group administrators, belie this claim. Rather, it promotes a hierarchical bilingualism with Russian given an elevated status, exemplifying the ideological orientation of 'democratic' bilingualism. As Spitulnik noted, '[i]n some cases ideologies do create appearances that mystify or falsify realities', (1998: 164) and the ideological site 'Ukrainian nation – bilingual' constitutes just such a case.[35]

The promotion of a bilingual Ukraine, a united country regardless of language choice, became particularly visible after the collapse of the Yanukovych regime and the new government's attempt to revoke the Regional Languages Law of 2012. Although this attempt was blocked, it did have immediate effects. Specifically, on 2 March 2014, all of Ukraine's national television channels began the 'Country with national unity' campaign, whose goal was 'to demonstrate unity during an imperative historical moment in the life of Ukraine, not allowing a destabilization of the situation'.[36] Some of these channels even produced a series of videos under the bilingual heading 'Ukraine is united!' (Nedashkivska 2015). Other events related to the campaign included code-switching flash mobs, bilingual language marathons on television and radio, students' public statements and mass demonstrations (2015: 307–8).

The 'Country with national unity' campaign illustrates the construction of an ideology of 'democratic' bilingualism that embraces bilingualism with a free individual language choice. As Bilaniuk notes, this 'bilingual trend can be seen as liberal, as on the surface it gives people freedom in language choice' (2017a: 140). However, in Ukraine, Ukrainian and Russian are not equally known by everyone, nor they are treated as socially and politically equal by all, which raises questions about the nature of this constructed bilingualism.

The 'ideological sites' discussed in this project oppose the one nation/one language ideology. Instead, they illustrate an ideology of 'democratic' bilingualism with the two languages presumably, but not in reality, functioning on equal footing while mediating national unity.

3.4 The ideology of pluralingualism and internal diversity

'[M]ass media build the communicative space of the nation-state, all of nation's languages, dialects and language varieties' (Spitulnik 1998: 165). Ukraine enjoys a discernible presence and vitality of language varieties and dialects, including minority languages.

The Maidan Revolution of Dignity of 2013–14 'spurred active play and innovation in language' (Bilaniuk 2017b: 352). These linguistic innovations and playfulness included neologisms for new phenomena that arose during the revolution, and also new linguistic vulgarities aimed at corrupt authorities[37] (2017b: 353). Another linguistic practice common on social media was the use of Surzhyk, a mixture of Russian and Ukrainian, as demonstrated by the site *Репка* ('Little Turnip' in Russian).[38] Participants on this site call their mixed language 'fighting' or 'martial Surzhyk' (2017b: 354).

Ukrainian regional dialects and minority languages have also become visible in discursive practices and online media projects such as video and animation. One such animation, *Наша Файта*,[39] depicts a case of multiple language varieties living in the Zakarpattia region: with Ukrainian as the leading voice, along with the distinct Zakarpattia dialect, Hungarian, Rusyn and Romani as minority languages, Surzhyk, and Ukrainian as spoken by foreigners with a heavy accent. The interplay of languages and language varieties in this animation clearly represents the multilingual map of the Zakarpattia region in particular, and the multilingual nature of Ukraine in general.

The online project *Наші без Раші* (Our [people] without Russia) is a production of sketch-videos by the *Kolegi Studio!* in Lviv,[40] which uses humour to showcase changes and reforms in Ukraine. The Canadian Ukrainian diaspora dialect is featured in the *Майкл Щур* (Michael Shchur)[41] satirical newscast, performed by the journalist Roman Vintoniv (Bilaniuk 2017b: 356).[42] A parody of a regional cultural talk show the *Дізель Шоу* (Diesel Show), in the programme *Від джерел до джерел* (From Roots to Roots),[43] uses the diverse language situation in Ukraine as a subject for humour.

The examples discussed here portray a pluralingual and linguistically diverse Ukraine. Relying on satire and humour, this ideological orientation mediates diversity and national unity by acknowledging the very existence of pluralingualism.

4 Discussion and conclusions

This study focuses on various discursive practices in online media texts that relate to language, particularly those that were triggered by the political unrest in Ukraine. The current war with Russia, disappointment with government policies and the perceived instability of the state constitute the particular social and political contexts for these texts. All the projects discussed here were created after the passing of the Regional Languages Law in 2012 and the Maidan revolution of 2013-4. The study examines various discursive practices of online media and how they endow and construct varying roles, statuses and images for the different languages spoken in Ukraine. These practices are ideologically invested in contributing to a multiplicity of language ideologies in Ukrainian society. A multilingual Ukraine, reflective of other multilingual and multiethnic societies, continues to face one of the fundamental problems of 'virtually every nation-state in the world today: the challenge of forging a unified national identity while simultaneously giving some recognition to national diversity' (Spitulnik 1998: 165). This fundamental reality of Ukrainian society, particularly in a time of war, foregrounds the role, status and functions of languages in Ukraine.

The online media texts that constitute the communicative space of Ukraine present a set of social meanings, values and relationships. They were studied as 'ideological sites' and advocates for transformation in language practices, beliefs about languages and language changes in Ukraine. These texts may be viewed as examples of a new online media sociolinguistic culture that cultivates shifts in status, roles and values of languages in Ukraine through the various language ideologies, movements and tendencies promoted in and by these 'ideological sites'.

The examination of these texts revealed four prominent language ideologies that are embedded in discursive practices of online media with respect to the role, function and image of language in social life. Importantly, all the language ideologies discussed in this project display the multilayered nature of this concept. The analysis of the text supports the four layers of significance outlined by Kroskrity (2000): (a) distinct language ideologies represent the interests of specific social groups in Ukraine, and discursive practices underlie the promotion, protection and legitimization of these interests; (b) language ideologies are multiple, reflecting varying social experiences; (c) language ideologies may be explicitly articulated or not explicitly articulated, but read from actual practices; and (d) language ideologies are mediators between the socio-cultural experiences of language users and their linguistic and discursive resources (2000: 195–200).

The ideology of language as a national and state symbol of Ukraine upholds Ukrainian as the only language that can secure Ukraine's sovereignty and political stability. The Ukrainian language is promoted as the heart and essence of the Ukrainian nation, thus directly linked to nation-building efforts for the good of all Ukrainians.

The ideology of the 'mother tongue', or native language activism, is illustrated by the multiple discursive practices in media and is especially prominent in online spaces. Native Ukrainian is constructed as the language of the Ukrainian people, as a language that is lively, vibrant, fun, and distinct from Russian, and as a fighting tool and defence weapon against Russia. These texts also demonstrated practices geared towards the rejuvenation of Ukrainian, ridding the language of unnecessary borrowings and mixed forms, including discursive practices of crowdsourcing and online language creativity. In addition, this ideological trend was related to calls for communication in Ukrainian in Ukraine and appeals for switching to Ukrainian in everyday practices.

The ideology of 'democratic' bilingualism promotes the idea of a bilingual and united Ukraine. In this ideological trend, the socio-cultural experiences of Russian-speaking Ukrainians are explicitly articulated as mediating between unity and bilingualism, thus projecting non-hierarchical power relationships between Ukrainian and Russian. The actual discourse practices show that this non-hierarchical relationship is questionable and often is showcased only on the surface.

The ideology of pluralingualism and internal diversity, on the one hand, is illustrated by the languages of protest representing interests of various social groups (Bilaniuk

2017b). Such examples, including vulgarities, obscenities and martial Surzhyk, are viewed as reactions to political events, corrupt authorities and the war with Russia. This ideology is also illustrated by the showcasing of diverse dialects and regional variants, including minority languages of Ukraine on various media 'ideological sites' and humorous portrayals of the pluralingual situation.[44]

Needless to say, this project does not preclude the possibility of establishing and categorizing other ideological tendencies emerging from the study of other texts and perspectives. One may also seek to investigate language ideologies that are absent from and neither produced or constructed in discursive practices of Ukrainian media. These investigations could have implications for studying and understanding other multilingual and multiethnic societies.

Even though the dataset in this project is relatively small, it nevertheless offers a view into the plurality of language ideologies in the online media communicative space of Ukraine, forming an interesting basis for future discoveries. In addition, future research may find statistically quantifying the findings of this study useful. A vivid plurality of language ideologies in Ukraine, as discussed earlier, may serve as a springboard for future investigations.

I conclude by stating that the multiplicity of language ideologies in Ukraine is pronounced, and, importantly, it is the society and its people that are the main driving force in these 'ideological sites'. Various online media communities take on language initiatives and facilitate transformations. The multiplicity of ideologies is directly related to the current discursive practices that contribute to the transformation of the society, its social identities, relationships, systems of knowledge and beliefs (Fairclough 1992: 65). Spitulnik stresses 'that language ideologies ... are never just about language. Language ideologies are, among many other things, about the construction and legitimation of power, the production of social relations of sameness and difference, and the creation of cultural stereotypes about types of speakers and social groups' (1998: 164). And because Ukraine remains in a state of relative political uncertainty and in the midst of societal changes and reforms, it remains to be seen how the language-ideological arena will evolve.

Notes

1 On language politics after 2004, see Kulyk (2006, 2010).
2 For the period preceding the Maidan revolution of 2014, see Moser (2013).
3 Kulyk's initial introduction of language ideologies classification defines a third ideology of purity, 'which translates the notion of identity/authenticity into the imperative of correspondence of language varieties and forms to a standard seen as an embodiment of the nation's true essence' (2010: 84).
4 This study is also informed by other prominent frameworks: see Silverstein (1979); Woolard (1992); Woolard and Schieffelin (1994), and theoretical developments in the study of language ideologies: see Kroskrity (2000); and Dailey O'Cain (2017).
5 In certain discussion threads, posts displayed conflicting themes. Each post, as a unit, was classified accordingly.

6 If the text displayed more than one theme, and these themes were both considered salient, the text was classified as belonging to all the themes identified. Therefore, the overall number of themes identified is higher than the number of units studied.
7 Although certain classifications may be subjective, a scholar must familiarize him/herself with what is taking place on these sites by becoming an insider to a certain extent prior to carrying out the study, which will inevitably include results that stem from the researcher's personal observations.
8 Two units, out of 152, were classified as 'neutral'.
9 The ideology of 'mother tongue' or native language activism stands out as most prominent and is reserved for future investigation.
10 Accessed 9/25/2018:https://www.facebook.com/Mova.Online/?tn-str=k*F&hc_location=group_dialog
11 This and similar quotations are cited and translated from the online sources, referenced when first introduced. Most are from the 'about', 'community' and 'info' sections found on a Facebook page.
12 Accessed 10/13/2018:https://www.facebook.com/groups/1013477292067876/about/
13 Accessed 10/22/2018:https://www.facebook.com/groups/1453810038227000/
14 Accessed 10/12/2018: https://www.facebook.com/groups/1453810038227000/
15 Accessed 09/12/2018:https://www.facebook.com/photo.php?fbid=435710680124082&set=g.1453810038227000&type=1&theater&ifg=1
16 In Ukrainian, the term 'native language' does not necessarily refer to one's first language. 'Ukrainians tend to use the term to refer to the language with which they most closely identify' (Friedman 2016:168). Therefore, one's native language is the language that generally corresponds to a person's ethnic heritage, even if the person is not proficient in the language he/she considers his/her 'native'.
17 Accessed 09/27/2018:https://www.facebook.com/groups/1173297849445774/
18 Accessed 10/01/2018:https://www.facebook.com/photo.php?fbid=417823015246182&set=g.1453810038227000&type=1&theater&ifg=1
19 Accessed 10/19/2018:https://ukr-mova.in.ua
20 Accessed 10/22/2018:https://www.facebook.com/chystamova/
21 Accessed 10/22/2018:http://myslovo.com
22 Accessed 11/24/2016:https://slovotvir.org.ua
23 Accessed 05/15/2018:https://www.facebook.com/photo.php?fbid=1655398194521740&set=g.1453810038227000&type=1&theater&ifg=1
24 Accessed 09/25/2018:https://www.facebook.com/groups/1453810038227000/about/
25 Accessed 0925/2018:https://www.facebook.com/photo.php?fbid=389670104836841&set=g.1453810038227000&type=1&theater&ifg=1
26 Accessed 09/25/2018:https://www.facebook.com/groups/367613903441695/about/
27 Accessed 10/17/2018:https://www.facebook.com/pg/perehodnamovu/about/?ref=page_internal
28 Bilaniuk (2017a), focusing on practices of conversions from speaking Russian to speaking Ukrainian by Ukrainian citizens, mentions this same campaign to illustrate the 'language matters' ideology.
29 Accessed 05/05/2018:http://movomarafon.in.ua/about-us/
30 Accessed 10/22/2018:https://www.facebook.com/pg/zahystukrmovy/about/?ref=page_internal
31 Accessed 09/25/2018:https://www.facebook.com/photo.php?fbid=433040317075214&set=g.1453810038227000&type=1&theater&ifg=1
32 Accessed 09/27/2018:https://www.facebook.com/groups/1857453157856494/

33 Accessed 10/16/2018:https://www.facebook.com/groups/964607810308733/
34 Accessed 09/25/2018:https://www.facebook.com/photo.php?fbid=2047877661920363&set=pcb.1263654943737350&type=3&theater&ifg=1
35 Spitulnik discusses democratic pluralism and hierarchical pluralism as two opposing language ideologies in mediating national unity and national diversity in Zambia (1998).
36 Accessed 04/02/2015:http://www.telekritika.ua/rinok/2014-03-03/91035
37 The analysis also relies on some examples from Bilaniuk's study (2017b) to demonstrate the ideology of pluralingualism and internal diversity in the discursive practices of Ukrainian media.
38 Accessed 05/15/2018:http://repka.club
39 Accessed 10/22/2018:https://www.youtube.com/user/KarMan2013?feature=watch
40 Accessed 10/16/2018:https://www.youtube.com/channel/UCGwARGVTJmetRpWEk2sIMYg
41 Accessed 10/22/2018:https://www.facebook.com/michael.shchur.3
42 Bilaniuk discusses other examples of pluralingual media texts (2017b: 355-357).
43 Accessed 11/20/2017:https://www.youtube.com/watch?v=5FCg-wW7Fxg
44 The grouping of language ideologies in present-day Ukraine into four categories does not deny other typologies with respect to the Ukrainian context. For example, Kulyk (2010, 2018) cites three ideologies: identification, understanding and purity, while Bilaniuk (2015, 2017b) identifies two: language does not matter and language matters. The group of four categories in this project offers a different method of classifying the themes identified in discursive practices of online media that project specific ideological positions, particularly in the wake of the Maidan revolution and the war with Russia.

References

Androutsopoulos, J. (2010), 'Ideologizing Ethnolectal German', in S. Johnson and T. M. Milani, *Language Ideologies and Media Discourse: Texts, Practices, Politics*, 182–202. London: Continuum.
Bachhi, C. and Bonham, J. (2014), 'Reclaiming Discursive Practices as an Analytic Focus: Political Implications', *Foucault Studies*, 17: 173-92.
Bilaniuk, L. (2015), 'Discourses of Language in the Zones of Conflict: Ideologies of Language in Wartime', Conference paper, *ASEEES Conference*, Philadelphia, November 20.
Bilaniuk, L. (2017a), 'Ideologies of Language in Wartime', in O. Bertelsen (ed.), *Revolution and War in Contemporary Ukraine*, 139-60, Stuttgart. Germany: ibidem-Verlag Press.
Bilaniuk, L. (2017b), 'Purism and Pluralism: Language Use Trends in Popular Culture in Ukraine since Independence', in M. S. Flier and A. Graziosi (eds), *The Battle for Ukrainian: A Comparative Perspective*, 343-63. Cambridge, MA: Harvard Papers in Ukrainian Studies.
Dailey O'Cain, J. (2017), *Trans-national English in Social Media Communities*. London, UK: Palgrave Macmillan.
Diuk, N. (2014), 'Finding Ukraine', *Journal of Democracy*, 25 (3): 83–89.
Fairclough, N. (1992), *Discourse and Social Change*. Cambridge: Polity Press.
Friedman, D. A. (2016), 'Our Language: (Re)imagining Communities in Ukrainian Language Classrooms', *Journal of Language, Identity & Education*, 15 (3): 165–79.

Kress, G. and van Leeuwen, T. (1996/2006), *Reading Images: The Grammar of Visual Design*. London: Routledge.

Kress, G. and van Leeuwen, T. (2001), *Multimodal Discourse: The Modes and Media of Contemporary Communication*. London: Arnold.

Kroskrity, P. V. (2000), 'Language Ideologies—Evolving Perspectives', in J.-O. Ostman, J. Verschueren and Ju. Jaspers (eds), *Society and Language Use*, 192–205. Amsterdam and Philadelphia: John Benjamins Publishing Company.

Kulyk, V. (2006), 'Constructing Common Sense: Language and Ethnicity in Ukrainian Public Discourse', *Ethnic and Racial Studies*, 29 (2): 281–315.

Kulyk, V. (2010), *Дискурс українських медій: Ідентичності, ідеології, владні стосунки. [Discourse of the Ukrainian Media: Identities, Ideologies and Power Relationships]*. Kyiv: Krytyka.

Kulyk, V. (2013), 'Language and Identity in Post-Soviet Ukraine: Transformation of an Unbroken Bond', *Australian and New Zealand Journal of European Studies*, 5 (2), 14–23.

Kulyk, V. (2014a), 'Ukrainian Nationalism Since the Outbreak of Euromaidan', *Ab Imperio*, 3: 94–122.

Kulyk, V. (2014b), 'What Is Russian in Ukraine?', in L. Ryazanova-Clarke (ed), *The Russian Language Outside the Nation*, 117–40. Edinburgh: Edinburgh University Press.

Kulyk, V. (2018), 'Between the "Self" and the "Other": Representations of Ukraine's Russian-Speakers in Social Media Discourse', *Language, Identity and Ideology in Ukrainian Media. Special Issues of East/West: Journal of Ukrainian Studies*, V (2): 65–88.

Moser, M. (2013), *Language Policy and the Discourse on Languages in Ukraine under President Viktor Yanukovych (25 February 2010–28 October 2012)*. Stuttgart: ibidem-Verlag.

Nedashkivska, A. (2010), 'Symbolic Bilingualism in Contemporary Ukrainian Media', *Canadian Slavonic Papers*, v. LII (3–4): 351–72.

Nedashkivska, A. (2015), '"Ukraine Is United" Campaign: Public Discourse on Languages in Ukraine at a Time of Political Turmoil', *Zeitschrift fur Slawistik*, 60 (2): 294–311.

Onuch, O. (2014), 'Who Were the Protestors?', *Journal of Democracy*, 25 (3): 44–51.

Osypian, A. (2014), 'Украина все же обрела собственное лицо [Ukraine Has Nevertheless Obtained Its Own Face]', *Ab Imperio* 3: 177–81.

Philips, S. (2000), 'Constructing a Tongan Nation-State through Language Ideology in the Courtroom', in P. V. Kroskrity (ed.), *Regimes of Language: Ideologies, Polities, and Identities*, 229–57, School of American Research.

Silverstein, M. (1979), 'Language Structure and Linguistic Ideology', in R. Cline, W. Hanks and C. Hofbauer (eds), *The Elements: A Parasession on Linguistic Units and Levels*, 193–247. Chicago: University of Chicago Press.

Spitulnik, D. (1998), 'Mediating Unity and Diversity: The Production of Language Ideologies in Zambian Broadcasting', in B. Schieffelin, K. Woolard and P. Kroskrity (eds), *Language Ideologies: Practice and Theory*, 163–88. New York: Oxford University Press.

Taranenko, O. (2007), 'Ukrainian and Russian in Contact: Attraction and Estrangement', *International Journal of Sociology of Language*, 183: 119–40.

Van Dijk, T. (1995), 'Discourse Analysis as Ideology Analysis', in C. Schäffner and A. Wenden (eds), *Language and Peace*, 17–33. Aldershot: Dartmouth Publishing.

Woolard, K. A. (1992), 'Language Ideology: Issues and Approaches', *Pragmatics*, 2 (3): 235–49.

Woolard, K. A. and Schieffelin, B. B. (1994), 'Language Ideology', *Annual Review of Anthropology*, 23: 55–82.

Unrecognized holidays

Old and new 'state' traditions in the self-proclaimed republics in the east of Ukraine

Yulia Abibok

1 Introduction

Since 2014, the inhabitants Donetsk and Luhansk regions of Eastern Ukraine with a total population of 7.5 million have been going through a forced transformation of their identities. The regions are divided by a frontline, and the parts of them that border Russia are not controlled by the Ukrainian government. In 2014, the unrecognized Donetsk People's Republic and Luhansk People's Republic were proclaimed in these parts of Donetsk and Luhansk regions. Since then, their de facto authorities have tried to develop new 'national' identities in these territories in order to legitimize and strengthen their 'statehood'.

1.1 Donbas: From conflict to war

The industrial Donetsk and Luhansk regions in the far east of Ukraine are commonly known as the Donbas region. The Ukrainian Donbas region is a phenomenon that originated in the nineteenth-century industrial revolution and the Soviet industrialization. Its main city, Donetsk, is just 150 years old. Donbas is the most urbanized of all Ukrainian regions (Studenna-Skrukva 2018). Its population burgeoned, thanks to migrants of various nationalities and backgrounds who moved to the region mostly from the territories of today's Ukraine, Russia and Belarus (Kuromìâ 2002).

As Kulìkov and Sklokìna point out, since the last decades of the Russian Empire, the young cities and towns of Donbas with highly mobile populations have been almost completely dependent on mines and factories. People involved in the management of these enterprises were actually more influential than the local authorities. Directors, engineers, and qualified and experienced workers at the region's mines and factories constituted the local elites. With its permanent workforce shortages, the region provided newcomers with high salaries and powerful means of social mobility. The local bosses cultivated ties with their most successful compatriots who left the region for the country's capital. Since the Soviet period, Donbas tended to have its own Moscow or Kyiv lobby (Kulikov and Sklokina 2018).

The particular character of the Donbas economy, dominated by collective labour, has facilitated the development of a distinct sense of local solidarity. The ethnic, linguistic and cultural differences have been eliminated by survival needs (Kulikov and Sklokina 2018) and the pursuit of success, in its Soviet version. Production volumes, high salaries and the development of local infrastructure have served as the criteria of success (Kuzina, Kulikov and Sklokina 2018). The Soviet propaganda cultivated the feeling of a mission and the sense of self-worth among Donbas workers. This led to unavoidable conflicts after the collapse of the USSR and the decline of the Donbas economy.

Therefore, since the early 1990s – the first years of Ukraine's independence – the city of Donetsk, with a population of approximately 1 million, became the locus of a years-long political strife between Ukrainian elites. It started with miners' strikes, which catapulted some representatives of the local establishment to power in Kyiv (Borisov 1999), and continued with mafia wars between two regional clans (Studenna-Skrukva 2014). Viktor Yanukovych, the former governor of Donetsk region, whose illegitimate election victory in 2004 caused the Orange Revolution and who was elected president in 2010, and Rinat Akhmetov, who was considered to be the richest man in Ukraine, hailed from this region and have rallied high levels of political support. An increase in mass promotion of a distinct, localized regional identity correlates directly with Viktor Yanukovych's rise to power in 1997 (Garmaš 2002; Wilson 2016). As research by Lviv and Donetsk sociologists showed, the regional identity was dominant, and rose from 55.6 per cent to 68.4 per cent in Donetsk in the decade after 1994. At the same time, the number of Donetsk residents who saw themselves as Ukrainians rose by less than 3 per cent from 39.3 in 1994–2004 (Černiš and Malančuk 2007).

Hence, by 2014, the Donbas regional identity, which was based in particular on the symbolic status of miner labour, the memory of the 1941– 5 Great Patriotic War between the Soviet Union and Nazi Germany, the Russian language, and close economic and cultural ties with Russia, was also linked to the images of local businesses and political elites (Zimmer 2004, 2007; Studenna-Skrukva 2014). The development of distinct cultural, social and historical value systems has, over time, set the region apart from the majority of other Ukrainian regions that, with their cultural, political and economic commitment to Ukrainization and the West, have a negative view of the 'Donetsk' elites. The long-standing conflict, which was already aggravated during the Yanukovych presidency, escalated amidst the turmoil of the Kyiv Maidan violence, the overthrow of Viktor Yanukovych and the annexation of the Crimean peninsula by Russia, and it sparked a pro-Russian separatist uprising (Wilson 2014; Sakwa 2015).

After weeks of seizures of local administrative buildings in Donetsk and Lugansk regions, and violence against officials and activists loyal to the Ukrainian state, the Ukrainian government launched the so-called anti-terrorist operation in the two regions, which was in fact a war. On 11 May 2014, the rebels and fighters in Donetsk and Luhansk regions conducted a poll, which they called a referendum, and then proclaimed independence of these regions from Ukraine. As a result of lack of rebel forces, local resistance and the 'anti-terrorist operation', parts of Donetsk and Luhansk regions have remained under the Ukrainian government control, while the biggest cities of Donbas, including Donetsk and Luhansk, have become parts of the unrecognized Donetsk People's Republic and Luhansk People's Republic. About 3.5 million people of the total population of 7.5 million in both Donetsk and Luhansk regions found themselves in a territory beyond the reach of the Ukrainian government power.

1.2 Legitimizing the statehood

The events of the first half of 2014 not only triggered a groundbreaking shift in the Ukrainian national and Donbas regional identities (Sasse 2017; Sasse and Lackner 2018; Pop-Eleches and Robertson 2018) but also, as a result of a new ideological vacuum, generated a need for new commemorative rituals and practices. The previous traditions related to the Ukrainian state have lost their meaning or require rethinking because of the emergence of the new 'states' in the Donbas region and their war against Ukraine. Luhansk and Donetsk People's Republics have had to 'invent traditions' (Hobsbawm 2015). Therefore, new holidays, commemorative dates and rituals have appeared in the part of the region beyond the control of Ukrainian government. Holidays are used as opportunities for political agitation when the leaders of the unrecognized Eastern Ukrainian republics report on their administrative successes, justify their failures, mobilize people, and proclaim their vision and mission statements. At the same time, they emphasize their high status by appealing to their 'nations' or other heads of states.

Attempts to introduce new holidays began in 2015 in the form of the first anniversary celebrations of the self-proclaimed Eastern Ukrainian republics. Since then, however, some of the initial ideas behind these holidays have changed and evolved. Some celebrations and commemorations have never been repeated, or have ceased in the next years. Some of these changes occurred due to the specifics of the local political landscape and its transformations, as well as particular political events of 2015–18. Some Soviet state and local holidays, like the Defender of the Fatherland Day, have gained a new political and social meaning because of the ongoing war. To some other events – mostly those pertaining to the Great Patriotic War of 1941–5 – local ideologists have added the new modern sense of the continuing fight against (Ukrainian or Western) 'Nazis' or 'fascists'. (The Western Ukrainian version of the Second World War history, which became dominant in Ukraine after 2014, glorifies the anti-Soviet underground, which collaborated with the Nazis in the first years of the German occupation of Ukraine. Supporters of this version were decried as 'fascists' by the pre-war political elites of Donbas that promoted the Soviet version of the Second World War history.)

The memory of the Great Patriotic War and of the current conflict is a key element of the attempts of Donetsk and Luhansk authorities to introduce a new local common ground. In both self-proclaimed republics, they actively reengage or even revive old Soviet practices and places of memory, as well as create new ones. For example, on 9 May, relatives and comrades of dead rebels join the ranks of the participants of the Immortal Regiment memorial march, in which descendants of the Great Patriotic War veterans carry portraits of their late relatives who fought in the war. The Savur-Mohyla hill in the far east of Donetsk region was a location of intense combat in both 1943 and

2014. Several new monuments have been built there since 2014, and Donetsk People's Republic's most symbolic tradition is to commemorate both wars 'against the Nazis' on Savur-Mohyla.

For Luhansk, the identification with 'statehood' was crucial for distancing itself from Donetsk, which has held absolute dominance over the two Eastern Ukrainian (or Donbas) regions. The specifics of the relations between the self-proclaimed republics and their leaders, as well as the intricacies of their very local traditions, have also had an impact on Donetsk and Luhansk commemorative practices. For example, the anniversary of the first 'election' in Luhansk is no longer celebrated, because its first leader fled the region after the 'coup' of November 2017. In Donetsk, after the assassination of the DPR self-proclaimed leader Alexander Zakharchenko in late August 2018, the day of his 'inauguration' became the day of his remembrance.

The Donbas Liberation Day on 8 September is the official date of the 1943 liberation of Stalino (today's Donetsk) from the Nazi occupation; it has not been celebrated in Luhansk region, which did not pick any date as the Donbas Liberation Day until 2018, but they celebrated the days of liberation of Voroshilovgrad (today's Luhansk) and other local towns instead. Officially, the whole region was liberated from the Nazi occupation on 4 September 1943, and in 2018, the local de facto authorities started to commemorate this date like the rest of the big holidays, with congratulatory addresses and popular celebrations. The Day of Luhansk/Voroshilovgrad Liberation is still celebrated as well, on 14 February. In 2018, the de facto authorities in Luhansk introduced the Day of the Unknown Soldier – the Defender of the LPR. Both Donetsk and Luhansk People's Republics have their Republic Days; however, while in Donetsk it is celebrated on the day of the internationally unrecognized referendum on independence, 11 May, in Luhansk, it is the day after the 'referendum', when the results of the improvised poll were declared. Both Luhansk and Donetsk self-proclaimed republics also commemorate the day of the 'liberation' of Debaltseve in Donetsk region, a town which has been under the rebel control since mid-February 2015. The Debaltsevo Operation, as it is called in Donetsk, is considered to be a single joint operation of the rebel forces of Donetsk and Luhansk People's Republics, but in Luhansk it is called the Debaltsevo-Chernukhino Operation after the neighbouring town of Chernukhino in Luhansk region, which is under the rebel control as well.

In Donetsk, the local de facto authorities have also introduced a tradition to celebrate the proclamation of the so-called Donetsk-Krivoy Rog Republic (actually the Donetsk-Krivoy Rog Soviet Republic, but in today's Donetsk and Luhansk ,it is mentioned exclusively as the DKR), which was supposed to have Kharkiv as its capital; this was an idea of the local Bolshevik leaders of the Civil War of 1917–22 period, which actually never materialized. While Luhansk still treats the DKR as the origin of the local 'statehood', it does not share the tradition to celebrate the DKR anniversary.

Donetsk, but not Luhansk, has made attempts to celebrate the Soviet anniversary of the so-called Pereyaslav Rada of the seventeenth century as the event that led to a 'reunification' of the lands which are now the territories of Ukraine and Russia. In his Pereyaslav Rada anniversary speech in 2018, Zakharchenko compared the current events to the mid-seventeenth-century period, and claimed that they both led to 'a revival of the (Ukrainian) state', with Donbas as the 'unification ground' (Donbas 2018). This meant that he had not abandoned the idea of Donetsk playing the leading role in Ukraine as a whole. Previously, in the summer of 2017, the self-proclaimed head of the Donetsk People's Republic declared the 'reestablishment' of Ukraine as Malorossia (the Russian name for a part of today's Ukrainian territory under the imperial rule) with the flag of its mid-seventeenth-century military leader Bohdan Khmelnytsky and the capital in Donetsk.

The de facto authorities of both Luhansk and Donetsk self-proclaimed republics have been surrounding the local holidays with similar rituals of celebration. These rituals, which are also crucial for creating and maintaining the group identity (Connerton 1989), include a wide variety of activities aimed to maximize participation, such as tours of duty and ceremonial guards at war memorials, sports competitions and art contests, film screenings, public prayers, issue of commemorative stamps, honorary decorations awards, concerts with inevitable performances by Russian pop stars, fairs, festivals, parades, marches, demonstrations, rallies, exhibitions, unveilings of memorials, quests, book presentations, floral offerings, flash mobs, car rallies, forums, conferences, dinners and openings of new museum expositions.

2 Data and methods

The Donetsk People's Republic and the Luhansk People's Republic emerged in extreme circumstances and under heavy Russian influence (Wilson 2016). As an April 2014 poll by the KIIS showed, the majority of residents of Donetsk and Luhansk regions became 'citizens' of the unrecognized republics by force rather than by choice (The views 2014). However, the deepening divide between the territories under rebel control and the rest of the country (Sasse 2017), the war and the unfavourable policies of Ukrainian government towards people from the territories beyond its control and towards internally displaced persons should affect their allegiance to the Ukrainian state and drive further transformations of the local identity.

This phenomenon is well-described in social psychology, for example, in Bar-Tal's work on the formation of societal beliefs, most of which is dedicated to 'dramatic collective experiences' as a key element for the emergence of such beliefs (which, in turn, constitute a group's identity). He stated that 'external threat heightens the feeling of solidarity and pressure to conform' (Bar-Tal 2000: 13). Attempts to introduce a kind of personality cults in both self-proclaimed republics are also visible in local commemorative practices. As Hale noted,

> the presence of a threat of some kind to group members that is based on the group categorization, as in intergroup conflict, tends to produce group cohesion, ingroup favoritism, distrust, a willingness of individuals to accept centralized group leadership, an emphasis on winning over considering the merits of the particular issue at stake, and a lack of intergroup communication. (Hale 2004: 469)

This phenomenon is especially well documented in wartime and clearly fits the current situation in the Donetsk and Luhansk People's Republics.

For a variety of reasons, we could not test whether the theory of group-identity formation during major upheavals has been proven true in the case of self-proclaimed statelets (Bar-Tal 2000; Hale 2004). There is no freedom of speech in the Donetsk and Luhansk People's Republics. There are also no conditions for independent opinion polls and direct interviews. Even in a more favourable situation, 'public identities' could differ from those which are expressed privately, in an inner circle (Gorenburg 1999). In the territories of the unrecognized Donbas republics, informal, private opinions of the inhabitants are impossible to assess. Thus, in this chapter, I study solely the attempts of the local de facto authorities to establish and promote the local 'state' identity in their speeches. In order to do this, I analyse 'official' texts from the ruling elites of the Donetsk and Luhansk People's Republics, who are forming a nuanced, top-down discourse around the new regional (or 'national') identity. The analysis does not provide an answer about the results of the elites' attempts.

In this work, I analyse speeches of representatives of de facto authorities of the self-proclaimed republics in the east of Ukraine on the occasion of the Russian National Unity Day and Russia Day holidays, as well as the Soviet holidays of Victory Day, the commemorative dates of the Donetsk and Luhansk cities and regions liberation from the Nazi occupation in 1943, the new Republic Days in Luhansk and Donetsk, and the main non-political holiday in the region, the Miner's Day.

I based this choice of dates on the assumption that the completely new holidays of the Russian National Unity Day and Russia Day could be used by the local leaders as a pretext to declare or define the newly established relations of Donbas territories with Russia as their key ally. In turn, the holidays related to Great Patriotic War victories should demonstrate the scale of ideological strife between Donetsk, Luhansk and Kyiv because of the different ideological approaches towards them in Russia, Donetsk and Luhansk People's Republics, and Ukraine.

The newly established Republic Days in Luhansk and Donetsk should provide insights about the views of the local de facto authorities on the past, present and future of these territories. And since miners' labour has a crucial symbolic meaning for the Donbas region, the 'official' speeches on the occasion of the Miner's Day must contain some clues about the perpetuation or transformation of the pre-war local identity markers, as well as the imposition of any new ones. By identity markers, I mean the collectively shared or imposed top-down views on a given group as an established community with common territory, history, values, enemies and allies, and alleged unique or exceptional features and vision for the future. Therefore, the analysis of speeches on the occasion of these holidays is expected to demonstrate the complete set of such identity markers.

The de facto authorities of the Luhansk and Donetsk People's Republics have developed different congratulatory approaches. In Donetsk, until the end of 2018, the head of the 'republic' was also the head of the 'government'. Until his death in August 2018, Alexander Zakharchenko was the single 'official' whose congratulatory speeches were published by the 'official' news media of the Donetsk 'republic'. The leader's congratulatory speech was not necessarily published in a news media. Thus, there were years when local 'official' news agencies did not publish any of Zakharchenko's addresses.

Each holiday in Luhansk, instead, usually starts with a commemorative speech by the de facto head of the 'republic.' It is followed by addresses of the heads of the 'council of ministers', 'people's council', local 'federation of trade unions', and sometimes also by addresses of several 'ministers', etc. Since 2015, Alexander Zakharchenko in Donetsk has delivered nine commemorative addresses, while the Luhansk de facto leaders and officials has delivered eighty-eight addresses. As some of them were repeated almost literally from year to year, or included no identity markers, the total of eighty-five texts (seventy-six by the Luhansk de facto officials and nine by Alexander Zakharchenko in Donetsk), each approximately 150 words long on average, have been analysed.

The premise of the study is that identities are interrelated and constructed discursively (Wodak et al. 2009). Therefore, the approach of the authors of *The Discursive Construction of National Identity*, which is based on critical discourse analysis, was adopted as the framework for this research (Wodak et al. 2009). Identities are based in particular on the 'we'/'they' juxtaposition; therefore, in my study, I focused on the 'we/us' aspect of this dyad by analysing the linguistic construction of the image of the self-proclaimed republics and their inhabitants, and on the 'they/them' aspect by investigating the representations of their rivals who bear the traits that are opposite to 'ours'.

I also analyse the war and peace topoi in the speeches, especially the promotion of 'siege beliefs', the perception of other nations as enemies (Bar-Tal 2000). According to Bar-Tal, siege beliefs

> satisfy society's need for a firm social identity, differentiating this group from others. By positioning the society in conflict with the rest of the world, siege beliefs clearly demarcate the boundaries of the society, differentiating between 'us' and 'them' – in this case, all others. (Bar-Tal 2000: 113)

They also satisfy a group's need for solidarity, freedom of action and superiority. Bar-Tal also states that 'those who hold the beliefs most strongly exert pressure on others for conformity and unity' (Bar-Tal 2000: 118).

This fits into the 'thematic areas' distinguished by Wodak et al.: the linguistic construction of the exemplary Donbas resident, shared political past, present and future of the people of the self-proclaimed republics, and their shared culture and territory, which, taken all together, the authors designate as constituents of a national identity (Wodak et al. 2009). Further, I also analyse the employment of constructive strategies and strategies of unification, perpetuation, transformation and dismantling, as well as the strategies of assimilation and dissimilation that are described in *The Discursive Construction of National Identity*, and the means and forms of their linguistic realization (Wodak et al. 2009).

3 War and peace

The war topos is present in seventy-seven of the eighty-eight texts, including all the nine speeches by Alexander Zakharchenko, either in the present, past or even in the future tense. I define the term *topos* as a common argumentative idea from which more specific arguments could be drawn. The war topos is usually used within the discursive strategies of unification, perpetuation and justification (of the establishment of the two statelets or their economic hardships). In most of the texts (in every speech on the occasion of the National Unity Day, a Russian holiday that commemorates a battle against the seventeenth-century Polish invasion) it is also synonymous with 'unity' and 'patriotism'. In their commemorative speeches, the leaders of the self-proclaimed republics usually draw a parallel between the Great Patriotic War and the ongoing war against the Ukrainian government, but at the big-picture level, they portray these wars as a conflict between the West and the Russian World.

This idea is especially clear from the National Unity Day greetings. In 2018, the Luhansk 'republic's' self-proclaimed leader Leonid Pasiechnik juxtaposed the 1612 and 2014 events, when 'our people' 'defended their liberty' (1). Igor Plotnitsky, in his 2015 Victory Day address, claimed that 'the foul western wind blew a new war into Ukraine' (2). The 'brotherly Russian people' came to rescue the people of Donbas from the new incarnation of Nazism, which is supported by the West (3). Sometimes the war is mentioned in the past or future tense. As Igor Plotnitsky stated in his 2016 Victory Day address, 'We did not allow to do this ("to erode the memory about the Great Victory") two years ago, we will not allow this today as well' (4). Thus, Nazism becomes an ahistoric phenomenon, an eternal evil to be repeatedly fought by new heroes of the Russian World. Donetsk and Luhansk are presented as a kind of besieged fortresses; the war has ended, but the enemy is still around somewhere.

A number of texts related to the Second World War include a topos of post-war reconstruction. 'The experience of our fathers and grandfathers' is introduced as a waymark for modern generations, who should not only fight but also work and endure hardships as their ancestors did in the name of victory. As, for example, the head of the 'people's council' Denis Miroshnichenko stated in 2018,

> (5) It's important to remember that behind the victory in the war lies the second and no less important victory, the reconstruction of the ruined cities and villages [...].[1]

The topos of labour is also present in twelve of the twenty-one speeches by Luhansk leaders on the Republic Day. For example, the head of the 'government' Sergey Kozlov stated in 2018:

> (6) 'Despite all the obstacles, the Luhansk People's Republic has succeeded and is developing. And this is, of course, your achievement – all of you who work honestly at plants and factories, in the agricultural sector, healthcare, educational and cultural institutions, who uphold the law and order and protect our peace. The credit goes to everyone who has endured so much trouble and suffering, and celebrates this holiday with confidence in our victory and his or her own abilities, with the persuasion that everyone's labour will bring prosperity and further development to our young state.

This position is very different from the public stance of the Donetsk de facto leadership, which has exclusively used the topos of reconstruction in order to give an account of its own administrative success. Thus, the Luhansk texts are designed not only to stoke the adversarial sentiment towards Ukraine but also to assign a set of qualities that every exemplary citizen of the self-proclaimed republic should obtain, such as endurance, fortitude, diligence, willingness to endure losses and make sacrifices, social cohesion and obedience, since the addresses emphasize the unanimity of the belligerent 'nation', and therefore do not allow for any dissent. These differences could be explained not just by Luhansk's heavier focus on 'patriotic education' but also by its much direr economic situation, since Luhansk region has always been much poorer than Donetsk region.

Both Donetsk and Luhansk speakers emphasize the example of post-war Soviet reconstruction in an attempt to justify the current circumstances in the self-proclaimed republics, which struggle with social and economic woes. For example, the head of the self-proclaimed government in Luhansk, Sergey Kozlov, claimed in 2016:

(7) Our duty is to be worth of their [our ancestors'] memory. To cherish peace, to be proud of our Homeland. To show unity and cohesion while rebuilding our Republic, as once, in the postwar years, our ancestors rebuilt their ruined cities and reclaimed the national economy virtually from scratch.

4 Who are 'we'?

There is still no public explanation for the existence of two self-proclaimed republics in the east of Ukraine. In their addresses, the de facto leaders of Luhansk and Donetsk called their counterparts 'the fraternal people'. At the same time, 'the Donbas people' within the whole Donetsk and Luhansk regions is constructed at least as a political community. However, in some messages, the region's inhabitants are presented rather as an ethnic community. Donetsk and Luhansk regions are portrayed as an exceptional (former) part of Ukraine because of their different language and heroes, as well as because of a distinct 'Donbas/Donetsk personality'. There is no mention of the neighbouring Russian-speaking regions of Ukraine, even though people in Kyiv are also predominantly Russian speakers. However, in one address, in the light of the ongoing war, Igor Plotnitsky mentioned 'neo-Nazis' who 'speak the same language as us' (8). Many greetings include statements about 'the right to self-determination'. In some addresses, the 'referendum' of May 2014 is referred to as 'nationwide', although it could be considered regional within Ukraine.

It is also clear that for the Donetsk and Luhansk de facto leaders, the 'imagined community' (Anderson 1991) is not the population of the whole Donetsk and Luhansk regions, but rather the residents of the self-proclaimed republics. As a rule, they address their speeches to 'compatriots', 'fellow citizens', 'countrymen' and 'the Donbas/Luhanshchina/Donetsk People's Republic inhabitants', but people in the part of the region that remained under the Ukrainian government control are usually mentioned in the third person, since 'they' are not 'us'. For example, as Pasiechnik stated in his 2018 speech for the anniversary of the Voroshilovgrad (today's Luhansk) region liberation:

(9) The Luhansk People's Republic has already proved that it can confidently resist the inhuman policies of the Kiev authorities, we are continuing to liberate

our area from invaders. I am sure that by virtue of joint efforts we will succeed in providing our citizens with the possibility to live in an independent and prosperous state!

In a 2016 address, Igor Plotnitsky also said:

(10) I know for sure that our fellow citizens from the districts which are temporarily occupied by the armed units sent by Kiev completely share our thoughts and feelings. Our duty is to attain liberation of all our lands and people.

The statements about Russia, the Russian World and the place of Donbas within it feature numerous contradictions. While in some addresses the region is 'coming back' to the Russian World or is going to be in the Russian World sometime in the future, in others it is already the Russian World vanguard. Even in congratulatory texts about the events of the Great Patriotic War, the word 'Soviet' is hardly mentioned, and the word 'Russian' is used instead, as in 'the Russian people' or 'the Russian land'. This highlights that 'Russian' is a rather extra-national and extra-ethnic category that applies to everyone who supports the ideas of the Russian World.

But it is still unclear whether the Russian World is a physical or an exclusively spiritual space. According to some speeches, the Ukrainian government's 'aggression' is to blame for the fact that the region still has not joined it. As Igor Plotnitsky stated:

(11) Unfortunately, the Maidan government has shown its inhuman and non-democratic essence; it did not take into account the expression of the people's will and launched an actual war against us. We acknowledge that we have not been ready for such mean cruelty. As a result, our path home, to the Russian World, has become longer and thornier.

This may mean that Donetsk and Luhansk regions could have followed the so-called Crimea scenario of annexation by Russia, but the war has put these developments on hold. Still, the Russia Day greetings from both Luhansk and Donetsk self-proclaimed leaders are addressed exclusively to citizens of the Russian Federation, sometimes still referred to as 'compatriots' (12), and/or to its president.

What being Russian means for the Donetsk and Luhansk people is also not generally clear, because in some addresses it is, among the other things, about common 'fathers' and history, while in others it is solely about a sense of spiritual belonging. In some texts, the word 'engagement' (with Russian history and culture) is used, which means that the speakers who have mentioned it are far from identifying Donetsk and Luhansk residents as Russian people. The people of Donbas and Russia have a 'shared Motherland', the Soviet Union and the Russian Federation itself. Also, the Russian empire may be implied in some texts, but has never been mentioned explicitly. In this context, it is also usually unclear what today's 'Motherland' actually means in different congratulatory addresses. Russians are 'the fraternal people' to 'us', who share 'our' traditions, culture and values, or 'we' as the people of the 'republic' are 'the same people' with Russians; the two interpretations are not the same, but both may be present in one statement:

> (13) Dear friends, compatriots! Please accept my cordial congratulations on the occasion of the National Unity Day, a holiday which we celebrate with our fraternal people of the Russian Federation [...] This nationwide Russian holiday is near and dear to all of us. It reminds us that we are a single people with a common historic destiny and, I strongly believe this, with a common future. In fact, our Republic is a part of the great Russian World.

In a 2015 address, Igor Plotnitsky spoke about 'the true Russians' who, in 2014, joined forces to send 'invaders from the West' away 'from the Russian land', hinting that the people who fled the region or refused to fight were not 'true Russians' (14).

While all the 'Donbas people' or the 'Donbas nation' are or should be a part of the Russian World or the Russian people, according to the speeches, the 'multinational', 'multicultural' nature of the region, as well as its religious diversity, are also emphasized in these texts. Sometimes it looks like a contradiction or even a potential threat to the local people's unity, as in one 2016 address where Donbas was presented as multiethnic, 'but the sense of spiritual commonality' 'consolidates all of us also in the present' (15). The multiethnic nature of Donbas is often emphasized in the National Day of Unity addresses in Luhansk, though the ideology around the holiday is not about interethnic unity. Thus, the Luhansk speakers use a quite-Soviet political topos that was also widely used by the local pre-war political elite as an argument against Ukrainization. In some greetings, the shared orthodox faith and the fight for it are mentioned, contradicting the claims about religious diversity in the region.

The Donetsk de facto leadership's vision of the region's geopolitical place is clearly different and more distinct. The self-proclaimed leader of the DPR, Alexander Zakharchenko, addressed the National Day of Unity greetings to Russians, but not to the people of the Donetsk 'republic'. The Russian holiday is important to the Donetsk People's Republic because

> (16) The Donetsk People's Republic, like the Russian militia army 405 years ago, is the vanguard of the Russian World, it defends our values, culture, traditions, language and faith. We have revolted against the Nazi threat and are countering it successfully. Volunteers from the Russian Federation have joined us in this fight, and that's why the National Unity Day is our holiday as well.

In 2018, in his congratulatory address to 'the people of the brotherly Russian Federation' on Russia Day, Zakharchenko claimed that Russian citizens and 'citizens of the Donetsk People's Republic' were all involved in 'rebuilding the geopolitical power, state ambitions and traditional canons of the Russian society'. According to Zakharchenko, Russia is 'our big Motherland' and 'we are the Russian people' (17). In other words, 'the Donbas people' do not claim to be Russian citizens, but they are an important part of the global Russian community.

5 Ukrainian authorities as hostile 'they'

In the addresses of the de facto leaders of Luhansk and Donetsk, the regions have been portrayed not just as the vanguard of the Russian World but also as the last outpost of a different, 'correct' version of the Ukrainian state with the 'right' Great Patriotic War memory. Their mission, as it is described in the speeches, has been to demonstrate the 'true' values to Ukrainians, to turn Ukraine back to 'the Russian World' where it belongs or even to lead Ukraine to a true democratic path. For example, in a 2017 address, Igor Plotnitsky stated that, just as in 1943, 'the rescue of Ukraine from Nazism will start with Luganshchina again' (18).

In some texts, Ukraine is not mentioned directly, but they contain the words 'fascists' and 'punishers' as the most common markers of the Ukrainian forces in the Russian and in the Donetsk and Luhansk media discourses. The label 'punishers', which is usually attached to the 'occupation regime', implies a local representation of the parts of Donetsk and Luhansk regions under the Ukrainian government control as 'occupied' territories. In his 2016 address on the Day of the Donbas Liberation, Igor Plotnitsky spoke about 'the previous, Hitlerite invaders' and the current task of the Donetsk and Luhansk 'republics' 'to fight for the liberation of all their lands and people' (19).

Sometimes, but not often, the celebratory and commemorative texts draw a line between today's Ukrainian state or authorities and ordinary Ukrainians. While Ukrainian soldiers are usually characterized as 'invaders' and 'punishers', their image in some addresses is rather grotesque. In a 2016 address, Igor Plotnitsky suggested that 'those who have come to us as Hitlerites should grease their heels with pork fat and run homewards headlong' (20): pork fat as an 'ethnic food' is a traditional sarcastic hint at Ukrainians.

Still, there is a clear difference in degrees of occupation between 'invaders' and 'punishers'. If Kyiv sent 'punishers' to the region in the spring of 2014, it meant that Donetsk and Luhansk were already 'occupied' by that time. It is not clear from the texts when the 'occupation' happened, given that many addresses contain statements about 'coming back home to the Russian World', although Donetsk and Luhansk regions had been a part of independent Ukraine for twenty-two years by the time when the war started.

Those who fight in the east of Ukraine on the Kyiv side are always portrayed as outsiders, while the population of Donetsk and Luhansk regions is seen as completely loyal to the self-proclaimed republics. Ukraine is commonly presented as an aggressor, and Luhansk and Donetsk people as those who have had to protect themselves from Ukrainian attacks. Some statements emphasize that the Luhansk and Donetsk people were 'forced' to defend themselves, and so the war was inevitable. They are in the right because they are the 'successors of heroic victors', according to the texts. Therefore, the speeches indicate that those in Ukraine who support Kyiv in the current conflict must be either 'successors' of the opposite side in the Great Patriotic War or people who do not know or have been made to forget the 'correct' history of the 1941–5 events.

The war narrative usually starts with a Kyiv military operation, and it skips the local political protests with seizures of administrative buildings in Donetsk and

Luhansk regions and violent attacks against local officials, politicians and activists, which preceded the Ukrainian 'anti-terrorist operation'. In his 2015 Victory Day address, Igor Plotnitsky once again blurred the time of the alleged 'occupation' by comparing the conflict with Kyiv with both 'a war for national liberation' and 'a patriotic war':

> (21) On 9 May 1945, our glorious grandfathers and great-grandfathers crushed the fascist beast in its Berlin seat. They saved the whole world from fascism and gave us 70 years of peaceful life, fruitful life for the benefit of our Homeland. [...] But the foul western wind brought a new war to Ukraine. And now we have to stifle it. We were not expecting the war and we were not preparing for the war. But when those uninvited people with weapons came to our land and started to behave like Germans in 1941, we had to defend ourselves [...]. A Russian soldier has never lost a national liberation war and a patriotic war.

At the end of his speech, Plotnitsky also employed a famous quote from the historic 1941 speech of a high-ranking Soviet official Vyacheslav Molotov, which marked the beginning of the Great Patriotic War between the Soviet Union and Nazi Germany. The quote became widely popular in the USSR, and has often been used in other speeches by the leadership of unrecognized republics in Donbas: 'The enemy will be defeated! Victory will be ours!' Plotnitsky used the typical Soviet greeting, 'comrades', which is never used in modern everyday speech (2).

The protests themselves, if mentioned, are justified with the Maidan 'military coup' of February 2014 in Kyiv. According to this version of the Maidan aftermatch, the legitimate government of President Viktor Yanukovych was violently ousted by Ukrainian far-right activists and politicians, and the Ukrainian state ceased to exist. 'The Donbas people', in turn, chose to exercise their right to self-determination by entirely peaceful means. Then, according to 'official' media narrative in Luhansk and Donetsk alike, 'the military junta' in Kyiv, with the help of 'Western mercenaries', launched an armed assault instead of negotiations and occupied parts of the newly proclaimed states. Consequently, on 11 May 2014, the people of Donetsk and Luhansk regions unanimously supported the declaration of the Donetsk and Luhansk People's Republics.

At the same time, in order to shift responsibility, many celebratory addresses for the Miner's Day – one of the most important holidays in the region – blame the government in Kyiv for not paying wages to miners, and for not supporting the local coal industry and introducing an economic blockade. In its 2016 greeting, the Mir Luhanshchine movement claimed that the Ukrainian authorities 'turned their backs to people and left only woes and ruin behind' (22).

Therefore, all the economic difficulties of the Luhansk and Donetsk 'republics' are also the fault of Ukrainian government. Igor Plotnitsky said in a celebratory address to miners that

> (23) Together with the whole republic, you are now bearing the hard times with fortitude. Our woes are of external origin. Kiev cannot help but buy our coal, although at the same time it can't buy it. However, you and me both know that it is

always darkest before the dawn. And it [the dawn] is unavoidable due to the very nature of things. The Kiev regime, which is equally hostile both towards Donbas and towards Ukraine, will soon disappear like dew in the sunshine. And the dawn will come to our homes as well as our mines, and then prosperity, well-being will follow.

6 Conclusions

The centralized efforts to construct 'the Donbas people' within the two self-proclaimed republics in the east of Ukraine are based on a standoff with the Ukrainian government and on self-identification with Russia. The de facto leaders of the Luhansk and Donetsk People's Republics use the topoi of war and external threat by applying constructive sub-strategies of unification, perpetuation and justification. In the congratulatory addresses of Luhansk and Donetsk de facto authorities, 'us' primarily means 'the people' of the self-proclaimed republics as well as Russian citizens. The opposite side, 'they', is the Ukrainian government supported by the West or the Ukrainian state in general. The strategy of transformation is also widely applied in the topoi about Russia and Russianness, despite the fact that the Russian identity was marginal in the region before the war and lagged far behind the regional and Ukrainian identities that had been growing stronger since the 1990s (Tablytsi odnovymirnykh rozpodiliv 2007). At the same time, it is still mostly impossible to define what being Russian or being a part of the Russian World means for the local speakers in Luhansk and Donetsk.

In addition, the congratulatory addresses of the Luhansk and Donetsk leaders have different approaches towards the statehood of the 'republics' and towards the position and role of an ordinary 'citizen'. Texts from different years, despite their numerous contradictions, show no signs of change of these positions. This means that the public positions of the leaders of the Luhansk and Donetsk self-proclaimed republics are not only underdeveloped but also inattentive to some details. First of all, having troubles with both their status and the 'reunification' with Russia, the self-proclaimed republics of the east of Ukraine have not found their place on the world map yet.

The local identity is constructed around the glorification of the 1945 Great Victory of the Soviet Union and the new commemorative practices related to the current war with the Ukrainian government, but also to the Great Patriotic War. The commemoration of the Great Patriotic War is not just needed for war propaganda. For the de facto authorities of Luhansk, it also supports the idea about objective post-war economic hardships that ought to be overcome by perseverance and labour, as it was done by their ancestors in the 1940s. While the war discourses are dominant, some of the Luhansk addresses are mostly or entirely about the peaceful agenda. Texts of this kind essentially describe the picture-perfect 'citizen'.

Note

1   All translations in the chapter are mine.

References

Anderson, B. (2006), *Imagined Communities: Reflections on the Origin and Spread of Nationalism*, Revised edn. London, New York: Verso.
Bar-Tal, D. (2000), *Shared Beliefs in a Society: Social Psychological Analysis*. Thousand Oaks: Sage Publications.
Borisov, V. (1999), *Nočnoe Domino na Oktâbr'skoj Ploŝadi: Sociologičeskie Zametki o Zabastovke v Donbasse (7-20 iûnâ 1993) [Night Domino at October Place: Sociologycal Notes on a Strike in Donbas (7-20 of June 1993)]*. Moscow: 'Rossijskaâ Političeskaâ Ènciklopediâ'.
Černiš, N. and Malančuk, O. (2007), 'Dinamìka ìdentičnostej meškancìv L'vova ì Donec'ka: komparativnij analìz' ['Dynamics of Identities of Lviv and Donetsk Inhabitants: The Comparative Analysis'], *L'vìv-Donec'k: Socìal'nì Ìdentičnostì v Sučasnìj Ukraïnì. Specìal'nij Vipusk. Ukraïna Moderna*, 12 (2): 61–92. Available online http://uamoderna.com/images/archiv/12_2/5_UM_12_2_Statti_Chernysh_Malanchuk.pdf (accessed 3 October 2019).
Connerton, P. (1989), *How Societies Remember*. Cambridge: Cambridge University Press.
'Donbass dolžen povtorit' vklad Pereâslavskoj rady v ob"edinenie bratskih narodov - Glava DNR' ['Donbas Shall Repeat the Contribution of the Pereyaslav Rada to the Union of the Fraternal People'] (2018), *DAN*, 1 January. Available online https://dan-news.info/politics/donbass-dolzhen-stat-povtorit-vklad-pereyaslavskoj-rady-v-obedinenie-bratskix-narodov-glava-dnr.html (accessed 3 October 2019).
Garmaš, S. (2002), 'Ânukovič pod zontikom, ili Perspektivy ukrainskoj žurnalistiki v "doneckij" period' ['Yanukovych Under an Umbrella, or the Prospects of Ukrainian Journalism in the 'Donetsk' Period'], *Ostrov*, 25 November. Available online https://www.ostro.org/general/politics/articles/38/ (accessed 3 October 2019).
Gorenburg, D. (1999), 'Identity Change in Bashkortostan: Tatars into Bashkirs and Back', *Ethnic and Racial Studies*, 22 (3): 554–80.
Hale, H. E. (2004), 'Explaining Ethnicity', *Comparative Political Studies*, 37 (4): 458–85.
Hobsbawm, E. (2010), 'Vstup: vinahodžennâ tradicìï' ['Introduction: The Invention of Tradition'], trans. M. Klimčuk, in E. Hobsbawm and T. Ranger (eds), *Vinajdennâ Tradicìï [The Invention of Tradition]*, 12–28. Kyiv: Nìka-Centr.
Kulìkov, V. and Sklokìna, I. (2018), 'Lûdi monomìst: paradoksi êdnostì ì podìlìv' ['People of Monotowns: Paradoxes of Unity and Divisions'], in V. Kulìkov and I. Sklokìna (eds), *Pracâ, Visnaženâ ì Uspìh: Promislovì Monomìsta Donbasu [Labour, Exhaustion and Success: Industrial Monocities of Donbas]*, 97–130. Lviv: FOP Šumìlovič.
Kuromìâ, H. (2002), *Svoboda ì Teror u Donbasì. Ukraïns'ko-Rosìjs'ke Prikordonnâ, 1870–1990-ì Roki [Freedom and Terror in the Donbas: A Ukrainian-Russian Borderland, 1870s–1990s]*, trans. G. K'orân and V. Ageêv. Kyiv: OSNOVY.
Kuzìna, K., Kulìkov, V. and Sklokìna, I. (2018), 'Cìna uspìhu' ['The Price of Success'], in V. Kulìkov and I. Sklokìna (eds), *Pracâ, Visnaženâ ì Uspìh: Promislovì Monomìsta Donbasu [Labour, Exhaustion and Success: Industrial Monocities of Donbas]*, 157–84. Lviv: FOP Šumìlovič.
Pop-Eleches, G. and Robertson, B. (2018), 'Identity and Political Preferences in Ukraine – Before and After the Euromaidan', *Post-Soviet Affairs*, 34 (2–3): 107–18.
Sakwa, R. (2015), *Frontline Ukraine: Crisis in the Borderlands*. London: I.B. Tauris.
Sasse, G. (2017). 'The Donbas – Two Parts, or Still One? The Experience of War Through the Eyes of the Regional Population'. *ZOIS Report*, 2. Available online https://ww

w.zois-berlin.de/fileadmin/media/Dateien/ZOiS_Reports/ZOiS_Report_2_2017.pdf (accessed 3 October 2019).

Sasse, G. and Lackner, A. (2018), 'War and Identity: The Case of the Donbas in Ukraine', *Post-Soviet Affairs*, 34 (2–3): 139–57.

Studenna-Skrukva, M. (2014): Ukraïns'kij Donbas: Obliččâ Regìonal'noï Ìdentičnostì. *[The Ukrainian Donbas. Faces of the Regional Identity]*, trans. A. Bondar. Kyiv: Laboratorìâ Zakonodavčih Ìnìcìativ.

Studenna-Skrukva, M. (2018), 'Carstvo vugìllâ ì zalìza. Rol' ìndustrìalìzacïï v procesì suspìl'nih zmìn na Donbasì' ['The Kingdom of Coal and Iron. The Role of Industrialization in the Process of Social Changes in Donbas'], in V. Kulìkov and I. Sklokìna (eds), *Pracâ, Visnažennâ ì Uspìh: Promislovì Monomìsta Donbasu [Labour, Exhaustion and Success: Industrial Monocities of Donbas]*, 21–42. Lviv: FOP Šumìlovič.

Tablicì odnovimìrnih rozpodìlìv trendovogo socìologìčnogo doslìdžennâ 'L'vìv–Donec'k: socìologìčnij analìz grupovih ìdentičnostej ta ìêrarhìj suspìl'nih loâl'nostej –1994, 1999, 2004 rr'. [Univariable Frequency Tables of the Trend Research 'Lviv-Donetsk: Sociological Analysis of Group Identities and the Hierarchy of Social Loyalties –1994, 1999, 2004'], compl. V. Susak, *L'vìv-Donec'k: Socìal'nì Ìdentičnostì v Sučasnìj Ukraïnì. Specìal'nij Vipusk. Ukraïna Moderna*, 12 (2): 299–356. Available online http://uamoderna.com/images/archiv/12_2/12_UM_12_2_Materialy.pdf (accessed 3 October 2019).

'The Views and Opinions of South-Eastern Regions Residents of Ukraine: April 2014' (2014), in *Kyiv International Institute of Sociology*. Available online: http://www.kiis.com.ua/?lang=eng&cat=reports&id=302&page=1&y=2014&m=4 (accessed 3 October 2019).

Wodak, R., de Cillia, R., Reisigl, M. and Liebhart, K. (2009), *The Discursive Construction of National Identity*. Edinburgh: Edinburgh University Press.

Wilson, A. (2014), *Ukraine Crisis. What It Means for the West*. New Haven and London: Yale University Press.

Wilson, A. (2016), 'The Donbas in 2014: Explaining Civil Conflict Perhaps, but Not Civil War', *Europe-Asia Studies*, 68 (4): 631–52.

Zimmer, K. (2004, December 21). 'Ukraine: The Donetsk Factor', *Transitions Online*.

Zimmer, K. (2007), 'Trapped in Past Glory. Selfidentification and Selfsymbolisation in the Donbas, in Adam Swain (ed.), *Re-Constructing the Post-Soviet Industrial Region: The Donbas in Transition*, 97–121. London: Routledge.

Sources

Pozdravlenie i.o. glavy LNR Leonida Pasečnika s Dnem narodnogo edinstva [Congratulations by the Acting LPR Head LEONID Pasiechnik on National Unity Day] (2018), *LIC*, 4 November. Available online http://lug-info.com/news/one/pozdravlenie-io-glavy-lnr-leonida-pasechnika-s-dnem-narodnogo-edinstva-39854 (accessed 3 October 2019).

Obrašenie glavy LNR k učastnikam i zritelâm parada v čest' 70-letiâ Velikoj Pobedy [The LPR Head's Address to Participants and Audience of the Parade on the Occasion of the 70th Great Victory Anniversary] (2015), *LIC*, 9 May. Available online http://lug-info.com/news/one/obraschenie-glavy-lnr-k-uchastnikam-i-zritelyam-parada-v-chest-70-letiya-velikoi-pobedy-3136 (accessed 3 October 2019).

Pozdravlenie Narodnogo Soveta LNR žitelâm Rossijskoj Federacii v čest' Dnâ Rossii [Congratulations by the LPR People's Council to Russian Federation Inhabitants on the Occasion of Russia Day] (2015), *LIC*, 12 June. Available online http://lug-info.com/news/one/pozdravlenie-narodnogo-soveta-lnr-zhitelyam-rossiiskoi-federatsii-v-che st-dnya-rossii-3888 (accessed 3 October 2019).

Pozdravlenie glavy LNR Igorâ Plotnickogo s Prazdnikom Velikoj Pobedy [Congratulations by the LPR Head Igor Plotnitsky on the Great Victory Holiday] (2016), *LIC*, 9 May. Available online http://lug-info.com/news/one/pozdravlenie-glavy-lnr-igorya-plotni tskogo-s-prazdnikom-velikoi-pobedy-13168 (accessed 3 October 2019).

Pozdravlenie predsedatelâ Narodnogo Soveta s 75-letiem osvoboždeniâ Luganšiny ot fašistov [Congratulations by the People's Council Chairman on the 75th Anniversary of the Luhansk Region Liberation from Fascists] (2018), *LIC*, 4 September. Available online http://lug-info.com/news/one/pozdravlenie-predsedatelya-narodnogo-sove ta-s-75-letiem-osvobozhdeniya-luganschiny-ot-fashistov-38088 (accessed 3 October 2019).

Pozdravlenie predsedatelâ Sovmina Sergeâ Kozlova s Dnem Luganskoj Narodnoj Respubliki [Congratulations by the Ministers Council Chairman Sergey Kozlov on Luhansk People's Republic Day] (2018), *LIC*, 12 May. Available online http://lug-info .com/news/one/pozdravlenie-predsedatelya-soveta-ministrov-sergeya-kozlova-s-dnem -luganskoi-narodnoi-respubliki-34869 (accessed 3 October 2019).

Pozdravlenie predsedatelâ Soveta ministrov Sergeâ Kozlova s Dnem Velikoj Pobedy [Congratulations by the Ministers Counsil Chairman Sergey Kozlov on Great Victory Day] (2016), *LIC*, 9 May. Available online http://lug-info.com/news/one/pozdravleni e-predsedatelya-soveta-ministrov-sergeya-kozlova-s-dnem-velikoi-pobedy-13077 (accessed 3 October 2019).

Pozdravlenie glavy LNR Igorâ Plotnickogo s godovŝinoj osvoboždeniâ Luganska ot fašistov [Congratulations by the LPR Head Igor Plotnitsky on the Anniversary of the Luhansk Liberation from Fascists] (2016), *LIC*, 14 February. Available online http://lug -info.com/news/one/pozdravlenie-glavy-lnr-igorya-plotnitskogo-s-godovschinoi-osv obozhdeniya-luganska-ot-fashistov-10590 (accessed 3 October 2019).

Pozdravlenie i.o. glavy LNR s 75-j godovŝinoj osvoboždeniâ Vorošilovgradskoj oblasti [Congratulations of the Acting LPR Head on the 75th Anniversary of the Voroshilovhrad Oblast Liberation] (2018), *LIC*, 4 September. Available online http://lug-info.com/news/one/pozdravlenie-io-glavy-lnr-s-75-i-godovschinoi-osvobozhde niya-voroshilovgradskoi-oblasti-38102 (accessed 3 October 2019).

Pozdravlenie glavy LNR Igorâ Plotnickogo žitelâm DNR s Dnem osvoboždeniâ Donbassa [Congratulations by the LPR Head to DPR Inhabitants on Donbas Liberation Day] (2016), *LIC*, 7 September. Available online http://lug-info.com/news/one/pozdravleni e-glavy-lnr-igorya-plotnitskogo-zhitelyam-dnr-s-dnem-osvobozhdeniya-donbassa-169 48 (accessed 3 October 2019).

Obraŝenie glavy LNR Igorâ Plotnickogo po slučaû Dnâ Respubliki [The LPR Head Igor Plotnitsky's Address on the Occasion of Republic Day] (2016), *LIC*, 12 May. Available online http://lug-info.com/news/one/obraschenie-glavy-lnr-igorya-plotnitskogo-po-s luchayu-dnya-respubliki-13273 (accessed 3 October 2019).

Obraŝenie i.o. glavy LNR Leonida Pasečnika k sootečestvennikam po slučaû Dnâ Rossii [The Acting LPR Head Leonid Pasiechnik's Address to Compatriots on the Occasion of Russia Day] (2018), *LIC*, 12 June. Available online http://lug-info.com/news/one/o braschenie-io-glavy-lnr-leonida-pasechnika-k-sootechestvennikam-po-sluchayu-dnya -rossii-35954 (accessed 3 October 2019).

Pozdravlenie Federacii profsoûzov LNR s Dnem narodnogo edinstva [Congratulations by the LPR Trade-Unions Federation on National Unity Day] (2018), *LIC*, 4 November. Available online http://lug-info.com/news/one/pozdravlenie-federatsii-profsoyuzov-lnr-s-dnem-narodnogo-edinstva-39838 (accessed 3 October 2019).

Pozdravlenie glavy LNR Igorâ Plotnickogo s Dnem narodnogo edinstva [Congratulations by the LPR Head Igor Plotnitsky on National Unity Day] (2015), *LIC*, 4 November. Available online http://lug-info.com/news/one/pozdravlenie-glavy-lnr-igorya-plotni tskogo-s-dnem-narodnogo-edinstva-8136 (accessed 3 October 2019).

Pozdravlenie predsedatelâ Narodnogo Soveta Vladimira Degtârenko s Dnem narodnogo edinstva [Congratulations by the People's Council Chairman Vladimir Degtiarenko on National Unity Day] (2016), *LIC*, 4 November. Available online http://lug-info.com/news/one/pozdravlenie-predsedatelya-narodnogo-soveta-vladimira-degtyarenko-s-dnem-narodnogo-edinstva-18721 (accessed 3 October 2019).

Pozdravlenie Glavy DNR Aleksandra Zaharčenko po slučaû Dnâ narodnogo edinstva [Congratulations by the DPR Head Alexander Zakharchenko on the Occasion of National Unity Day] (2017), *DAN*, 4 November. Available online https://dan-news.info/official/pozdravlenie-glavy-dnr-aleksandra-zaxarchenko-po-sluchayu-dnya-narodnogo-edinstva.html (accessed 3 October 2019).

Pozdravlenie Glavy DNR Aleksandra Zaharčenko po slučaû Dnâ Rossii [Congratulations by the DPR Head Alexander Zakharchenko on the Occasion of Russia Day] (2018), *DAN*, 12 June. Available online https://dan-news.info/official/pozdravlenie-glavy-dnr-aleksandra-zaxarchenko-po-sluchayu-dnya-rossii.html (accessed 03 October 2019).

Pozdravlenie glavy LNR Igorâ Plotnickogo s 74-j godovŝinoj osvoboždeniâ Luganska [Congratulations by the LPR Head Igor Plotnitsky on the 74th Anniversary of the Luhansk Liberation] (2017), *LIC*, 14 February. Available online http://lug-info.com/news/one/pozdravlenie-glavy-lnr-igorya-plotnitskogo-s-74-i-godovschinoi-osvobozh deniya-luganska-21451 (accessed 3 October 2019).

Pozdravlenie šahteram LNR ot obŝestvennogo dviženiâ 'Mir Luganŝine' [Congratulations to LPR Miners by the Civic Movement 'Mir Luhanshchine'] (2016), *LIC*, 28 August. Available online http://lug-info.com/news/one/pozdravlenie-shakhteram-lnr-ot-obsch estvennogo-dvizheniya-mir-luganschine-16609 (accessed 3 October 2019).

Pozdravlenie glavy LNR Igorâ Plotnickogo s Dnëm šahtëra [Congratulations by the LPR Head Igor Plotnitsky on Miners Day] (2016), *LIC*, 28 August. Available online http://lug-info.com/news/one/pozdravlenie-glavy-lnr-igorya-plotnitskogo-s-dnem-shakht era-16441 (accessed 3 October 2019)

Andriy Biletsky's Ukrainian order

Discourse, actions and prospects of democracy in Ukraine

Halyna Mokrushyna

1 Introduction

The Euromaidan protests in Ukraine, actively supported by Western politicians, drastically changed the social and political situation within Ukraine itself and the larger geopolitical context of relations between Russia and the collective West. Russia's annexation of Crimea and the support of anti-Maidan rebellion in Donbas triggered a wave of unseen patriotism in large parts of the Ukrainian population and led to the emergence of the unprecedented volunteer movement in the country. The extreme-right elements of the Ukrainian society that remained marginal so far gained more prominence in the society thanks to their involvement in the Euromaidan and the active participation in the war against Donetsk and Luhansk insurgency. Probably, the best known or the most publicized in the media example of the far right is Azov battalion. The initiator and the first commander is Andriy Biletsky, a long-time active member of the Ukrainian far right. After the incorporation of the Azov into the National Guard of Ukraine, Biletsky united former members of the battalion and its followers in a new political party – National Corps – while Biletsky himself became a deputy of Verkhovna Rada.

This article analyses the political discourse of Andriy Biletsky and of his party, as manifested in Biletsky's blog on Ukrayinska Pravda website, interviews and his earlier writings, as well as in the programme and statements of the National Corps. The content analysis of the material reveals the main themes of the discourse, whereas the linguistic analysis shows how these themes are developed.

The discourse analysis of Biletsky's texts shows that his Ukrainian nationalism is a classical 'blood and land' nationalism, and it draws on the 'integral' nationalism of the Organization of Ukrainian Nationalists. Biletsky's nationalism has also a strong socialist component that translates in economic and social justice for all. The analysis of the National Corps programme reveals the traditional conservatism, directed against neoliberal values, including those of LGBT and transgender rights.

Biletsky's nationalistic discourse is directed against Putin and Russians who support his actions. It inscribes itself into a widespread anti-Russian sentiment within Ukrainian society. Biletsky's frequent appearances in various mainstream TV and radio shows feed into this sentiment, which works against attempts to establish a direct dialogue with Donetsk and Luhansk. What is more dangerous is that they contribute to the legitimization of extreme-right nationalism among the public at large.

Biletsky and his fellow members of the National Corps act on their nationalist discourse, and although they claim that their actions are non-violent and directed at re-establishing social justice and public order, some of these actions do the opposite – they intimidate left-wing, feminist, LGBT activists, and threaten the development of Ukraine as an open, inclusive democracy. Therefore, it is important to examine their discursive practices to understand their motivation and ideology. This task will be undertaken here.

2 Theoretical framework

In this article, the term 'discourse' is used in the largest meaning – as a social practice of using a language to represent a certain understanding of reality (Cameron and Panovic 2014: 3). It is a social practice because the primary material of the representation – language or what we say – is learned by us through socialization. Since childhood, we not only learn words and sentences but also assimilate certain perspectives on reality. We form our individual voices out of the range of social voices already present in society (Lemke 1995: 24–5).

The variety of these perspectives is shaped by the historical experience of a given society, and the predominance of certain interpretations, of certain discourses, is the reflection of the distribution of power within society. By framing reality from a given point of view, using certain linguistic means, we describe and make sense of reality; we also construct it to a certain extent. As Michel Foucault famously noted, we systematically form the objects of which we speak (Foucault 1972: 49). When a group accesses power, it gains the control of not only what to say but also about what and how. This group, the elite, does not need brute physical force or economic coercion; it does it through the symbolic means of language and a certain representation of reality.

One famous demonstration of this symbolic power at work is George Orwell's *Politics and the English Language* (1946) in which he shows, in part, how political discourse is used 'in defense of the indefensible' (p. 8). For example, bombarding unprotected villages from the air, setting fire to huts and machine-gunning cattle is called pacification; the Soviet deportations and imprisonment in gulags is called 'elimination of unreliable elements' (p. 8–9). Such neutral or even positive representations (pacification) mask human pain and suffering (Wilson 2015: 777). The political elites not only impose their own representations but also try to discredit alternative representations in order to retain control of discourse and through it their control of power.

However, politicians do not just produce a certain type of discourse. They are also products of this discourse in the sense that in the process of describing and explaining through the discourse what they do, why and how, they build their own individual and political group identities (Wilson 2015: 786; Wodak 2011).

The critical discourse analysis (CDA) focuses not so much on the discourse itself as on the social problems and political issues. It not only describes the discourse but also tries to explain it as a product of social interaction and social structure (Van Dijk 2015: 467). Since I am interested in the view of the far-right nationalist groups on the post-Euromaidan developments in Ukraine, which is a political issue, I will study the discourse of Andriy Biletsky and the right nationalist party that he leads, National Corps, from the CDA perspective.

First the language and imagery of Biletsky political discourse will be analysed. Then the ideology underpinning this discourse will be determined and an attempt to outline its historical roots will be made. Since discourse is a social practice and people act on their words, I will provide examples of the actions by National Corps and National Militias, affiliated with them. I will show how these actions are directly linked to the political programme of the National Corps and Andriy Biletsky's blog. I will conclude with the role the extreme-right plays in the politics of post-Euromaidan Ukraine, and the threat it poses to the young Ukrainian democracy.

3 Andriy Biletsky – From Trident to National Corps

Andriy Biletsky has been involved in the Ukrainian extreme right since his university years. He studied history at the Kharkiv Karazin State University. His dissertation was about the Ukrainian Insurgent Army (UPA) – the Ukrainian nationalist and later partisan guerilla in Western Ukraine during the Second World War.[1] Biletsky mentions in one of the interviews that in his childhood he was influenced by a book presenting Ukraine as a victim of Moscow/Russian imperialism. Biletsky recalls how in the last days of the Soviet Union, in 1990, when he was twelve, he refused to join the ranks of the Young Pioneer organization and together with several schoolmates raised the Ukrainian flag on his school (Bereza 2014).

After graduating from the university, Biletsky became the commander of the Kharkiv branch of the Stepan Bandera's Trident, a Ukrainian nationalist organization. He actively collaborated with the Social-Nationalist Party of Ukraine that mutated into the extreme-right party Svoboda. In 2005, after the first Maidan, Biletsky founded the 'Patriot of Ukraine' organization with the goal of propagating the Ukrainian nationalism in Eastern Ukraine – Kharkiv, Luhansk, Donetsk, Odessa and Crimea (Bereza 2014). It was registered in January of 2006 as a civil society organization. Biletsky became the 'commander-in-chief', planning, coordinating and participating in all activities, from marches and protests to acts of civil disobedience and riots. He also led raids on the drug dealers and arrested illegal migrants.

In December 2011, he was arrested on the charge of planning a group beating and assassination, and remained in prison till February 2014 when the Verkhovna Rada adopted a decree to free all 'political' prisoners. Upon release from prison, Biletsky and his Patriot friends immediately got involved in fighting the Anti-Maidan groups in Kharkiv. In May 2014, they came to Berdiansk in Zaporizhia region to help stop the advancement of pro-Russian insurgency. Biletsky had been advocating for the incorporation of the volunteer battalion within the Ministry of Interior, but, in his words, the bureaucrats were too slow and undecided. The worsening situation in Donbas forced them to act more swiftly, and the 'Azov' battalion of territorial defence was officially registered (Pylypchuk 2018). The Azov battalion became instrumental in defending Mariupol in June of 2014 from the attacks of the pro-Russian insurgency. For his military achievements, in August 2014, Biletsky was awarded an order and received the rank of the lieutenant colonel of police extraordinary ('Andriy Biletsky' 2015). In November 2014, the Azov battalion was officially incorporated into the National Guard of Ukraine.

Azov is ill-famed for its crimes against the civilian population, such as mass looting, unlawful detention and torture. These crimes were reported in several reports of the Office of the United Nations High Commissioner for Human Rights and in the reports of Human Rights Watch (see, for instance, OHCHR reports of February and May 2016 or the Human Rights Report of July 2016 – 'You don't exist').

In September 2014, at the assembly of the party People' Front, Biletsky together with commanders of other volunteer battalions was admitted to the Military Council of the party ('Narodny front'). Biletsky intended to run as a member of the party in the parliamentary elections of October 2014, but he had to abandon his plans because of the mounting international pressure, caused by the indignation at the explicitly ultra-nationalist and racist programmes of the Biletsky's Patriot of Ukraine and the Social-Nationalist Assembly. Biletsky withdrew his candidacy and instead run as an independent candidate in one of the districts of Kyiv. He was elected by one-third of votes.

In October 2016, Biletsky left the army. At the same time, he announced the creation of the political party National Corps based on Patriot of Ukraine. The day of the announcement of the new party was highly symbolic – 14 October, the day of the creation of the Ukrainian Insurgent Army, and the day of the Defender of the Fatherland. The Patriot/National Corps marched through the downtown Kyiv in several thousands, carrying torches and banners of the newly created party (Pietsukh 2016).

4 Political programme of the National Corps

The home page of the party's website greets visitors with three words, 'strength, prosperity, order', which are declared the cornerstones of future Ukraine. Members of the party claim to be the only ones capable of saving Ukraine from its present catastrophic condition through decisive actions and honest work. They present themselves as the builders of a 'new Ukrainian world' with advanced medicine, high salaries, space programmes, nuclear weapons and the most interesting culture. The diplomatic corps of new Ukraine is skilful, the army is powerful and there is no corruption, no 'corruptionaries' and no chaos ('Nacional'nij Korpus'), the Ukrainian dream come true.

In its programme, the party sees Ukraine as part of Europe and member of the 'intermarium' geopolitical space stretching from the Baltic to the Black sea:

> *We feel part of European civilization, but we do not strive to join Brussels bureaucracy. Therefore, the priority of Ukrainian external policy is the creation of a new community of European nations based on the harmonious integration of traditional values and innovative ideas. The cradle of the new European Union should become the commonwealth of countries, situated in the geopolitical space which connects the Baltic and the Black Sea* ('Proġrama').[2]

The central focus of Ukraine's foreign policy is to improve, deepen, expand and strengthen relations with all countries belonging to this space, except Russia. The latter is declared a state-aggressor on all levels of international relations. All cooperation with Russia must be suspended until Russia returns Crimea and other 'annexed territories', pays reparations to Ukraine and the leadership of Russian Federation is tried in the international tribunal court for having launched the war against Ukraine.

Internally, the National Corps intends to nationalize all of the important enterprises that were privatized after the dissolution of the Soviet Union, to deregulate economy, to decentralize power, to train Ukrainian 'warrior', the sole real guardian of Ukrainian sovereignty and territorial integrity, and to educate population in traditional values, while implementing innovative ideas through an advanced technology ('Proġrama').

5 Biletsky's blog on Ukrayinska Pravda

These principles reverberate in Biletsky's blog on *Ukrayinska Pravda* (Ukrainian Truth), one of the leading Ukrainian web media. Biletsky started writing his blog in August 2016, around the same time when he announced the creation of his political project – the National Corps. In his first, programmatic post (Biletsky, 24 August 2016) he raises the essential 'blood' theme of the nationalistic discourse saying that it is only after the Ukrainian blood was spilled in the Revolution of Dignity and then later in the East that Ukrainians started creating the true Ukrainian State, the incarnation of the Ukrainian Dream. 'The state is not given as a gift – the State is fought for, fought for with blood', says Biletsky (24 August 2016). During the twenty-five years of the Ukrainian independence (Biletsky's post is dated 24 August, the Day of Ukrainian independence), Ukrainians did not have a true Ukrainian state – it was a post-Soviet state machine, coupled with a 'kleptocratic' oligarchic regime that was plundering national resources. The old system is still alive and is fighting back. Corrupted bureaucrats in Ukrainian public offices are not true citizens; they are 'parasites on the body of the Nation'. They occupied Ukraine from inside, while Russia tries to occupy Ukraine from outside, and conscious Ukrainians must fight on both fronts (24 August 2016).

According to Biletsky, foreign nationals who defended Ukraine on the Eastern front are much more worthy of the Ukrainian citizenship than bureaucrats with the Ukrainian passports. Foreign fighters earned this right through the blood that they shed for Ukraine (Biletsky, 27 July 2017).

All of Biletsky's sworn brothers (*pobratymy*), who shed their blood on Maidan and on the Eastern front defending Ukrainian land from the Russian invaders, are heroes. They are fearless and noble people, legionaries of the twenty-first century, who obtained heroic victories. They sacrificed their lives for the Fatherland. They are conscious Ukrainians who realized their responsibility before the nation. 'There are no greater patriots of our Fatherland than those first volunteers who, unarmed, went to an internecine battle for Ukraine', writes Biletsky (Biletsky, 14 January 2017).

These heroes come from the common people – ordinary men and women, students, athletes, managers, lawyers, combine operators and painters who never served in the army. They became volunteers, organized themselves in an incredibly short time, built an efficient military machine, built a real people's home front and defended the country[3].

The tone of Biletsky's posts, when he talks about those who died on the Eastern front, is solemn and elevated. The words that he uses (heroes, sacrifices, to lay down one's life, faith and devotion) conjure images of valiant warriors of ancient sagas who cleave the sea waters on their way to Troy. The defenders of the Ukrainian independence are also likened to heroes of Cossack ballads rushing to Istanbul through the stormy Black Sea (Biletsky, 13 June 2018).

Through their sacrifices in the name of the nation, they transcended the ordinariness, the materiality of life here and now, and acquired the heroic spiritual power. They incarnate the Ukrainian phenomenon: free will, devotion, fanaticism and faith in people and the country, all that stands against the material world with its moral feebleness, greed, and egoism (Biletsky, 5 May 2017).

Biletsky turns to history to underline the continuity of the heroic spirit of his brothers-in-arms. Many times, he mentions that contemporary defenders of Ukraine are backed up by the warriors of the Kievan prince Sviatoslav, Khmelnitsky's Cossacks and young cadets who died at Kruty,[4] soldiers of the Ukrainian Insurgent Army. All those who died on the Eastern front in 2014–2018 joined the millions-strong Immortal Army of the defenders of powerful, united, primordial Ukraine (Biletsky, 14 March 2017).

It is also noted in history that modern Ukrainians should look for the inspiration for the fight for and the restoration of the Ukrainian state as it existed in the times of the Kievan Rus, for which the noble hetmans in the seventeenth—eighteenth centuries or the soldiers of the Ukrainian Insurgent Army fought during the Second World War. The dawn of this Ukrainian state has begun, and the elite that will build this state was born on the frontline (Biletsky, 24 August 2017). Here, again, Biletsky verbalizes the topic of fight through blood, through sacrifice and through suffering. Only in this way can the truly Ukrainian state, the truly independent and powerful Ukraine, be built.

This antithesis of an elevated, sacred world of Heroic Spirit and weak, corrupted materialism magnifies the nobility, the fortitude and the selfishness of Biletsky's brothers-in-arms, and accentuates the moral decay and baseness of Ukrainian power and Ukrainian bureaucracy. Ukrainian political leaders are 'midgets', 'profiteers' and 'pawnbrokers'. They make deals with the enemy, they steal and lie, and they sell out Ukraine. Biletsky depicts a disgusting portrait of the Ukrainian leadership: a 'clique of thieves'; a group of greedy billionaires who usurped the 'power; a 'political terrarium'; and a 'bestial system'. They sell Ukraine's national interests in bulk and in retail. Because of them, Ukraine is perceived as a street prostitute by the international community (Biletsky, 11 October 2017). Ukraine became a political currency at the hands of Poroshenko and his likes who care more about their business than about Ukraine. The political leadership of Ukraine is not true national leadership, it is a local colonial administration that was directed from Moscow yesterday, and now receives orders from Washington.

As Biletsky reminds his readers, a fish starts rotting from the head, and if the head, that is the political leadership of Ukraine, is rotten, people of Ukraine have the right to cut off the rot (Biletsky, 29 June 2017) either through legal means, such as the impeachment, or through another Maidan. He argues that deputies of Verkhovna Rada should also be deprived of their parliamentary immunity. They not only they from people but also place their kids in lucrative posts within the state apparatus. Sons and daughters of ordinary Ukrainians die on the front line defending Ukrainian freedom and sovereignty; volunteers help the army with food and equipment, purchased on the money from public fundraising campaigns; and Ukrainian soldiers buy ammunition with their own money and for years rotate between the front line and their homes. At the same time, bureaucrats and their kids, sitting in safe and cosy offices in Kyiv, rob the army and fill up their pockets through shady deals and schemes. President Poroshenko promised that he will cut hands of those who steal in the defence industry. If he forgot his promise, it is time to do it without him (Biletsky, 26 February 2019). Cut, chop off – Biletsky uses radical verbs when he talks about the need to punish the corrupted officials. 'The cleansing of power must be pitiless, just, and all-embracing', declares bluntly Biletsky (Biletsky, 16 March 2017).

In posts of Biletsky's blog on Ukrayinska Pravda, it is not only the Ukrainian political leadership that is depicted as usurious and rotten. Financial extortioners from the West are twisting the hands of Ukraine, imposing draconian requirements on her and pushing anti-Ukrainian reforms. European businesses are no better – they are lobbying for the removal of sanctions against Russia because they suffer from the shortage of Russian petrodollars (Biletsky, 22 February 2017).

Russia, in its turn, is verbalized in Biletsky's writings as a financial and military invader, a nuclear monster. It rewrites Ukrainian history and spreads lies about the Ukrainian liberation movement in an attempt to discredit Ukraine on the world stage (Biletsky, 4 October 2016).

6 Ukrainian social nationalism of the Patriot of Ukraine

Social justice or social equality is a prominent theme in Andriy Biletsky's writings on the Ukrainian social nationalism, the doctrine of the paramilitary organization Patriot of Ukraine, one of his earlier projects. In the programmatic article 'Ukrainian racial social-nationalism', Biletsky explains that sociality or social equality means the creation of the harmonious National community. A sharp inequality leads to the rotting of the National spirit. The principle of sociality means the negation of democracy and liberalism as they break the unity of the nation and install the rule of a mediocre crowd over prominent personalities. The basis of the new society should be not the democratic voting of the crowd, but the natural selection of the best representatives of the nation – innate leaders. The modern political system degrades people who work hard and achieve goals because it equates a vote, say, of a professor and a vote of a prostitute, a vote of a drug addict and a vote of a military commander. 'People by nature are born with different abilities and capabilities, and so the greatest happiness of a person is when (s)he finds his/her own place in the National hierarchy and consciously fulfill his/her life's task', affirms Biletsky (Biletsky 2007).

Another principle of social nationalism is raciality (the word *racism* is not used in the text at all). Contrary to the post-OUN Ukrainian nationalism, which proclaims language, culture or territory as the basis of the Ukrainian nation, Biletsky considers them all secondary to the Race, the Racial nature of Ukrainians. Spirituality, language and culture are derivative of the unique Ukrainian racial nature. The Ukrainian nation needs to undergo racial purification, and only then will a healthy Ukrainian Spirit be regenerated in a healthy Racial body (Biletsky 2007).

The third principle of the Ukrainian social nationalism is the great power/statehood. Biletsky affirms that Ukraine is a nation with an old imperial history – it is a descendant of at least two superpowers, the Great Scythia and Kievan Rus. The mission of the current generation of Ukrainians is to create the Third Empire – a Great Ukraine. Such lexis is reminiscent of Russia as the Third Rome. And here, again, Biletsky resorts to the social Darwinist determinism: 'If we are strong, we will take everything that belongs to us by right and even more; we will build our own Superpower – Empire – Great Ukraine …. If we are weak, we belong among conquered, dying peoples because such are the laws of Nature' (Biletsky 2007).

Biletsky returns to the 'organized' or 'integral' nationalism of the OUN based on the postulate of the organic nature of the nation. The radical nationalist ideology of the OUN was a totalitarian, anti-democratic and anti-communist revolutionary movement, based on the cult of action, military idealism and voluntarism. The nation was considered the most natural and the most organic form of the organization of human society. National prevailed over universal, all-human and over the individual. The state was seen as the main institution responsible for solving social and economic problems. The state together with corporate-professional unions (trade-unions) should also ensure the societal consensus. The radical nationalist programme combined political elitism and social egalitarianism. The social programme was based on principles of social justice (Kasianov 2004: 37).

7 Social justice in action – National Militia

Biletsky in his blog raises many times the theme not of social justice, but injustice, when he talks about ordinary Ukrainians. These people organized themselves into volunteer battalions to defend Ukraine from the aggressor in the East, collected funds to buy equipment and weapons for fighters and donated to the army the last pennies from meagre salaries while the corrupted leadership continued to conduct business in blood with the aggressor and make profits on the shady schemes of weapon purchases. While expressing his indignation by the fact that Russian banks continue to work in

Ukraine, Biletsky declares: 'If the state does not react and does not fulfill its duties before the people in the time of war, people have the right to take the cause of justice in their own hands. We ourselves, by our own decision, close Sberbank of Russia in Ukraine' (Biletsky, 13 March 2017). On 13 March 2017, members of the National Corps gathered in front of the Sberbank branch in Kyiv and started to lay a brick wall in front of the windows ('Nacional'nij Korpus zamuruvav').

This and other actions of the 'activists' of the National Corps are reminiscent of the OUN's cult of action. If the state is not capable of acting in the national interests of Ukraine, nationalists are ready to step in. In the spirit of this 'social activism' Biletsky inspired the creation of National Militia, a paramilitary organization of volunteers whose goal is to secure order on the streets, as indicated on their website ('Nacional'ni družini'). The goals of this grass-roots organization, according to one member, are also 'to assist in emergency situations and help with any existing problems in the society' ('Tak zvani nacional'ni družinniki'). Members come from the former volunteer battalions, from the 'patriotic' youth and simply active citizens eager to bring back safety to the country ('Nacional'ni družini').

The examples of the National Militia's actions include patrolling and detaining poachers doing illegal fishing; organizing and practising rock climbing; cleaning the territory of natural reserves; upon reports by residents, checking stores involved in non-licensed commerce of alcohol and cigarettes; and organizing marches-protests against corruption in the military. Their actions follow the logic of voluntarism in which ordinary people organize themselves to support an institution, in this case, the state's function of securing public order. Not coincidentally, users of social media likened the units of the National Corps marching in the streets of Kyiv to volunteer people's militia of the Soviet Union (Shramovych 2018). Some others compared members of the National Corps to storm troopers of Nazi Germany because of the evident ideological affiliation with Biletsky and his extreme-right ideology.

8 A strong leader for Ukraine

Biletsky in his first post on Ukrayinska Pravda discusses the subject of a strong leader for the nation, which echoes the OUN's cult of the leader (Kasianov 2004: 37). Biletsky once again turns to history to remind his readers that 'in times of the greatest danger, Ukrainians always entrusted their lives and destiny to the only leader – a prince, a hetman, a commander-in-chief, a president' (Biletsky, 24 August 2016). Ukrainian sovereignty is now under a serious threat from Russia, the country-aggressor. Therefore, the form of political governance of Ukraine must be changed from the parliamentarian-presidential to presidential-parliamentarian republic so that president has more power to protect the country. The president will have more power, but he will also have a higher responsibility before the people of Ukraine, and if he fails, the measure of punishment will be not only impeachment but even execution in war times (ibid). To this effect, Biletsky promises to introduce a bill to make an amendment to the Constitution of Ukraine on increasing the responsibility of the president of Ukraine (Biletsky, 24 August 2016).

9 Anti-oligarchic, anti-Russian and anti-liberal nationalism of Andriy Biletsky

The word choice of the Biletsky's discourse shows that he draws upon the Ukrainian integral nationalism of the OUN–UPA and the classical nationalism of land and blood. He identifies internal and external enemies. The former is the corrupted, rotten elite and bureaucrats who are Ukrainians only by passports. The latter is Russia with its never-ending imperial claims and the usurious Western financial structures. Russia is not only an external military invader but also an internal invader through the financial capital and culture.

Biletsky's blog abounds in the salute 'Glory to Ukraine' that has OUN as origin and was considered a Nazi salute until it became a mainstream salutation in post-Euromaidan Ukraine. He also uses strictly ethnic qualifiers written with a capital letter such as Ukrainian Spirit, Ukrainian Dream, Ukrainian Phenomenon, Ukrainian State, Ukrainian Order, Ukrainian Peace and Ukrainian Victory.

Biletsky's resort to the nationalist Ukrainian discourse of the OUN is logical and expected as many parties build on the rhetoric from the past, especially when the modern-day political entities share the same ideology with their like-minded predecessors (Żuk and Żuk 2018: 139–42). In the post-Soviet Ukraine, when communism lost its prominent position, nationalism started gradually growing in importance. After the Euromaidan and the following annexation/departure of Crimea and the pro-Russian uprising in Donbas, communism was equated by the ruling regime with the Soviet/Russian occupation, and a mild version of Ukrainian nationalism was included in the platforms of mainstream parties. The Communist Party of Ukraine was banned, and the hammer and sickle were likened to the Nazi Swastika and declared illegal. Moreover, any pro-Russian rhetoric or critic of the Poroshenko regime was silenced through arrests and physical and online intimidations by extreme-right militants. Under such conditions, the left-wing parties and socialist/communist ideology in Ukraine were reduced to a marginal, insignificant presence in the political and public space, as they were in Poland of the 1990s (Żuk and Żuk 2018: 136). As a result, the Marxist framing of the post-Euromaidan developments in Ukraine as an increasing social and economic inequality and class struggle between pro-European, transnational Ukrainian oligarchy, and more and more impoverished working class is almost absent from intellectual and political debates.

However, such framing is very much present in Biletsky's nationalist discourse. One of the central themes of his writing is the activism of ordinary Ukrainians, activism that is full of heroism, unselfishness and determination. They step in to defend the homeland, to take care of their army, to ensure order on the streets and to draw attention to illegal activities of corrupt bureaucrats and businessmen with 'unclean hands'. Ukrainian oligarchs and non-patriotic, corrupted bureaucracy continue to enrich themselves at the expense of the ordinary people. Biletsky's image of Ukraine as a prostitute is a striking allegory of Ukrainian people being exploited and sold by the greedy, usurious elites. In this regard, Biletsky and his comrades are closer to left-wing populist parties in Europe than to extreme-right European parties whose ideology is based on the right-wing nationalism and exclusion of the ethnically different other (see, for instance, Stavrakakis et al. 2017; Akbaba 2018; Żuk and Żuk 2018).

There is no single mentioning of ethnic minorities or of their languages in the National Corps programme. Ukrainian culture is declared the basis of the Ukrainian nation. And this culture is Ukraine-centred. It means the development of the Ukrainian language and the popularization of traditional national values and ideals by all kinds of state-supported initiatives – from renaming geographical locations to the vast promotion of 'high' culture ('Proğrama'). In an interview to Ukrainian news website gordon.ua, Biletsky stated that he is not a racist, nor an anti-Semite, and for him the main criteria of defining a Ukrainian patriot/nationalist is not the mastery of the Ukrainian language, but the deeds that a person did for Ukraine. He remarked that half of the Ukrainians who fought on the Eastern front are Russian-speaking (Batsman 2018).

However, he and his party enthusiastically supported the 'historic' law on the Ukrainian language that practically banned Russian from public spaces in Ukraine. Such a contradictory attitude towards the Ukrainian language is probably rooted in Biletsky's bilingualism and biculturalism. Just like millions of Ukrainians and as a native of Kharkiv, he is perfectly bilingual. There are many videos on YouTube of his interviews where he speaks Russian, including a very recent one recorded in March 2019 ('V gostâh' 2019). At the beginning of this interview, Biletsky explains that although Ukrainian undoubtedly must be the only state language in Ukraine, for him the Ukrainian language is not the only marker of a true Ukrainian. The language question is a 'complex' one, as he admits ('V gostâh' 2019), but he proposes no other solution than the one formulated in the new language law: to eliminate Russian from all spheres of life, except private communication in the family and between friends.

For Biletsky and his followers, the divide between Us and Them runs through the support of Putin's Russia. They confronted the enemy, the Russia-backed insurgents of Donetsk and Lugansk on the frontlines; they staged street protests against the functioning of Russian businesses in Ukraine; they criticized and denounced Ukrainian politicians with the pro-Russian position, such as Viktor Medvedchuk. As director-general of the Ukrainian Jewish Committee, Edward Dolinsky noted, the Ukrainian extreme-right groups avoid public anti-Semitic rhetoric and violence, but instead they attack the left on the ground that they are 'pro-Russian'; they also attack LGBT minorities (Colborne 2019).

For instance, in May of 2018 in Poltava, members of the National Corps disrupted training for psychologists working with the LGBT people ('Nackorpus zirvav'). In June 2018, National Corps militants were among a group of people who tried to disrupt the LGBT pride parade 'March of Equality' in Kyiv. In a statement issued a couple of days before the event, National Corps declared that just as they did not let Putin turn Ukrainians into slaves, they will not allow the LGBT to disregard the traditions of Ukrainian society and Ukrainian family, and to transgress Ukrainian moral principles. For centuries, Ukrainians fought for freedom and independence of their Fatherland so that a healthy and happy Ukrainian nation could live in it, not the LGBT. 'You are a deadlock of the evolution of humanity! A final dot in its existence, since after you only your material creations will remain on Earth, and any material creation is nothing without the man!' – said National Corps, addressing the LGBT ('Nacional'nij korpus za zdorovu'). LGBT cannot produce children, and there is no future for a nation without children. Only the traditional Ukrainian family is the basis of a healthy and strong nation. National Corps has defended and will continue to defend the traditional ways of Ukrainian family and nation (Colborne 2019).

National Corps' embrace of traditional values is clearly verbalized in their request to ban a transgender march in Kyiv. Under a telling title, 'Disease should be treated, not propagated', the National Corps declares that transgender identity is a disease, and it is mean and cruel to tell a person who suffers from this mental illness that he/she is normal. These persons should receive an appropriate medical treatment. And it is out of the question to let these people adopt children, as they will cripple them. The only family where children should live and grow is the traditional nuclear family with a man as a father and a woman as a mother ('Pozyciya').

10 Discussion

Based on the analysis of Biletsky's blog and the programme and statements of his party, National Corps, as well as by their actions, one could say that their nationalism is more restrained and more 'respectable' than the radicalism of extreme-right groups such as S 14, Tradition and Order, and others, known for their aggressive propaganda and illegal actions. After all, National Corps is a party and has parliamentary aspirations. They tried to unite their efforts with two other far-right parties, Svoboda and the Right Sector, and present one candidate for the presidential elections of March-April 2019 in Ukraine, but failed to do so because of ideological differences and leaders' personal ambitions.

Andriy Biletsky's frequent participation as a guest of various talk shows on mainstream TV channels testifies to the fact that perception of the far right in the Ukrainian society changed. Before the Euromaidan and the war in Donbass, right-wing groups in Ukraine were marginal. But through their involvement in the Euromaidan revolution and the fight against Russia-backed insurgency in Donbas, they won a significant legitimacy with the wider public (Likhachev 2018: 5). They rode the wave of patriotism and contributed to the general acceptance of the nationalistic symbols and language of OUN–UPA. As the example of the Azov battalion shows, extreme-right elements were also integrated into the state structures, becoming part of the National Guard. Ukrainian law-enforcement forces oftentimes remain passive and do not intervene when members of far-right groups show aggressive behaviour towards others and even towards the police.

Although right nationalist parties like Andriy Biletsky's National Corps can be considered marginal in terms of political power (they do not have sufficient support of the population to enter the Ukrainian parliament), they do have a certain social authority and presence through the street activism.

The most massive act of the National Corps denouncing the corruption within the Ministry of Defense were marches through downtown Kyiv to the presidential administration and headquarters of public security ministries with the demands to arrest high-ranking bureaucrats implicated in multi-million dollar shady deals with weapon purchases ('Vduy Svynarchukam'). In all these public actions, militants of the National Corps present themselves as defenders of the ordinary people, fighters for justice and crusaders against the corrupted, profit-seeking Ukrainian bureaucrats and 'pseudo-elites'. National Corps activists often initiate and participate in street protests against unauthorized constructions in various cities throughout Ukraine. Often these protests become violent, and 'activists' of the National Corps are arrested by the police. All these actions of Biletsky's far-right party contributed to the acceptance of violence in the Ukrainian society, traumatized by the revolution and the war (Likhachev 2018: 5).

The biggest threat that Biletsky and his party pose is their anti-Russian rhetoric, as it feeds into the anti-Russian sentiment in the Ukrainian society and diminishes their chances of a reconciliation with Donetsk and Luhansk and a peaceful resolution of the conflict that would come from the direct negotiations with the rebelled republics.

It also prevents the re-identification of pro-Russian Ukrainians with the pro-European Ukrainians after the deepening of the split, caused by the March 2014 banning of the language law that granted Russian the status of regional language, and by the tragedy of Odessa on 2 May 2014, among others. In Odessa, forty-two people of pro-Russian Ukrainians from the Anti-Maidan groups were killed and burned in a fire in the Trade Union building when far-right nationalists drove them into it. The investigation of this tragedy is dragging on. For many pro-Russian Ukrainians, the violent death of their fellow citizens and the evident procrastination of post-Euromaidan authorities to establish the truth and bring to justice the culprits became a symbol of the exclusive, anti-Russian nationalism of the new post-Euromaidan Ukraine. On 2, May when residents of Odessa were commemorating these tragic events, the National Corps marched through the streets of the city in the March of Ukrainian Order, celebrating the fifth anniversary of the victory over 'Kremlin stooges' ('V Odesi rozpochavsia'). 'Odessa is a Ukrainian city', concluded a short article on National Corps website, while in the photos accompanying the article one could see 'activists' with torches and portraits of two far-right militants who died in the clashes on 2 May 2014 ('V Odesi rozpochavsia'). It is another reminder of the cleavage that still exists within the Ukrainian society and is a clear illustration of how difficult it will be to heal that cleavage in the presence of active extreme-right nationalists in Ukraine.

11 Conclusions

Discourse analysis of Andriy Biletsky's writings, and of the programme and statements of his party, National Corps, reveals a classical 'soil and blood' nationalism and social conservatism, coupled with technological modernism. Ideologically, they continue to develop the OUN nationalism of the late 1930s.

Biletsky and his followers legitimate themselves and their actions through the lexis of historical links between them and heroic defenders of Ukraine from the past. Present-day Ukraine is the heir of the great forms of Ukrainian statehood in history. Biletsky continues to verbalize the topic of the fight for independence by stating that the true

Ukrainian state can be born only through blood, and that only in 2014, when ordinary Ukrainians spilled their blood and defended the motherland from Putin's troops, the did Ukrainian nation and Ukrainian state truly came into being. However, Ukraine is still under the grip of corrupted elites whose only interests are self-enrichment and profit, and Ukrainians must get rid of their oligarchic regime.

Biletsky's nationalism has a strong anti-Russian component, the result of Russia's annexation of Crimea and support of Donetsk and Luhansk insurgency. It is directed not against Russian-speaking Ukrainians or Russian people, but against Putin and his supporters, the so-called Russian World (*Russkij mir*).

An essential component of Biletsky's nationalism is a socialist vision of the Ukrainian social and economic order, based on welfare and social justice for all. He is against bureaucracy and oligarchy both in Ukraine and in the European Union.

Ukrainian society is consolidated though Ukrainian culture and language. There is no mentioning of ethnic minorities in Biletsky's blog or the programme of the National Corps.

Biletsky's nationalism is conservative and embraces traditional values of the nuclear family. They are against the neoliberal ideology of feminism, transgender and LGBT rights.

National Corps and its leader, Andriy Biletsky, not only talk and write about their nationalism, but they act on it. Their presence and active participation in Ukrainian politics continue to legitimize traditional Ukrainian nationalism, which impedes Ukraine's progress towards European style neoliberal democracy, while their vocal anti-Russian stance prevents Ukraine's engagement in a direct dialogue with Donetsk and Luhansk.

Notes

1. UPA was a situational ally of the German Nazis during the occupation of Ukraine in the Second World War, but also fought against them and against the Soviet Army during and after the war.
2. Translations from Ukrainian and Russian are the author's own.
3. This image evokes Soviet era depiction of the all-patriotic drive to fight the fascist invaders under the slogan 'All for the front! All for Victory!'
4. Battle of Kruty took place on 29 January 1918 between the Bolshevik Forces of about 4000 men under the command of Mikhail Muraviev and a small, hastily assembled detachment of 500 men who were sent to defend the Ukrainian People's Republic (UNR) in Kyiv. Kruty is a small town in Chernihiv oblast, around 130 km northeast of Kyiv. The two enemy forces clashed near Kruty railway station. The Bolshevik forces were advancing towards Kyiv and the detachment sent by the UNR had to stop that advance. It consisted mainly of young cadets, not trained for military actions, and soldiers of the Haidamaka unit of the Army of the UNR. In an unequal battle half of the Ukrainian soldiers were killed ('Kruty'). In the post-Soviet Ukraine, the battle of Kruty became a symbol of self-sacrifice for the Ukrainian independence. It is commemorated on the official level every year.

References

Akbaba, S. (2018), 'Re-narrating Europe in the Face of Populism: An Analysis of the Anti-immigration Discourse of Populist Party Leaders', *Insight Turkey*, 20 (3) (Summer 2018): 199–218.

'Andriy Biletsky'. (2015), *Natsiolnalny korespondent*, 8 December 2015. https://nackor.org/en/andrey-bileckiy (accessed 7 April 2019)

Batsman, O. (2018), 'Andrìj Bìlec′kij: Polovina lûdej, âkì voûvali za Ukraïnu, rozmovlâê rosìjs′koû movoû' ['Andriy Biletsky: Half of the People Who Fought for Ukraine Speak Russian'], *Gordonua.com*, 20 November 2018. https://gordonua.com/ukr/publicatio ns/-biletskij-507346.html (accessed 6 April 2019).

Bereza, A. (22 October 2014), 'Andrej Bileckij. Kak vojna prevratila polituznika v komandira batal′ona Azov' ['Andrei Biletskiy. How the War Transformed a Political Prisoner into the Commander of Azov Battalion']. *Novoie vremia*. https://web.archive.org/web/2015011 9152837/http:/nvua.net/ publications/Andrey-Bileckiy-Kak-voyna-prevratila-polituznik a-v-komandira-batalona-Azov--17031.html (accessed 13 April 2019).

Biletsky, A. (2007), 'Ukraïns′kij rasovij socìal-nacìonalìzm' ['Ukrainian Racial Social-Nationalism'], *Patriot Ukrayiny*. Retrieved on 3 April 2019 from https://web.archive. org/web/20080409023834/http:/www.patriotukr.org.ua/index.php?rub=stat&id=267

Biletsky, A. (24 August 2016), 'Mi v borot′bì stali spravžn′oû Nacìêû – nastav čas navesti porâdok ta stvoriti spravžnû Deržavu' ['In the Fight We Became a Real Nation – Time Has Come to Put Things in Order and Create a Real State'], *Ukrayinska Pravda*. Retrieved on 27 March 2019 from: https://blogs.pravda.com.ua/authors/bileckyj/57bda c213349d/

Biletsky, A. (4 October 2016), 'Zaâva Andrìâ Bìlec′kogo z privodu ostannìh dìj RF' ['Statement of Andriy Biletsky Concerning the Latest Actions of the Russian Federation']. Retrieved on 27 March 2019 from https://blogs.pravda.com.ua/authors/bileckyj/57f3775e209c6/

Biletsky, A. (14 January 2017). 'Zaâva Andrìâ Bìlec′kogo z privodu Nacìonal′noï gvardìï' ['Statement of Andriy Biletsky Concerning National Guard']. Retrieved on 27 March 2017 from: https://blogs.pravda.com.ua/authors/bileckyj/587a3805370f5/

Biletsky, A. (22 February 2017), 'Ul′timatum vladì' ['Ultimatum to Power']. *Ukrayinska Pravda*. Retrieved on 27 March 2019 from: https://blogs.pravda.com.ua/authors/bile ckyj/58ad8182b1970/

Biletsky, A. (13 March 2017), 'Čomu mi boremosâ z rosìjs′kimi bankami' ['Why We Fight Against Russian Banks'], *Ukrayinska Pravda*. Retrieved on 27 March 2019 from: https ://blogs.pravda.com.ua/authors/bileckyj/58c6b861f0e18/

Biletsky, A. (14 March 2017), 'Do Dnâ ukraïns′kogo dobrovol′câ' [On the Occasion of the Day of Ukrainian Volunteers', *Ukrayinska Pravda*. Retrieved on 27 March 2019 from: https://blogs.pravda.com.ua/authors/bileckyj/58c83e09b4eba/

Biletsky, A. (16 March 2017), 'Po Nasirovu' ['On Nasirov']. Retrieved on 27 March 2019 from: https://blogs.pravda.com.ua/authors/bileckyj/58cafd7be1d8e/

Biletsky, A. (5 May 2017), 'Do tret′oï rìčnicì zasnuvannâ polku "Azov"' ['On the Occasion of the Third Anniversary of Regiment "Azov"'], *Ukrayinska Pravda*. Retrieved on 27 March 2019 from: https://blogs.pravda.com.ua/authors/bileckyj/590c6167be0a6/

Biletsky, A. (29 June 2017), 'Ŝodo zaâv prezidenta pro nedotorkannìst'' ['On President's Statements about Immunity'], *Ukrayinska Pravda*. Retrieved on 27 March 2019 from: https://blogs.pravda.com.ua/authors/bileckyj/59549ed58d7c9/

Biletsky, A. (27 July 2017), 'Pro ġromadânstvo' ['About Citizenship']. *Ukrayinska Pravda*. Retrieved on 27 March 2019 from: https://blogs.pravda.com.ua/authors/bileckyj/5979b7e02ad0f/

Biletsky, A. (24 August 2017), 'Do Dnia nezalezhnosti Ukrayiny' ['On the Occasion of Ukraine's Independence Day'], *Ukrayinska Pravda*. Retrieved on 27 March 2019 from: https://blogs.pravda.com.ua/authors/bileckyj/58c83e09b4eba/

Biletsky, A. (11 October 2017), 'Čes′kij lâpas Porošenku či vse domovleno?' ['Czech Slap in the Face of Poroshenko or Everything Is Settled?'] *Ukrayinska Pravda*. Retrieved on 27 March 2019 from: https://blogs.pravda.com.ua/authors/bileckyj/59de5a548ad39/

Biletsky, A. (13 June 2018), 'Mariupol', *Ukrayinska Pravda*. Retrieved on 27 March 2019 from: https://blogs.pravda.com.ua/authors/bileckyj/5b20eee127d57/

Biletsky, A. (26 February 2019), 'Čas rubati ruki' ['Time to Chop Off Hands']. Retrieved on 27 March 2019 from: https://blogs.pravda.com.ua/authors/bileckyj/5c751d08a30fb/

Cameron, D. and I. Panovic. (2014), 'Discourse and Discourse Analysis', in Debora Cameron and Ivan Panovic (eds). *Working with Written Discourse*, 3–14. London: Sage Publications.

Colborne, M. (2019), 'Ukraine's Far Right Is Growing Increasingly Violent –Why Aren't Local Jews Concerned?' *Haaretz.com*, 4 February 2019. https://www.haaretz.com/world-news/europe/.premium-ukraine-s-far-right-is-increasingly-violent-why-aren-t-local-jews-concerned-1.6852878 (accessed 14 April 2019).

Foucault, M. (1972), *The Archaeology of Knowledge and the Discourse on Language*. New York: Pantheon.

Kasianov, H. (2004), 'Ideolohia OUN: istoryko-retrospektyvnyi analiz' ['OUN Ideology: A Historical-Retrospective Analysis'], *Ukrayinskyi istorychyi zhurnal*, 1: 29–42.

'Kruty, battle of'. (n/a), *Internet Encyclopedia of Ukraine*. http://www.encyclopediaofukraine.com/display.asp?linkPath=pages\K\R\KrutyBattleof.htm (accessed 5 April 2019).

Lemke, J. (1995), *Textual Politics: Discourse and Social Dynamics*. London: Taylor & Francis.

Likhachev, V. (May 2018), 'Far-Right Extremism as a Threat to Ukrainian Democracy'. *Nations in Transit Brief*. Freedom House.

'Nacìonal′nì družini' ['National Militia']. (n/a), https://ndrugua.org/

'Nacìonal′nij korpus'. (n/a), https://nationalcorps.org/

'Nacìonal′nij korpus zamuruvav "Sberbank Rossii" ['National Corps Bricked Up "Sberbank Rossii"'], *Hromadske telebachennia*, 13 March 2017. https://www.youtube.com/watch?reload=9&v=MI9vLCMl-pc (accessed 3 April 2019).

'Nacìonal′nij Korpus za zdorovu i šaslivu ukrainsku naciù' ['National Corps Is for a Healthy and Happy Ukrainian Nation']. *National Corps*, 15 June 2018. https://nationalcorps.org/blog/naconalnij-korpus-za-zdorovu-shhaslivu-ukransku-nacju (accessed 9 April 2019).

'Nackorpus zìrvav trenìng pro LGBT-spìl′notu u Poltavì' ['National Corps Disrupted a Training About LGBT Community in Poltava'], *Hromadske Radio*, 31 March 2018. https://hromadske.radio/news/2018/03/31/nackorpus-zirvav-trening-pro-lgbt-spilnotu-u-poltavi-foto-video (accessed 11 April 2019).

'Narodny Front sformiroval voyenny sovet' ['People's Front Has Formed Military Council'], *Focus.ua*, 10 September 2014. https://focus.ua/politics/315018/ (accessed 7 April 2019).

Orwell, G. (1946), *Politics and the English Language*. Downloaded on 24 April 2019 from http://post.queensu.ca/~leuprech/docs/writing_guide/writingOrwell.pdf

Pietsukh, M. (2016), 'Andrìj Bìlec'kij: Avakov – lûdina sistemi, a cû sistemu â vvažaû vkraj negativnoû' ['Andriy Biletsky: Avakov Is a Man of the System, and I Consider This System Extremely Negative'], *Ukrayinska pravda*, 18 October 2016. http://pda.prav da.com.ua/articles/id_7123983/ (accessed 7 April 2019).

Pietsukh, M. (2017), 'Vìjna ì mir mìž ukraïns'kimi nacìonalìstami' ['War and Peace between Ukrainian Nationalists'], *Ukrayinska Pravda*, 27 March 2017. https://www.pra vda.com.ua/articles/2017/03/27/7139384/ (accessed 5 April 2019).

'Poziciya Nacionalnoho Korpusu stosovno transhendernoho marshy' ['Position of National Corps Regarding the Transgender March'], *National Corps*, 16 November 2019. https://nationalcorps.org/blog/pozicja-naconalnogo-korpusu-stosovno-transge ndernogo-marshu (accessed 20 April 2019).

'Proġrama polityčnoï partiï 'Nacionalnij korpus' ['Program of the Political Party "National Corps"'] (n/a). https://nationalcorps.org/section/program

Pylypchuk, R. (2018), 'Andriy Biletsky: "Našì hlopcì – ukraïnofìli, a ne ksenofobì' ['Andiy Biletsky: "Our Guys Are Ukrainophiles, Not Xenophobes"']. *Konkurent.in.ua*, 7 August 2018. https://konkurent.in.ua/publication/29175/andrij-bileckij-nashi-hlopci-ukra yinofili-a-ne-ksenofobi/ (accessed 5 April 2019).

Shramovych, V. (2018), 'Nacìonal'nì družini: hto ì navìšo ïh stvoriv' ['National Militia: Who and Why Created Them'], *BBC*, 30 January 2018. https://www.bbc.com/ukrai nian/features-42859649 (accessed 5 April 2019).

Stavrakakis, Y., Katsambekis, G., Nikisianis, N., Kioupkiolis, A. and T. Siomos. (2017), 'Extreme Right-Wing Populism in Europe: Revisiting a Reified Association'. *Critical Discourse Studies*, 14 (4): 420–39.

'Tak zvanì nacìonal'nì družinniki, v nedìlû u Kiêvì, sklali prisâgu' ['The So-Called National Militia Members Were Sworn In']. *Spetskor/Novyny 2+2*, 30 January 2018. https://www.youtube.com/watch?v=PClGIhlElKI (accessed 6 April 2019).

'V gostâh u Dmitrija Gordona. Andrei Biletsky'. *V gostâh u Gordona*. https://www.you tube.com/watch?v=paQBjBdAmbY (accessed 5 May 2015).

'V Odesi rozpochavsia marsh ukrayinskoho poriadku' ['March of Ukrainian Order Started in Odessa']. *National Corps*, 2 May 2019. https://nationalcorps.org/blog/v-odes-ro zpochavsja-marsh-ukranskogo-porjadku (accessed 2 May 2019).

Van Dijk, T. A. (2015), 'Critical Discourse Analysis', in Deborah Tannen, Heidi E. Hamilton and Deborah Schiffrin (eds), *The Handbook of Discourse Analysis*, Vol. I, 466–85. Malden, MA and Chichester, West Sussex: Willey Blackwell.

'"Vduj Svinarčukam razom z nami": Aktsiya 9 kvitnia v Kyevi vid Natsionalnoho Korpusu' ['"Ram It Up to Svynarchuks Together With Us": A Public Protest in Kyiv on 9 April by the National Corps'], 8 April 2919. *Natsionalny Korpus*. https://nationalcorps.org/blog /34vduj-svinarchukam34-razom-z-nami-akcja-9-kvtnja-v-kiv-vd-naconalnogo-kor pusu (accessed 20 April 2019).

Wilson, J. (2015), 'Political Discourse', in Deborah Tannen, Heidi E. Hamilton and Deborah Schiffrin (eds). *The Handbook of Discourse Analysis*, Vol. II, 775–94. Malden, MA and Chichester, West Sussex: Willey Blackwell.

Wodak, R. (2011), *The Discourse of Politics in Action*. Basingstoke: Palgrave Macmillan.

'You Don't Exist'. Arbitrary Detentions, Enforced Disappearances, and Torture in Eastern Ukraine'. (2016), *Human Rights Watch*. https://www.hrw.org/report/2016/07/21/ you-dont-exist/arbitrary-detentions-enforced-disappearances-and-torture-eastern (accessed 8 April 2019).

Żuk, P. and Żuk, P. (2018), 'Multimodal Analysis of the Nationalist Discourse and Historical Inspirations of the Spectacle of the Populist Right in Poland Between 2015 and 2017'. *Discourse, Context & Media*, 26, 135–43.

11

The art of the insult

(Re)creating Zaporizhian Cossacks' letter-writing on YouTube as collective creative insurgency

Alla Tovares

1 Introduction

In 2014, Russia's annexation of Crimea, a Ukrainian territory, escalated the growing tensions between the two countries and prompted the upsurge in crisis communication, including (online) conflict discourse in which adversarial messages are used as political weapons (Knoblock 2016). To elucidate the complexity of conflict discourse, I analyse a YouTube video in which Ukrainian soldiers (re)create a well-known painting that depicts Zaporizhian[1] Cossacks writing an insulting reply to the Turkish sultan. The YouTube version, however, is adapted to show Putin and his allies as the addressees, and a derogatory anti-Putin song-chant serves as a *post scriptum*. The question that this chapter aims to answer is how in the context of a Russian-Ukrainian geopolitical conflict, Ukrainian soldiers use repetition across different modalities, or resemiotization (Iedema 2003), to engage in creative insurgency, a combination of activism and artistry (Kraidy 2016).

In my analysis, I draw on prior work on conflict talk and impoliteness (e.g. Culpeper 2011; Grimshaw 1990; Tannen 2002; Tracy 2008, 2010) and frames theory, especially how it has been developed and applied in sociolinguistics (e.g. Gordon 2002, 2009; Tannen 2006; Trester 2012). I also mobilize the notion of intertextuality and its related concepts of dialogicality (Bakhtin 1981, 1986) and prior text (Becker 1995), and build on the extant work that considers the relationship between language and other semiotic resources (e.g. Iedema 2003; Kress 2009; Kress and van Leeuwen 2001). The analysis shows how by drawing on multimodal resources, the soldiers situate their (re) enactment in multiple embedded and overlapping frames that simultaneously refer to past and present, to play and real life, and in so doing, create what elsewhere (Tovares 2005) I call intertextuality in action, or when 'texts' become actions. Specifically, by deploying multimodal repetition and using stylization, lexical choices and a deliberate use of Ukrainian or Russian–heteroglossia with awareness (Bakhtin 1981), Ukrainian soldiers collaboratively perform an insult, or situationally appropriate reasonable hostility (Tracy 2008, 2010), against Russian President Putin and Russia's aggressive policies towards Ukraine. Thus, this work adds to our understanding of the relationship between discourse and action by demonstrating how social actors mobilize multimodal resources to engage in creative insurgency.

In what follows, I begin by offering a brief sociohistorical background of the current conflict between Ukraine and Russia followed by a discussion of the mythology of Zaporizhian Cossacks in relation to Ukraine's national consciousness and identity. I then review the theoretical underpinnings of this work and introduce the data and methodology. The analysis shows how in a video posted on YouTube Ukrainian soldiers deploy multimodal repetition to laminate frames that allow them to manoeuvre between frontstage and backstage, past and present, and in so doing not only creatively challenge Putin's aggressive policies towards Ukraine but also promote solidarity among those who share anti-Putin and pro-Ukrainian sentiments. The concluding remarks discuss the main contributions of this study, point out its limitations and offer directions for future research.

2 Sociohistorical background

2.1 Russia and Ukraine: From 'brotherly' states to adversaries

After the collapse of the Soviet Union in 1991, Russia and Ukraine – two successor states with shared cultural, ethnic and linguistic backgrounds – embarked on divergent trajectories, with Ukraine moving closer to the West and Russia trying to maintain its influence over the former Socialist Republics, including Ukraine. In 2014, Russia aggravated the tensions between the two countries by annexing Crimea, an aggressive move further compounded by Russia's covert support of the separatist forces in the ongoing armed conflict in Eastern Ukraine. All this has escalated conflict discourse between the former 'brotherly' states in which not only the present-day but also past actions and events are revisited and re-evaluated. Specifically, Russia nostalgically venerates Soviet symbols and rituals (Ryazanova-Clarke 2016). In contrast, Ukraine – in search of its cultural roots and new national identity – institutes 'decommunization' laws[2] to eliminate any reminders of Soviet rule and mythologizes pre-Soviet times. The Russian-Ukrainian geopolitical conflict has heightened the national awareness among many Ukrainians, promoting symbolic expressions of national pride such as wearing traditional Ukrainian embroidered shirts, *vyšyvanky*. However, no other symbol is more inextricably linked to Ukrainian national consciousness than that of the independent, egalitarian and democratic brotherhood of the Zaporizhian Cossacks[3] (Sysyn 1991).

2.2 The Cossack mythology

The military fraternity of Zaporizhian Cossacks lived beyond the rapids of the Dnieper River (now Eastern Ukraine) from the twelfth till the late eighteenth century. The fifteenth century witnessed the rapid expansion of the Cossack settlement, known as Zaporizhian Sich, which harboured many runaway serfs fleeing the Polish-Lithuanian

Commonwealth and later the Russian Empire (Subtelny 2005: 108). In addition to runaway serfs, Zaporizhian Sich also included 'defrocked priests, and impecunious or adventure-seeking noblemen', and '[a]lthough Poles, Belorussians, Moldavians, and even Tatars joined the ranks of the Cossacks, the overwhelming majority of those who lived in the Dnieper basin were Ukrainians' (Subtelny 2005: 108–9). Squeezed between the oppressive conditions of serfdom and the lack of national loyalty among the Ukrainian nobility who adopted Polish culture, Ukrainians looked up to the Cossacks to provide leadership (Subtelny 2005: 105). Thus, since early times, Zaporizhian Cossacks were associated not only with bravery and defiance but also with Ukrainian national consciousness.

The Zaporizhian Sich was a well-organized political entity with a parliamentary system of government whose strong political and military force presented a challenge to the oligarchy of the Polish-Lithuanian Commonwealth and the autocratic Russian Empire (Sysyn 1991: 849). Additionally, with the Ottoman Empire to the south, Sich was a battleground and a buffer zone between the diverse political and religious interests, and the Cossacks – free and independent – fought with and against various political entities, commanding respect and instilling fear. Therefore, it is not surprising that the Cossacks were glorified and their myth outlasted not only its heroes but also the changing regimes, and was often co-opted for varying sociopolitical goals. For instance, in the nineteenth century, the Cossack mythology was used by Ukrainian intellectuals to promote Ukrainian national liberation; it became a symbol of Soviet patriotism during WWII, a dangerous manifestation of Ukrainian nationalism during various periods in Soviet history, and an inspiration for Ukrainian nation-building and identity construction after the collapse of the former Soviet Union (Plokhy 2012; Sysyn 1991). Thus, the Cossack myth has been circulating in Ukraine and its neighbouring countries for some time. Two of the most enduring and recognizable cultural artefacts of the myth are the 'Reply of Zaporizhian Cossacks to the Turkish sultan' (hereafter 'The Reply') and Repin's painting depicting the act of writing 'The Reply'.

2.2.1 'The Reply' and Repin's painting as embodiments of the Cossack mythology

'The Reply' can be described as an apocryphal story (Friedman 1978), as Kostomarov (1872: 451) puts it, '[i]t is difficult to decide whether such a reply was in fact given or if it is fiction' (my translation). Because there exist several variants of the document (with different dates and signatures), it is safe to assume that the reply is fiction, but 'old, Zaporizhian' fiction (Kostomarov 1872: 451). The story behind 'The Reply' is that sometime between 1676 and 1680, after the Cossacks defeated the Ottoman forces in a battle, the Turkish sultan sent a letter demanding the Cossacks submit to Turkish rule. Instead, the Cossacks wrote 'The Reply' (Text 1), a defiant letter laced with insults and profanities. Reportedly, when Ilya Repin (1844–1930), a well-known painter who was born in Ukraine but lived in Russia, learned about the story, he exclaimed, 'A holy people! No one in the world held so deeply freedom, equality, and fraternity', and decided to paint the scene of the Cossacks writing 'The Reply'. The painting, of which there are two copies[4] and numerous sketches (not unlike several versions of

Figure 11.1 Ilya Repin. 'Zaporožcy/Zaporozhians' also known as 'Reply of the Zaporizhian Cossacks to Sultan Mehmed IV of the Ottoman Empire' (1880–1891) The State Russian Museum, St. Petersburg, Russia.

'The Reply' itself), took over a decade to complete (1880–1891), and it depicts the Cossacks gleefully enjoying the pleasure of coming up with various insults directed at the Turkish sultan (Figure 11.1). Both 'The Reply' and Repin's depiction have become inextricable parts of Ukrainian culture, including popular culture. While during Soviet times the Cossack mythology was viewed as old history, in contemporary Ukraine, it serves as 'an instrument for building a modern Ukrainian political culture on the basis of native traditions' (Sysyn 1991: 861).

3 Theoretical background

3.1 Pre-battle taunts and insults, reasonable hostility and creative insurgency

'Taunt him with the license of ink: if thou thou'st him some thrice, it shall not be amiss' (Shakespeare, *Twelfth Night*).[5] This is how the Shakespearian character Sir Toby instructs Sir Andrew to write a letter challenging a rival to a duel. Of interest, and relevant to this analysis, calling someone – and repeatedly – by the informal *you* ('thou') is metadiscursively identified as one of the strategies used to insult. Bax's (2010: 68) research corroborates that the informal 'thou' was often mobilized as an insult in Europe in 1600s. Additionally, the above example from Shakespeare (circa 1601) anecdotally indicates that pre-battle taunts and insults have a long history of provocation and impoliteness (see Culpeper and Kádár 2010 for a discussion of historical impoliteness).

Adversarial or confrontational exchanges have been of interest to a number of linguists and communication scholars who explore such behaviours through the lenses of (im)politeness (e.g. Bousfield and Locher 2008; Culpeper 2011), conflict talk (e.g. Grimshaw 1990), agonistic discourse (Tannen 2002) or ritual insults (Labov 1972). In many of the aforementioned studies, confrontational or impolite interactions are presented as breaking the rules of conduct (cf. Labov 1972), thus indicating that polite and amicable interactions are viewed as the norm. In contrast, Tracy (2008, 2010) argues that in a number of contexts, conflict talk is not a deviation from a norm but rather *is* the norm. In her study of disagreements during school board meetings, Tracy (2008) introduced the notion of reasonable hostility to refer to the 'emotionally marked criticism of the past and future actions', especially of public officials (for a discussion of reasonable hostility online, see Al Zidjaly 2012). In this analysis, I build on Tracy's (2008, 2010) argument by suggesting that in the context of a geopolitical conflict, the mutually adversarial communication between Russia and Ukraine is expected, with Ukrainians framing their contributions as responses to the aggressive politics and actions of Russia. While Tracy (2008, 2010) focuses on peaceful contexts (e.g. courtrooms and public hearings), where parties in disagreement typically follow basic rules of civility, the level of hostility in the context of Russian-Ukrainian conflict 'matches the perceived wrong to which it responds' (Tracy 2010: 203). In other words, what is perceived as 'reasonable' in hostile exchanges is context-dependent.

Because Russian-Ukrainian conflict is marked by power imbalances (Ukraine as the less powerful country whose territory [Crimea] was annexed by the more powerful Russia), I also draw on the notion of creative insurgency that Kraidy (2016) developed in the context of the Arab Spring. The focus on the subversion of power through creative acts of provocation allows the notion of creative insurgency to capture the expressions of dissent and political resistance in diverse geographic contexts, including Ukraine. As I suggest elsewhere (Tovares 2019), in the context of Russian-Ukrainian conflict, anti-Putin online trolling can be understood as creative insurgency by the supporters of Ukraine. Related, Knoblock's (2016) research shows how, in the context of the Ukrainian crisis, creativity (especially sarcasm and irony) is used as a political weapon on social media. It is worth noting that acts of resistance and provocation, such as online political trolling, not only serve to delegitimize the trolling target but also create alliances and collective identities (Tovares 2019). Similarly, the recreation of 'The Reply' by the contemporary Ukrainian soldiers can be understood as collective creative insurgency that simultaneously provokes and delegitimizes the adversary, and unites and reassures the supporters. In their collective creative insurgency, the soldiers mobilize an array of multimodal resources to recreate prior 'texts'.

3.2 Intertextual and multimodal repetition of prior 'texts': From entextualization to resemiotization

A number of researchers (e.g. Fairclough 1992; Gasparov 2010; Gordon 2009; Tannen 2007, to name but a few) have investigated the relationship between fixity and novelty in discourse by focusing on *intertextuality* (Kristeva 1986) or the related notions of *dialogicality* (Bakhtin 1981, 1986) and *prior text* (Becker 1995). Collectively, the extant studies highlight the intricate texture of human interaction where, as Becker (1995: 185) suggests, the old bits of language are taken from memory and reshaped into new contexts. Such reshaping can be understood through the lens of repetition. Tannen (2007) views repetition as a source of new meaning and interpersonal involvement and identifies play and humour as strategies of how involvement is achieved by repetition. Similarly, Norrick (1994: 15) suggests that repetition is a 'fertile ground for verbal joking' because of the duality of repetition – it is simultaneously similar to and different from the original. The researcher views repetition as a type of variation in which the second speaker changes the frame introduced by the first speaker. This echoes Bakhtin's (1986: 110) assertion that only the second speaker, the second voice, is truly creative as such a voice engages and incorporates other voices. Repetition, especially when it occurs across time and space, also involves the processes of entextualization, decontextualization and recontextualization (Bauman and Briggs 1990). Entextualization makes a segment of discourse extractable; decontextualization divorces it from its 'original' context; and recontextualization situates it in a new context (see Trester 2012 for a discussion).

Furthermore, what is often referred to as intertextual repetition is not restricted to language and includes other semiotic resources. As Bakhtin (1986: 103) indicates, *text* can refer to 'any coherent complex of signs – then even the study of art (the study of music, the theory and history of fine arts) deals with texts (works of art)'. A number of researchers (e.g. Jewitt, Bezemer and O'Halloran 2016; Kress 2009; Kress and van Leeuwen 2001; Norris 2004) who study meaning-making within the framework of multimodal analysis emphasize the dynamic relationship between various 'textual' modes, without privileging language. Put differently, by blurring the traditional boundaries between various semiotic modes, these researchers aim to capture the complexity and materiality of practices, actions and representations. To gain a better understanding how socially recognizable artefacts are constructed, Iedema (2003: 41) adds a sociohistorical dimension to multimodality and introduces the notion of resemiotization, which centres on how 'meaning making shifts from context to context, from practice to practice, or from one stage of a practice to the next'. In this chapter, building on the aforementioned body of work, repetition is conceived broadly to include recycling of any semiotic unit (from phonetic to narrative) and in any semiotic mode (from linguistic to visual).

3.3 Framing

Like repetition, framing is also concerned with meaning-making. Goffman (1974) developed the notion of a frame, broadly understood as a definition of a situation, to better understand how people make sense of everyday activities. Goffman (1981) also observed that people could simultaneously engage in various activities and thus that frames can be nested within other frames. Put differently, frames can be layered or laminated. For example, Gordon (2002, 2008, 2009), in her exploration of the intersection of intertextual repetition and framing in family discourse, demonstrates how frames can be embedded (constructed as more specific) or overlapping (simultaneously indexing present and past contexts).

Among the main framing mechanisms, Goffman (1981) identifies footing and keying. While footing refers to the 'alignment we take up to ourselves and the others present as expressed in the way we manage the production or reception of an utterance' (Goffman 1981: 128), keying indicates a transformation of an already meaningful activity into another or, using Tannen's (2006: 601) articulation, keying establishes 'the tone or tenor of an interaction'. Exploring framing in interaction, Tannen and Wallat (1993: 59–60) introduce the term 'interactive frame' to denote 'a definition of what is going on in interaction, without which no utterance (or movement or gesture) could be interpreted'. These researchers, in addition to demonstrating that in interactions people may attend to numerous shifting frames, also put forth the notion of *knowledge schema* to indicate structures of expectations, or 'participants' expectations about people, objects, events and settings in the world' (Tannen and Wallat 1993: 59–60). Mismatched knowledge schemas can lead to reframing, or change of an interactive frame. Tannen and Wallat (1993) view schemas, as well as frames, as dynamic. It is this dynamism that allows capturing the complex relationship between familiar and novel in meaning-making.

4 Data and methodology

The data for this study include a YouTube video titled *Letter to the Tzar[sic] / List do Carâ / Pis'mo k Carû* in which Ukrainian soldiers (re)create Repin's painting of Zaporizhian Cossacks' writing an insulting reply to the Turkish sultan. It was uploaded on 29 August 2014 with the caption 'Modern reflection acted out by the soldiers of 95th airmobile brigade of a famous painting of Ilya Repin'. As noted earlier, in this 'modern reflection', the sultan and his army are replaced with Russian President Putin and his allies. The video is professionally produced by Babylon'13, defined by the Institute of Documentary Film (IDF) as 'a documentary filmmakers collective' established in 2013 ;to highlight the struggle for democracy and human rights in Ukraine during the Maidan protests, and oppose the Russian propaganda during annexation of Crimea and the war in Donbas region'. Babylon'13 has a YouTube channel and a wide social media presence (Facebook, Twitter and Instagram), all serving as co-referencing mechanisms to amplify the collective's presence online and to reach a broader audience. In fact, the goal of these cinematographers is to share their art, and its message, as widely as possible. The organization's Facebook page states: 'Ukrainian cinematographic community couldn't step aside from events, that are happening in Ukraine. We will publish our films, make subtitles for them in English, so that not only Ukrainians but the world community could observe and judge what is happening all around the country'. In sum, the Babylon'13 cinematographers are pro-Ukrainian activists who use their art as creative insurgency (Kraidy 2016) against Russian aggression.

It is worth noting that there is a plethora of online videos of 'The Reply' with Putin as the addressee, including a more recent (October 2018) and very popular

Lyst moskovs'komu šajtanu/Letter to the Moscow devil, produced and distributed by the Ukrainian radio station *Krajina FM*. The video under analysis was chosen for a number of reasons: (a) at the time of the analysis (June 2018), it was the most popular recreation of 'The Reply' on YouTube: it had 260,932 views, 3,300 likes and 142 dislikes; (b) while many recreations – including the aforementioned *Letter to the Moscow devil* – feature famous actors and musicians, as well as other celebrities, and offer a more faithful and seemingly rehearsed repetition of the 'original' (both visual and textual), in Babylon'13's version the soldiers appear to engage in a spontaneous collective creation of their own contemporary take on 'The Reply'; finally, and more importantly, (c) in the age of notoriously short news cycles, I would like to remind the reader about the protracted armed conflict in Eastern Ukraine in which regular people, including Ukrainian soldiers, are at the frontline and 'frontstage'.

Following prior studies (Bauman and Briggs 1990; Trester 2012), I take up a process approach to the study of multimodal repetition. Specifically, I trace how 'The Reply', as well as other resources used in the video, became entextualized, decontextualized and recontextualized in various semiotic modalities and in different contexts. To gain a better understanding of the complexity of meaning-making in interaction, framing is used as both a theoretical underpinning and an analytical tool. Finally, in the analysis, the 'original' text of 'The Reply' (Text 1) and a reproduction of Repin's painting (Figure 11.1) are used for comparison.

5 Analysis

As noted earlier, Babylon'13's (re)creation of 'The Reply' by the Ukrainian soldiers is one of the countless recontextualizations. Although it is impossible to determine when the text of 'The Reply' was first entextualized, its several decontextualized versions have been circulating since the nineteenth century, and – after Repin 'entextualized' the images of the Cossacks – the reproductions of his work, often together with the text of 'The Reply', have joined the recontextualization circuit. While in the video under analysis the textual and visual modalities are simultaneous and interconnected, for the ease of exposition and taking into consideration the linear nature of written academic discourse, I present the analysis of the visual and textual elements sequentially, first focusing on the visual followed by the analysis of the textual elements, and bringing the two together in the last section on framing.

5.1 Visual repetition as embodiment and intertextuality in action

The video opens by showing the behind-the-scene preparations for the re-enactment of 'The Reply' and Repin's painting. First, several tables are set up on the territory of a military base (with heavy weaponry in the background). Then a group of soldiers in summer uniforms appear (most carry heavy machine guns) and continue setting the scene: one bandages a fellow soldier's head, while two others observe and comment; two soldiers bring two boxes of ammunition and place them on the tables; two more soldiers (with naked torsos) practice holding guns in various ways; another soldier puts on a Cossack-styled red coat and a hat while the rest of the group put on hats. The set-up completed, the (re)creation starts.

By staging the scene in front of the audience and transforming their appearances to resemble those depicted in the painting, the soldiers deliberately blend frontstage and backstage regions (Goffman 1959), and in so doing not only invite the audience to be a part of the action but also create a leaky frame. Tannen and Wallat (1993) introduced the notion of a leaky frame to show how a paediatrician, while simultaneously juggling several frames (examining the child, consulting with the mother, teaching medical students, etc.), occasionally let the register used in one frame 'leak' into the other. Whereas Tannen and Wallat (1993) view 'leaky' frames as an unintentional slippage, I – similar to Gordon (2008, 2009) who refers to such frames as blended – suggest that leaky, or blended, frames can be intentional. Specifically, unlike actors, who appear in front of the audience already in character and retreat to the backstage after the performance, the soldiers – and the filmmaker – do not allow the audience to forget who they are and where they are. In this way, they intentionally blend frames of play and real life, a discussion to which I will return later.

A side-by-side comparison of the 'original' painting (Figure 11.1) and a still from the YouTube video (Figure 11.2) reveals similarities in the overall composition, including the position of people and the objects in space (e.g. in both the armed men are sitting or standing around the table), the characters and their roles (e.g. a scribe), the clothes and naked torsos, the bandaged and shaved heads, and the mischievously smiling or laughing faces. The aforementioned similarities (visual repetition) help to create conceptual linkages between the Cossacks and the soldiers, their appearances, beliefs and actions. The soldiers in the video use the material objects (a piece of paper, guns, a table, clothes, etc.) and their bodies as meditational means or cultural tools (Scollon 2001) to (re)create the painting. Furthermore, as Kraidy (2016) argues, the human

Figure 11.2 YouTube video 'Letter to the Tzar[*sic*] / List do Carâ / Pis'mo k Carû', Babylon'13.

body is the nexus of resistance and subversion of power. In the same subversive spirit, Ukrainian soldiers use their bodies to literally embody the painting and to reactivate the knowledge schema of bravery and defiance associated with the Cossacks ,and in so doing frame their own actions as collective creative insurgency.

In her work on multimodal interactional analysis, Norris (2011: 273) refers to material objects, including paintings, as frozen actions of those who created them. In this work, I suggest that by recreating – embodying – the painting, the soldiers reactivated, or 'thawed out', the frozen actions not only of the painter but also those of the sitters and, by doing so, actively engaged in what elsewhere (Tovares 2005) I identify as intertextuality in action, or when 'texts' become actions. The soldiers' embodiment of a recognizable cultural artefact can also be understood as layered resemiotization: 'The Reply' becomes Repin's painting; the painting is embodied in the actions of the soldiers, and that embodiment becomes the video that circulates on YouTube. In the video, not only is the painting (re)created but also the text that inspired the painting, thus producing a complex semiotic aggregate with fluidity between the different modes. In the next section, I analyse, often in comparison with those of the 'original' text of 'The Reply', the linguistic and paralinguistic strategies deployed by the soldiers.

5.2 Recontextualization and resemiotization of 'The Reply' as collective creative insurgency

While on the surface the two letters may appear quite different, the Ukrainian soldiers' 'letter' (Text 2) can be viewed as a recontextualization, or shaping an old and widely circulated text of 'The Reply' (Text 1) into a new context. The letter is also a type of resemiotization as the recontextualized text in the video is produced in an oral mode (we do not even know if the scribe actually wrote anything down) while the text of 'The Reply' has been circulating in a number of written versions.

Text 1: 'The Reply' or the 'original' letter. In Kostomarov (1872: 451) translated in Friedman (1978: 27–28); the lines are numbered for ease of reference]

(1) You Turkish Satan, brother and comrade of the damned devil and
(2) secretary to Lucifer himself! What the hell kind of knight are you?
(3) The devil s[hit]s and you and your army swallow [it].
(4) You aren't fit to have the sons of Christians under you;
(5) we aren't afraid of your army, and we'll fight you on land and sea.
(6) You Babylonian busboy, Macedonian mechanic, Jerusalem beerbrewer,
(7) Alexandrian goatskinner, swineherd of Upper and Lower Egypt, Armenian pig,
(8) Tatar goat, Kamenets hangman, Podolian thief, grandson of the Evil Serpent
(9) himself, and buffoon of all the world and the netherworld, fool of our God,
(10) swine's snout, mare's asshole, butcher's dog, unbaptized brow, may the devil
(11) steam your ass!
(12) That's how the cossacks answer you, you nasty glob of spit!
(13) You're unfit to rule true Christians. We don't know the date

(14) because we don't have a calendar, the moon [month] is in the sky,
(15) and the year is in a book, and the day is the same with us as with you,
(16) so go kiss our butt!

Chief Hetman Zakharchenko with all the Zaporizhian Host

Text 2: Transcript of 'Letter to the Tzar[sic] / List do Carâ / Pis′mo k Carû'

(1) Soldier 1: Якщо ти, падлюка, сюди прийдеш, ми тобі дамо копняка під зад
     If you, scumbag, come here, we'll kick your ass,
(2) Разом із Мішкою своїм,
     together with your 'Mishka' ((Russian Prime Minister Medvedev)),
(3) Жиріком паршивим
     lousy 'Zhirik', ((Russian ultranationalist politician Zhirinovsky))
(4) Soldier 2: Яника, Яника не забудь
     'Yanyk', do not forget about 'Yanyk' ((former – now exiled – Ukrainian President Yanukovych known for his pro-Russian stance in politics))
(5) Soldier 1: і всією твоєю армією. А Яника, собаку цю
     and all of your army. As for 'Yanyk', that dog-
(6) Soldier 3   Яника на палю!
                   impale 'Yanyk'!
(7) Soldier 1: Яника на палю або віддай нам, ми його на кол посадимо
     Impale 'Yanyk' or give him to us, and we'll impale him
(8) Solider 4: А опосля-
     And later-((mock old Slavonic))
(9) Soldier 1:   На ялинку посадимо.
                   on a Christmas tree.
(10) Soldier 2: На 'йолку'.
     On a Christmas tree ((Russian)). ((everyone laughs))
(11) Soldier 1 ((laughing)): На 'йолку'.
     On a Christmas tree. ((Russian)).
(12) Scribe: Ну и пост-скриптом шото давай. ((Russian nonstandard))
     Well give something as a post scriptum.
(13) Soldier 5: Ла-ла-ла-ла-ла-ла-ла-ла-ла
     La la-la-la-la-la-la-la-la ((a refrain from an insulting song about Putin)).
(14) Soldier 1: пост-скриптом ((all soldiers)) ла-ла-ла-ла-ла- ла-ла-ла-ла
     post scriptum: ((all soldiers)) la-la-la-la-la-la-la-la-la
(15) ((laughing, to Scribe)): Пиши, пиши.
     Keep writing, keep writing. ((Russian)).

A closer analysis reveals linkages and similarities between the 'original' text (Text 1) and its recontexualized and resemiotized version (Text 2). For instance, in both texts, the Cossacks (Text 1, line 5) and Ukrainian soldiers (Text 2, line 5) frame their messages as defiance by stating that they are ready to fight the aggressor's army. To insult and provoke, the Cossacks and the soldiers utilize not only abusive words but also what Bakhtin (1984), in the context of carnival, identifies as a string of abuse, or when abusive words/phrases are clustered together for emphasis. However, in the 'original' text a string of sixteen abusive phrases refers only to the sultan (Text 1, lines 6–10), while in the contemporary version, a shorter string of abuse (folksy nicknames used as personal references) is used to list Putin's allies: Mishka, Zhirik and Janyk (Text 2, lines 2–4). In so doing, the soldiers provoke not only Putin but also his associates. The nicknames of Putin's allies require further discussion. Mishka, used in reference to Russian Prime Minister Medvedev (Text 2, line 2), is also a popular, informal, folksy way Russian speakers reference a *bear* or *teddy bear*. The Russian word for *bear* is *medved'*, thus sharing the same root as the last name *Medvedev*. In fact, in countless online memes and other satirical representations, such as the Ukrainian political cartoon *Skazočnaja Rus'/Fairy-tale Rus'*, Medvedev is depicted as a bear. Prior research of Ukrainian traditional curses and oaths (Demjanova 2011; Vojcehivs'ka 2014) finds that using zoonyms, or animal metaphors to describe humans and/or their actions, is a typical feature of conflict talk. Moreover, by choosing Mishka over a *bear/medved'*, Ukrainian soldiers use familiarity as a strategy to humiliate and insult a high-ranking Russian official. In a similar way, as signals of defiance and disrespect, Zhirik (Zhirinovsky) and Janyk (Yanukovych), the informal 'street' nicknames typically reserved for old friends (Text 2, lines 3–6), are used to refer to a seasoned Russian politician with known anti-Ukrainian sentiments (Zhirinovsky) as well as to the ousted pro-Russian ex-President of Ukraine (Yanukovych). By using familiar referring terms and zoonyms, Ukrainian soldiers not only create an insult but also challenge power hierarchies. It is worth noting that in the soldiers' letter, Russian President Putin is not even mentioned by name; instead, he is referenced by an insulting referring term *padl'uka/scumbag* (Text 2, line 1). Nonetheless, the word 'tzar' [*sic*] in the title of the video immediately identifies Putin as the addressee because 'tsar' is a popular mock-aggrandizement term (a meme) used in Ukraine to refer to, and mock, the Russian President. All these abusive words 'repeat' the impolite and hostile style of 'The Reply', and in so doing also frame the recreation as an insult.

The analysis shows that both letters (Text 1 and Text 2) rely on similar strategies (summarized in Table 11.1) to create an insulting message. Namely, they mobilize (a)

Table 11.1 Examples of strategies used to cause insult

Insulting strategies	Old Cossacks' letter (Text 1)	Ukrainian soldiers' letter (Text 2)
Abusive referring terms	hangman, fool, thief	scumbag, Miška, lousy žyrik, Janyk
Zoonyms (animal metaphors)	swine, mare, dog, pig, evil serpent	Miška(medved'), dog
Body parts and violent acts	kiss our butt, steam your ass	we'll kick your ass, impale
Informal pronominal reference	exclusive use of the informal (T) form of the second person pronoun	exclusive use of the informal (T) form of the second person pronoun

abusive personal references, (b) zoonyms, (c) references to body parts and violent acts, and (d) repeated use of the informal (T) form of the second person pronoun (see Section 3.1).

Although there are similarities in linguistic strategies between the two letters (Table 11.1), the 'original' letter is more vulgar than its contemporary (re)creation. Perhaps this is because the excessive obscenities would not fit the decorum of the soldiers of the Ukrainian Army. This also points to the fact that the soldiers' letter is not a mere repetition of 'The Reply', but rather is a creative engagement with the prior text in which some elements are changed or discarded while others are preserved. For instance, by using the archaic 'A oposl'a' (and later) in line 8, Soldier 4 helps to stylize (Coupland 2007) the letter in the manner or the 'original', thus reinforcing linkages between the soldiers and the Cossacks, and between present and past events.

It is important to address not only the style and lexical choices but also the choice of language in the video. Because of various political, socio-cultural, and historical reasons (too numerous and complicated to address in this study, but see Bilaniuk 2005, 2017; Pavlenko 2013), Russian-Ukrainian bilingualism is widespread in Ukraine. The events of the 2013 (Maidan) revolution, Russia's annexation of Crimea and the armed conflict in Eastern Ukraine further complicated, and problematized, the language situation in Ukraine. Specifically, while Ukrainian remains the official language of the country, because people of diverse linguistic backgrounds support Ukraine's pro-European course and oppose Russian aggression, one's national identity is not directly linked to one's linguistic practices (Kulyk 2016; Bilaniuk 2017). Therefore, it is not surprising, or unusual, that the Ukrainian soldiers in the video used both Ukrainian and Russian. However, it is their manoeuvring between the language varieties that requires further exploration. While Russian was predominantly used during the set-up, when the act of the letter-writing started, there was an immediate switch to the Ukrainian language (Text 2, line 1). This deliberate use of Ukrainian – Bakhtin's (1981) 'heteroglossia with awareness' (see also Coupland and Jaworski 2004: 27) – not only provides a closer intertextual link to the 'original' letter, which was in Ukrainian, but also reinforces the collective creative insurgency by the Ukrainian soldiers who use Ukrainian as a symbolic tool to simultaneously oppose Putin and his supporters and to align with one another and a larger pro-Ukrainian audience.

In their (re)creation, the soldiers weave together old and new resources. For instance, another deliberate switch, now to Russian (Text 2, lines 10 and 11) intertextually refers to, and recontextualizes, the 2011 instance when in his speech delivered in Ukrainian, the now ousted Ukrainian President Yanukovych, a Russian speaker, seemingly forgot the Ukrainian word *jalynka/Christmas tree* and after a long pause substituted it with the Russian word *jolka*. This incident became part of Ukrainian popular culture, and is widely used in online *jolka* (in Ukrainian transliteration of the Russian word) memes. During the events of the 2013 (Maidan) revolution, *jolka* acquired a more serious, even grave, key when over 1,000 anti-government protesters were violently dispersed by the special police who used the pretext that the area occupied by the protesters was reserved and thus needed for holiday festivities, including setting up a Christmas tree. After the Maidan events, the newer versions of *jolka* memes refer to punishing Yanukovych (Janyk) for the violence against the protesters, including using *jolka* as an instrument of punishment, which is also referenced by the soldiers (Text 2, line 7). Thus, in the soldiers' letter-writing, invoking *jolka* created an overlapping frame that connects the already complex and layered past and present events.

Another use of a decontextualized artefact from Ukrainian popular culture is the repetition of 'La-la-la-la-la-la-la-la' in lines 13 and 14 (Text 2), which is a refrain from a popular insulting song-chant about Putin in which Putin is called *hujlo/a* dickhead. Initially a chant that Ukrainian soccer fans used to taunt rival teams, their owners and coaches, the song-chant – after Russia's annexation of Crimea and its covert support of the military aggression in Eastern Ukraine – has become a popular, and recognizable, expression of anti-Putin sentiments. The refrain serves as a shorthand, a multimodal memory trigger, used to metonymically reactivate the entire provocative, even vulgar, schema of the song in which Putin is ridiculed by being reduced to a body part, further contributing to the overall defiant and humorous key of the recreation marked by repeated laughter.

Laughter, a paralinguistic feature, performs several functions in the video. During the set up (when the soldiers are transforming their appearances to resemble Cossacks), laughter helps to establish a humorous key that frames the entire video as a joking provocation. During letter-writing (Text 2), laughter – in addition to maintaining the humorous key of the (inter)action – is also a part of the multimodal repetition, or resemiotization: in the painting the Cossacks are laughing and so are the soldiers in the video, thus adding 'authenticity' to their performance. Laughing at the adversary, by both the Cossacks and the soldiers, is also a sign of bravery that is shared by both groups, reinforcing their similarities. As Sørensen (2016) indicates, political humour not only exposes and ridicules those in power but also diminishes fear among the less powerful. Furthermore, laughing at the adversary creates both linkages between past and present 'texts' and an affinity between Ukrainian soldiers and the online audience that shares anti-Putin and pro-Ukrainian sentiments. The third function of laughter is that of signalling the uptake. In her work on intertextual repetition, Sierra (2016) suggests that laughter signals the hearer's recognition of a shared prior text that is often sourced from popular culture. In Text 2, when in line 10 Soldier 2 switches to Russian to index the prior history of *jolka*, everyone's laughter indicates that his contribution was recognized as an intended intertextual reference. Finally, everyone's laughter (line 10), including that of Solider 1 (in line 11) when he engages in savouring repetition (Tannen 2007), is polysemous: it could be about Yanukovych's 'Christmas tree' debacle or about appreciating a clever contribution made by Soldier 2 to the insulting nature of the letter.

Taken together, all these linguistic and paralinguistic strategies, from referring terms to laughter, make it possible for Ukrainian soldiers to construct collective creative insurgency that is rooted in history and shared (popular) culture that allows citizens of a less powerful country, Ukraine, to challenge the autocratic leader of a stronger country, Russia. Additionally, by drawing on resources ('The Reply' and Repin's painting) familiar to the majority of Ukrainians and adding contemporary elements to their (re)creation, the soldiers not only preserve but also contribute to the Cossack mythology, and in so doing simultaneously construct their (re)creation in multiple frames, connecting past and present, play and real life.

5.3 Multimodal intertextual repetition as a semiotic aggregate and a resource for framing

While prior studies at the intersection of intertextuality and framing (e.g. Gordon 2002, 2008, 2009; Trester 2012; Sierra 2016) tend to focus on how repetition of shared bits of language such as individual utterances is used to create and manipulate frames, in this work, I explore how the entire semiotic aggregate of multimodal intertextual repetition(s) is deployed to construct and laminate frames. Specifically, I suggest that by (re)constructing 'The Reply' and the painting, and by adding references from contemporary Ukrainian popular culture, Ukrainian soldiers – in their letter-writing – create embedded (Figure 11.3) and overlapping (Figure 11.4) frames. For instance, Figure 11.3 shows that by re-enacting the Cossacks' letter-writing, the soldiers create a play frame that is embedded in a larger frame of real-life resistance against Russia's aggressive actions. Furthermore, the soldiers' re-enactment can be simultaneously (as indicated by the arrows) viewed as a play and as a real-life pre-battle insult directed at the adversary, Putin. In this way, the frames are not only embedded but also blended

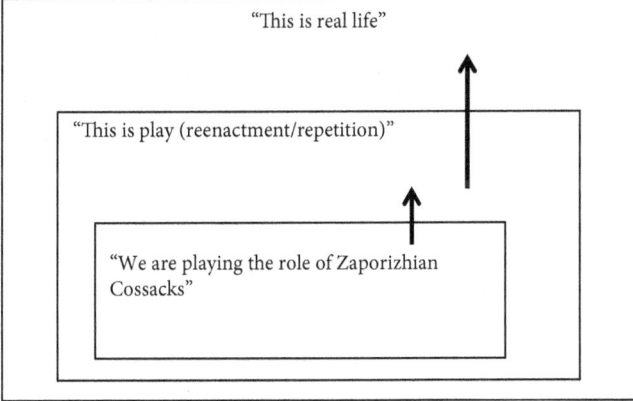

Figure 11.3 Embedded (and blended) frames.

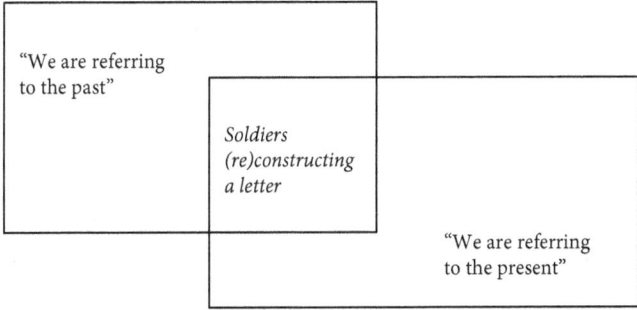

Figure 11.4 Overlapping frames.

(Gordon 2008, 2009), with play and real life inextricably intertwined and brought about by the same resources.

The multimodal (re)construction of 'The Reply' creates not only embedded but also overlapping frames (Figure 11.4). Specifically, it is simultaneously oriented towards the past, the time of the Zaporizhian Cossacks, and the present, when Ukrainian soldiers, the present-day Cossacks (and several written comments below the YouTube video call them as such), have to face – ironically – the same aggressive neighbour as did the Cossacks several centuries ago. As with the embedded frames (Figure 3), this simultaneous orientation also laminates frames, connecting past and present actions of Ukrainians defending their territory.

6 Conclusion

In this chapter, I have considered how repetition across different modalities, or resemiotization (Iedema 2003), is deployed as creative insurgency (Kraidy 2016) in the context of Russian-Ukrainian geopolitical conflict. Specifically, I have analysed a YouTube video in which Ukrainian soldiers (re)create the iconic painting of Zaporizhian Cossacks writing an insulting reply to the Turkish sultan, but in the soldiers' re-enactment, the addressees are Russian President Putin and his allies. My analysis demonstrates that by mobilizing various meditational means (Scollon 2001) – referring terms and 'heteroglossia with awareness', stylization and laughter, guns and their own bodies – Ukrainian soldiers collaboratively perform an insult, or 'reasonable hostility' (Tracy 2008) against, Putin and his policies towards Ukraine. Furthermore, the soldiers' use of multimodal intertextual repetition, including the embodiment of recognizable cultural artefacts, creates a complex semiotic aggregate with fluidity between 'texts'. By theorizing the soldiers' (re)creation as intertextuality in action (Tovares 2005), or when 'texts' become actions, this study adds to our understanding of repetition as wells as the relationship between 'texts' and actions by demonstrating how social actors draw on multimodal intertextual resources to engage in the act of creative insurgency.

The analysis also adds to prior work on framing, especially studies that consider intertextual repetition as a resource for framing (Gordon 2002, 2008, 2009; Trester 2012; Sierra 2016), by showing how the soldiers' (re)creation, as a complex semiotic assemblage that includes but does not privilege language, constructs embedded and overlapping frames, often blending frames, and in so doing simultaneously signals play and real life, as well as the past and present of Ukraine.

Tannen (2007) underscores that repetition provides a key to our understanding of both creation and perception of discourse. In this chapter, I have addressed only the production side of multimodal repetition. To achieve a more comprehensive understanding of multimodal meaning-making, future research needs to explore how multimodal repetition is perceived by the audience by, for instance, analysing written YouTube comments posted in reaction to the video. Another limitation of this study is that it mobilizes repetition (broadly conceived) and framing primarily from a discourse-analytic perspective. The data – with its richness and complexity –

can be approached from other theoretical standpoints, such as blending theory (e.g. Fauconnier and Turner 2002; Karpenko-Seccombe 2016). Put differently, the current investigation offers a contribution rather than an exhaustive answer to the ongoing academic dialogue on meaning-making in interaction.

Finally, this work suggests that by creatively drawing on the familiar to most Ukrainians multimodal 'texts', from 'The Reply' and Repin's painting to online memes, the soldiers reinforce the link between the mythologized military fraternity of Zaporizhian Cossacks and Ukrainian national consciousness, and in so doing emphasize the common loyalties of Ukrainian people in a time of crisis.

Acknowledgements

I am grateful to Natalia Knoblock and the anonymous reviewer for their helpful suggestions on earlier drafts of this chapter. I am forever thankful to Raul Tovares for his support of my research.

Notes

1 'Zaporizhian' is a transliteration of a Ukrainian word while 'Zaporozhian' reflects Russian pronunciation. In this study I use 'Zaporizhian'.
2 https://en.wikipedia.org/wiki/Decommunization_in_Ukraine
3 In this work the term Cossacks is used in reference to Zaporizhian (Ukrainian) Cossacks. The confusion often stems from the parallel and later intertwined histories of Zaporizhian and Russian Cossacks. During the same time when Zaporizhian Cossacks were establishing their settlement, Zaporizhian Sich, '[a] Russian variant of Cossackdom evolved farther to the east, along the Don River' (Subtelny 2005: 109). In the second half of the 18th century, after Zaporizhian Sich was destroyed and its members disbanded under the auspices of the Russian empress Catherine II, Zaporizhian Cossacks and/or their descendants – after years of exile and temporary settlements – settled in the Kuban area of Russia and together with their Russian counterparts form what came to be known as the Kuban Cossacks (Subtelny 2005: 176).
4 One copy of the painting is in the State Russian Museum in St. Petersburg; the other (slightly unfinished) is in Ukraine, in the Kharkiv Art Museum.
5 I am grateful to Elisa Oh, a specialist in Early Modern British literature, for bringing this example to my attention.

References

Al Zidjaly, N. (2012), 'What Has Happened to Arabs? Identity and Face Management Online', *Multilingua*, 31: 413–39.
Bakhtin, M. (1981), *The Dialogic Imagination*. Austin: University of Texas Press.
Bakhtin, M. (1984), *Rabelais and His World*. Bloomington: Indiana University Press.

Bakhtin, M. (1986), *Speech Genres and Other Late Essays*. Austin: University of Texas Press.
Bauman, R. and Briggs, C. (1990), 'Poetics and Performance as Critical Perspectives on Language and Social Life', *Annual Review of Anthropology*, 19: 59–88.
Bax, M. (2010), 'Epistolary Presentation Rituals: Face-Work, Politeness and Ritual Display in Early Modern Dutch Letter-Writing', in J. Culpeper and D. Kádár (eds), *Historical (Im)politeness*, 37–86. Bern: Peter Lang.
Becker, A. L. (1995), *Beyond Translation: Essays Toward a Modern Philology*. Ann Arbor: University of Michigan Press.
Bilaniuk, L. (2005), *Contested Tongues: Language Politics and Cultural Correction in Ukraine*. Ithaca: Cornell University Press.
Bilaniuk, L. (2017), 'Purism and Pluralism: Language Use Trends in Popular Culture in Ukraine Since Independence', in M. Flier and A. Graziosi (eds), *The Battle for Ukrainian: A Comparative Perspective*, 343–63. Cambridge: Harvard University Press.
Bousfield, D. and Locher, M. A. (eds) (2008), *Impoliteness in Language: Studies on Its Interplay with Power in Theory and Practice*. Berlin: Mouton de Gruyter.
Coupland, N. (2007), *Style: Language Variation and Identity*. Cambridge: Cambridge University Press.
Coupland, N. and Jaworski, A. (2004), 'Sociolinguistic Perspectives on Metalanguage: Reflexivity, Evaluation and Ideology', in A. Jaworski, N. Coupland and D. Galasínski (eds), *Metalanguage: Social and Ideological Perspectives*, 15–51. Berlin: Mouton de Gruyter.
Culpeper, J. (2011), *Impoliteness: Using Language to Cause Offence*. Cambridge: Cambridge University Press.
Culpeper, J. and D. Kádár (eds) (2010), *Historical (Im)politeness*. Bern: Peter Lang.
Demjanova, J. O. (2011), 'Zlopobažann'a Jak Cinnyj Component Etnolingvistyčnoji Svidomosti' ['Curses as a Valuable Component of Ethnolinguistic Consciousness'], *Aktual'ni Problemy Slovjans'koji Filologiji*, 24 (2): 457–68.
Fairclough, N. (1992), 'Intertexuality in Critical Discourse Analysis', *Linguistics and Education*, 4 (3–4): 269–93.
Fauconnier, G. and Turner, M. (2002), *The Way We Think: Conceptual Blending and the Mind's Hidden Complexities*. New York: Basic Books.
Friedman, V. A. (1978), 'The Zaporozhian Letter to the Turkish Sultan: Historical Commentary and Linguistic Analysis', *Slavica Hierosolymitana*, 2: 25–38.
Gasparov, B. (2010), *Speech, Memory, and Meaning: Intertextuality in Everyday Language*. Berlin: De Gruyter Mouton.
Goffman, E. (1959), *The Presentation of Self in Everyday Live*. Garden City: Doubleday.
Goffman, E. (1974), *Frame Analysis*. New York: Harper & Row.
Goffman, E. (1981), *Forms of Talk*. Philadelphia: University of Pennsylvania Press.
Gordon, C. (2002), '"I'm Mommy and You're Natalie:" Role-Reversal and Embedded Frames in Mother-Child Discourse', *Language and Society*, 31 (5): 679–720.
Gordon C. (2008), 'A(p)parent Play: Blending Frames and Reframing in Family Talk', *Language in Society*, 37 (3): 319–49.
Gordon, C. (2009), *Making Meanings, Creating Family: Intertextuality and Framing in Family Interaction*. New York: Oxford University Press.
Grimshaw, A. (ed.) (1990), *Conflict Talk: Sociolinguistic Investigations of Arguments in Conversations*. New York: Cambridge University Press.
Iedema, R. (2003), 'Multimodality, Resemiotization: Extending the Analysis of Discourse as Multi-Semiotic Practice', *Visual Communication*, 2 (1): 29–57.

Jewitt, C., Bezemer, J. J. and O'Halloran, K. L. (2016), *Introducing Multimodality*, London: Routledge.

Karpenko-Seccombe, T. (2016), 'Intertextuality as Cognitive Modeling', *English Text Construction*, 9 (2): 244–67.

Knoblock, N. (2016), 'Sarcasm and Irony as a Political Weapon: Social Networking in the Time of Crisis', in D. O. Orwenjo, O. Okerch and A. H. Tunde (eds), *Political Discourse in Emergent, Fragile, and Failed Democracies*, 11–32. Hershey: IGI Global.

Kostomarov, M. (1872), 'Sultan Tureckij i Zaporožcy' ['Turkish Sultan and Zaporozhians'], *Russkaja Starina [Russian Antiquities]*, 6: 450–1.

Kraidy, M. (2016), *The Naked Blogger of Cairo: Creative Insurgency in the Arab World*. Cambridge: Harvard University Press.

Kress, G. (2009), *Multimodality: A Social Semiotic Approach to Contemporary Communication*. London: Routledge.

Kress, G. and T. van Leeuwen (2001), *Multimodal Discourse*. London: Bloomsbury.

Kristeva, J. (1986), 'Word, Dialog and Novel', in T. Moi (ed.), *The Kristeva Reader*, 34–61. New York: Columbia University Press.

Kulyk, V. (2016), 'Language and Identity in Ukraine after Euromaidan', *Thesis Eleven*, 136 (1): 90–106.

Labov, W. (1972), 'Rules for Ritual Insults', in W. Labov (ed.), *Language in the Inner City*, 297–353. Philadelphia: University of Pennsylvania Press.

Norrick, N. (1994), 'Repetition as a Conversational Joking Strategy', in B. Johnstone (ed.), *Repetition in Discourse: Interdisciplinary Perspectives*, 15–28. Norwood: Ablex Publishing Corporation.

Norris, S. (2004), *Analyzing Multimodal Interaction: A Methodological Framework*. London: Routledge.

Norris, S. (2011), *Identity in (Inter)action: Introducing Multimodal (Inter)action Analysis*. Berlin: de Gruyter Mouton.

Pavlenko, A. (2013), 'Multilingualism in Post-Soviet Successor States', *Language and Linguistics Compass*, 7 (4): 262–71.

Plokhy, S. (2012), *The Cossack Myth: History and Nationhood in the Age of Empires*. New York: Cambridge University Press.

Ryazanova-Clarke, L. (2016), 'Linguistic Mnemonics: The Communist Language Variety in Contemporary Russian Public Discourse', in P. Petrov and L. Ryazanova-Clarke (eds), *The Vernacular of Communism: Language, Ideology and Power in the Soviet Union and Eastern Europe*, 169–95. London: Routledge.

Scollon, R. (2001), *Mediated Discourse: The Nexus of Practice*. London and New York: Routledge.

Sierra, S. (2016), 'Playing Out Loud: Videogame References as Resources in Friend Interaction for Managing Frames, Epistemics, and Group Identity', *Language in Society*, 45 (2): 217–45.

Sørensen, M. J. (2016), *Humour in Political Activism: Creative Nonviolent Resistance*. London: Palgrave Macmillan.

Subtelny, O. (2005), *Ukraine: A History*, 3rd edn. Toronto: University of Toronto Press.

Sysyn, F. (1991), 'The Reemergence of the Ukrainian Nation and Cossack Mythology',. *Social Research*, 58 (4): 845–64.

Tannen D. (2002), 'Agonism in Academic Discourse', *Journal of Pragmatics*, 34 (10–11): 1651–69.

Tannen, D. (2006), 'Intertextuality in Interaction: Reframing Family Arguments in Public and Private', *Text & Talk*, 26 (4): 597–617.

Tannen, D. (2007), *Talking Voices: Repetition, Dialogue and Imagery in Conversational Discourse*, 2nd edn. Cambridge: Cambridge University Press.

Tannen, D. and Wallat, C. (1993), 'Interactive Frames and Knowledge Schemas in Interaction: Examples from a Medical Examination/Interview', in D. Tannen (ed.), *Framing in Discourse*, 57–76. Oxford: Oxford University Press.

Tovares, A. (2005), '*Intertextuality in Family Interaction: Repetition of Public Texts in Private Settings*', Ph.D. diss., Georgetown University, Washington, DC.

Tovares, A. (2019), 'Trolling as Creative Insurgency: The Carnivalesque Delegitimization of Putin and His Supporters in Online Newspaper Commentary', in A. Ross and D. Rivers (eds), *Discourses of (De)legitimization: Participatory Culture in Digital Contexts*, 228–47. New York: Routledge.

Tracy, K. (2008), '"Reasonable Hostility": Situation-Appropriate Face-Attack', *Journal of Politeness Research*, 4: 169–91.

Tracy, K. (2010), *Challenges of Ordinary Democracy: A Case Study in Deliberation and Dissent*. University Park: Pennsylvania State University Press.

Trester, A. M. (2012), 'Framing Entextualization in Improv: Intertextuality as an Interactional Resource', *Language in Society*, 41: 237–58.

Vojcehivs'ka, N. K. (2014), 'Prokljony ta zlopobažannʹa v ukrajinsʹkomu konfliktnomu dialogičnomu dyskursi' ['Curses and Oaths in Ukrainian Conflict Dialogic Discourse'], *Naukovyj Visnyk Mižnarodnogo Gumanitarnogo Universytetu*, 12: 4–8.

12

Fighting fear with humour

The linguistic-pragmatic aspects

Yaroslava Sazonova

1 Introduction

The project examines the linguistic-pragmatic aspects of humour used in a popular Ukrainian blog to help readers cope with fear. Blogs and blogging have become popular and socially influential in contemporary society, and they successfully compete with traditional media. In 2014–6, Ukraine experienced an outburst of debate and sharing controversial ideas via printed and internet media as well as social media. It was prompted by sociopolitical renewal, which began with Maidan[1] as the starting point and included the war with Russia. The obvious inability of the Ukrainian authorities prior to 2014 to pursue national policies independent from Russia provoked dissatisfaction in the society and finally resulted in Maidan. Russia's annexation of the Ukrainian Crimea and the beginning of the war destroyed the people's long held worldviews, causing confusion in people's minds and full or partial destruction of the traditional / prior world and society ontology.

This vortex of political events and news from battlefields, complicated by the intrigues and manipulations of politicians, instilled fear in the population and provoked polarization of the Ukrainian society. The variety of opinions in blog texts of that time presents pro- and anti-Maidan views; both make wide use of humour in representing the opponents. As emphasized by Seçil Deren van het Hof (2015: 44):

> Members of the group, based paradoxically on both the sarcastic and optimistic language of humour, overcome political apathy and alienation naturally. <…> Like OWS,[2] Otpor,[3] the Zapatistas[4] and actually many others, Gezi events[5] has been an example how humour functions as a rhetorical element in turning cynical citizens into politically potent individuals.

In this chapter, I intend to demonstrate how humour is successfully employed for pragmatic purposes of non-violent resistance.

2 Theoretical framework: Humour research in human sciences

Humour has received considerable attention from humanities scholars, starting with Aristotle. My research is informed by the views on the communicative value and functions of humour developed by Balaban (2015), Day (2011), van het Hof (2015), Haugerud (2013), Hutcheon (1994), Sørensen (2016) and others. They take into account psychological factors of humorous communication and describe it through the Relief Theory focusing on tension reduction, the Superiority Theory focusing on power, the Incongruity Theory focusing on the mental representation of what is funny, and others. The communicative approach helps address the value of humour in the circumstances of problematic or frightening situations.

Victor Raskin's *Script-based Semantic Theory of Humor* (2017) is used in this chapter as a source of ideas for the analysis undertaken in this project. He suggests that a joke begins when two different scripts are opposed to one another. Raskin lists the types of opposition, among which 'normal VS abnormal' (2017: 112) is the one regularly exploited in the analysed blog texts. I also rely on the studies of the linguistic aspects of humour by Oaks (1994), Hetzron (1991), Norrick (1989) and others.

In this research, I use the term 'humour' as an umbrella term, bearing in mind its psychological nature and social functions relying on researchers (Berger 1997; Hageseth 1988; Lefcourt 2001) who cast light on the difference between the positive and negative effects of humour, funny and hostile humour in communication. Researchers (e.g. Billig 2005) stress that humour in the form of ridicule plays a necessary role in maintaining social order; they identify the disciplinary function of ridicule and its social significance as rebellious humour.

This study relies on the definition of ridicule given by the representatives of Discourse Analysis: it is a discursive strategy aimed at undermining the legitimacy of some object or process (mainly of sociopolitical value) or at stigmatizing it to provoke change (Payne 2018: 5). Pragmatically, ridicule is opposed to raillery; these two strategies of humorous communication have different aims and lead to opposite effects. The objects that are ridiculous in the eye of the speaker bear vices and incongruities: 'Nothing is ridiculous except what is deformed' (Shaftesbury, cit. in Billig 2005: 77). Deformities can be both physical and moral or mental (like overconsumption (Eriksson 2015) or arguments for the necessity of nuclear deterrence (Payne 2018)). In the communicative-pragmatic reasoning of applying the strategy of ridicule to a frightening object, the key role belongs to the emphasis on its incongruity and gaining superiority over it.

We differentiate irony and sarcasm as linguistic-pragmatic mechanisms of the realization of ridicule and mockery as an overarching discursive strategy. They find their realization in various linguistic means such as puns, all types of malapropism, metathesis, hyperbole and other techniques. We use the terms 'irony' and 'sarcasm' interchangeably, like other researchers (Attardo et al. 2003). Both sarcasm and irony are often used to express negative evaluation, as 'a vehicle for expressing an attitude /

evaluation and it emphasizes a discrepancy between what the speaker hopes / expects to happen / to have happened and what he / she believes to be the case, based on the evidence at hand' (Dynel 2018: 130).

As history shows, merciless satire can become the weapon of those who cannot fight physically, which is represented in the Ukrainian culture by the literary heritage from Ivan Vyshenskyi[6] to Les Podervianskyi, Ivan Semesyuk[7] and other modern writers. Humour can play a prominent role in non-violent resistance in political struggle. Following Bergson's ideas (2005), Sørensen (2016: 2) states that mocking the dominant ideas about what is true and right in the 'other axiology', ridiculing them or turning them upside down shows solidarity in opposing the alien axiology. Sørensen (2016: 3) emphasized the following functions of humour in such circumstances:

- It facilitates outreach and mobilization and contributes to sustaining a culture of resistance;
- It reduces the levels of fear;
- It exposes, ridicules and influences the opposed power.

Mocking the political opponent may be performed in abusive practices in the opponent's description (Zhao 1987) or in the delegitimization of the threatening object by means of 'other-presentation' via such mechanisms as blaming, scapegoating, marginalizing, excluding, attacking the moral character, attacking rationality and sanity, and others (Cap 2017). Piotr Cap suggests that the emphasis on the abnormality of the threatening object helps draw a line between *us* and *them*, which is achieved by friendly irony towards *us* and hostile sarcasm and mockery towards *them*. As Sanders claims (2001: 75), 'Mockery can draw a clear demarcation line between us and them'.

Another abusive practice is profanity, which, in the context of non-violent resistance to aggression, has a lot in common with humour. Researchers (Stapleton 2010) show that abusive vocabulary also performs the social function of showing solidarity and aligning oneself with a certain group. Stapleton claims that feeling involved and accepted in a group is of vital importance for a person; Gibbs and Izett (2005) metaphorically compared people who share the same idea and understand the irony to wolves, and the opposing group to sheep. Profanity as well as humour may have laughter as a common response, but this response is of secondary emotional and communicative value.

Another important factor prominent in the blogs under analysis is language floating. Researchers (Rosina Lippi-Green and others 2012) stress that intentional adoption of another language or dialect may lead to unpredictable results: from complete failure in communication to a complementary effect. The blog texts under analysis constantly switch from standard Ukrainian to Surzhyk. This language phenomenon is strongly stigmatized among people who apply a sociopolitical attitude to this living blend of languages. However, linguists are compelled to admit the fact of Surzhyk's vitality, and have paid much attention to its roots, linguistic features or sociolinguistic factors of functioning (Braga 2012; Bilanuik 1997, 2005).

3 Materials and methods

The analysis uses the framework of discourse analysis and linguistic-pragmatic approach to studying language phenomena and the process of communication. The materials of this study are blog texts by Did Svyryd Opanasovych dating from 2014 to 2016 (the total number of texts is twenty-five; the approximate number of words is 30,000).[8] The texts collected from these blogs were checked for humorous descriptions of people and phenomena that are considered scary and/or dangerous but ridiculous using the method of total sampling. The descriptive and contextual-interpretative method allowed to group the examples according to the aspects of the opponent's abnormality and then to analyse them in terms of linguistic-pragmatic means of expressing irony and sarcasm.

The object of analysis is the linguistic-pragmatic mechanisms of humorous presentation of the enemy in blog texts of sociopolitical orientation. The research questions are:

(1) What is the communicative basis of ridiculing the target object in the blog texts under analysis?
(2) What are the linguistic-pragmatic mechanisms and language means of achieving a humorous effect in the blog texts under analysis?
(3) What are the pragmatic functions of humour in the blog texts under analysis?

4 Results and discussion

4.1 General characteristic of Did Svyryd's blog. Communicative and structural specificity

The Repka Club, with Did Svyryd Opanasovych as one of its founders, claimed to be a website for those who respond to thorny problems in a humorous way using Surzhyk: its subtitle was 'The Club of Battle Surzhyk'. The roots of Did Svyryd Opanasovych's[9] image lie in Les Podervianskyi's humorous play *Repka, abo Huli ne Yasno?* (*Turnip, or What the Fuck is Unclear?*) (Karpenko 2014). Moreover, Surzhyk is reinforced with swearing from time to time, making the blogger's comments as close to the perception and expression of common people as possible. Humour and swearing are two inseparable characteristics of the image of Did Svyryd, who is supposed to be an elderly but strong and wise villager whose mindset is pragmatic and logical ,and whose heart is full of passion and love for his country and fellow citizens. The credibility of Did Svyryd's persona is based on the constantly growing distrust of the media, politicians and representatives of the authorities, who have the lowest credibility ratings according to numerous sociological surveys, whereas people / neighbours, the army, volunteers and clergy are seen as reliable.[10] Did Svyryd's language is close to the language of common people: he verbalizes the most complicated ideas in a simple, understandable manner; moreover, he is never in a hurry and always advises:

(1) *Спокійно наблюдаєм –*
Let's observe calmly.[11]

Did Svyryd's blog posts are different from the traditional humorous texts with a punch line, that have no classical linear structure, no beginning or ending, and no plot. They are not intended to make people laugh (like jokes, humorous short stories, novels, etc.). Instead, they are a blend of a blog and a letter, with a greeting that is traditional for the epistolary genre:

> (2) *Доброго здоров'я, друзі! Надворі чудовий осінній ранок, який просто створений для фізкультури і спорту, тому всім, хто зранку потренувався – мої найщиріші вітання.*
> *Good day, friends! It's a wonderful autumn morning that is made for exercising and sports, that's why I send my best wishes to those who have exercised since morning*

Saying goodbye is accompanied by didactic statements and wishes:

> (3) *Сохраняєм бадьорий бойовий дух, держим кулаки за полонених, всячеськи допомагаємо Армії, ведемо здоровий спосіб життя і спонукаємо розумних та чесних людей іти в політику. Ну і привично слєдім, шоб візде порядок був! А не то, шо січас* [smile]
> *Keep your spirits up, fingers crossed for the captives, help our army in every way, lead a healthy lifestyle and encourage smart and honest people to go into politics. And, as usual, mind that order is kept here! Unlike now!*

The functioning of Surzhyk in these blogs is intentional and mostly limited to the narration and comments about the aggressor: here, the author wears the mask of Did Svyryd and toys with the language, mocking the frightening enemy. However, when the communicative aim changes (comments on gruesome events or news from battlefields, sharing information about help necessary for the wounded or some other serious problem), the personality of the author comes forward. It is linguistically marked by the use of standard Ukrainian in stylistically impeccable passages.

These blogs appeared regularly, and if the author skipped a day or two, he gave explanations why, as it is usually done in personal letters. Their letter-like composition and the communicative intention to build friend-like relations with the readers, as well as the discussion of current problems, resemble friendly correspondence. The blogger is open for communication, so comments are allowed after the blog is published; he also answers the readers or thanks them for their support.

The blog, as an influential format of communication, helps the author create texts with the specific pragmatic intention to consolidate readers in opposing the frightening enemy and to share a balanced point of view on current events. The personality of a credible elderly man is a mask the blogger wears to win the confidence of his readers as well as to give advice to fellow citizens or to ridicule the enemy. The structure of the blog texts and their linguistic features contribute to the realization of these intentions; humour and swearing are intentionally verbalized in Surzhyk while referring to the enemy.

4.2 Abnormality of the frightening / threatening opponent in Did Svyryd's texts

Humorous representation of the threatening object in the blog texts outlines the 'normal/abnormal' opposition. The discursive strategy of ridiculing abnormality is realized via irony and sarcasm as linguistic-pragmatic mechanisms. Initially, sarcasm is implicated in the psychological presupposition that is based on normal expectations of civilized behaviour of a country or people and of its leader. Insofar as what is presupposed contradicts the reality, a gap appears that facilitates the textual actualization of ridicule. In the course of the blogger/readers communication, the processes of actualizing abnormality and ridiculing it are simultaneous; this abnormality is revealed in the following characteristics:

(1) Unmanly personality and treacherousness;
(2) Mental disability and unpredictability;
(3) Aggressiveness;
(4) Loneliness and misery;
(5) Non-democratic character.

A linguistic-pragmatic analysis of ridiculing these characteristics of the aggressive object follows.

4.2.1 Unmanly personality and treacherousness

In the analysed texts, the trigger that activates the ridicule and serves as a precondition to understanding the ideological component of the author's pragmatic intentions is the nomination *hujlo*[12] (putz) in a range of derivatives applied to Vladimir Putin. These texts and the whole communication trend in patriotic circles use the nomination *hujlo* (a kind of antonomasia, or an expressive name in the Russian stylistic tradition) that is correctly deciphered when used in the context of the Ukrainian-Russian conflict. The 'normal/abnormal' opposition actualizes the idea of moral abnormality of the Russian leader, thus facilitating all the psychological effects of humorous communication – reclaiming power, letting out steam, and emphasizing mental and moral incongruity.

Generally, the swearword *hujlo* is very strong and is applied to a person treated with contempt for his sneakiness and unworthiness (*čmo*[13] is close to it, but is much milder and refers mostly to a person's appearance, physical condition or low social status). An expression like *botoksne čmo* (botox prick) implies Putin's unmanly personality and fake appearance.

In the blogs, the word is capitalized (*Hujlo*), which marks it as a personal name, individual and impossible to confuse:

(4) *С етім фамілійом [Hujlo] йому жить і с ней он і помрьот*
    He is destined to live with this surname, and he will die with it.

Also, this nomination has derivatives showing diminutive attitude (the Russian suffix *-uš* is usually used to express tenderness towards little children or very dear people), though in this political context the diminutive meaning is converted into moral immaturity (*Hujluša*):

(5) *І де би яка херня не случилася, сразу шукають чи не наслідив там бува мілдруг* **Хуйлуша**.
Whatever shit happens somewhere, people wonder if dear friend **Hujluša** has left his trace there.

To emphasize the extent of abnormality, not only is the Russian leader the target of this mockery but is related people as well: phrases like *pičalʹna lošadʹ Lavrov / Pičalʹna lošadka* (a sad horse Lavrov[14] / a sad horsie) mock the similarity of the Russian Foreign Minister's elongated face with a horse head and its sombre expression. Referring to a person (who is associated with a threatening country) as a horse is an insult that dehumanizes him; the diminutive suffix –*k* turns 'a horse' into 'a small / toy horse' and adds a sense of pity to the target of ridicule. These techniques make the situation grotesque and diminish fear.

A blend of pity and ridicule also is achieved by nominating Vladimir Putin's press secretary Peskov as *skomoroh Pisʹkov* (doofus Pisʹkov[15]). His appearance of a doofus with straw hair and pink cheeks, and his usual job of verbalizing the most absurd of Putin's ideas make Peskov a puppet that deserves pity in Ukrainian opinion. The phonetic pun maximizes scorn: the surname is intentionally misspelled to make it sound similar to the noun *pisʹka* (slang for female genitalia). The emphatic predicative end-position of adjectives expressing the pitiful condition of the joke's targets makes the whole sentence sound like a verdict:

(6) *І Лавров, і Піськов виглядали в телевізорі* **жалко й безпорадно**
Both Lavrov and Pisʹkov looked **miserable and helpless** on the TV.

Separate comments are necessary to explain the use of neuter gender to refer to a person. Grammatically, this strategy is actualized when the personal pronoun *vono* (it) refers to men and, less often, to women to manipulate with gender distinctions. The grammatical meaning of this pronoun is 'object, countable/uncountable, singular, neuter gender' (Velykyi 2005), though in colloquial speech in Ukrainian it may be used with disdain or caress or their mixture with reference to a person of any gender, for example:

(7) **Воно** *ж не просихає: дивна поведінка* **Савченко**[16] *потрапила в об'єктив*
It is always drunk: **Savchenko**'s strange behavior attracts attention (Tsaruk 2018);

(8) *та ще, на лихо,* **сердешне** *хита головою*[17]
unfortunately, **the poor thing** has its head shaking (Shevchenko 1844).

This use may be explained by the similarity of a drunk or ill person with a body[18] that is partially immobilized, partially unconscious, and so on:

(9) *зненацька металеві двері відчиняються й до кімнати ледве не карачкиввалюється дивне **'тєло'**: **воно** п'яне, потаскане, за спиною – щось, схоже на крила, але прим'яті та перекошені*

suddenly the metal door opens and **a 'body'** barges into the room, nearly on all fours: it is drunk, shabby, and behind **its** back there is something similar to wings, but crumpled and twisted (Humennyi 2011);

(10) *поїзд їде – **воно** лізе*

the train is moving, **it** is crawling (a well-known phrase by Verka Serdiuchka[19] about a drunk passenger trying to catch a train).

Grammatically, the word *hujlo* is referred to as *vono*, which can be seen from a number of examples where gender distinctions are marked by verbal forms:

(11) ***Хуйло** по обикновенію **тянуло** резіну до послєднєго, всіма силами показуючи, шо **оно** тут вообще ні при чом*

Huylo was stalling as usual, doing **its** best to show that **it** has nothing to do with this;

(12) ***Хуйло витерло** мармизу і **пошло** откровенічати з пресою. Хотя дуже **не хотіло** ето дєлать*

Huylo wiped **its** muzzle and went to open **itself** up to the press. Though **it** really did not want to do it;

(13) ***Хуйло притихло** і **начало** заісківать перед Обамою –*

Huylo calmed down and **began** to curry favour with Obama.

These examples (7–13) not only illustrate the unmanly personality of the frightening object and pity towards it but also reflect the psychological basis of the actualized superiority over the target of ridicule. Further Did Svyryd plays with other shades of unmanliness, even hinting at possible homosexual relations. The circle of Vladimir Putin's close people, in public opinion, is limited to the Prime Minister Dmitriy Medvedev, who is called *komnatna sobačka* (a pet dog) in the blogs, metaphorically emphasizing Medvedev's dependence and inseparability from Putin. Here is how this relationship is perceived:

(14) *Впереді уже ясно маячить могилка, а шо за спиною? Та ніхера. Сім'ї нема, діти на папу чхать хотіли, а онуків Хуйло і сам не любить. Даже женщини порядної рядом нема, разве шо Діма Медвед. Та й **Діма** вічно в айфон погружена, слова ласкового від **неї** не дождешся. І некрасіва **вона** якась в послєднє врем'я*

A grave is looming clearly ahead, but what has been done? Nothing [abusive]. He has no family, his children don't care for him [emotionally coloured], he doesn't like his grandchildren. He doesn't even have a respectable woman near him, except for **Dima Medved**. But **Dima** is constantly immersed in **her** phone, she is not tender. And **she** hasn't seemed beautiful at all lately.

The grammatical pun is made with feminine gender forms of the personal name and pronoun (consider the homonymous endings –a in nouns of feminine and masculine gender, like in *Dima* (male name) / *Maša* (female name) (Nom. Case)) and the further use of feminine gender forms of verbs and adjectives. With this grammatical transformation, the lack of feminine behaviour is sarcastically referred to (Dima is not beautiful and not tender).

The treacherous and immature behaviour of the Russian leader is implied by referring to him as *gad'oniš* ('baby snake', or 'little bastard' metaphorically) or *kris'oniš* (baby rat). The Russian suffix *–oniš* means 'a child of', and hints at minimum current threat but possible future harm, like from a child of a snake (Efremova 2000). Whole text passages actualize the negative attitude of representatives of the civilized world to Putin's treacherousness by metaphoric representation of diplomatic negotiations like deadly animal games:

(15) Ми мали удовольствіє наблюдать як **американська шаблезуба киця**[20] *ігралася із кремльовським крисьонишем*, цапаючи його то пазурями, то іклами, намекаючи, шо ні малазійського боїнга Хуйлу ніхто не забув, ні розбомблених гумконвоїв у Сирії прощать йому ніхто не намерен

We enjoyed watching how **an American sabre-toothed kitty** was **playing with the Kremlin baby snake**, picking him up with its claws and fangs and hinting that nobody forgets or forgives Hujlo, either for downing the Malaysian Boeing or for humanitarian convoys bombed in Syria.

The comparison of Samantha Power to a sweet but dangerous pussycat not only compliments the high professional competence of this politician and appreciation of her womanly appearance and style but also highlights Vladimir Putin's inability to confront her and reclaim power.

In the circumstances of a real war with tangible deaths, threat and fear, a hybrid war suggests new aggressive actions in addition to the traditional ones. This war-like hybrid influence is mostly imposed by Russia via mass media and the Web. Did Svyryd uses a lot of profanities in his blogs, and in the following examples he is directing them towards Russian mass media:

(16) Вся подобна **херня**[21] *придумуєцця* в Москві **і вбрасуєцця в інфопростір**

All this **shit is invented** in Moscow and **infiltrated into the information space**;

(17) долгоіграюща **медіабитва**

a long-lasting media **battle**.

The swearword *hernâ* is used to emphasize the incredibility of the lie produced by Russian journalists and official representatives.

Putin's treacherousness is obvious in passages where the Russian leader's deceitful and dishonourable behaviour is verbalized:

(18) *десантніки **кажецця заблудилися**, **но точно він не знає**, бо Шойгу ще не доложив*

*the paratroopers **seem to have lost their way**, **but he doesn't know for sure**, as Shojgu22 hasn't reported yet23*

(19) *Хуйло **високомєрно йорнічав** по поводу сомнітєльной лєгітімності власті на Українє*

*Huylo was **arrogantly kidding around** about doubtful legitimacy of Ukrainian authorities.*

More attention should be paid to Example (18), where sarcasm of the highest degree borders and blends with absurdity, since a president cannot be unaware of what his soldiers are doing in another country. The quoted passage reveals the refusal of the target of ridicule to accept responsibility for his actions. It is emphasized in the following example as well:

(20) *всю жізнь **бздів**²⁴, шо легіони НАТО будуть маршірувати коло російських кордонів **і пожалуйста** – сам признається, що ...*

*he has **been afraid** [derogatory] his whole life that NATO legions will be marching near the Russian border, **and here you go** – he confesses on his own that ...*

The use of the lexeme *bzdíty* (to fart) bears a derogatory connotation. Using a vulgarism while describing Putin's feeling of fear may serve to diminish his position and, as a result, to reduce the fear the readers might feel; the causative-consecutive relations between the predicates *has been afraid* and *and here you go* emphasize the mental inability of this president to foresee events and make logical decisions.

In contrast, the author's intention is to balance the chaotic cries 'betrayal!' and 'victory!',²⁵ and to present a logical analytical point of view, anticipating unpredictable actions of the frightening target of ridicule:

(21) *готувати асиметричний удар по хунті*²⁶

to prepare an asymmetrical blow to the junta;

(22) *війна штука дорога, гривня нестабільна, вопрос з газом так і не вирішений, тому взимку, в крайньому случаї навесні **Україна дозріє** і тагда вже Хуйло **буде діктувать условія**. А пока він **буде грати роль непрічасного і кругом невінного***

*war is an expensive thing, hryvnia is volatile, the natural gas problem has not been solved yet, so by winter, by spring at most, **Ukraine will be ready**, and then Huylo **will dictate the terms**. Meanwhile, he will **pretend to be innocent and uninvolved.***

In the text, Did Svyryd often uses the lexeme *junta* (21), showing how ridiculous it is to refer this word to the Ukrainian authorities. It is an example of echoing sarcasm aiming at the Russian media that accuse Ukraine of having President and government that took power illegally. Echoing sarcasm helps show false accusations, on the one hand, and restores power, on the other, meaning 'we are organized and strong'.

4.2.2 Mental disability and unpredictability

Moral and mental abnormality is ridiculed in nominations like *zažravšyjsâ kreml'ovs'kyj debìl, moskovs'kyj duračok* (retarded Kremlin[27] glutton, Moscow fool) referring to the president of Russia. They are abusive, although the noun *duračok* has a derivational morpheme *-ok,* which adds a diminutive meaning to the phrase. Sarcasm is implied in applying the lexeme with the derogatory and diminutive meaning to the person who is supposed to be the wisest or the most reliable and rules the whole country.

Restoring the readers' resilience in the time of hardship and keeping people's spirits up becomes possible by stressing the perception of Vladimir Putin as a person who has no common sense:

(23) *Ми вже давно нічому не удівляємся, а дєйствія Хуйла давно опровергли антинаукову гіпотезу, шо етот* **дєятель дружить со здравим смислом**

We are no longer surprised by anything, and Huylo's actions refuted the anti-scientific hypothesis that **this personage has common sense** *long ago.*

The contemporary political situation is perceived as a madhouse where the patient is the Russian leader while the doctors are world leaders who have been treating the patient to no avail:

(24) *В* **тупенькій** *голові Хуйла созрел план*

Huylo's **stupid** *head bore a plan;*

(25) *Вообще-то він мріє порішать всьо з* **главврачом Обамою**, *но у главврача неприйомні дні і Хуйлу сказано сначала обійти* **профільних врачей**. **Профільні дохтора в нормандськом форматі** *готові осмотреть* **пацієнта**, *но лише єслі він продємонстрірує готовность сотрудничать з медиками*

Actually, he dreams to solve all the problems with **the Chief of Medicine Obama***, but today is not a visiting day, and Huylo was told to see* **medical specialists** *first. The* **specialists** *are ready to see* **the patient in the Normandy format**[28] *only if he shows readiness to cooperate with the doctors.*

As the examples show, disdain and humour are often accompanied by pity – the adjective *tupen'kyj* is a diminutive derivative that helps blend pity, misery and abjection, actualizing incongruity. Such nominations as *pacijent, debìl, duračok, duren'* emphasize the inadequacy of the threatening object, and the level of fear falls as these nouns either bear a diminutive connotation (the Russian suffix *–ok*) or are attributed by disdainful adjectives (Ukr.) *myršavyj* (unattractive, unhealthy, miserable, weak), (Rus.) *zažravšyjsâ* (glutton), and so on.

In Did Svyryd opinion, mental disability of the Russian leader spreads over the country and is perceived as a catching disease. Moreover, active support of Putin by

Russian politicians and by journalists in media bears the connotation of irreversible changes in Russian society. Their looming threat and its apocalyptic character is verbalized by the lexeme *pandemija* (pandemic) or *čuma* (plague):

(26) *Модна в Росії етом сєзонє* **шизофренія** *має всі ознаки* **пандемії**

The **schizophrenia** that's trendy in Moscow this season has all the features of a **pandemic**;

(27) *метаморфози колорадської* **чуми**, *яка охопила нашого північного сусіда*

metamorphoses of the **Colorado plague**[29] that has **engulfed** our northern neighbour.

Incurability of their disease is implied in **patologìčnì** *brehuncì* (**pathological** liars) – the diminutive suffix *-c* makes the phrase humorous by using the understatement 'little liars'.

Mental disability is also characteristic of other representatives of the threatening object: for example, *gosdura* is a mocking nomination of Gos**duma**[30] (phonetic pun): the word *Duma* is derived from the verb *dumat'* (to think) and sarcastically changed into *dura* (a fool (fem.)). The next passage sarcastically emphasizes this feature when an action seen as foolish is done by 'wonderful' people (prototypical irony):

(28) **Еті прекрасниє люді** *вчора прийняли в третєм і окончатєльном чтєнії закон, запрещающій россіянам хранить свої персональниє данниє за рубєжом!*

Yesterday, these wonderful people [Russian MPs] passed a law in the third and last reading which forbids Russians to keep their personal data abroad!

The sarcastic expression of the mental disability of the target of humour is found here:

(29) *Тєм временєм,* **Москва радосно сообщає**, *шо в Росії пойман український* **супершпіон** *Роман Сущенко, который* **притворяючись** *французьким журналістом* **викрив** *усі секрети Кремля,* **внєдрився** *у росгвардію і* **здобув** *точні свєдєнія, шо Путін – Хуйло. При чому зробив це все находясь в отпуске, в качествє хобі, для душі*

Meanwhile, **Moscow happily reports** that a Ukrainian **superspy** Roman Sushchenko[31] has been caught in Russia; **pretending** to be a French journalist, he **infiltrated** the Russian armed forces, **exposed** all Kremlin secrets and **got** precise information that Putin is Huylo. Moreover, he did it while on vacation, as a hobby, for the fun of it.

The passage contains a set of sarcastic exaggerating expressions, such as 'superspy', 'pretending', 'infiltrated', 'exposed secrets', 'did it as a hobby'; catching this man is depicted as a victory of Russia which reports about it happily. The 'obvious' secret exposed by the Ukrainian 'spy' is also ridiculed.

4.2.3 Aggressiveness

Bullying is getting more and more attention as a form of abusive behaviour in different social groups, and it is considered a crime in many countries. The author metaphorically transfers this model of abnormal behaviour to the sphere of international relations when a country with powerful military potential treats others in an aggressive way:

(30) *Світові відмінники згуртувалися для серйозної відсічі ізвесному* **хуліґану** *і двойошнику Хуйлу, який взяв собі за моду теорізірувать маленькіх*
The world's straight-A students gathered to stand up to a well-known hooligan and F student Huylo, who got used to terrorizing the weak.

Here, the leader of a powerful country is humorously compared to a school bully and opposed by a consolidated group of good guys. Unworthy behaviour towards smaller and weaker countries like Ukraine makes humorous metaphoric nominations of this kind possible (the attribute *izvesnyj* (well-known) also hints at repetitive bullying and reminds us of the annexation of Georgian and Moldovan territories).

Furthermore, this type of mindset results in the belief in having an exclusive right to act aggressively, which is stigmatized as characteristic of criminals:

(31) *svâto свято уверовал в ефективність чотирьохчленного алгоритму:*
'*приезд – наезд – откат – от'езд*'
he has got sacred faith that a four-step algorithm '*come-hit-payoff-run*' *is effective.*

The linguistic representation of this abnormal feature is a combination of the Church-Slavonic verbal form *uveroval* (had sacred faith) and the Russian transliteration of a criminal slang expression '*prijezd – najezd – otkat – otjezd*'. The mocking effect is produced by wordplay with lexis from different stylistic registers. Putin's narcissism and semblance of God is reflected in the use of stylistically coloured lexis of high register, on the one hand; on the other, he is described as a criminal whose behavioural pattern is verbalized by low register lexemes.

4.2.4 Loneliness and misery

The president who is getting older but trying to look very manly, who divorced his wife and hides his personal life from the public, multiplies reasons for rumours and ridicule, so he is called *plûgavyj mačo* (shabby macho) or *lysyj starikaška na arênê cyrka* (a bald geezer on the circus arena), drawing attention to the discrepancy between his age and efforts to hide it.

Following the tradition of Ukrainian classics, Did Svyryd artfully blends fear, humour and pity for the object of fear. In our opinion, this strategy helps reduce fear – the higher the level of pity, the lower the fear:

(32) *А сначала обратим вніманіє, шо Хуйла* ***дето тоже можна понять*** *– його ніхто не любить, ніхто йому не вірить і всерйоз його слова ніхто*

*не воспринімає. Він стоїть посреді трясіни, **одін, голий і жалкий**. Болото його постепенно засмоктує, комарі дошкульно і больно кусають, а сліпні безстижо ссуть кров. **Но горде Хуйло** по-прежнєму **старається ізлучать уверенность**, хотя получається все хуже і хуже*

*But first let's pay attention to the fact that **Huylo can also be understood somehow – nobody loves him, nobody believes him or takes his words seriously**. He is standing in the middle of the bog, **lonely, naked and miserable**. He is being sucked into the bog, mosquitoes are biting him violently, and horseflies are sucking his blood. **But proud Huylo is still trying to show self-confidence**, although it is becoming more and more difficult.*

Incongruity as the logical basis of sarcasm as the mechanism of mockery is fully revealed in this passage. First, the sarcastic effect is achieved by the use of oxymoron *proud Huylo* that reveals a paradoxical combination of qualities in the object of ridicule; here the author uses opposing attributes *naked and miserable* VC *proud* to emphasize it. Second, extreme hyperbolization by means of repeated negation is aimed at maximizing the inadequate self-perception of the target. Moreover, repetitive use of the pronoun *nobody* opposed to *he* shows contrast and stresses Putin's loneliness. Metaphoric representation of current political events as a bog emphasizes the whole absurdity of the situation when a person refuses to admit that he is wrong and his further actions that only make the situation worse are worded by Continuous tense forms to show continuity and development (*is being sucked into* – *is still trying*). I may also suggest that international criticism and implementation of sanctions is metaphorically expressed as violent bites of mosquitoes and horseflies.

4.2.5 *Non-democratic character*

Another feature of the target of ridicule – lack of democracy – reveals the basic ideological difference between Russia and Ukraine. To outline this difference and distance from the frightening object, the author shows his strong disapproval of this trait by naming Russia *Moskvabad*, *Hujlostan* and *Zaporêbrik*. The first two imply the Asian tradition of state building (compare, *Afghanistan, Pakistan, Islamabad*, etc.). The nominations *Moskvabad* and *Hujlostan* are perceived as mocking due to a morphological pun and the use of a profanity; *Zaporêbrik* is a result of holophrasal compounding.[32]

The blog texts contain notions of notorious Russian ideas like the 'Russian world'. 'Russian world' is an ideologeme rooted in the nineteenth-century Russian ultra-nationalist movements that aimed at uniting vast conquered territories under the Russian Empire; later, it became the dominant political doctrine to unite these territories as a monolithic orthodox Russian-speaking world. The phrase 'Russian world' (in Examples 33–35) is intentionally and sarcastically used in Surzhyk to form a logical malapropism based on the homonymy of two Russian nouns, *mir* (world) and *mir* (peace).[33] The sarcasm may be rendered as 'the Russian world is not peace' (e.g. *oskal russkogo mira* or the grin of the Russian world): the author implies that nations that agree to live in accord with 'Russian world' are endangered. Intentional use of the stylistically marked lexeme *oskal* (grin) hints at the predatory nature of Russia. This cultural-historical background finds its realization in nominations like *a crystal dream*, mocking at the unlikeliness of its realization and the non-democratic character of this Russian set of mind:

(33) *хрустальна мечта по созданію* **'*русского міра*'**
a crystal dream about the **'*Russian world*'** *creation.*

Non-democratic and old-fashioned ideology is stigmatized as *bigotry* by Did Svyryd; he mocks at the persistence of Russia to pursue the aim of world domination on the lexical and syntactic levels, using the metaphor *to stand up from its knees* in a generic-impersonal sentence (the type existing in the Ukrainian language system):

(34) **мракобесіє** *на теми геополітіки і* **великаго русскаго міра,** *якому* **не дають приподніматься с колєн**
bigotry *when considering geopolitical topics and the* **great Russian world that is not allowed to stand up from its knees.**

Mocking is maximized with orthographic puns (in Example 34) *velìkago russkago* (great Russian), or *velìk ì vsêmoguŝ* (great and powerful), where the spelling and word forms typical of the eighteenth–nineteenth century hint at the imperialistic roots of Russia and at its divinity and blessing. The grotesque pathos (in Examples 33–35) sounds sarcastic when applied to the pitiful humanitarian state of Lugansk and Donetsk: in the modern Russian-speaking world, these grammatical forms are used mostly in religious services:

(35) *пребывая у* **благости од епохальной победи русскаго міра** *в отдєльно взятих районах Луганської і Донєцкой областєй*
being in **a divine trance from an epochal victory of the 'Russian world'** *in individual parts of Lugansk and Donetsk regions.*

Lack of democracy and appropriation of an exclusive role in the world politics is sarcastically actualized in the phrases *spasìtêl' ì mirotvorêc'* (saviour and peacemaker) and *mêčtatêlì o mìrovom gospodstvê* (dreamers about world supremacy), as well as in the frequent use of derivatives of the lexeme *vêra* (belief):

(36) **уверенность,** *шо Господь Бог йому шото должен*
confidence *that God owes him something;*

(37) *окончатєльно* **уверовали** *в свою 'звізду'*
have **got faith** *in their 'star'.*

Taking into account the number of war conflicts Russia is involved in, the sarcasm is revealed through logical malapropism that shows the inadequacy of the President's ambitions.

5 Conclusion

The pragmatics of non-violent humorous resistance to actual fear in blog texts of post-Maidan and at-war Ukraine finds its realization in the exemplary blog texts by Did Svyryd. The analysis of the texts of Did Svyryd Opanasovich's blogs revealed that ridicule is a commonly used discursive strategy. In the blog under study, it serves the function of non-violent political and social resistance. The examples presented in this chapter reiterate the previously noted functions of ridicule as facilitating solidarity in opposing the enemy, mobilizing like-minded people, stigmatizing the opponent, restoring order and reducing fear. Ridicule highlights the abnormality of the target.

The research presented here has led to the following conclusions:

(1) The communicative basis of ridicule of the target object in the analysed blog texts is based on the opposition of a norm and a deviation from it. It emphasizes the difference between the behaviour of ridiculed characters and the normal expectations of civilized behaviour of a country or people and of its leader. The abnormality of the target of ridicule is revealed in the following characteristics:

   a. Unmanly personality and treacherousness;
   b. Mental disability and unpredictability;
   c. Aggressiveness;
   d. Loneliness and misery;
   e. Non-democratic character.

(2) The linguistic-pragmatic mechanism of actualizing ridicule is irony and/or sarcasm. These mechanisms are activated in various ways at different language levels via specific linguistic means of creating a humorous effect. At the phonetic level, the author practices phonetic and orthographic puns. The lexical level is the most intensively used in verbalizing the enemy's abnormality. The profanity *hujlo* triggers the ridicule; later the author derives other nominations of the object of fear to render the shades of irony and sarcasm (immaturity and unmanly character). Dehumanization and understatement are the means of mocking at the key figures in Russian politics; animalistic metaphors and personification help mark the objects of ridicule as treacherous or dependent, create intentional emotional effect; or compliment the appearance and skills of Ukrainian allies. Other stylistic means like hyperbolization, oxymoron and shifts in register and language floating allow the author to toy with senses expressing false pathos. The use of clichés and ideologemes help the author create the objective mage of the enemy tying it up with Russian historical-cultural background. The grammatical level presents examples of puns, the use of multiple negation, emphatic end-position of meaningful elements, comparative constructions and generic-impersonal sentences. In addition to all this, we observed pragmatic implications that resulted in prototypical irony, echoing sarcasm and logical malapropism.

(3) These texts and the extra-lingual factors that motivated their production make it possible to outline the main intentional implications of the author's influence on the readers: to emphasize the abnormality of the threatening object, delegitimize it and distance oneself from it; to minimize the actual threatening effect and provide psychological comfort and support for the like-minded people in at-war and post-Maidan Ukraine; and to unite the people in their resistance to the invader. The pragmatic means of this intentional influence are the personality of the author (a respectable and credible elderly commoner), the epistolary-like structure of the blog texts that makes the author–readers communication more friendly and confidential. The analysis shows a pitiful and merciful attitude even to a threatening object, which is traditional for Ukrainian culture. As a result, the emotional colouring of the blog texts is that of ridicule and disgust blended with pity.

Notes

1 Maidan (*square* in Ukrainian) – the central square in Kyiv (its full name is Maidan Nezalezhnostі) that became the centre of popular resistance to Yanukovych's regime in 2013-2014. It is an old Ukrainian tradition to gather on the central square to elect local leaders by voting or solve other problems that require unity in decision.
2 OWS (Occupy Wall Street) – a left-wing movement against economic inequality.
3 Otpor (*resistance* in Serbian) – a popular movement against Milošević's regime.
4 Zapatista is an extreme-left socialist movement in Mexico.
5 Gezi Park events – a civil protest in Turkey in 2013, held in Gezi Park in Taksim Square, Istanbul, against government interference with secularism, freedom of the press, and so on.
6 Ivan Vyshenskyi (1550-1621) – a Ukrainian religious leader, an orthodox monk, a polemicist.
7 Les Podervianskyi, Ivan Semesyuk – contemporary Ukrainian writers.
8 As the Repka Club website is not accessible anymore, we rely on texts at forum. durdom.in.ua and espreso.tv/blogs/author/opanasovych_spiridon/.
9 The personal names *Svyryd* (Ukr. *Свирид*) and *Opanas* (Ukr. *Опанас*) were popular in Ukraine before the Second World War, but they are rare nowadays – in this way, the blogger is associated with wisdom that goes far back in centuries. Out of this context, the lexeme *did* (Ukr. *дід*) is used to identify or address a male elderly person; here, it is a part of the character's personal name.
10 See https://www.pravda.com.ua/news/2019/02/20/7207175/ and https://www.pravda.com.ua/news/2019/01/29/7205183/.
11 This and further translations are mine; they render the content of the utterance.
12 https://dic.academic.ru/dic.nsf/dic_synonims/267627/%D1%85%D1%83%D0%B9%D0%BB%D0%BE%BE
13 https://dic.academic.ru/dic.nsf/proverbs/10269/%D0%A7%D0%9C%D0%9E%9E
14 Lavrov is the Russian Minister of Foreign Affairs.
15 Skomorokh (En.*doofus*) – an actor and a musician in the East Slavonic culture of the 11th -17th centuries. 'Settled' actors served in aristocratic families to entertain the master's family and his guests. These actors could breach the boundaries of the norm

and decency; they sometimes expressed problematic issues in the artistic form of various performances.

16 About a Ukrainian woman-deputy N. Savchenko (Tsaruk 2018).
17 Taras Shevchenko about the Russian tsarina in his poem (Shevchenko 1844).
18 The word *têlo* (Rus) / *tilo* (Ukr.) (body) is of neuter gender and is substituted by the pronoun *ono* / *vono* (it).
19 Verka Serdiuchka (Andriy Danylko) – a well-known male comedy actor, singer and composer. His most successful image is a middle-aged woman, a common sleeping car attendant Verka. She speaks Surzhyk. In Europe, he is known for his participation in Eurovision 2007, where he took second place.
20 Samantha Power – United States Ambassador to the United Nations from 2013 to 2017.
21 Херня [her´nia] – an incredible thing or fact or idea.
22 Sergey Shoygu – the current Russian Minister of Defense.
23 This is a reference to the first cases of Russian soldiers imprisoned in the Ukrainian territory. It is an indirect quotation of Vladimir Putin's words.
24 *Бздіти* is a vulgarism meaning 'to fart' or 'to be afraid of'.
25 Public opinion of modern Ukraine divides into two trends called 'betrayal – victory'. dominated in the first years of war and is still quite influential in the society. According to the former ('betrayal') point of view, all failures or non-resultative actions of the representatives of any governmental institution or anything that is non-consistent with the public opinion are suspected of 'betrayal' and labelled in this way (mind that it is a metaphorical expression that has nothing to do with real traitors). The latter attitude ('victory') represents the set of mind of those who see positive changes and effective steps forward and emphasize that everything might have been worse.
26 The reference is made to the clichéd phrases of V. Putin and the Ministry of Foreign Affairs in response to each case of sanctions from EU or USA.
27 Kremlin (Rus. Кремль) – the official residence of Russian presidents in Moscow.
28 Normandy Contact Group – a diplomatic group of senior representatives of four countries (Germany, France, Ukraine and Russia) created to resolve the war conflict in Eastern Ukraine; in this context, the phrase refers to three of its members (except for Russia).
29 Colorado plague – a metaphoric expression referring to the symbol of anti-Maidan, a striped ribbon of orange and black colour which resembles Leptinotarsa decemlineata, or a Colorado potato beetle.
30 Gosduma (Gosudarstvennaya Duma) – the lower house of the Federal Assembly of Russia as it is commonly abbreviated in Russian.
31 Roman Sushchenko – a Ukrainian journalist kept in captivity in Russia.
32 The word *Zaporêbrik* appeared when the Web showed the first days of the Russian invasion in Eastern Ukraine, when one of the soldiers without any insignia ('a green man') cried out to the locals, *Za porêbrik otojdi!* (Step behind the curb!). The word *porêbrik* marked him as a bearer of the lingual culture which was not characteristic of either Ukrainian-speaking or Russian-speaking Ukrainians, especially if pronunciation is taken into account ([par`´ebr`ik]) (the discussion can be found here https://rus.stackexchange.com/questions/32507/%D0%A3%D0%BA%D1%80%D0%B0%D0%B8%D0%BD%D1%81%D0%BA%D0%B8%D0%B9-%D0%BF%D0%BE%D1%80%D0%B5%D0%B1%D1%80%D0%B8%D0%BA).
33 In Ukrainian, *world* is *світ (svit)*, and *peace* is *мир (myr)*.

References

Attardo, S., Eisterhold, J., Hay, J. and Poggi, I. (2003), 'Multimodal Markers of Irony and Sarcasm', *Humor: International Journal of Humor Research*, 16 (2): 243–60.
Balaban, U. (2015), 'Vernacular Utopias: Mimetic Performances as Humour in Gezi Park and on Bayındır Street', in A. Yalcintas (ed.), *Occupy Movements: Intellectual Disobedience in Turkey and Beyond*, 48–74. London: Palgrave Pivot.
Berger, P. L. (1997), *Redeeming Laughter: The Comic Dimension of Human Experience*. Berlin and New York: Walter de Gruyter.
Bergson, H. (2005), *Laughter: An Essay on the Meaning of the Comic*. Mineola and New York: Dover Publications, Inc.
Bilaniuk, L. (1997), 'Speaking of "Surzhyk": Ideologies and Mixed Languages', in *Harvard Ukrainian Studies*, 21 (1/2): 93–117.
Bilaniuk, L. (2005), *Contested Tongues: Language Politics and Cultural Correction in Ukraine*. Ithaca and London: Cornell University Press.
Billig, M. (2005), *Laughter and Ridicule: Towards a Social Critique of Humour*. Thousand Oaks, CA: Sage Publications.
Braga, I. (2012), 'Surzhyk u sociolingvistychnomu vimiri' ['Surzhyk in the Sociolinguistic Dimension'], in *Visnyk Zaporizkogo nacionalnogo universitetu. Filologichni nauky*, 1: 82–7.
Cap, P. (2017), *The Language of Fear: Communicating Threat in Public Discourse*. Basingstoke: Palgrave.
Day, A. (2011), *Satire and Dissent: Interventions in Contemporary Political Debate*. Bloomington: Indiana University Press.
Dynel, M. (2018), *Irony, Deception and Humour: Seeking the Truth about Overt and Covert Untruthfulness*. Berlin, Munich and Boston: Walter de Gruyter GmbH.
Efremova, T. (2000), *Sovremennyi tolkovyi slovar russkogo yazyka* [*Modern Russian Language Dictionary*]. Available online: https://dic.academic.ru/dic.nsf/efremova/136432/%D0%BE%D0%BD%D1%8B%D1%88 (accessed 18 November 2018).
Eriksson, G. (2015), 'Ridicule as a Strategy for the Recontextualization of the Working Class', in *Critical Discourse Studies*, 12 (1): 20–38.
Gibbs, R. and Izett, C. (2005), 'Irony as Persuasive Communication', in H. Colston and A. Katz (eds), *Figurative Language Comprehension: Social and Cultural Influences*, 131–52. Mahwah, NJ: Erlbaum.
Hageseth III, C. (1988), *A Laughing Place: The Art and Psychology of Positive Humour in Love and Adversity*. Fort Collins, CO: Berwick.
Haugerud, A. (2013), *No Billionaire Left Behind: Satirical Activism in America*. Stanford, CA: Stanford University Press.
Hetzron, R. (1991), 'On the Structure of Punchlines', in *Humor: International Journal of Humor Research*, 4 (1): 1–108.
Hof van het, S. D. (2015), 'Political Potential of Sarcasm: Cynicism in Civil Resentment', in A. Yalcintas (ed.), *Occupy Movements: Intellectual Disobedience in Turkey and Beyond*, 30–47. London: Palgrave Pivot.
Humennyi, D. (2011), *Selo. Evolyuciya (8-y poverh)* [*Village. Evolution (the 8th floor)*], Available online: http://teatre.com.ua/ukrdrama/selo-evoljutsija-8-jpoverx-nadsja-dengumennyj/ (accessed 18 November 2018).
Hutcheon, L. (1994), *Irony's Edge: The Theory and Politics of Irony*. London and New York: Routledge.

Karpenko, O. (2014), *5 ukrainskih blogerov, virtuozno vladeyushchih Surzhikom* [*5 Ukrainian Bloggers Who Demonstrate Master Ability to Write in Surzhyk*]. Available online: https://ain.ua/2014/11/15/5-ukrainskix-blogerov-virtuozno-vladeyushhix-surzhickom (accessed 18 November 2018).

Lefcourt, H. M. (2001), 'The Humor Solution', in C. R. Snyder (ed.), *Coping with Stress: Effective People and Processes*, 68–92. New York: Oxford University Press.

Lippi-Green, R. (2012), *English with an Accent: Language, Ideology, and Discrimination in the United States*. New York: Routledge.

Norrick, N. R. (1989), 'Intertextuality in Humour', in *Humor: International Journal of Humor Research*, 2 (2): 117–40.

Oaks, D. D. (1994), 'Creating Structural Ambiguities in Humour: Getting English Grammar to Cooperate', in *Humor: International Journal of Humor Research*, 7 (4): 377–401.

Payne, R. A. (2018), 'Stigmatization by Ridicule: From Dr. Strangelove to Donald Trump', *Presentation at the Workshop on Non-Nuclear Peace*, University Centre Saint Ignatius, Antwerp (UCSIA), University of Antwerp, Belgium, 23–25 May 2018.

Raskin, V. (2017), 'Script-Based Semantic and Ontological Semantic Theories of Humor', in S. Attardo (ed.), *The Routledge Handbook of Language and Humor*, 109–25. New York and London: Routledge.

Sanders, B. (2001), *Kahkahanın Zaferi. Yıkıcı Tarih Olarak Gulme*. İstanbul: Ayrıntı.

Shevchenko, T. (1844), *Son* [*Dream*]. Available online: http://litopys.org.ua/shevchenko/shev128.htm (accessed 18 November 2018).

Sørensen, M. J. (2016), *Humour in Political Activism: Creative Nonviolent Resistance*. London, UK: Palgrave Macmillan.

Stapleton, K. (2010), 'Swearing', in Miriam A. Locher and Sage L. Graham (eds), *Interpersonal Pragmatics. Handbook of Pragmatics*, 6, 289–305. Berlin and New York: Walter de Gruyter GmbH & Co. KG.

Tsaruk, N. (2018), *Vono zh ne prosyhaje: dyvna povedinka Savchenko potrapyla v objektyv* [*It Is Never Sober: Savchenko's Strange Behaviour Recorded on Camera*]. Available online: https://znaj.ua/politics/vono-zh-ne-prosyhaye-dyvna-povedinka-savchenko-potrapyla-v-obyektyv (accessed 18 November 2018).

Velykyi tlumachnyi slovnyk ukrayinskoyi movy [*Big Ukrainian Language Dictionary*] (2005). Available online: http://irbis-nbuv.gov.ua/cgi-bin/ua/elib.exe?I21DBN=UKRLIB&P21DBN=UKRLIB&S21STN=1&S21REF=10&S21FMT=fullwebr&C21COM=S&S21CNR=20&S21P01=0&S21P02=0&S21P03=ID=&S21STR=UKR0000989 (accessed 18 November 2018).

Zhao, Y. (1987), *The Information-Conveying Aspect of Jokes*, Unpublished MA thesis, Purdue University, West Lafayette, IN.

13

Assimilative representations of Ukrainian refugees in the Russian and Ukrainian press

A 'burden' or a 'gain'?

Ludmilla A'Beckett

1 Introduction

The Western mass media are often concerned with representations of migrants who do not share their hosts' language, religion or cultural traditions. In such instances, migrants are often depicted in the press as dehumanized and deindividualized masses of aliens who can potentially destroy Western civilization (Kopytowska and Chilton 2018; 2010; Musolff 2012, 20112018; KhosraviNik, Krzyzanowski and Wodak 2012). Such constructions of images of migrants frequently rely on the use of numbers and metaphors of moving water. The dehumanized and de-individualized images evoke fear and the desire to prevent any influx of migration (cf. Musolff and Viola 2017).

Can these views prevail in situations when the host country is party to the military conflict from which the refugees are fleeing? Can such representations be consistent with the state goal to gain or to maintain political control over the disputed territory? Under circumstances in which the refugees are claimed to have some common identity with the host community, the negativization of the migrants backfires.

The military conflict in South-Eastern Ukraine ostensibly started as a dispute over the identities of the people who live in Ukrainian regions bordering on Russia. The political tensions between Russia and Ukraine triggered a separatist movement and then initiated the bloodiest conflict in Europe since Yugoslavia (Operation: Russian Federation 2017; Ukraine, Fact sheet 2017). The official narrative in both countries is that the people from these regions belong to 'our kith and kin' and, therefore, expressions of doubts about the duty of care owed to the residents of South-Eastern Ukraine are deemed inappropriate.

President of Russia Vladimir Putin persistently calls Ukrainians 'brothers', implying that Russia and Ukraine can be the one and the same nation again (Putin 2018; A'Beckett 2017: 375), while the President of Ukraine, Petro Poroshenko, assures his audience that he is 'listening' to the people from Eastern Ukraine and honours their pleas (Poroshenko listens 2014; Poroshenko 2018). Residents of Ukraine and Russia often express similar sentiments and pledge to support the escapees from the southeast of Ukraine (UNIAN 2014; Kuzmin 2014).

These persistent empathetic claims in the press can indicate that the shared ideological platform of publications about refugees from Eastern Ukraine differs from beliefs about migration expressed in the Western media. The publications in the Russian and Ukrainian media advocate humanitarianism, that is, accepting measures that legalize the status of refugees (Felberg and Saric 2017: 228; Horsti 2012). If the discourse ideology, otherwise known as microcontext (KosraviNick, Krzyzanowski and Wodak 2012: 293) changes, it is reasonable to expect a shift in interpretation of text microelements. Van Dijk (2006: 115) argues that a modification of ideological principles primarily affects the construction of self-representation images and images of incomers to the country. Even though linguists are aware of the influence of ideological orientation of texts on the meaning of microelements, the changes have not been analysed substantially.

This investigation seeks to answer the following question: If the host community has to accommodate refugees who are culturally similar or are of the same ethnic and cultural background as the hosts, would this experience have an effect on the production and understanding of discourse strategies that have been used as a tool of migrants' negativization in discourses portraying differences between hosts and migrants?

2 Migration discourse in the UK and countries of Western Europe

In this chapter, I deal with the discourse strategies which KosraviNick, Krzyzanowski and Wodak (2012) analyse in their investigation of representations of newcomers to the United Kingdom in the British press. The patterns they analyse are very common ways of portraying migrants in other countries of Western Europe, that is, in the Austrian press (Reisigle 2018; Krzyzanowski and Wodak 2008), in the Italian press (Taylor 2009), in the French press (Van der Valk 2003) and in many European countries that are on migration routes (Barlai et al. 2017).

Two approaches to the analysis of representations of migrants in the press have been used in most of the investigations. The first one draws on categories of social actors that were introduced by Van Leeuwen (1996, 2008) and Van Dijk (1987). The representation of social actors can be linked to the following semantic parameters: collectivization/individualization, personalization/impersonalization, humanization/dehumanization, passivization/activization and foregrounding/backgrounding. The analysis of agencies attributed to migrants largely involves answering the following question: How are persons and their actions named or referred to linguistically?

KosraviNick, Krzyzanowski and Wodak (2012: 289) argue that the most widespread discursive strategies in negative representation of migrants throughout the ten-year period in the British media are aggregation, collectivization and functionalization processes. These are defined as 'the linguistic processes through which these groups of people are systematically referred to and constructed as one unanimous group with all the members sharing similar characteristics, backgrounds, intentions, motivations, and economic status, or reducing these groups to their "functions", e.g. "entrants"' (2012: 289).

The aggregation is usually understood as a quantification or statistical representation of a group of participants (Van Leeuwen 2008: 37). The use of numbers and numerical references became a tool of objectivizing people, that is, of equating them with physical items undergoing an inventory. Such a presentation dehumanizes and depersonalizes migrants. This technique introduces into texts a hostile 'other' who confronts 'us' – the group of insiders.

The strategy of collectivization can be illustrated by the representation of migrants in terms of masses of moving water. The lexical manifestations of moving water are the nouns 'waves', 'tsunami', 'flow' and 'river' (Pohl and Wodak 2012: 206; Musolff 2015: 4; Van Dijk 2012: 26; Taylor 2009: 25; Kainz 2016; Schrover and Schinkel 2013). This metaphor depicts a large group of migrants sharing the same characteristics. Individual features of members of this group are hidden.

Moreover, many researchers (Musolff 2012; Pohl and Wodak 2012; Schrover and Schinkel 2013) argue that the metaphor dehumanizes migrants by presenting them as a 'liquid'. The metaphors of moving waters not only dehumanize the arriving migrants, but also attribute to them a possession of a destructive force, which either demolishes the foundation of civilization, or form a water basin in which representatives of the host community could drown (Musolff 2012; Leeuwen 2008: 58, 63; Kopytowska and Chilton 2018: 135). Thus, the collective representation becomes a powerful tool of negativization of refugees. Both collectivization and aggregation' represent the assimilative strategy that is consciously or subconsciously used to dehumanize, deindividualize and depersonalize people (Van Leeuwen 2008: 26; KosraviNick, Krzyzanowski and Wodak 2012: 283).

On the other hand, the negative representations of migrants provoke an argumentative flow, which can lead to the conclusion, 'We do not wish to accept migrants, we should stop or minimize the intake of refugees'. The analysis of argumentative schemata in discourse was launched by a Discourse Historical Approach, a branch of critical discourse analysis (Wodak and Meyer 2001). These scholars pioneered the theory of topoi, which has become a popular research tool of deconstructing chains of reasoning developed throughout texts.

The generally accepted definition of topoi suggests that topoi are the content-related warrants or conclusion rules that connect arguments with the conclusion (KosraviNick, Krzyzanowski and Wodak 2012: 287; Reisigle and Wodak 2001). The pioneers of the topoi analysis have offered a list of basic topoi, which can serve as a background for inspection of arguments in discourse (cf. Reisigle and Wodak 2001: 74–80). KosraviNick, Krzyzanowski and Wodak (2012: 291) suggest that assimilative representations of migrants are connected with '*topos of numbers* (along with the relevant metaphors such as the metaphors of 'flood' and 'disease'); *topos of economic burden* (abuse of the welfare system and expenditure); *topos of threat* (threat to cultural identity and threat to community values and violence); *topos of danger;* and *topos of law*'. These negative topoi are commonly associated with implicit decisions that 'one should act in order to diminish those problems or to counter them' (Reisigle and Wodak 2001: 76;). In the context of migration, such claims are interpreted as a prohibition or limitation of migration.

However, the mechanism of reasoning that connects the premises, that is, group representations of migrants, with the implicit claim of prohibition or limitation, has not been explained sufficiently (see criticism in Zagar 2010). For instance, problems represented as the *topos of burden* can be solved by the attraction of additional funds or charity efforts rather than through diminishing or expulsion of migrants. In other words, the generalized key idea of expenditures on migrants or economic burden can also lead to a conclusion that highlights an effective use of scarce resources by the host community rather than advocates a policy of intolerance.

In the context of Russia-Ukraine confrontation, the problems with migrants that the host societies in Russia and Ukraine face may be similar to those encountered in Western countries. However, the flow of arguments initiated by an acknowledgement of these problems seems different. For instance, KosraviNick, Krzyzanowski and Wodak (2012: 292–3) and Horsti (2012: 299) report that from time to time, the assimilative representation of refugees has been used to compliment the host community on their effort to rescue many individuals who go through a harsh ordeal. It is possible to suggest that the Russian and Ukrainian press can orient their readers towards a similar message. It can be expected that the Russian and Ukrainian media portray migrants as victims of circumstances or as people in need, whereas the host community is praised for their humanitarianism and cooperation.

3 Data

A corpus of Russian and Ukrainian publications from the mainstream media has been compiled to check the research hypothesis. Initially the data were collected through a google search that used Russian keywords such as *bežency Ukraina* (refugees Ukraine) or *pereselentcy ATO* (displaced persons *ATO*[1]). The texts were collected from 2014 to mid- 2018. The total size of the corpus is 145,388, out of which there are 78,323 words from the Russian press and 67,065 words from the Ukrainian mass media.

Among the Russian media outlets that emerged in my pilot google search there were five Russian newspapers. These are as follows: a Russian government daily newspaper *Rossiyskaya gazeta*; *Argumenty i fakty*, the weekly newspaper with the largest circulation in Russia; *Komsomolskaya pravda*, the second-largest tabloid; *Pravda.ru*, an internet newspaper that has a name similar to the broadsheet published by the Communist Party of Russia; and *Izvestia*, the biggest daily broadsheet (The Press in Russia 2008).

Among the most frequent Ukrainian hits there were two internet newspapers – *Censor.net* and *Ukrainskaja pravda*, followed by *Ukrainian Informational News Agency* (UNIAN), and *Zerkalo nedeli* – a weekly newspaper in Ukrainian, Russian and English, which is regarded as the best analytical newspaper in Ukraine (The Press in Ukraine 2006). Publications from all the above newspapers were included in the data for analysis.

Even though the official language in Ukraine is Ukrainian, many media outlets are bilingual, since Russian was and remains the language of interethnic communication (A'Beckett and David 2018). Ninety per cent of the population know Russian and many prefer reading in Russian (Pavlenko 2008). None of the selected publications mentions problems with the choice of language for communication between migrants and hosts in Ukraine. It led to an assumption that the language of publication, that is, Russian rather than Ukrainian, did not affect the contents and stances towards internally displaced people.

The juxtaposition of Russian and Ukrainian data reveals that their genres and topics are similar. The tokens 'refugees' and 'internally displaced people' frequently feature in the following genres: discussions of the conflict, interviews with state and local officials, interviews with refugees, information about hot lines and services for refugees, discussions of problems and achievements of host communities, as well as reports about criminal activities, fraud and embezzlement.

In the Russian and Ukrainian media, everyday lives of refugees and their stories became one of the central topics for discussions in the media. Contrary to this, researchers of the Western media report that 'the everyday lives of the Others are seldom portrayed in the press, even on topics that would be covered for European people' (Van Dijk 2012: 24; see also KosraviNick, Krzyzanowski and Wodak 2012: 294). Thus, there is a mismatch between the themes in the Western European press and the ones in Russia and Ukraine. At the same time, the Russian and Ukrainian media seem to express analogous concerns and appraisal, for example, mutual or reciprocal accusations of Russia and Ukraine, self-flattering comparisons with the other and the EU, as well as healing and blessings of refugees amidst members of the generous host community. Problems, disadvantages and exploitation experienced by refugees are also common topics for discussion in the press.

The role of assimilative strategies of migrant representations in all these publications is discussed in the following sections of the paper.

4 Research procedures

A set of research procedures was developed in order to investigate ideas and flows of arguments that were introduced to the texts by assimilative representations of refugees.

The first step was to locate assimilative representations in the data collected. For this purpose, a basic search for stems of the words whose meanings roughly correlate with the following English counterparts: 'million', 'thousand', 'hundred', 'number', 'digit/figure', 'quantity' and 'ten' was performed. In addition to it, the metaphors of moving water were located through the search for the Russian counterparts of the English words 'flow' and 'wave'.

In total, 241 numerical expressions in Russian and 189 numerical expressions in Ukrainian were found. However, not all expressions were relevant, as they were often used to denote money, distance, age, years, residents of the host community, frequency and so on. On the other hand, several numerical expressions about refugees could relate to one and the same argument or, on the contrary, a single numerical expression could underscore different considerations. Such instances contradicted the expectation that each numerical expression corresponds to a single argumentative pattern. Hence, the decision was made to focus solely on a qualitative analysis and use extensive contexts.

As for numbers of 'masses of water' metaphors, overall, 28 'waves' were found in the Russian data and 19 'waves' in the Ukrainian data. 34 'flows' were found in the Ukrainian texts and 33 in the Russian texts. All 114 occurrences were analysed in order to establish whether this conceptualization induced negativization and dehumanization of migrants. Arguments and inferences were compared with those offered by KosraviNick, Krzyzanowski and Wodak (2012) and Musolff (2012).

For the study of numerical expressions, fifty randomly selected passages from the Russian share of the corpus and fifty from the Ukrainian share were taken. Thereafter, common co-occurrences of nouns with numbers were established. Among popular numerical co-occurrences the following emerged: *X number of / people / Ukrainians / residents of Y place / arrivals / entrants / refugees / displaced persons / compatriots*.

Superficially, the samples contained many similarities with patterns discussed by Van Leeuwen (1996: 208) and KosraviNick, Krzyzanowski and Wodak (2012: 289), as the scholars regarded references to people via notification on their residential status as a form of objectification, dehumanization and functionalization of migrants (see Section 2). Nevertheless, several reasons can be given why these Russian and Ukrainian examples are not exactly a manifestation of dehumanization.

First, when the extended context of numerical expressions was explored, it was found that the initial numerical reference to refugees was followed by a further characterization, for example, specification of age, gender, profession and other personal traits in subsequent parts of texts. Second, grammatical features of the Russian language position these nouns in the class of animate beings. The system of endings in the plural form of the words suggests an animate status of their referent. Furthermore, the aggregate representations of migrants in such instances introduce topics that convey empathy to refugees. Basically, the collective references were often used as evidence of a humanitarian catastrophe.

The next stage of analysis required identification of ideas supported by or illustrated by numerical elements. A textual pattern was recognized on occasion when at least five examples from both Russian and Ukrainian data emerged. The main ideas represented in a group of patterns were named as follows: (a) humanitarian crisis and allotment of responsibility for the tragedy; (b) testimony of humanitarianism of the host community; (c) critiques of public offices and authority; and (d) numbers as a basis for comparison. The names of these textual patterns were used as headings of sections in which findings were presented.

Lastly, a check for consistency of the examples with negative topoi of burden, threat and numbers was performed. Findings were presented and discussed in further sections.

5 Allotment of responsibility for the humanitarian catastrophe

The most common inference or conclusion induced by numerical elements in the material under study is that the armed conflict has reached epic proportions and endangers neighbouring countries or even humanity as a whole. In the Russian press, the numbers of casualties and refugees testify to the necessity of the Russian intervention and thus justify the Russian support of rebels. The Ukrainian press focuses on the role of Russian revanchist aspirations in disrupting the peace in Post-Soviet countries. The human tragedy is unfolded in front of the readers who can see the scale of the disaster and are 'invited' to agree with authors and 'their' suggestions for the conflict resolution.

(1) **1.2 million Ukrainians**[2] arrived in our country because of the Kiev-launched war in the Donbass. 'In general, the share of Ukrainian citizens is more than half of the **total number** of compatriots [Russophone people from countries which were the Soviet Republics before – L.A.] who have arrived in Russia', the Russian Foreign Minister observes. Kiev launched the military operation against the self-proclaimed Donetsk and Luhansk People's Republics in April 2014. According to the UN, during this time more than **eight thousand people** became victims of the conflict ... The Russian authorities made an exception for refugees from the Donbass (RP 1).[3]

(2) According to Vitaly Muzychenko, director of the Social Protection Department of the Ministry of Social Policy, as of today, more than **900 thousand** people have left the Ukrainian territories occupied by Russia. 'We say that the **number of the ... immigrants** will increase very rapidly as soon as the aggression [**quantity of aggression** – in the original, L.A.] intensifies,' Muzychenko said (UP 1).

In Example 1, the Russian foreign Minister Sergei Lavrov accuses Ukraine for unleashing violence, whereas in Example 2, the Ukrainian representative of the Ministry of Social Policy, Vitaly Muzychenko, blames Russia for fuelling the conflict. In fact, many statements about numbers of refugees serve the communicative purpose of pinning the blame on the adversary. Numbers serve as an instrument of conveying objective information about the conflict. Big numbers testify to the level of suffering and misery caused by the enemy. Compare Examples 3 and 4.

(3) According only to official data, about **1.3 million Ukrainian refugees** have already moved in, but their actual number is, of course, much larger. What are these people running from? From the 'dignity' that was brought to the Maidan? Or rather, from poverty, war, lack of hope for the future and rulers who have become the laughingstock of the whole world? Following two recent years, the new government brought its people only social and economic problems and the war in the southeast, where some citizens of Ukraine shoot at other citizens of Ukraine (RP 2).

(4) At around 9:40, during the withdrawal of refugees from the settlements of Gryaschevatoe and Novosvetlovka, the militants struck with a massive attack using mortars and rocket artillery against this column. ... As a result, there are a **large number of casualties**. People burned right in the cars that they were taken in ... **This column of refugees** was led out by our command so as to avoid

human casualties. Because in those cities there are intensive hostilities ... The **exact number of casualties** is still unknown (UP 2).

It transpires from these examples that the aggregate presentation of people does not deprive them of their human essence. People suffer in large numbers and the party that caused this suffering is held responsible. Both countries assume that they have a responsibility to take care of the refugees and thus make all possible concessions to them. The acceptance of refugees is not negotiable. The hosts show that they are a humane society that treats the suffering of other people as their own. The common message is that the problems with refugees can be solved only if the conflict is extinguished. Russia and Ukraine, however, view the way to achieve peace differently.

6 Numbers as a testimony of the humanitarianism

When discussed in the Western media, the use of numbers in references to refugees often triggers the *topos* of *economic burden*, which is shown as state expenditures or abuses of the welfare system (Wodak and Van Dijk 2000; KosraviNick, Krzyzanowski and Wodak 2012). Massive expenditures and fraudulent schemes are discussed in the Russo-Ukrainian data as well. However, these topics do not necessarily cause a negativization of migrants or lead to a conclusion that acceptance of refugees should be minimized. Quite often, the discussion of expenditures on masses of displaced people leads to praising the efficiency of the host community as well as the willingness of the people to donate their financial resources and possessions to the newcomers.

(5) When we are told that a **million Ukrainian refugees** are now in Russia, this **figure** does not fit in the mind, and many do not believe it. However, neither Russian nor Western experts have any doubt that this **grandiose figure** is close to reality. But it is hard to imagine how many human tragedies there are, how many helpless old people, children, disabled ... They all need a roof over their heads, food, medical assistance, and no one, thank God, has stayed outside. I repeat: The Federal Migration Service reported the other day that Russia accepted a bit more than **a million refugees** from the south-east of Ukraine ... I made a comforting conclusion for myself: in Russia, it's not so bad with humanity as we, the journalists, write (RP 3).

(6) Railway workers continue to take away people from the dangerous territory of the East of Ukraine on trains. In particular, on 7 August, **100 children** were transported free of charge from the city of Yasinovataya to Odessa. They were orphans; children from large and low-income families. Over this period, more than **285 thousand passengers** were transported from the Donetsk region and the Luhansk region. Railway workers efficiently fulfilled all orders received from inter-regional headquarters (UP 3).

Examples 5 and 6 show the praise for 'caring and protecting people'. Big numbers, such as 'a million', are impressive and commendable on their own; nevertheless, an explicit statement of praise for humanitarianism was added. When the numbers are not so big, they can be 'embellished' with individualization of migrants in terms of 'orphans', 'children' and 'low-income families', which add more respect for the humanitarianism displayed. It should be noted that none of the statements with numerical elements in Russo-Ukrainian discourse lead to the conclusion that is common in the Western press: 'The numbers speak for themselves! We can't afford many more intakes of people' (see KosraviNick, Krzyzanowski and Wodak 2012: 290).

Reports of authorities is another common 'genre' featuring different ranges of numbers and expressing pride for the actions of the hosts. In such reports, the authorities usually present their 'achievements' in a positive light, state multiple facts and share concerns. Public officials also reflect on difficulties they overcome and usually express a readiness to meet new challenges.

(7) According to the premier, almost five thousand **refugees** from the South-East of Ukraine have arrived on the peninsula (Crimea-L.A.). People are placed in resorts and children's camps. In addition, many refugees are accommodated free of charge in the private sector at the expense of the patrons. At the same time, the authorities promised that they would do everything possible to accommodate and feed people fleeing from the war (RP 4).

(8) Over the past year, the **number of migrants** from the occupied territories receiving pensions has increased by **80 thousand**. This was announced on Radio Liberty by the Minister of Social Policy of Ukraine Andrei Reva, 'To say that the government creates obstacles and does not allow people to receive pensions is at least incorrect,' the minister stressed. According to him, in total almost **570 thousand internally displaced persons** receive pensions (UP 4).

Examples 7 and 8 show that the numbers in reports of public officials certify efficiency of their work. By no means can the numbers and the increases in expenditures be interpreted here as a matter of economic burden that needs to be diminished or eliminated. Even when there are explicit indications that caring for migrants puts strain on state capacities, arguments are put forward as to how the facilities and services can be improved without additional expenses.

(9) According to the UN, there are already more than **one million of such people** in Ukraine. These people have lost everything. They lost their jobs and their housing was either destroyed or degraded. It goes without saying that the state, which is currently in a quandary, will not be able to provide everyone with work and housing. However, it is necessary to start small, or create a special body or an authorized person for immigrants, like in Georgia where, with **250 thousand refugees**, a whole ministry was created with a state programme and international assistance. In addition, there are a number **of measures** to help immigrants that need to be carried out and which do not require skyrocketing financial injections (UP 5).

In many other articles, speakers appeal to volunteers, patrons and sponsors to improve conditions for migrants and relieve the humanitarian crisis. The strategy of victimization, that is, showing migrants in a sympathetic light has been deployed frequently. The adopted strategy can hardly be seen as a carrier of the negative topoi. On the contrary, it allows authors to communicate achievements and expectations in accommodating refugees in the community.

7 Criticism of authorities

Van Dijk (2012: 24) comments that the Western press does not reflect much on the conduct of the host society towards immigrants, such as prejudice or lack of hospitality. As for the Russo-Ukrainian discourse, a multitude of texts can be found that criticize authorities for the lack of hospitality, coupled with inefficiency, rather than prejudice. Voices of refugees describing particular problems with their hosts are also present in the discourse. But the most unpleasant facts about the host communities are exposed by the neighbouring country, for example, Russia would criticize Ukraine and vice versa.

Here are some samples of internal criticism when the state authorities are questioned and denounced:

(10) 'So where do **500–900 thousand fake** migrants come from? You did not learn yesterday about the existence of "pension tourism". Your employees did not issue certificates, did not register **people**, for almost two years turned a blind eye to the scheme of paying pensions .... Before the March remittance, when, as you said, all mistakes will be eliminated, families and children need to live somehow.' (UP 6)

(11) [A list of the Federal Migration Service] does not indicate which work they invite refugees to, and the conditions of their housing are generally blurred. It is clear, in general, that they do not have anything good in terms of housing. And they will live in about the same way as other migrant workers live with us – packs of them in basements. Why then invite them to 49 Russian regions? I think the governors were ordered from above, they saluted to their superiors, 'We will let them go, and then we'll see' ... No one has any idea what awaits those **hundreds of thousands of refugees** in the vast spread of their new homeland (RP 5).

The questions from the public and journalists do not point at the ultimate impossibility of hosting migrants. They are meant to expose the inefficient ways which bureaucrats adopted dealing with the problems of refugees. Russian and Ukrainian journalists, unlike their Western counterparts, do not argue that their countries cannot cope with such problems and do not advocate for stopping the intake of refugees from the conflict zone. Instead, they point out areas neglected by bureaucrats. Again, the use of numbers cannot be interpreted as a tool of dehumanization and negativization since the basic needs of a large group of people are highlighted.

8 Numbers as a basis for comparison

Another popular technique of the journalists is the use of numbers referring to people for comparing their country to the others. Most often this comparison is more favourable for the country of publication. Russians argue that Ukrainians are cruel when they deal with the needs of their compatriots. Ukrainians show how unhospitable Russia is in relation to the people who have lost their homes because of Russian aggression. Both countries draw a flattering comparison between their own attitudes towards refugees and the EU handling of migrant crises. Numbers play an important role here as the presented proportion always looks flattering compared to the 'minuscule' problems of the other.

(12) **Hundreds of thousands of people** left their homes and became refugees. Most of the refugees from Donetsk and Lugansk are seeking salvation from the war in Russia. And we have repeatedly published reports from the camps on the border of the Rostov region. But there are those who decided not to leave Ukraine and left for other parts of the Independent country [a Russian ironical name for Ukraine – L.A.]. How do they live there? About a **hundred refugees** settled in Nikopol ,... One of these days ,... four drunken men came and began shouting 'Glory to Ukraine!' And 'Where are the separatists here? We will sort them out!' A 15-year-old guy ... asked them not to scream, so the hooligans grabbed him by the neck and nearly strangled him. Well, what kind of 'terrorists' can be there if only women and children are living in that place ... Their native Kiev is not happy to host their refugees ... (RP 6).

(13) About **two hundred immigrants** from Ukraine were misinformed and found themselves in a difficult situation in Yakutia: without documents, practically without money, without work and without clear prospects on the eve of a harsh winter. Before being sent there, the Federal Migration Service staff provided the displaced people with false information that the Sakha Republic is among the regions where the programme of support for the voluntary relocation of compatriots living abroad is being implemented. The programme provides a number **of benefits** ... However, after arriving in Yakutia, it turned out that the programme does not work in Yakutia. 'Our republic is not included in that list, on the contrary, we have a law in place that helps those who want to leave the territory of the Far North,' says the Vice-Premier of the Republic (UP 7).

Examples 12 and 13 demonstrate that problems of refugees in a neighbouring country have been highlighted and contrasted against the excellent conditions in the country of publication. The neighbours cannot cope with even a small number of people while their own country deals with a more intense flow of newcomers. Each country considers its citizens to be more sympathetic to the misfortunes of other people.

At the same time, the numbers do not look flattering for the EU, which allegedly has more resources and experience.

(14) And if you compare [a million of Ukrainians in Russia] ... In the European Union, for example, there are now disputes about how to distribute only **40 thousand Africans** among their countries. At one time I had the opportunity to attend a PACE meeting in Strasbourg, when the issue of refugees from Africa was discussed. They arrive in fragile boats, hide in the holds of ships, and drown in masses. The terrible numbers of the dead were heard, and international conventions and European values came to mind. But representatives of prosperous countries stubbornly did not agree to accept 'extra' people (RP 3).

It is possible to see that the use of numbers does not lead to the objectification of refugees. Instead, more nuanced arguments and mental pathways were built in the Russian and Ukrainian press with the help of the assimilative strategy.

9 Collective representation of refugees as 'masses of moving water'

Section 2 showed that in Western discourses, metaphors of masses of water function as a manifestation of dehumanization of migrants since 'liquidity does not even belong to the realm of living beings' (Pohl and Wodak 2012: 206). However, not all analogies with inanimate objects are unflattering, for example=, 'Juliet is the sun' or 'A mighty fortress is our God' (Gluksberg and Keysar 1993: 415), and not all metaphoric comparisons with humans are complimentary, for example, 'Ivan the Terrible' or 'Ivan Demjanjuk', who was a sadistic guard at the Treblinka death camp during WW2 (Gluksberg and Keysar 1993: 409). In Russo-Ukrainian discourse, some intertextual metaphors, which refer to social organizations and roles of people in such organization, for example, 'fascists', 'Nazi', 'chasteners' and 'junta' (A'Beckett 2019: 282), are more stigmatizing than the notorious 'water movement' metaphors.

When we analyse 'waves' and 'flows', which acquired the sinister reputation of indicating an imminent 'flood' and ultimate 'destruction' (Musolff 2015: 45; Felberg and Saric 2017: 237; Taylor 2009: 25–26; Kainz 2016), it is probably worth taking the view that the scene of the destruction is not so much a fixed assumption, but rather an entailment which can be overridden or eliminated by context. By entailment I understand this to be the rich encyclopedic knowledge or complex of features that can be evoked by the metaphoric vehicle or source domain, but which is not always fully projected onto the topic or target domain (Kovesces 2002: Chapter 8).

For instance, there is a tradition in Russian culture of referring to the three waves of Russian migration to the West. In many contexts, descriptions of these three waves of migration in English yield a positive entailment, which contains information about an enrichment of the host community:

Since the immigrants were of the higher classes of the Russian Empire, they contributed significantly to American science and culture. Inventors Vladimir

Zworykin, often referred to as the 'father of television', Alexander M. Poniatoff, the founder of Ampex, and Alexander Lodygin, arrived with this **wave** (Wikipedia, Russian Americans, accessed 1 November 2018).

In such contexts, waves are not perceived as destructive elements but rather as 'transporters' bringing to the shore 'treasures'. 'Waves' and 'flows' tend to be used in a positive sense in relation to investors, buyers, clients, tourists and admirers when they make a positive contribution to different industries, trades and to the esteem of public figures.

In the Russo-Ukrainian discourse of displaced Ukrainians, some other contextual elements override the cataclysmic implicative complexes of 'waves' and 'flows'. As a rule, in this discourse, the metaphors of masses of water are followed by descriptions of community efforts that try to resist 'the destructive forces of nature'. The people who come with waves and flows are themselves victims of cataclysmic events. The heroic actions of hosts prevent a further tragedy. Consider Examples 15 and 16.

(15) In recent days, more of the new refugees — **wave after wave** — are coming and coming to us from the west. And they are coming because the Kiev criminal junta is firing at more and more of their cities and villages with all kinds of weapons. More and more civilians, including old people and children, are dying under Ukrainian shelling. In many tents one can hear how women are crying and cursing the notorious Kiev executioners. Only in this camp there are up to **2,600 people**. But the Ministry of Emergency Situations copes. Nobody complains about anything. The food is superb. For each person, including the able-bodied, around **800 roubles** a day is spent on food (RP 7).

(16) The occupation of the Ukrainian Crimea by 'fraternal' Russia and the destabilization of the situation in the Donetsk and Luhansk regions forced Ukraine to face a new problem – the problem of refugees ... In these regions, the peaceful population, fleeing from local gangs and terrorists on Putin's payroll are forced to leave their homes, leave their jobs and property, and travel to other regions in the country. Most are looking for security in the capital and in the central regions of Ukraine. The whole country tries to assist them: from volunteers to people's deputies and ministers. 'We had the **first wave** of immigrants from the annexed territory of the Crimea and the city of Sevastopol since March ...,' said Victoria Krupskaya, the deputy of the Head of the Department of Social Protection of the Dnipropetrovsk Regional State Administration. Since May, 'the **second wave of immigrants** are from the eastern regions of Donetsk and Lugansk regions. Today we have more than a **thousand people** from the eastern regions. We try our best to create conditions for these people,' she assured. To help all these people, in Dnepropetrovsk as well as in all cities of the region, special centres for coordination have been created. '[The centres] involve volunteers, public organizations and all the appropriate services ...; doctors, and social workers, and employees of the employment centre. Psychologists also work [there]. All necessary assistance is provided,' said Victoria Krupskaya (UP 8).

In these examples, the authors attempt to evoke empathy from readers and appeal for readers' assistance rather than emphasize differences between hosts and migrants or to activate a negative entailment which equates refugees with a calamity.

10 Discussion and conclusions

The results show that numerical references and moving water metaphors were used in the Russian and Ukrainian press for purposes that have not been discussed by researchers of migration discourse before. Numbers and water metaphors in the Western discourse of migration served as a sign of dissociation from the human needs and wants of migrants, and represented 'fearsome masses' without distinct characterization. However, Russo-Ukrainian discourse uses numbers and water metaphors differently: to show a disaster of epic proportions, praise heroic actions of the host community and evaluate the preparedness for coping with the disaster. Numerical expressions and water metaphors also play an important role in denouncing the party responsible for the brutal conflict in which masses of people became homeless, even though the Russian and Ukrainian press disagree on the part each country played in this tragedy.

In the material analysed for this project, it was hard to find negative topoi in relation to migrants that were represented as masses and numbers. Both host communities acknowledged expenses and problems, but they were looking for optimal solutions that could allow for an expedient allocation of scarce resources. The topos of danger and threat was developed in relation to the neighbouring state, rather than in relation to migrants fleeing from this 'danger'. The topos of numbers supported the conclusion that society must mobilize its resources to resist the threatening activity of the neighbouring state, rather than the conclusion that the intake of migrants should be reduced.

Some readers may make further inferences, 'Large numbers of refugees is evidence of the scale of violence in the region'; 'the number of refugees will continue to grow if the conflict is not stopped'; 'to stop the conflict those responsible should be held accountable'; and finally several variants can emerge as a conclusion that 'only the international community is capable to stop this crime' or 'our country who treasures humanitarian values can stop it'. However, they are just possible inferences rather than obligatory conclusions.

In Russo-Ukrainian discourse, the group identity of refugees often emerged in interviews with public servants and state officials. The so-called bureaucrats usually use numbers together with references to broad categories of people, events and actions. They draw a global picture rather than reveal individual concerns. Still, the public officers try to demonstrate that they are in touch with reality by acknowledging the most urgent needs of migrants through compassionate statements regarding refugees' ordeals and by special attention to individual cases. When public officers take the floor for their statements, they often refer to people by giving names to groups of individuals, for example, students, doctors and medical workers, patients, investors, employees, proprietors, pensioners, flat and house owners, spectators and fans. They de-individualize their fellow citizens just as much as newcomers to the country.

The dichotomy of 'a group representation' versus 'individualization' does not consistently build the correlations between 'negativization' and 'a sign of positive attitude'. For instance, in the Russian press, the refugees who were named 'brothers' have been assigned a positive collective or aggregate identity, whereas bandits, saboteurs and provocateurs were discussed as unrepresentative individuals.

This investigation demonstrates that all the language facts need to be assessed carefully in the broad context of their use, because relying on the work of other scholars, adopting their research models and an overemphasis on quantitative research can mislead investigators about the meaning-inductive forces in texts. The strong linkage previously identified between numerical elements and the topoi of burden, danger and threat may not be relevant for contexts oriented towards an appraisal of community efforts.

Notes

1 An antiterrorist operation, which was launched in Ukraine on 14 April 2014.
2 In this chapter, relevant expressions were marked in bold. Only translations were provided because of the considerable length of the originals. All translations are of my own.
3 The cited sources are marked as RP for Russian publications and UP for Ukrainian publications. The number after the index corresponds to the number of the article in the lists of Russian and Ukrainian newspaper articles in the Appendix.

References

A'Beckett, L. (2019), 'Displaced Ukrainians. Russo-Ukrainian Discussions of Victims from the Conflict Zone in Eastern Ukraine', in L. Viola and A. Musolff (eds), *Media and Migration: Discourses About Identities in Crises*, 265–89. Amsterdam: John Benjamins.

A'Beckett, L. (2017), 'Fragmentation of the Discourse Community Through the Lens of Metaphor Analysis: A Case Study of Russians and Ukrainians are Brothers', in K. Bros and G. Kowalski (eds), *Discourse Studies—Ways and Crossroads*, 365–87. Frankfurt am Main: Peter Lang.

A'Beckett, L. and David, M. K. (2018), 'National Language and Social Cohesion: Focus on Ukraine and Malaysia', in Y. Ning, J.-G. Turi and C. Le (eds), *Proceedings of The Fifteenth International Conference on Law and Language of the International Academy of Linguistic Law (IALL 2017)*, 195–207. Marietta, GA: American Scholar Press.

Barlai, M., Fähnrich, B., Griessler, C. and Rhomberg, M. (2017), *The Migrant Crisis: European Perspectives and National Discourses*. Berlin: Lit Verlag.

Felberg, T. and Saric, L., (2017), 'Representations of Migration on the Balkan Route. Discourse Analysis of Croatian and Serbian Public Broadcasters (RTS and HRT online)', *Journal of Language Aggression and Conflict*, 5 (2): 227–50.

Glucksberg, S. and Keysar, B. (1993), 'How Metaphors Work', in A. Ortony (ed.), *Metaphor and Thought*, 401–24. Cambridge: Cambridge University Press.

Hart, C. (2010), *Critical Discourse Analysis and Cognitive Science: New Perspectives on Immigration Discourse*. Basingstoke: Palgrave Macmillan. Available online: https://doi.org/10.1057/9780230299009 (accessed 1 November, 2018).

Horsti, K. (2012), 'Humanitarian Discourse Legitimating Migration Control: FRONTEX Public Communication', in M. Messer, R. Schroeder and R. Wodak (eds), *Migrations: Interdisciplinary Perspectives*, 297–308. Vienna: Springer Science & Business Media.

Kainz, L. (2016), 'People Can't Flood, Flow or Stream: Diverting Dominant Media Discourse on Migration'. Available online: https://www.law.ox.ac.uk/research-subject-groups/centre-criminology/centreborder-criminologies/blog/2016/02/people-can%E2%80%99t (accessed 1 November 2018).

KhosraviNik, M., Krzyzanowski, M. and Wodak, R. (2012), 'Dynamics of Representation in Discourse: Immigration in the British Press', in M. Messer, R. Schroeder and R. Wodak (eds), *Migrations: Interdisciplinary Perspectives*, 283–95. Vienna: Springer.

Kopytowska, M. and Chilton, P. (2018), '"Rivers of Blood": Migration, Fear and Threat Constructions', *Lodz Papers in Pragmatics*, 14 (1): 133–61.

Kovesces, Z. (2002), *Metaphor: A Practical Introduction*. Oxford, UK: Oxford University Press.

Krzyzanowski, M. and Wodak, R. (2008), *The Politics of Exclusion. Debating Migration in Austria*. New Brunswick, NJ: Transaction publishers.

Kuzmin, V. (2014), 'Putin and Medvedev obsudili problem s bežencami' ['Putin and Medvedev Discusses the Refugee Problem'], *Rossiyskaia Gazeta*, 9 June. Available online: https://rg.ru/2014/06/09/bejenci-site-anons.html (accessed 20 March 2019).

Musolff, A. (2011), 'Migration, Media and "Deliberate" Metaphors', *Metaphoric.de*, 21: 7–19.

Musolff, A. (2012), 'Immigrants and Parasites: "The History of a Bio-Social Metaphor"', in M. Messer, R. Schroeder and R. Wodak (eds), *Migrations: Interdisciplinary Perspectives*, 249–58. Vienna: Springer. Available online: https://doi.org/10.1007/978-3-7091-0950-2_22 (accessed 1 November 2019).

Musolff, A. (2015). 'Dehumanizing Metaphors in UK Immigrant Debates in Press and Online Media', *Journal of Aggression and Conflict*, 3 (1): 41–56. Available online: https://doi.org/10.1075/jlac.3.1.02mus (accessed 1 November 2018).

Musolff, A. and Viola, L. (2019), 'Introduction. Migration and Crisis Identity', in L. Viola and A. Musolff (eds), *Migration and Media: Discourses about Identities in Crises*, 1–13. Amsterdam: John Benjamins.

'Operation: Russian Federation'. (2017), UHNCR (United Nations High Commissioner For Refugees), 24 November. Available online: http://reporting.unhcr.org/sites/default/files/pdfsummaries/GA2018-Russian Federation-eng.pdf (accessed 28 April 2018).

Pavlenko, A. (2008), 'Russian in Post-Soviet Countries', *Russian Linguistics*, 32 (1): 59–80.

Pohl, W. and Wodak, R. (2012), 'The Discursive Construction of Migrants and Migration', in M. Messer, R. Schröder and R. Wodak (eds), *Migrations: Interdisciplinary Perspectives*, 205–12. Vienna: Springer. Available online: https://doi.org/10.1007/978-3-7091-0950-2_18 (accessed 1 November 2018).

Poroshenko, P. (2018). 'Žyteľam okkupirovannyh territorij: My Vas ne ostavim i nikomu ne otdadim' ['To Residents of Occupied Territories: We Will Never Leave You and We Will Not Give You to Anyone'], *Gordon*, 2 September. Available online: https://gordonua.com/news/war/poroshenko-zhitelyam-okkupirovannyh-territoriy-my-vas-nikogda-ne-ostavim-i-nikomu-ne-otdadim-331533.html (accessed 12 March 2019).

'Porošenko slyšit i uvažajet golos Donbassa' ['Poroshenko Listens to and Respects the Voice of Donbass']. (2014), *Correspondent*, 20 June. Available online: https://korresp

ondent.net/ukraine/politics/3381580-poroshenko-slyshyt-y-uvazhaet-holos-donbassa-rukovodstvo-metynvesta (accessed 1 November 2018).

Putin, V. (2018), 'Russia and Ukraine Will Have a Common Future' ['U Rossii i Ukrainy obŝeje buduŝeje'], *RT (Russian TV)*, 8 June. Available online: https://russian.rt.com/ussr/news/520821-putin-ukraina-buduschee-rossiya (accessed 1 November 2018).

Reisigl, M. (2018), 'Normative Standards for Critical Discourse Analysis – A Discourse-Historical Model', Keynote lecture presented at the 7th Conference On Critical Approaches To Discourse Analysis Across Disciplines, Aalberg, Denmark, 4–6 July.

Reisigl, M. and Wodak, R. (2001), *Discourse and Discrimination: Rhetorics of Racism and Antisemitism*. London and New York: Routledge.

Schrover, M. and W. Schinkel (2013), 'Introduction: The Language of Inclusion and Exclusion in the Context of Immigration and Integration', *Ethnic and Racial Studies*, 36 (7): 1123–41.

Taylor, C. (2009), 'Representation of Immigrants in the Italian Press', *Occasional Papers*, 21: 2–39.

'The Press in Russia' (2008), *BBC Monitoring*, 16 May. Available online: http://news.bbc.co.uk/2/hi/europe/ 4315129.stm (accessed 20 June 2017).

'The Press in Ukraine' (2006), *BBC News*, 31 October. Available online: http://news.bbc.co.uk/2/hi/europe/ 4073375.stm (accessed 20 June 2017).

UNIAN (Ukrainian Informational News Agency) (2014), 'Kak Ykraina možet rešit'problemu peresencev' ['How Ukraine Can Solve the Problem of Internally Displaced People?']. Available online: https://www.unian.net/politics/931010-bolshoe-pereselenie-kak-ukraine-reshit-problemyi-bejentsev.html (accessed 20 February 2019)

'Ukraine. Fact Sheet' (2017), UNHCR (United Nations High Commissioner for Refugees), 31 December. Available online: http://reporting.unhcr.org/sites/default/files/UNHCR%20Ukraine%20Fact%20Sheet%20-%20December%202017.pdfhttp://reporting.unhcr.org/sites/default/files/UNHCR %20Ukraine%20Fact%20Sheet%20-%20December%202017.pdf%20 (accessed 28 April 2018).

Van der Valk, I. (2003), 'Right-Wing Parliamentary Discourse on Immigration in France', *Discourse and Society*, 14 (3): 309–48.

Van Dijk, T. A. (1987), *Communicating Racism: Ethnic Prejudice in Thought and Talk*. Newbury Park, CA: Sage Publications.

Van Dijk, T. A. (2006), 'Ideology and Discourse Analysis', *Journal of Political Ideologies*, 11 (2): 115–40.

Van Dijk, T. A. (2012), 'The Role of the Press in the Reproduction of Racism', in M. Messer, R. Schroeder, R. Wodak (eds), *Migrations: Interdisciplinary Perspectives*, 15–29, Vienna: Springer.

Van Leeuwen, T. (1996), 'The Representation of Social Actors', in C. R. Caldas-Coulthard and M. Coulthard (eds), *Text and Practices: Readings in CDA*, 32–70. London: Routledge.

Van Leeuwen, T. (2008), *Discourse and Practice. New Tools for Critical Discourse Analysis*. Cambridge: Cambridge University Press.

Wodak, R. and M. Meyer (2001), 'The Discourse-Historical Approach', in R. Wodak and M. Meyer (eds), *Methods of Critical Discourse Analysis*, 63–93. London: Sage Publications. Available online: https://doi.org/10.4135/9780857028020 (accessed 1 Nov. 2018)

Wodak, R. and T. Van Dijk (2000), *Racism at the Top*. Klagenfurt: Drava.

Zagar, I. (2010), 'Topoi in Critical Discourse Analysis', *Lodz Papers in Pragmatics*, 6 (1): 3–27.

Appendix

List of cited newspaper articles

Russian articles
1. 'More Than 1 Million Ukrainians Fled to Russia from the War in the Donbass', in *Argumenty i fakty*, 2 November 2015.
2. 'Revolution against Dignity', in *Argumenty i fakty*, 26 February 2016.
3. 'How We Can Help Ukrainian Refugees to Settle in Russia?' in *Rossijskaja gazeta*, 2 August 2015.
4. 'Extremists Come to Crimea in Disguise of Refugees', in *Komsomolskaya pravda*, 9 June 2014.
5. 'Refugees from Donbass: "We Will Never Go Back"', in *Komsomolskaya pravda*, 23 August 2016.
6. 'Ukrainian Refugees: "We Were Afraid to Leave for Russia as We Were Threatened That in This Case, Our Flats Would Be Taken Away from Us', in *Komsomolskaya pravda*, 3 August 2014.
7. 'Exiles Seek Shelter in Russia, Otherwise They Will Simply Be Killed at Home', in *Komsomolskaya pravda*, 24 August 2016.

Ukrainian articles
1. 'Over 900 Thousand People Have Left the Territory Occupied by the Militants', in *Zerkalo nedeli*, 23 January 2015.
2. 'Militants Shelled Refugees from "Grads"', in *Censor.net*, 18 August 2014.
3. '"Ukrainian Railways" Took Away from the Eastern Regions of Ukraine Almost Three Thousand Displaced Persons Free of Charge', in *Censor.net*, 12 August 2014.
4. *Reva*: 'The Number of Immigrants Receiving Pensions Has Increased', in *Ukrainskaja pravda*, 30 June 2018.
5. 'Donbass: What to Start With?' in *Ukrainskaja pravda*, 16 March 2015.
6. 'Internally Displaced Persons and Underdeveloped Policy', in *Zerkalo nedeli*, 26 February 2016.
7. 'Authorities of the Russian Federation Misled Ukrainian Refugees', in *Censor.net*, 6 September 2014.
8. 'A Massive Relocation: How Ukraine Can Solve Problems of Internally Displaced People?' in *UNIAN*, 20 June 2014.

Index

abnormality 7, 108, 109, 111, 112, 236, 238–49
   aggressiveness 245
   loneliness and misery 245–6
   mental disability and unpredictability 243–4
   non-democratic character 246–7
   unmanly personality and treacherousness 238–9
abusive words/phrases 224, 235
affective meaning 17, 18, 22, 23, 31
aggression 1, 2, 15, 19, 23, 24, 26, 27, 31, 45, 71, 113, 219, 227. *See also* explicit aggression; implicit aggression
agonism 102, 103, 113, 114
agonistic discourse 113, 217
Akhmetov, Rinat 178
analogical reasoning 118
antagonism 2, 3, 5, 56, 109, 113
antagonistic discourse 84
   Carpentier's 102–3, 111
   context 103–5
   destruction of enemy 109–11
   homogenization 106–8
   pro- and counter-Maidan 111–12
   radical difference between self and enemy 108–9
   research design 105–6
anti-Maidan articulations 107–12, 114
'anti-terrorist' military operation (ATO) 104, 105, 178, 189
Argumenty i fakty 256
Aristotle 234
Association Treaty 130
Atlas of the Polish presence abroad (*Atlas polskiej obecności za granicą*) 66
Austria 21
Avakov, Arsen 113
axiological profile 68, 70, 76, 77
Azov Battalion 195, 198, 206

Babylon'13 219, 220
Bandera, Stepan 197
Bartmiński, Jerzy 67
Battle of Kruty (1918) 208 n.4
Biletsky, Andriy 6, 195–6
   anti-oligarchic/-Russian/-liberal nationalism of 204–6
   blog on Ukrayinska Pravda 199–201
   discussion on strong leader for nation 203
   National Corps 197–9
   political discourse 195–7, 207
   social justice in action 202–3
   Trident 197–8
   writings on Ukrainian Social-Nationalism 201–2
bilingualism 87, 163, 169–70, 172, 205, 225
blended names 5
   cross-linguistic 84
   data analysis 89–97
   formal and semantic characteristics 84–5
   hypotheses 85–6
   methodology 86–9
   semantics 83
blogs 86, 195, 197, 199–202, 204, 206, 208, 233, 235–8, 240, 241, 246, 249
Bolshevik Forces 208 n.4
Brexit campaign 131
British Parliament 45
bullying 245

Canada 49–52, 59
Canada diaspora community 139, 142–4, 153
Cap, Piotr 235
Carpentier, Nico 101–3, 111, 112
categories of violence 47, 48, 51, 60, 61
   mobilization 50, 51, 55, 59–61

obligation hierarchies   50, 51, 53–5, 58–61
targeting   50, 51, 53, 55–7, 59, 61
values   50–3, 54, 55, 57–61
victimhood   50, 51, 53, 54–5, 58–61
categorization   46, 68, 79, 181
Censor.net   256
Chechen separatism   18
Civil War (1917–22)   180
'The Club of Battle Surzhyk'   236
cognitive frame   128–9
collectivization   254–5
collocations   13–15, 19–24, 27–31, 72, 73, 78, 87, 89, 92, 95, 98
colloquialisms   85, 88, 97
communication   1, 2–4, 32, 101, 109, 161, 163, 166–9, 181, 205, 213, 217, 234–8
communism   204
Communist Party of Ukraine   204
comparative cross-linguistic approach   12
conceptualization   75, 79, 111, 118, 132, 258
conceptual mapping   5, 117–19, 127, 131
conceptual metaphor theory   49, 118
conflict discourse   4–5, 84, 213, 214
analysis and transitivity   12
of annexation *vs.* reunification   19–22
of brotherhood   29–31
corpora and methods   12–14
corpus analysis and findings   12, 14–15, 31
cross-linguistic corpus studies   12, 31, 32
of fascism   28
participants   26–7
of separatism   15–18
of truce   18–19
'conflictual togetherness'   102, 113
connotation   15–18, 31, 120, 122, 244
Constitution of Ukraine   203
corpus   75, 86–7, 256
analysis and findings   12, 14–15, 31
context (CC)   69, 71, 73
cross-linguistic studies   4, 12, 31, 32
reference (RC)   69, 70, 73
Cossack mythology   214–16, 226

'Country with national unity' campaign   179
creative insurgency   6, 213–14, 216–17, 219, 222–6, 225, 226, 228
Crimea   29, 51, 55–6, 60–1, 138, 199, 214, 265
annexation of   11, 19–22, 71, 76, 95, 108, 117, 121, 127, 131, 137, 150, 157, 178, 186, 195, 204, 208, 213, 219, 225, 226, 233
events   46, 49, 50, 53, 57, 59
critical discourse analysis (CDA)   2, 4, 48, 129, 183, 197, 255
critical metaphor analysis   4, 5, 118
cross-linguistic corpus studies   12
culture   3–6, 17, 71, 142, 145, 146, 157, 164, 166, 172, 183, 186–7, 204, 205, 208, 215, 216, 225–7, 235, 264

Day of Luhansk/Voroshilovgrad Liberation   180, 185
Day of the Donbas Liberation   188
Day of the Unknown Soldier   180
Debaltsevo-Chernukhino Operation   180
decision tree analysis   88, 93–7
decommunization   214
decontextualization   218, 220
Defender of the Fatherland Day   179, 198
dehumanization   2, 5, 102, 108, 109, 112, 113, 239, 248, 253, 255, 258, 262, 264
democracy   52, 53, 59, 103, 197, 201
demonization   102
Demoskop Weekly   65
denotative meaning   15, 31
derogation   83, 85, 88, 90, 96, 97, 104, 105, 112, 213, 242, 243
dialogicality   213, 218
diaspora. *See also* Ukrainian diaspora
Polish in Ukraine   65–7, 70
war discourse in   148–50
Diesel Show (Дізель Шоу)   171
diplomatic discourse   46, 47
discourse   1, 3–4, 57, 65, 76, 118, 142, 145, 162, 217, 228. *See also individual discourses*
and action   214
analysis   12, 234, 236

of annexation *vs.* reunification   19–22
'anti-other'   111
of brotherhood   29–31
corpus-assisted studies   12, 31, 32
family   218
of fascism   28
historical approach   255
ideology   254
media   79, 83, 188
migration   254–6, 266
nationalist   196, 199, 204
'the other'   22–8
press   71, 77
public   1, 157, 158
Russo-Ukrainian   261, 262, 264–6
of 'self'   27–8
of separatism   15–18
sociolinguistics   139
of 'them' and 'us'   140 (*see also* 'us' and 'them')
theory   102, 106, 109, 114
of truce   18–19
of Ukrainians   4, 17, 145, 147, 151, 152 (*see also* Ukrainian diaspora)
war   146–50
Western   264, 266
discursive image   65, 70–8
discursive image of the world (DIW)   67
discursive practices of online media
  analysis   162–71
  data   161–2
  language ideologies   160–1 (*see also* language ideology in Ukraine)
Dolinsky, Edward   205
Donbas Liberation Day   180
Donbas region   14, 29, 46, 177–9, 181, 182, 186, 187, 189, 190, 195, 198, 204, 206, 259. *See also* Donetsk People's Republic (DPR); Luhansk People's Republic (LPR)
Donetsk-Krivoy Rog Republic   180
Donetsk People's Republic (DPR)   11, 16, 18, 103–4, 120, 125, 137, 142, 146, 148, 149, 177–8, 180–2, 184–8, 196, 205, 207, 208, 247, 259, 263, 265
Duma   12–22, 24–30

embedded frames   228
embodiment   215–16, 220–2, 228
emotional involvement   31, 139, 141, 146, 148, 150, 153
'an empty signifier'   59, 60
entextualization   218, 220
ethnicity   138, 164
ethnic minorities   20, 205, 208
ethnonyms   84
Eurasian Customs Union   103
Euromaidan. *See* Revolution of Dignity (Революція гідності/Revolûciâ gìdnost, 2014)
Europeanization   111

Facebook   105, 106, 109–14, 139, 161, 164, 166, 167, 219
Fairy-tale Rus' (*Skazočnaja Rus'*)   224
family metaphor   5
  cognitive frame   128–9
  methodology   118–19
  motherhood and birth models   123–6
  siblings   120–3
  Ukraine as whole family   126–7
  Ukrainian voices   129–31
Federal Migration Service   260, 263
footing and keying   219
foreign policy   46, 48, 199
forum discussions   85, 86, 87
Foundation Freedom and Democracy   65–7, 71
framing   213, 218–20, 227–8
freedom   52–4, 59, 75, 77–9, 183, 201, 205, 215
From Roots to Roots (*Від джерел до джерел*)   171
frontstage and backstage   214, 220, 221
functional grammar   22, 24, 85, 87, 239–41, 247, 248, 258

Gezi Park events   249 n.5
globalization   164
Governmental programme for cooperation with the Polish communities and Poles living abroad in 2015-2020 (*Rządowy program współpracy z Polonią i Polakami za granicą w latach 2015-2020*)   66
Great Patriotic War (1941–5)   178, 179, 182, 184, 186, 188–90

Great Victory of the Soviet Union (1945)   190
Grounded Theory approach   139

hate speech   45
hegemony   106, 108, 111, 113
heteroglossia   213, 225, 228
holidays
   data and methods   181–3
   Donbas region   177–9
   existence of self-proclaimed republics   185–7
   legitimizing statehood   179–81
   Ukrainian authorities as hostile   188–90
   war and peace   183–5
homogenization   102, 106–8, 111
House of Trade Unions   110
humanitarianism   254, 256, 258, 260–2
humanity   59, 109, 205, 259
human rights   20, 219
Human Rights Watch   198
humour   6, 171, 173, 218, 226, 233, 248
   abnormality   238–47
   Did Svyryd's blog   236–7
   research in human sciences   234–5
hyperonyms   69, 70
hyponyms   86

identity/identities   3, 6, 47, 253. See also in-group identity; out-group identity
   anti-oppression conflict   55–9
   approach   46
   collective   54, 57, 106, 138, 145, 217
   group   46–8, 53, 54, 159, 181–2, 197, 266
   imagined   138, 153
   'liquid'   153
   local 'state'   6, 182
   national   6, 132, 137, 138, 141, 142, 145, 153, 163, 172, 177, 179, 183, 214, 225
   negotiation   137, 141–6
   political   53–5, 58–60
   post-Soviet   28
   pro-values conflict   51–5
   public   182
   regional   178, 179, 190

   of self and other   102
   social   139
   values-based   61
'ideological square'   47, 48, 84
ideology   3, 18, 22, 31, 47. See also language ideology in Ukraine
   conflict   46, 54, 55
   patterns   46
   principles   138
   radical nationalist   202
   representation   55
   socialist/communist   204
   value   48
imagined community   138, 185
Immortal Army   200
Immortal Regiment memorial march   179
incongruity theory   234
Independence Square   69, 72
in-group identity   1, 47, 52–60, 137, 138, 140–53, 181
Initiative 'Language Security' (Ініціатива 'Мовна безпека')   169
Institute of Documentary Film (IDF)   219
insult   5, 6, 213, 216–17, 219, 224, 226–8, 239
intentional action   23, 26
interactive frame   219
internally displaced persons (IDPs)   7
intertextuality   213, 217–18, 220–1, 226–8
irony   119, 122, 234, 236, 238, 248
Izvestia   256

'Jacobin imaginary'   102
'jumpers'   104, 106–9, 111

Karaims   20
keywords   13–15, 18–19, 21, 31, 69, 89, 90, 161, 256
Khmelnytsky, Bohdan   181
Kievan Rus'   121
Kiev International Institute of Sociology (KIIS)   103, 181
Kiev/Kyiv   15, 57, 66, 69, 72, 79, 104, 121, 129, 182, 188–90, 198, 201, 203, 208 n.4, 249 n.1, 259
'Kill Kolorady!'   109, 114

Kiseliov, D.   121
Kolegi Studio!   171
'kolorady'   104–6, 110–13
Komersant   120, 129
Komsomolskaya Pravda   105, 256
Korpusomat   69
Kozlov, Sergey   184, 185
Krajina FM   220
Kravchuk, L.   128
Kuchma, Leonid   158
Kurier Galicyjski (KG)   65, 66

Laclau, Ernesto   59, 102, 106, 112
language   1–2, 13, 153
   of communication   32, 257 (*see also* communication)
   discriminatory   45
   floating   235
   phenomena   236
   policy   140, 142, 157–8
   Russian   7, 157, 158, 167–70, 172, 178, 205, 225
   Ukrainian   6, 7, 143, 157–9, 163–70, 172, 205, 225
language ideology in Ukraine   6, 8, 172–3
   democratic bilingualism   169–70
   language situation and   157–60
   'mother-tongue'/native language activism   165–9
   as national and state symbol   163–5
   pluralingualism and internal diversity   171
   theoretical framework and methodology   160–2 (*see also* discursive practices of online media)
laughter   226
Lavrov, Sergei   259
legitimization   46, 47, 52, 53, 58, 179–81
Letter to the Moscow devil (*Lyst moskovs'komu šajtanu*)   220
Letter to the Tzar[sic] (*Lyst do Čar'a/Pis'mo к Čar'u*)   219
LGBT   205–6, 208
linguistic-pragmatic mechanism   233, 234, 236, 238, 248
'Little Turnip' (*Репка*)   171. See also Repka Club

loans   84, 85
Luhansk People's Republic (LPR)   11, 16, 18, 103–4, 120, 137, 142, 146, 148, 149, 177–8, 180–90, 196, 205, 207, 208, 247, 259, 263, 265
Lutsenko, Yuri   113

Maidan   65, 70
   event-based profile   73–4, 79
   locative profile   72–3, 79
   temporal profile   75–7, 79
Maidan Revolution (2013–2014). *See* Revolution of Dignity (Революція гідності/Revolûcìâ gìdnost, 2014)
'maidowns'   104–9, 111
'March of Equality'   205
material processes   23, 26
media
   discourse   79, 83, 188
   mass   105, 158, 241, 253, 256
   online   159–63, 167, 171–3
   Russian   85, 243, 256
   social   101, 139, 161, 162, 165–6, 171, 203, 219, 233
   traditional   6, 7, 233
   Ukrainian   5, 83, 95, 98, 173, 254, 256, 257
Medvedchuk, Viktor   205
Medvedev, Dmitriy   224, 240
memes   101, 102, 114, 224, 229
metaphor   46, 58, 59, 106, 255, 257
   conventional   119, 131
   expressions   48–51, 55, 74
   novel   117, 119
   political   47–8
   relationship   57
   scenario   46, 48, 50, 59, 60
   use   53
   violence   47, 50–1 (*see also* categories of violence)
   water   264–6
metaphor identification procedure (MIP)   49, 118
metonymy   106, 118
Michael Shchur (*Майкл Щур*)   171
microcontext   254
migration   48, 253–6, 264, 266
military conflict   1, 13, 27, 253
Military Council   198

Miner's Day   182, 189
Ministry of Emergency Situations   265
Minsk I agreement (2014)   12–13
Mir Luhanshchine movement   189
Miroshnichenko, Denis   184
mockery   234, 235, 239, 246
modality   162, 213, 220, 228
modernization   111
modifiers   90, 91, 93
Molotov, Vyacheslav   189
Monitor Wołyński (*MW*)   65, 66–7
'mother-tongue'/native language activism   165–9
Movement to defend Ukrainian (*Рух захисту української мови*)   168
multimodal repetition   213, 217–18, 220, 226–8

Nakhimov Square   123
national consciousness   214, 215, 229
National Corps   195–9, 203, 205–8
National Guard of Ukraine   195, 198, 206
nationalism   58, 60, 195, 197, 202, 204–8, 215
National Militia   197, 202–3
national policies   233
National Unity Day   184, 187
nation-building   132, 164, 165, 173, 215
nationhood   60, 138
Nazi Germany   21, 178, 189, 203
negativization   253–5, 258, 260, 262, 267
neo-liberal democracy   208
neologisms   84, 105, 171
New Zealand diaspora community   139, 143, 150, 153
non-blended names   90–1, 94. *See also* unblended names
'non-intended' effects   101
Normandy Contact Group   250 n.28
North America diaspora community   139, 145, 153
Novorossia   125
Nurturant Parent model   120, 131

obscene words   86, 88, 90, 95, 96
Occupy Wall Street (OWS)   249 n.2
October Revolution   124
Office of the United Nations High Commissioner for Human Rights   198

online political trolling   217
onomasiology   68, 69, 84
oppressive 'expansionism'   56
Orange Revolution   158, 159, 178
Organization of Ukrainian Nationalists (OUN)   195, 202–4, 206, 207
'other'   22–8, 45–7, 53, 55, 59, 101–3, 108, 111, 112, 137, 138, 151, 153, 159
'othering'   30, 45, 109, 111, 113, 114, 138, 140, 142–3, 148–51
Otpor   249 n.3
out-group identity   1, 47, 54, 55, 56, 59, 60, 137, 138, 142, 144, 146–50, 153
overlapping frames   213, 226, 228

pacification   196
'panheads'   104, 106–9, 111, 114
Parliamentary Assembly of the European Council   21
parliamentary debates   4, 11, 12, 15, 23, 27, 31, 117
Pasiechnik, Leonid   184, 185
patriotism   57–8, 60, 195, 206, 215
Patriot of Ukraine   197, 198, 201–2
pejorative lexis   84
Pereyaslav Rada   180
personification   54, 56, 57, 58
physical space and motion concept   56
Plotnitsky, Igor   184–9
pluralingualism   163, 171, 172–3
Podervianskyi, Les   235, 236, 249 n.6
point of view   67, 68
Poland   45, 66, 70, 71, 78, 79, 204
Polish communities   66, 70, 78
Polish-Lithuanian Commonwealth   214–15
Polish media, Ukrainian crisis in   5, 65–79
    diaspora   65–7, 70
    discursive image   70–8
    research procedure   69–70
    theoretical basis for research   67–8
Polish Ministry of Foreign Affairs   66, 71
Polish minority in Ukraine   5, 65–6, 70–1, 76–9
political conflict   46–7, 50, 54, 61, 512
political discourse   45, 83, 85, 121, 141, 153, 207
    Biletsky's   195–7
    data and method   48–50

metaphor 47–8
research 50–9
violence and its complexity 46–7
popular culture 216, 225, 226, 227
populism 45, 57
Poroshenko, Petro 5, 7, 46, 48, 50, 51–6, 59, 60, 83, 110, 130, 201, 204, 253
post-Maidan period 159, 160, 163
Pravda.ru 256
prepositional phrases 72–3
prior text 217–18
profanity 235
profiling of concepts 67–9, 72–7
pro-Maidan articulations 107–14
Pure Language (Чиста мова) 166
Putin, Vladimir 5, 29, 46, 48, 50, 51, 55–61, 83, 84, 91, 121, 123, 128, 130, 131, 149, 151, 196, 205, 208, 213–14, 219, 224, 226–8, 238–43, 245, 246, 253, 265

raciality 202
Rada 12– 22, 26–8, 30
radicalism 45, 206
radicalization 5, 114
radical othering 102, 109, 111, 114
Radio Liberty 110
raillery 234
reasonable hostility 216–17
recontextualization 218, 220, 222–6
refugees representation in Russian and Ukrainian press 7, 253–67
 criticism of authorities 262
 data 256–7
 humanitarian catastrophe 258–60
 as 'masses of moving water' 264–6
 migration discourse in UK and Western Europe 254–6
 numerical references 260–4
Regional Languages Law (2012) 171, 179
relational process 24–6
relief theory 234
repetition 139, 141, 145, 147, 213–14, 217–18, 220–1, 226–8
Repin, Ilya 215–16, 219–20, 222, 229
Repka Club 236
'Reply of Zaporizhian Cossacks to the Turkish sultan' 215–16, 219, 220, 222–9
resemiotization 6, 218, 222–6, 228

Reva, Andrei 261
Revolution of Dignity (Револю́ція гідності/Revolûcìà gìdnost, 2014) 2, 5, 69, 71, 76, 77–9, 102–3, 107–110, 112, 113, 137, 138, 141, 148, 157, 159, 161, 171, 195, 199–200, 206, 225, 233. *See also* antagonistic discourse
ridicule 234, 238–40, 246, 248
Right Sector 206
Rossiyskaya gazeta 256
Russia 58–60, 104, 113, 122–4, 145, 166, 190, 199, 201, 203, 204, 241, 246, 247, 259–60, 263, 265
 annexation of Crimea 11, 19–22, 71, 76, 95, 108, 117, 121, 127, 131, 137, 150, 157, 178, 186, 195, 204, 208, 213, 219, 225, 226, 233
 Empire 215
 perception of Ukraine 128–9, 131, 132
 political identity 58
 TV debates 5, 117, 119, 121, 128, 132
 and Ukraine 5, 46–8, 57, 76, 84, 103, 137, 157, 158, 168, 213–14, 217, 228, 238, 253, 256
Russia Day 182, 186
Russian National Corpus (RNC) 119
Russian National Unity Day 182
Russian Poroshenko-Putin corpus (RPP) 86, 88–93, 96–8
'Russian World' (*Russkij mir*) 29, 184, 186–8, 190, 208, 246–7
Russification 145, 157, 169
Russophone ideology 158

sarcasm 123, 188, 233, 234, 236, 238, 241–3, 246–8
satire 171, 224, 235
schema 55–9, 61, 219, 222, 226, 255
Script-based Semantic Theory of Humor (Raskin) 234
'self' 27–8, 45–7, 53, 59, 102, 112, 159, 165
self-identification 138, 190
self-representation 47, 50, 59, 254
semantic-lexical relations 68, 95
semantization 68, 69. *See also* symbolic semantization
semasiology 68

Senate of the Republic of Poland   65
Serdiuchka, Verka   250 n.19
Shevchenko, Taras   166, 250 n.17
'siege beliefs'   183
Sketch Engine   86, 87
'Slovopedia'   16
Słowo Polskie (*SP*)   65, 66
social activism   203
socialization   196
social justice/equality   201-3
social media   101, 139, 161, 162, 165-6, 171, 203, 219, 233
Social-Nationalist Assembly   198
Social-Nationalist Party of Ukraine   197
social networks   5, 7, 101, 105, 110, 138
social relations   77, 106, 109, 160, 173
societal beliefs   181
Solidarity Movement   71
'Solidarity' Trade Union (1980)   78
source words   84-6, 89, 94-5, 97, 98
sovereignty   159, 173, 199, 201, 203
Soviet Union   71, 78, 108, 120, 124-5, 144, 145, 157, 178, 186, 189, 190, 197, 199, 203, 214
'sovki'   104-6, 109, 111, 112
Stalin, Joseph   20
statehood   121, 124, 177, 179-81, 190, 202, 207
Strict Father model   120, 131
Surzhyk   6, 87, 163, 171, 173, 235-7, 246
Sushchenko, Roman   250 n.31
Svoboda   197, 206
Svyryd Opanasovych   236-7, 240, 242, 243, 245, 247, 248
symbolical names and values   77-8
symbolic semantization   68, 79
symbolization   2, 68
synecdoche   106, 108
synonyms   68-70, 86, 89, 95, 98, 106

target words   87, 88, 89-94, 96-8
Tatars   20
territorial integrity   14, 16, 17, 29, 52, 132, 199
terrorism   48, 114
traditional values   205-6, 208
transitivity   12, 22, 23, 26, 31
Trident   197-8

Turchinov, O.   130, 131
Tyahnybok, O.   130

Ukraine. *See also individual entries*
   and EU relations   132
   history   8, 69, 75, 79, 121, 200-2
   language situation and ideologies in   158-60
   and Polish relations   65-7, 70, 71
   post-Maidan   4, 197, 204, 207, 249
   post-Soviet   204, 208 n.4
   and Russia conflict   5, 46-8, 76, 84, 103, 137, 158, 168, 213-14, 217, 228, 238, 253, 256
   Russian immigrants in   145
   Russian perception of   128-9, 131, 132
   'us' and 'them' in   139-42
   voices   129-31
   as whole family   126-7
Ukrainian diaspora
   identity negotiation and othering   142-3
   method of study   139
   'us' and 'them' in Ukraine   139-42
   war discourse   146-50
Ukrainian Informational News Agency (UNIAN)   256
Ukrainian Insurgent Army (UPA)   197, 198, 200, 204, 206, 208 n.1
Ukrainian People's Republic (UNR)   208 n.4
Ukrainian Poroshenko-Putin corpus (UPP)   86-93, 96-8
Ukrainian Social-Nationalism   201-2
Ukrainophone ideology   158
Ukrayinska Pravda   195, 199-201, 203, 256
unblended names   85, 87, 89, 92, 93, 95-7. *See also* non-blended names
unintentional action   23-6
United Nations General Assembly Resolutions   20
United States   49, 54, 56, 59, 60, 66, 128, 139, 142, 153
'us' and 'them'   138, 139-42, 144-5, 149, 167, 183, 205
US Congress   50, 53

Van Dijk, T. A.   47, 48, 84, 162, 262
'vatniki'   104-6, 109, 111-14

verbal analysis   162
verbal attacks   84
verbs   26, 72, 90–3
Verkhovna Rada   197, 201
Victory Day   182, 184
Vintoniv, Roman   171
violence   31, 45, 46, 103
   and its discursive construal   46–7
   in Odessa   104, 110–11, 207
   physical   114
   political   5, 58–60
visual analysis   162
visual repetition   220–1
vocabulary analysis   12
vulgarism   85, 88, 90, 171, 225, 226, 242

war   3, 14–15, 19, 23, 24, 31, 83, 139, 150, 183–5, 188
WebBootCat   86
Westernization   111
WeWord (*Мислово*)   166

wildcard searches   27
Word creator (*Словотвір*)   166
word-formation processes   84
Wordwriter (*Словопис*)   166
World War II   65, 84, 184, 197, 200, 208 n.1, 215

Yanukovych, Viktor   103, 129–31, 158, 170, 178, 189, 225, 249 n.1
YouTube   66, 205, 213, 214, 219, 220–2, 228

Zakharchenko, Alexander   180, 182–3, 187
Zaporizhian Cossacks mythology   213, 219–22, 224, 227–9, 229 n.3
Zaporizhian Sich   214–15, 229 n.3
Zerkalo nedeli   256
Zhirinovsky, V.   124, 125, 127
zoonyms   224

www.ingramcontent.com/pod-product-compliance
Lightning Source LLC
Chambersburg PA
CBHW072128290426
44111CB00012B/1820